Heine and Critical Theory

ALSO AVAILABLE FROM BLOOMSBURY

Plato and Nietzsche, Mark Anderson
Foucault and Nietzsche, edited by Alan Rosenberg and Joseph Westfall
Inheriting Walter Benjamin, Gerhard Richter
Aesthetic Marx, edited by Samir Gandesha and Johan Hartle

Heine and Critical Theory

Willi Goetschel

BLOOMSBURY ACADEMIC
LONDON • NEW YORK • OXFORD • NEW DELHI • SYDNEY

BLOOMSBURY ACADEMIC
Bloomsbury Publishing Plc
50 Bedford Square, London, WC1B 3DP, UK
1385 Broadway, New York, NY 10018, USA

BLOOMSBURY, BLOOMSBURY ACADEMIC and the Diana logo are trademarks of Bloomsbury Publishing Plc

First published in Great Britain 2019

Cover design by Maria Rajka
Cover image: Portrait of Heinrich Heine (1797–1856) 1831 (oil on paper on canvas), Oppenheim, Moritz Daniel (1800–82) / Hamburger Kunsthalle, Hamburg, Germany / Bridgeman Images

A catalogue record for this book is available from the British Library.

A catalog record for this book is available from the Library of Congress.

ISBN: HB: 978-1-3500-8729-3
ePDF: 978-1-3500-8726-2
eBook: 978-1-3500-8727-9

Typeset by Newgen KnowledgeWorks Pvt. Ltd., Chennai, India
Printed and bound in Great Britain

CONTENTS

ABBREVIATIONS

[. . .]	texts in brackets have been added in quotes and translations.
B	Heinrich Heine, *Sämtliche Schriften*, ed. Klaus Briegleb. Munich: Hanser, 2nd ed., 1975–85 and Munich: Deutscher Taschenbuchverlag, 1997.
D	Hal Draper, *The Complete Poems of Heinrich Heine*. Boston: Suhrkamp/Insel, 1982.
DHA	Heinrich Heine, *Historisch-kritische Gesamtausgabe der Werke*, ed. Manfred Windfuhr. Hamburg: Campe. 1973–97.
GS	Theodor W. Adorno, *Gesammelte Schriften*, ed. Rolf Tiedemann in collaboration with Gretel Adorno, Susan Buck-Morss, and Klaus Schultz. Frankfurt am Main: Suhrkamp, 1970–86.
GS	Walter Benjamin, *Gesammelte Schriften*, ed. Rolf Tiedemann and Hermann Schweppenhäuser in collaboration with Theodor W. Adorno and Gershom Scholem. Frankfurt am Main: Suhrkamp, 1972–99.
HSA	Heinrich Heine, *Säkularausgabe*, ed. Nationale Forschungs- und Gedenkstätten der klassischen deutschen Literatur and Centre Nartionale de la Recherche Scientifique: Berlin and Paris, 1970–.
KSA	Friedrich Nietzsche, *Sämtliche Werke: Kritische Studienausgabe*, ed. Colli and Montinari. Berlin: Walter de Gruyter 1967–77 and Munich: Deutscher Taschenbuch Verlag, 1980.
KSB	Friedrich Nietzsche, *Sämtliche Briefe: Kritische Studienausgabe*, ed. Giorgio Colli and Mazzino Montinari. Berlin and Munich: Walter de Gruyter 1975–84 and Deutscher Taschenbuch Verlag, 1986.
L	Heinrich Heine, *The Works of Heinrich Heine*, vol. 1–8, trans. Charles Godfrey Leland. London: Heinemann, 1906.

Marx, *Selected Writings*	Karl Marx, *Selected Writings*, ed. Lawrence H. Simon. Indianapolis and Cambridge: Hackett, 1994.
MEW	Karl Marx and Friedrich Engels, Werke, ed. Institut für Marxismus-Leninismus beim ZK der SED. Berlin: Dietz, 1956–68.
ND	Theodor W. Adorno, *Negative Dialectics*, trans. E. B. Ashton. New York and London: Continuum, 2005.
OH	Heine, *On the History of Philosophy and Religion and Other Writings*, trans. Howard Pollack-Milgate, ed. Terry Pinkard. Cambridge Texts in the History of Philosophy. Cambridge: Cambridge University Press, 2007.
S	Heinrich Heine, *Ludwig Börne: A Memorial*, trans. Jeffrey Sammons. Rochester and Woodbridge, UK: Camden, 2006.
SA	Sigmund Freud, *Studienausgabe*. Frankfurt am Main: Fischer, 1969–75.
SE	Freud, Sigmund, *The Standard Edition of the Complete Psychological Works of Sigmund Freud*. London: Hogarth Press and the Institute of Psychoanalysis, 1953–74.

All translations unless otherwise indicated are mine with the occasional assistance of John Koster.

ACKNOWLEDGMENTS

"To read what was never written" can be a challenging task. Hugo von Hoffmannsthal's enigmatically suggestive line gains particular salience when the blindness concerns the elephant in the room. Or a few elephants. For only death bound elephants travel alone. The others move together in formations or constellations similar to the movement of critical concerns whose freely roaming associations are not always easily compartmentalized.

Heine and his poignantly provocative writing represents the sort of elephant to which scholarship—and not just historians of Critical Theory—have turned a blind eye. But avoiding the elephant has made the quarters only more cramped and led to the impediment of free critical movement that is Critical Theory's first and foremost concern. This is a concern that does not travel alone but moves in close association with questions such as Critical Theory's relationship to its various sources, including Jewish tradition, identity, and the German Jewish experience "at home," abroad, and in exile—issues that circle around the role of what can be called the role that Jewish difference plays in the Critical Theory of the Frankfurt School.

This book seeks to track the fundamental significance of these issues for a critical understanding of Critical Theory. It does so by attending to what I argue is a key link in the emergence of Critical Theory that helps rendering central issues legible that a selective scholarship has, over time, made hard to read, and so allows us to approach the question of the critical significance of Jewish difference unhampered by the disciplinary blindness that has marginalized Jewish Studies: with Jewish Studies, for its part, having assimilated the paradigm it once sought to challenge in the first place.

While it could be said that Critical Theory equals Heine without the humor, highlighting the critically reflective force that humor brings to the project of critique, Critical Theory can help track the critical thrust in Heine. To bring out this nexus, the book reads Heine with the Frankfurt School while highlighting the multiple reflections that Heine evokes in reading the Frankfurt School. But this is easier said then done. Exploring this relationship has become a project that commanded more time, more research, and more analysis than initially anticipated—but in return it also yielded more than formerly expected. The journey of this book has been an experience that has lasted longer than anticipated and I owe thanks to all who so generously indulged me in what might have seemed an unending pursuit.

The book could not have become what it now is without the accompaniment of David Suchoff's continuously generous and illuminating feedback, with numerous and always helpful discussions that opened up ever-new views and connections. Thanks are also due to all those who commented on parts of earlier versions of talks, essays, and book chapters that have become part of the book, those who helped me clarify particular issues, or those who simply lent a sympathetic ear to my elaborations. They include Asaf Angermann, Gérard Bensussan, Agatha Bielik-Robson, Roger F. Cook, Karen Feldman, Robert Hulot-Kentor, Martin Jay, Gerhard Höhn, Moshe Idel, Miriam Leonard, Adam Lipszyc, Tracie Matysik, Warren Montag, Harro Müller, Nils Roemer, Jeffrey Sammons, Gilad Sharvit, Oliver Simons, and Fred Unwalla.

A special thanks goes to the students of my Heine seminars with whom I was allowed to explore many of the aspects of this study. Manda Vrkljan and her librarians' team, especially Caroline Silva and Sarah Stiller, were most helpful in chasing down research literature. Thanks go also to Elisa Ho at the Jacob Rader Marcus Center of American Jewish Archives of the Hebrew Union College in Cincinnati for sharing material of the Adolph S. Oko Papers and to Marlo Burks for looking for copies of *Das Neue Deutschland* in Berlin. I thank Will Ohm for putting together the bibliography. I thank Andrew Warren for editing earlier versions of the manuscript and John Koster who did an outstanding job of editing the final version.

Chapter 3 is based on my essay "Heine's Aesthetics of Dissonance" that appeared in *The Germanic Review* 90, no. 4 (2015): 304–34. A part of Chapter 4 is based on a section from "Displaced Philologies: Introduction" cowritten with David Suchoff (the introduction to the special theme issue "Displaced Philologies," *The Germanic Review* 93 (2018): 1–6. A part of Chapter 7 is based on a section of "Secularization Theories and Their Discontents," the introduction to a special theme issue of *The Germanic Review* 95 (2015): 2–5, cowritten with Nils Roemer. I thank Taylor & Francis for permission to publish these texts. Chapters 4 and 5 include parts from my paper "Nightingales Instead of Owls: Heine's Joyous Philosophy" that appeared in *A Companion to the Works of Heinrich Heine*, ed. Roger F. Cook (Rochester, NY: Camden House, 2002), 139–68. I thank Camden House for permission to publish them. Sections of Chapters 2 and 5 are based on parts from my paper "Heine and Freud: Deferred Action and the Concept of History" in *Freud and Monotheism: Moses and the Violent Origins of Religion*, ed. Karen Feldman and Gilad Sharvit (New York: Fordham University Press, 2018), 65–86. I thank Tom Lay from Fordham University Press for granting me permission to include these sections. Chapter 8 is based on my paper "Another Abraham, Another Sarah: Heinrich Heine's *The Rabbi of Bacherach*" that appeared in *Judaism in Contemporary Thought: Traces and Influence*, ed. Agata Bielik-Robson and Adam Lipszyc (New York and London: Routledge, 2014), 39–50. I thank Routledge for granting me permission to include this paper.

Liza Thompson has been a wonderful editor and her assistant Frankie Mace a reliable support at Bloomsbury.

Last but not least my wife Denise deserves a very special thanks not just for her unflinching support, critical attentiveness, and generous patience—and not just with this project. I dedicate this book to her.

Introduction: Heine's Jewish Difference and the Project of Critical Theory

This book traces Heine's formative role for Critical Theory and explores the ways in which Heine's playful negotiations assert Jewish difference as a critically constitutive aspect of modernity—one that no longer requires erasure but instead embraces difference as a creative and liberating force. Heine's Jewish comedy employs the creative force of difference as an emancipatory lever in a way that went on to inform the central ideas that, from Marx, Nietzsche, and Freud to Benjamin, Adorno, and the Frankfurt School, have become the hallmark of Critical Theory. In examining Heine's part in the formation of Critical Theory, his writing becomes legible as a central source text for rethinking the project of modernity.

Tracing Heine's seminal role in the formation of Critical Theory makes it possible to situate the trajectory of the Frankfurt School in the experience of Jewish modernity as Heine had modeled it: as a critical model for a poetics of liberation with a universal address made possible precisely by its open reliance on the specificity of Jewish experience. This universalism with a difference was to prove paradigmatic for Critical Theory. Recognizing Heine's role in turn allows for a historically and theoretically more accurate understanding of the project of Critical Theory. *Heine and Critical Theory* recovers the vigorously humorous and pleasurable aspects of the Frankfurt School's strenuous efforts to reimagine a liberated form of continuous, open-ended negative dialectic—a style of thinking whose features have been vaguely associated with Jewish tradition, but whose Jewish difference can now, with recourse to Heine, be addressed with greater specificity.

Examining the relationship between Heine and the Frankfurt School more closely does not only lead to a better grasp of the critical importance of Heine's Jewish difference for the project of the Frankfurt School, it also allows us to rethink the Frankfurt School itself in broader, critically more engaging terms. This book seeks to recapture those aspects of the critical thrust and energy that drive Critical Theory, which come into full view with critical recourse to Heine. Restoring this connection—of which Critical Theory has become forgetful—makes it possible to reconnect Critical Theory with the pleasure and emancipatory verve that were once its most powerful impulses—impulses that of late have been obscured, if not completely eclipsed, in the process of institutionalization that has assimilated Critical Theory to the academic pastime it was once meant to critically expose as repressive.[1] Recapturing the Frankfurt School's emancipatory thrust by recourse to Heine, it becomes possible to understand how the dialectic of difference makes Critical Theory critical.

The trajectory of the Critical Theory's project comes into fuller view when its intersection with the history of modern German Jewish intellectual history is considered more attentively. For this context constitutes a formative aspect of the background story of the rise of the Frankfurt School. But historians of the Frankfurt School have met with resistance to the question of what to make of the fact that the initial members and associates of the Frankfurt Institute for Social Research were almost exclusively Jewish. Martin Jay conducted extensive interviews with some of the founding members, including Felix Weil, whose family fortune provided the funds for founding and running the institute. In *The Dialectical Imagination: A History of the Frankfurt School and the Institute of Social Research 1923–1950*, the first study of the history of Critical Theory, Jay concluded that "in the face of this vehement rejection of the meaningfulness of Jewishness in their backgrounds, one can only look for indirect ways in which it might have played a role."[2] And indeed, as Jay and others have suggested, the issue of its Jewish "background" loomed over the Frankfurt School as a prominent but curiously silenced presence. To ignore the many direct and indirect allusions and references to Jewish traditions and experiences in the writings of its early members and associates would be tantamount to muting the very critique they suggest, for the subtly subliminal wave of German Jewish connotations that runs through their writings presents a critical dimension of their form of argumentation. While there have been efforts to acknowledge this context, the question remains of how exactly this undercurrent can be properly addressed.[3] Various figures have displayed a range of attitudes, from unbroken silence to open expression of their Jewish sentiments. Given their otherwise critical commitment to clarity and precision when it comes to exploring the finer points of their genealogy (see Benjamin's *Berlin Childhood* and Adorno's *Minima Moralia*), the often elusively coded and almost esoteric way of addressing their Jewish experience continues to pose a particular challenge.

In the lives of Walter Benjamin, Leo Löwenthal, Siegfried Kracauer, Herbert Marcuse, Erich Fromm, Max Horkheimer, and Theodor W. Adorno—just as in the lives of their contemporaries Ernst Bloch, Hannah Arendt, and Georg

Lukács—Jewish heritage played a varied but irreducible role. Those who, like Lukács, sought to ignore it altogether, were promptly reminded of it in a sometimes perilous manner. If Critical Theory's intuitive impulse was to resist any form of intellectual assimilation to hegemonic forms of public and academic discourse, its exponents' personal experience of negotiating the pressures of assimilation suggested at least some basic existential nexus. The Weimar Germany that provided the culturally invigorating backdrop for the emergence of the Frankfurt School was also the setting for a Jewish Renaissance deeply interwoven with the fabric of Weimar culture, where Jewish artists, intellectuals, and scholars worked side by side with creative non-Jewish talents, thus highlighting the promise of broader social and cultural activity with a proudly self-conscious insistence on the universal address of Jewish particularity.[4]

While the founding of the Institute for Social Research began to make its mark, another "Frankfurt School" began to play an equally decisive role in the social fabric of the city: the Jewish House of Study directed by Franz Rosenzweig and later by Martin Buber, which was a central force of the Jewish Renaissance in Weimar Germany. Remarkably, the impact of both "schools" continues to the present day in their respective shaping of modern Jewish experience on the one hand and Critical Theory on the other. Side by side, the two movements present an illuminating juncture that highlights the intensity of the synergies of two innovative institutions of Weimar Germany's Jewish experience in 1920s Frankfurt, two stellar initiatives in the panoply of Frankfurt's rich cultural life that occasionally involved the same people, as in the case of Erich Fromm. The vivacity of the Weimar intellectual scene is a reminder that the Institute for Social Research did not operate in a cultural vacuum but within a larger fabric of intersecting projects. Horkheimer's and Adorno's fierce opposition to the reappointment of Martin Buber at the University of Frankfurt after the Shoah—Buber having held the first chair in Jewish Studies at a German university—is, like Adorno's admiration for Scholem, a case in point of this often conflicted complexity.[5]

But the Jews of Weimar Germany were not the first generation of German Jewish intellectuals. It was Heine's generation that had first seen the emergence of a group of Jewish intellectuals. While a group of Jewish intellectuals organized in the 1820s as the Verein für Cultur und Wissenschaft der Juden had been the first to attempt to make their voices heard, it was only after one of its members, Heinrich Heine, had begun to establish the role of the public intellectual in Germany, that it became possible to address the modern German Jewish experience in a wider sphere of circulation.[6] In a remarkable simultaneity, the emergence of the modern German intellectual was linked to the voice of a poet and critic whose Jewish identity was unmistakably recognizable. Heine's persona combined the figure of the exile, the estranged, and the modern literary author in a voice whose Jewish timbre—to German ears—linked the critical stance and Jewish perspective irreducibly to the figure of the modern cultural critic.

Aside from the deep level at which the Jewish experience helped form the figure of the modern German intellectual, Heine was at the same time also the poet and critic who reminded his readers that his Jewish difference was less a problem for modernity than an invigorating chance to imagine and create modernity with a difference, as his Jewish difference became his most empowering characteristic. It was this emancipatory thrust, embraced so paradigmatically by Heine, that Adorno would recognize in his exile in Los Angeles as the liberating force that positioned Heine at the cutting edge of a hopeful modernity that no longer required the erasure of the particular and its individuality. Rather, with Heine, an individual's Jewish difference could be grasped as its most liberating resource. It is no coincidence that "it was with Heinrich Heine that Adorno most deeply identified" in his years of exile in California, as Harvey Gross so strikingly put it.[7] And it is noteworthy that Martin Jay concludes his essay "Adorno in America" with a reference to this remark by Gross, but with a curious twist. For according to Jay, reading "Heine's wound"—an interpretation that critics had taken for Adorno's reading of Heine—into Adorno's exacting diagnosis of "Heine the Wound" neutralized the emancipatory thrust that Adorno's reappraisal of Heine had sought to recover:

> For not the least of Adorno's gifts to his émigré asylum, a country known for receiving rather than generating refugees, was the knowledge that in some sense we too are still suffering from Heine's wound, we too are still leading the damaged lives of men unable to find their way home.[8]

For Adorno, Heine became not a wound but the paradigmatic voice that demonstrated the liberating force of dissonance as an empowering instrument of critique. The Heine Adorno encountered in exile in the United States had, by the time of his own arrival, long since struck roots in the land of the free. Unencumbered by the nationalism of the German philological tradition, this different, American Heine could be embraced for his bold and irreverent aspects, for which his censors and critics in Europe, from Metternich to Karl Kraus, had so relentlessly persecuted him. The critical role the American Heine came to play for Adorno illustrates the crucial significance that the exile in New York and Los Angeles had for the development of Critical Theory.

If—contrary to the claims of much of Adorno scholarship—Adorno was the only one who embraced Heine openly, as Chapters 1 and 3 will show, others like Benjamin, Löwenthal, and Horkheimer were no less affected by their own negotiations of Heine's legacy, though in a more strikingly conflicted manner. Yet Adorno's close affinity with Heine should not come as a surprise for those willing to distinguish, with Adorno's "Heine the Wound," the critical diagnosis of the problem that Heine's readers face from the desire to blame Heine, the messenger, for his message. If Adorno exposed the poignant wound that blocked Heine's reception, the reception of both Heine and Adorno chose to ignore Adorno's critical point: that the wound was not Heine's. It resided instead in the kind of reaction that had become anesthetic to its own pain while keeping the wound open. Like the phenomenon of stupidity, the wound that marked Heine's reception remained a scar that would not heal even as it kept the senses numb. Chapters 1 and 3 will address the question in more detail of how stupidity as a scar figures in the concluding aphorism of Max Horkheimer and Theodor W. Adorno's *Dialectic of Enlightenment* and how this connects to the argument in Adorno's essay "Heine the Wound." Read this way, Jay's suggestion regarding "Heine's wound" appears as a substitution for the more serious diagnosis of the wound called Heine, a substitution that has become symptomatic for the misreading of an entire generation.[9]

Read with an eye to the fragment "On the Genesis of Stupidity," the final section of *Dialectic of Enlightenment*, Adorno's analysis of the complex he calls "Heine the Wound" appears as a traumatizing blockage that projects the numbness it produces onto the source that presents it with its diagnosis, that is, Heine's radically subversive exposure of the repressive character of the culture industry that his mimetic imitation so brutally denounces. This different reading suggested by Adorno's work on Heine is recovered not only by recognizing Adorno's insistence on treating the wound more aggressively but also by opening Critical Theory to the liberating power of Heine's embrace of pleasure and joy—an aspect that Adorno appreciated as the affective force that powers the project of Critical Theory.

In his terse commentary on the failure of Heine reception during the Cold War in Germany, Adorno's "Heine the Wound" identifies the anesthesia surrounding Heine as a wound that numbs German readers, preventing them from recognizing the repression of their cultural memory imposed by the rejection of Heine from the German canon.[10] In Adorno's diagnosis of this traumatic reaction, Heine had become the name for the conflicted manner in which the German Jewish experience appeared at the moment of German reconstruction. As Adorno puts it, "Heine's name is an irritant, and only someone who addresses that without whitewashing it can hope to be of aid" (80). For Adorno, "what in Heine and his relationship to the German tradition causes us pain and what has been repressed, especially since the Second World War" (80), was the wall of silence that had made it impossible to address the German Jewish experience in the frank and open fashion that Heine had elevated to the art of disruptive comedy. In Adorno's view, Heine's celebration of Jewish difference as a pleasurable distinction with a liberating thrust had become an episode that seemed to have been erased from German memory. In its place there remained a wound that would not heal, a wound whose diagnosis hurt so deeply that Adorno's painful soul-searching was mistaken for a verdict on Heine rather than an expression of critique of the repressive reaction formation that would assimilate even its most irreverent critic, Heine, to its own image. If Adorno had cautiously gestured toward Heine's Jewish difference, his readers hastened to reduce

Heine's critical ingenuity to the failure of assimilation that Heine, after all, so provocatively exposed as the lie of hegemonic culture. Adorno's cautiously couched elegy on the German elites' failing of Heine testifies to the virulence of the sustained trauma that the essay "Heine the Wound" addresses as the phantom pain that mistook the limb it had lost for the cause of its pain.

While Adorno's 1956 Heine essay addressed the critical condition of postwar German culture and politics and its anesthetic relationship to the past, its readers mistook Heine's Jewish difference for the fault of the poet and critic instead of acknowledging postwar Germany's cultural bankruptcy, which Adorno's essay took great pains to relentlessly expose. Marked by the aporia to grasp what had been lost, German culture after the Shoah remained numb to the distinction between the wound and its cause, mistaking the diagnosis for the symptom and setting up Adorno, who had so clearly called this failure by its name, as the fall guy for the debacle of the maintenance of the German literary canon he had so openly sought to defy.

Adorno's call for the liberation of Heine from the repressive regime of German literary history was, however, not just an appeal to resist the normalization of the repressive tendency of cultural memory, but also a call for Critical Theory to resist the dangers of assimilation to the industry norms of the administered world of postwar culture. For where there was no room for appreciating Heine's Jewish difference, Adorno felt, the project of Critical Theory would be doomed as well. However, both Heine scholarship and the reception of Critical Theory remained unresponsive to Adorno's appeal. The posthumous publication of Adorno's earlier, 1948 essay—with which he had begun his reappraisal of Heine—almost four decades later in 1985 did not change much, because the initial perception of the later essay had already taken root in critics' imaginaries on both sides of the Atlantic.

Returning to this earlier reappraisal of Heine, which Adorno pursued in exile in Los Angeles during the 1940s, allows us to reappraise, along with Adorno's estimation of Heine, also Adorno's own work as an opening to reexamine Heine's significance for Critical Theory. During the 1930s and 1940s, the exiled members and associates of the Institute for Social Research encountered Heine in Paris and New York as the archetype of their own experience as exiles.[11] In New York, this occurs at the moment when the New York Intellectuals associated with the magazine *Commentary* and the members of the Institute for Social Research encounter common ground in Heine as a paradigm for their postwar debate on the prospects of a more inclusive American culture, as shown in Chapter 1.

This book is thus not only a call to reexamine the narratives of German literary history and Weimar intellectual history but is also a call to attend to the legacy of German Jewish experience that informs the history of the Institute for Social research and the projects of its members and associates for the purpose of recovering a dialectically more sophisticated openness with regard to the Jewish difference that had been obscured by the complicated identity politics of the exponents of the Frankfurt School.

Attending to the formative role of Heine's "inward dissonance"—as Emma Lazarus, one of Heine's first American Jewish translators, characterized it—in shaping Critical Theory, this study argues that Heine's significance for Critical Theory "lives on because the moment to realize it was missed," to paraphrase Adorno's opening line of *Negative Dialectic*.

Heine's Jewish Comedy

Heine has enjoyed a curiously conflicted literary double life. On the one hand, his searing voice has been resounding ubiquitously in literary, cultural, and political discourse from the nineteenth century to the present. But while resonating with many aspects of a critically understood project of modernity, Heine's significance has, on the other hand, remained oddly unacknowledged, as he was cast as either a fluke or a misfortune of German literature and culture.[12] While critics have claimed from the time Heine entered the literary scene that he was at best of no great consequence and at worst detrimental for the German literary and intellectual scene, Heine's infectious style and diction continue, with their exuberant tropes, turns, phrases, images, and ideas, to invigorate literary and intellectual discourse. In fact, Heine's literary voice has been so completely assimilated that his voice, even more so than Goethe's, has become an indistinguishable part of modern German thought and expression. This thorough naturalization has made it difficult to recognize how deep the appropriation of Heine goes—even and especially with his fiercest adversaries.

Praised and cursed as the author who, in the eyes of many of his readers, enriched—but according to their opponents, impoverished—German poetry and prose with his jubilantly open form, pulsating rhythm, and diction, some readers celebrated as Heine's virtuosity what in the eyes of others had simply become signs of a pernicious frivolousness and a degenerate lack of propriety. What some critics identified as an utter lack of any sort of decency and morality, other, more enthusiastic readers recognized as Heine's unique exposure of the lie of hypocrisy and repression.

Championing a bold new literary style, Heine played an instrumental part in the invention of modern High German. His unparalleled mastery of language brought out the dialectical—that is, dialectal and dialectic—internal differences and otherness that the national language family romance of nineteenth-century philologists strove to domesticate. As he forged new forms of dialectically open prose and poetry, the insistent pushing of the limits of what would, with Heine's assistance, emerge as modern High German ironically cast Heine as the quintessential stranger, exile, and Jew.

While claiming the mantle of Goethe as his rightful heir and presenting himself as Germany's new voice, Heine approached the difference between the German and the Jewish cultural, literary, and intellectual traditions as a productive chance to explore new forms of expression. Recognizing the underlying affinities, this difference allowed Heine to launch his literary and intellectual project as a German poet and critic not only despite but also because he resolutely embraced Jewish tradition and his Jewish difference in no less assertive ways. Heine anchors the emancipatory vision of his project in an unflagging insistence on his Jewish difference. His recurrent recourse to this difference becomes the spring that drives the open and dynamic vision of a modernity that encompasses the German and European project as part of a larger vision of worldwide emancipation.

Heine's poetry and prose, his fiction and his critique, assumed their unique thrust as he began to embrace his Jewish difference, while the distinctly German sound of his voice allowed multiple sources of the Jewish voice to spring forth in creative new ways. The liberating force of Heine's song of freedom received its thrust from the openly attuned attention to Jewish and many other sources that inform his open vision of modernity. This gave the emerging dialect of High German in the first half of the nineteenth century its distinct character. Its forthright assertion of the multiplicity of linguistic origins exposed the repressive character of the nationalist agenda and its imagined linguistic homogeneity that sought to erase the diversity of its multiple linguistic treasures and cultural sources. For Heine, the lively abundance of modern languages' and cultures' multiple origins drove the dynamic verve of modern life and exposed the purportedly normative function of homogeneity as difficult to sustain.

Allowing Jewish difference its own voice in German poetry, prose, and critique created a powerfully articulate form of dissonance that brought home the multiplicity of origins informing Heine's open vision of modernity in a way that resonates with Adorno's insight that such dissonance would be the truth of harmony.[13] It was Heine's dissonant aesthetics that made him the paradigmatic figure in modern German literature, as his voice stood its ground as a resolute reminder of the multiple origins of the many sources that created modern German literature, culture, and thought.

Heine's voice articulates Jewish difference dialectically with an "inward dissonance." But while this "inward dissonance" represented for Emma Lazarus a troubling aspect, it enabled Heine to give a distinct voice to the particularity of Jewish experience in modernity; an experience whose carefully staged performative character highlights the challenges of the precariously supplementary character of the marginal position to which Jewish difference was reduced. Reduced to minor status, Jewish forms of assertions of any form of difference had only one way to express themselves without submitting to the pressures of assimilation: that of comedy. According to the classic canonical distinction between tragedy and comedy, Jewish forms of expression had no place in tragedy. Comedy was all that was left for Jews. Shakespeare's Shylock signaled that while Jewish life might be abjectly tragic, a critique of its condition could only be addressed in the genre of comedy, or so Shakespeare's classification of *The Merchant of Venice* as comedy suggests. By the time Lessing's *The*

Jews and *Nathan the Wise* entered the scene, the minorization of the Jewish voice by its reduction to comedy had been painfully brought home. The conflicted attitudes highlighted by the reception history and the stage productions of Lessing's two plays constitute a sobering commentary on this issue. Remarkably, Heine inserted his redemptive reading of Shylock at the end of his discussion of Shakespeare's tragedies and at the point of intersection with his discussion of the comedies, as if to highlight Shylock's uncomfortable position caught between comedy and tragedy. The conventions of literary representation simply did not allow for a Jew to appear as a central character in a tragedy.[14]

Heine's novella *The Rabbi of Bacherach* showcases Heine's approach, albeit in a literary genre atypical of his oeuvre. The novella tells the story of the Ashkenazi rabbi Abraham and his wife Sarah, named after the archetypes of the patriarchal ancestry of Jewish tradition, and Isaac Abarbanel, the Sephardi scion of a prominent dynasty of scholars, rabbis, and poets. His father, Yehuda Leon Abarbanel, who seems to stand behind Heine's figure of Don Isaac, was the celebrated author of the famous *Dialoghi d'Amore* and better known by the name Leone Ebreo. The novella presents a version of the story of the prodigal son in which the allegorical figures that stand for the normative strand of Jewish tradition (the pious rabbi and his wife Sarah) welcome Abraham's intimate friend, the renegade Spaniard Isaac, into their family as the lost son that makes their family complete.

Echoing the biblical matriarch's laughter and pleasure upon learning that she is to expect a son—the joy of her old days—the novella's Sarah opens her heart to welcome the modern day Isaac, whose difference is marked by the joyous laughter of the renegade who returns to infuse Abraham's and Sarah's marriage with new life. It is with the couple's embrace of Isaac and his pleasurably liberating laughter that their life comes to completion as their openness reclaims Jewish tradition's most pleasurable, enduring, and liberating moment as the celebration of the difference within. Sarah's embrace of Isaac, the novella signals, recognizes that Jewish tradition will live on because it opens itself to its own otherness within—Lazarus's "inward dissonance"—as the most powerful and liberating force of the life of tradition. Heine's alter ego, Don Isaac, figures the internal Jewish difference as the inner spring of the dialectic of tradition that keeps it alive.

In his landmark study *Heine's Jewish Comedy: A Study of Portraits of Jews and Judaism*, Siegbert Salomon Prawer called attention to the critical function of humor and comedy in Heine. Heine's literary project, he argued, is best understood in terms of a Jewish comedy, a permanently genre-defying intervention. Prawer's study suggests that we consider Heine's Jewish comedy as his response to the repressive features of the classic distinction between tragedy and comedy and the particular regime this distinction entails. Heine's provocatively uncompromising break with the classic canon of literary forms and norms liberates comedy, travesty, upstaging, and the comic relief of slapstick and physical humor as modern literary forms whose dissonant aesthetics break free from the repressive hold of the classical conventions with their obsolete form and genre distinctions.

Heine's Jewish comedy thus responds to the challenge of rethinking modernity in Jewish terms, a comedy that mobilizes his Jewish difference as critical leverage to articulate a vision of a modernity that no longer requires aesthetic compliance and assimilation by, or exclusion of, the Jews.[15] Heine not only redefines and reinvents modern literary form and praxis, but also liberates comedy from the nineteenth-century neoclassical normative scheme of culture as an exclusionary and repressive regime of control and authority. In Heine, comedy becomes the open form of a praxis of critique and emancipation whose challenge and defiance pose resistance against the normative commitments of Western culture while pointing out alternative ways of reimagining modernity as a project that recognizes difference and alterity as its most promising features.

In aesthetic terms, Heine's Jewish comedy performs a critical turn. Its change of perspective subverts the repressive character of the regime of canonical aesthetic norms. Along with the slapstick-inspired exposure of the false claims to cultural supremacy, Heine's Jewish comedy implodes the hegemonic character of the classical canon from within. Heine enters the literary scene with his style of performative critique at the moment when the notion of the tragic is being renegotiated as the underlying feature of modernity.[16] As a result, Heine's Jewish comedy challenges the terms that define the claims and counterclaims of the discourse of modernity by comically upstaging the hegemonic assumptions of a Hellenocentric discourse that puts Jewish and other differences under categorical erasure. He thus gives voice to a dissonant aesthetics that enacts and acts out Jewish difference to renegotiate the terms of the discourse of modernity. Heine's Jewish comedy exposes the tragic as a notion whose universal claim comes at the price of an aesthetics that relentlessly crushes the pleasures of individual aesthetic expression by subjecting the individual to the destructive force of an equalizing universalism that can accommodate for difference only as a form of failure and aberration.

Heine's Jewish comedy does not simply reverse the hierarchy between tragedy and comedy but challenges the casting of the discourse of modernity in terms of the tragic in the first place.[17] Heine's mantra that "after the tragedy comes the farce"[18]—given notoriety by Marx's citation and erroneous attribution to Hegel[19]—signals a transformative approach that moves beyond the classical distinction between tragedy and comedy and its canonical privileging of the tragic as the paradigm for theorizing modernity. For Heine, comedic articulation of Jewish difference subverts the convention of literary genres and liberates the particular and its singularity from the pressure of assimilation and the anxiety of being forced to submit to a universalism fixated on the erasure of the individual's difference as its distinctive feature.

To counter the repressive dominance of the aesthetics of the hegemonic culture, Heine's Jewish comedy seeks to redeem what the notion of the tragic abnegates. It does so by consistently and stubbornly attending to the multiple aspects of the sources of Jewish traditions with a critical grasp of their dynamic development and transformation into ever-changing manifestations of Jewish life. Heine's comedy thus traces tradition as a dynamic process of change and innovation that produces ever-new instantiations of the "old."

In a critical gesture that anticipates Benjamin's and Adorno's responses to the problematic character of a universalism that would exclude them, Heine's comedy drives home the difference that exposes the exclusionary character of the universalism of single origins and authoritatively hypostatized sources. If Critical Theory translates Heine's play of difference into a more stable and refined philosophical vernacular, Heine's playfully dissonant, colorful, and burlesque comedy travels cheerfully under the radar of the coercive control of the discipline of philosophy and its obsessive anxiety about noncompliance with academic protocol. In its depiction of life in the university town of Göttingen, the opening of his *Travel Pictures* takes this critique to its extreme in exposing the curiously parochial forms that can be assumed by academic universalism. By highlighting its attendant anti-intellectualism and shameless suppression of what it preaches but ultimately betrays, Heine reveals its repressive character as the only universal feature it seems to claim as its own. Heine's prototype of negative dialectic is thus already, if playfully, built into his writing as it moves under the umbrella of a comedically staged vaudeville of resistance.

Critical Theory purchases stringency of reason the way Odysseus escapes the clutches of the sirens, or so the analysis of Horkheimer and Adorno's *Dialectic of Enlightenment* suggests: by submitting to the force of a logic that requires the suppression of pleasure. The seductive lure of the conceptual rigor that Critical Theory otherwise so resolutely decries looms large. But the price is the forfeiture of the liberating dynamic of the affective resources that drive humor, which, as Freud has shown, supplies the critical impetus that invests critique with its emancipatory force. However, by domesticating Heine's subversive use of humor, comedy, and laughter, Critical Theory barters away its best bet for a mess of pottage. While Critical Theory shares with Heine the particular way in which difference comes into play as catalyst for critique as emancipatory praxis, Critical Theory is prone to rarefy difference into a generalized concept. But by assimilating the specificity of Jewish difference that informs its critical impulse into a universalized concept, Critical Theory obscures the source of its critical thrust: the specificity of the historically particular constellation of many of its exponents' German Jewish experience.

In Heine, on the other hand, the performative insistence on his Jewish difference serves as a constant reminder that the critical force of his dialectic rests on the specificity of this particular difference, from which it gains its critical thrust to push against what it critiques. In other words, while the movement of critique relies on the specificity of the difference and the particularity of its articulation, that is, the thinking of difference and the difference that it makes, the erasure of one's own traces of multiple origins, that is, the decontextualization of the trajectory along which one's difference operates, incapacitates the movement of the dialectic that owes its precise meaning and critical force to the particularity of the difference that drives it. In all its farcical theatricality, Heine's Jewish comedy reminds us that difference that does not dare to speak its name loses with its specificity its dialectically precise grip and critical edge.

Heine's Jewish comedy suggests that Critical Theory at its best deserves to be read otherwise. Contrary to the various attempts to urge Critical Theory into the straitjacket of unambiguous thinking, the reminder of Heine's comedic resistance facilitates a recovery of Critical Theory's insistence that the concept's sedimentation in the process of conceptualization is a danger that needs to be handled carefully. To lose sight of this aspect is to jeopardize the momentum of Critical Theory's emancipatory impetus. With Heine, it becomes intelligible how the exponents of the Frankfurt School gain the most momentum where they allow recognition of the specificity of their Jewish difference to openly enter and affect the critical project; whereas every sort of domestication, compromise, containment, or, more precisely, any reading that dilutes or obscures the particularity of their Jewish difference results in a neutralization of the critical force of the dialectic. Losing sight of the singularity that drives the dialectic in its thrust to counter the exclusionary form of philosophical universalism and its theological-political implications results in submission to the repressive character it challenges in the first place.

As a result, Heine's Jewish comedy gives voice to the critical power of the dialectic of the play of difference that Critical Theory will later develop in a theoretically more sophisticated, but conceptually more rigid and therefore subdued fashion—for it risks erasing the very pleasure it seeks to set free. While the trace of Heine's Jewish difference lives on in the Frankfurt School's critical project even where its exponents seem to submit to the dictate of assimilation to a degree that renders it nearly illegible, it is the Frankfurt School's boldest and most potent moments that testify to the significance of Heine's instrumental role—pun intended—in the formation of Critical Theory.

Heine's Jewish comedy brings Jewish difference into play as emancipatory leverage to challenge the repressive containment of tradition and its narratives and to liberate the project of modernity from within. The way in which Heine reimagines the function of tradition and the multiple sources of Jewish tradition in particular reflects an open and creative approach that frees tradition's fluid, dynamic, differential, and dialogical character. An open-ended work in progress, tradition thus comes into view as defined by translation, transformation, and change that rests on the dynamic process of innovation. In other words, there is no one tradition. Traditions occur in the plural only, as they emerge in relation and dialogue with, and differentiation from, each other as they negotiate their multiple origins. Traditions are historical artifacts and, as such, exist in time. They are constituted by a continuous process of negotiation. They continue, that is, are transmitted, by a process of reinvention, reimagination, and renewal. Continuity and discontinuity constitute each other. Or, as Benjamin put it,

> It may be that the continuity of tradition is mere semblance. But then precisely the persistence of this semblance of persistence provides it with continuity.[20]

> Mag sein, daß die Kontinuität der Tradition Schein ist. Aber dann stiftet eben die Beständigkeit dieses Scheins der Beständigkeit die Kontinuität in ihr.[21]

Heine's Jewish comedy creates the space for a level playing field where Jewish difference can address the exclusionary tendencies of the regime of conceptual thought. Insisting on the irreducibility of the singularity of its experience, Heine's Jewish comedy highlights Jewish and other forms of difference as critical reminders of the nonnegotiability of the singularity of the particular, giving striking expression to its resistance to conceptualization. Heine's dialectic of Jewish difference thus anticipates Benjamin's and Adorno's form of negative dialectic in literary form. But given the Frankfurt School's theoretical ambitions, Critical Theory shies away from gesturing toward its Jewish difference otherwise than in conceptually coded fashion. While Heine's Jewish comedy prefigures with its unrelenting insistence on the specifics of the particularity of its Jewish difference the critical move of negative dialectic, the Frankfurt School's attitude no longer explicitly reflects the necessity of recognizing the contingency of its protagonists' singularity as the condition of the negative dialectic to which it aspires. Its deeply linked nexus with the Jewish comedy paradigmatically figured by Heine is a critical reminder that to name the silenced and repressed can—with Freud read closely—be not only pleasurable and liberating but also epistemologically decisive.

At the heart of Heine's literary project stands an insistent rethinking or, more precisely, a reconfiguration of the relationship between theory and praxis, not unlike that of Hegel, Heine's great teacher from whom he learned by watching. Heine, in other words, intuitively grasped the great philosopher's power by thinking in movement. True to Hegel's thought, however, Heine did not adopt, embrace, or adapt particular aspects of his teachings but demonstrated his intuitive grasp as he moved away from it. If the critical moment of truth resides in the movement of thought, Heine's thought proved itself to be in constant motion powered by the dialectic's counterthrust, which Hegel recognized as the force that drives the movement of thinking.

Heine's radical move was to reinvent poetry and prose as a praxis that critically engages theory on its own "practical" terms, that is, performatively.

Following Hegel's cue that theorizing means always following the praxis whose reflection it is, Heine's writing responds to, plays with, and reimagines theory as it rewrites it through praxis. Resonating with Benjamin's implicit and Adorno's explicit approach to rethinking the relationship of theory and praxis,[22] Heine's writing exhibits at the same time a distinctively "philosophical" and "theoretical" impulse, precisely because it consciously acts out its issues while reflecting playfully on the conditions of its own possibility. In other words, Heine's writing performatively reflects the interplay of theory and praxis in its form.

Heine and the Frankfurt School: Dialectic of a Constellation

Yet, while the central tenets of Heine's comedy speak to concerns and sensitivities that resonate with some of the most cherished theoretical commitments of the Frankfurt School, neither Heine research nor scholarship on the Frankfurt School have shown much interest in examining this connection more closely. Turning a blind eye on it, however, deprives us of the possibility to comprehend the critical role that the Jewish connection plays for both Heine and Critical Theory. An adequate understanding of this nexus is not just of historical interest but also has theoretical relevance that goes to the core of the project of Critical Theory. Examining the wider implications of the connections between Heine and Critical Theory allows for a more nuanced grasp of Critical Theory's ambivalent and occasionally conflicted identification with Jewish tradition. When the various positions regarding Heine are traced as they found expression in Walter Benjamin, Leo Löwenthal, Max Horkheimer, Theodor W. Adorno, and Hannah Arendt; when the crucial role is examined that Heine played for Jewish New Yorkers, from Emma Lazarus to the New York Yiddish poets "Di Yunge" and the intellectuals associated with the seminal student journal *Menorah*; when Heine's importance for the New York Intellectuals who wrote for *Commentary* and for the German Jewish exiles in New York during the 1930s and 1940s is considered: Heine emerges as the paradigmatic figure for the debate about the cultural identity of Jews in Europe and America.

Chapter 1, "Displacement, Relocation, and the Dialectic of a Constellation: Heine, Critical Theory, and the New York Intellectuals" examines this historical context in which Heine assumes a paradigmatic role for Jewish intellectuals in Europe and America. Manifesting unexpected family resemblances between the discussions and cultural concerns of Jews in Weimar Germany and of the New York Intellectuals, Heine becomes a critical figure for rethinking Jewish identity at a moment when new visions of culture are being renegotiated. On both sides of the Atlantic, Jewish critics rally around Heine as the paradigmatic case that enables renegotiation of

Jewish identity in the face of the pressures of a hegemonic notion of culture. At the moment when the New York exponents of the Institute for Social Research and the New York Intellectuals see eye to eye, they turn to Heine as the paradigm for a self-conscious approach to Jewish life in modernity.

Heine's signal importance as the paradigm for modern secular Jewish existence in general and for Critical Theory in particular was no coincidence; it was the result of Heine's far-reaching and profound impact on his most influential readers. In examining Heine's role in Critical Theory, we need to be aware of the fact that Critical Theory did not stumble naively upon Heine: for Heine had already left his mark on the language and thought that are ready at hand the moment Critical Theory begins to form itself in relation to Marx, Nietzsche, and Freud. Heine is thus already part of the tradition that shapes Critical Theory and, knowingly or unknowingly, a critical source from its start. These three "masters of suspicion"—all of them close readers of Heine—reflect more than just a deep appreciation of Heine's style and critical flair: there are clear indications that Marx, Nietzsche, and Freud made productive appropriations of Heine's writing.[23] Channeled through their various forms of intervention, Heine enters the language of Critical Theory in their three different projects that together form the theoretical constellation that decisively informs the Frankfurt School's thought. Heine, as it were, becomes the literary force that informs the language, style, diction, and occasionally the mode of expression in which Critical Theory learns to speak.

Heine had made it clear that style, diction, air, and flair are anything but merely formal properties. Rather, form formulates content dialectically. Reading Marx, Nietzsche, and Freud with an eye and ear attuned to Heine's voice, Chapter 2, "Heine's Readers: Marx, Nietzsche, and Freud," traces the multiple resonances in three of Heine's most attentive readers and shows how they appropriate and reconfigure Heine's insights, whose transformative impulse powerfully informs their own work and thought in ways that will go on to shape the project of Critical Theory. All three readers highlight the theoretical promise of Heine's intuitions, demonstrating how the recourse to Heine allows us to rethink their respective projects critically. But more importantly, this constellation of Heine readers makes Heine's formative significance more legible. As a result, Heine emerges as the unacknowledged voice that inspired Critical Theory.

Recovering Heine as a critical source at the multiple origins of Critical Theory bores multiple passageways through the wall that the canonical forgetting of Heine has produced, inviting us to further the "reappraisal" of Heine that Adorno began. Chapter 3, "Heine's Dissonant Aesthetics," examines Adorno's 1948 lecture "Toward a Reappraisal of Heine." Prepared as a manuscript for publication in 1949, the text remained unpublished until 1985, when it appeared tucked away in the last volume of Adorno's collected works. Widely ignored, yet of critical importance, this talk has continued to receive curiously little attention. It calls for a reexamination not only of Adorno's later, notorious essay "Heine the Wound," but also of Adorno's thought and the project of Critical Theory more generally. Adorno's embrace of Heine as an early model for critical thinking challenges the dominant narratives. Attending to Heine's paradigmatic role for Adorno, Adorno's advocacy for a reappraisal of Heine emerges as more than an incidental digression. At the moment of the critical debate about the future of Jewish culture and identity in America, which saw exponents of the Frankfurt School participating along with New York Intellectuals and affiliates such as Hannah Arendt in the culture war of Cold War politics, Adorno enthusiastically claimed Heine as his ally. It was during this period that Adorno began to theorize dissonance as a musical as well as a critical theoretical concept, using Heine's dissonant aesthetics as a paradigmatic model for countering the repressive character he had diagnosed just a year earlier—in *Dialectic of Enlightenment* of 1947—as the deadly dynamics of culture. Adorno's early reappraisal demonstrates how central Heine is to the heart of Critical Theory's project, and how Heine's distinct voice became assimilated to that of the Frankfurt School as Critical Theory began to speak.

Still widely perceived through the bifocal optics of the nineteen- and twentieth-century dichotomy of culture and aesthetics on the one hand, and social and political history on the other, Heine fell prey to an increasingly problematic distinction that continues to define the way he is viewed today. This division continues to inform what little attention he is given outside of German Studies. In German Studies itself he has become subject to a politics of commemoration that has stuck him somewhere between German and Jewish worlds carelessly linked by a hyphen. Neither here nor there, Heine has become canonically enshrined as a figure of displacement. But this displacement has become one of philological study as well as of intellectual history, thus minimizing, if not altogether obfuscating, the critical challenge Heine presents to any such politics of displacement—a marginalized position he shares with the figures of the Frankfurt School.

Looking beyond the disciplinary divisions of academic labor that have kept Heine's critical voice apart from the Frankfurt School's radical redeployment of aesthetic theory, there emerges a nexus of interconnected circuits whose flow of critical impulses highlights the dialectic of the constellation that informs their relationship and sheds new light on the Frankfurt School's Critical Theory. Adorno's description of philosophy as what "lives on because the moment to realize it was missed" thus comes into view as a comment that seems apposite also with regard to Heine.[24]

In the wake of a culture war that approached the construction of the German literary and aesthetic canon as a nation-building affair, Heine's reception reflected the deep split dividing the German reading public into pious consumers of classicist aestheticism on the one hand and, on the other, into a politically alert audience for whose ears Heine became the voice of social justice and political change that would overcome the paralyzing lure of aestheticism. In an effort to secure Heine's place in the high literary canon, Weimar Germanists sought to assimilate Heine to the cultural norms that the dominant nationalist discourse imposed.[25] As German Jews were increasingly entering the ranks of the bourgeoisie, Heine became the exemplary figure for exposing this painful process of assimilation. As Heine found welcome inclusion in the German literary canon only as a poet of pleasingly soothing lyric poetry, his prose and political lyrics, set to a harsher beat, were excluded, their message deemed inopportune with regard to the literary expectation of what would be considered good taste. Heine had reimagined literary aesthetics with a difference and placed his new poetics front and center, but his bold challenge was marginalized as aesthetic blunder, appreciated only by a minority of literary scholars. Heine's writing had circumspectly intertwined form and content into an irreducible dialectic, but Goethe-centric philology pigeonholed him as a lyric poet, aligning Heine's poetry—despite its palpable resistance—with a conservative aesthetic and national agenda that ignored his modernist approach to form and content and instead imposed a rigid distinction between aesthetics and politics.

"Content" and "prose"—the crumbs from the high table of the German canon—were left to readers with socially and politically more progressive preferences. For many liberals, socialists, Marxists, and Jewish readers, Heine had given their highest aspirations a voice. His provocative and subversive stance articulated their visions of emancipation. With the division of Heine's legacy into two parts that aligned poetry with form and prose with content, the former with noble claims of aesthetics and the latter with the less fancy and mundane sphere of politics, Heine's critical insistence on the poetic irreducibility of form and content fell by the wayside for many readers. Separating the aesthetic from the political dimension ignored the very purpose of Heine's writing, which pointedly interweaves politics and aesthetics. It is the dialectic of the aesthetic and the political that drives every line of Heine's writing, from the most "poetic" to the most "prosaic," generating its distinctly emancipatory movement. For Heine, this is the defining point that animates literature, culture, and intellectual life in general, and not just in modernity.

To put it differently: Heine's literary project presents a critical exploration of the interplay between prose and poetry, content and form. Inattention to the programmatic significance of this dialectic has led to reductive readings of Heine by both the aesthetically inclined and politically minded readers. What they fail to appreciate is that Heine's writing dwells on the interface that both connects and divides the aesthetic and the political as it engages with novel, creative literary forms and effects. Like a master weaver, Heine produces his texts shooting the shuttle through the frame interlinking the distinct and separate threads into a fabric that both holds them together and serves as the structure that allows contrast and tension to do their work. As a result, however, Heine has been taken to task for displaying unreliable and morally dubious (if not obscene) and politically suspect and philosophically flawed and shallow (if not trivial) views. But such classifications result from the collapse of the author and his fictional personae.[26] Ironically, it is precisely the playful leveling of this distinction that serves Heine as a literary strategy to give the issues of morals, politics, culture, aesthetics and their intertwined relation provocative expression.

As a result, Heine's view of the function of language assumes central importance as a critical site where these issues are played out. Chapter 4, "The Signifying Lizard: Language, Sign, and Play," examines the way in which Heine's play with language as a complex weave of metaphors, linguistic glitches, and double entendres within and in between dialects and languages gives voice to a sustained critique of the repressive character of the concept. Heine's language games and politics resonate strongly with Benjamin's and Adorno's approach to language, including Adorno's insistence, examined in Chapter 3, that there is no *Sprachontologie*, no ontology of language, as the metaphysically invested linguistic nationalism of German cultural discourse assumed. Objects and animals may choose to speak or not. It is not insignificant that Heine's signifying lizard speaks, whereas the monkeys refuse to do so in order to elude human exploitation, by escaping exposure to the regime of language; nor that the paragon of German high canonical literature, Goethe, turns out to use the vernacular dialect of the Frankfurt in which he was raised, undaunted by, and dismissive of, perceived notions of linguistic purity. In a move that anticipates Nietzsche's insight into the pervasive metaphoricity of language and thought, Heine's play with language—like Wittgenstein's language games—preludes Adorno's reminder of the nonconceptual as the limit of the epistemological reach of the concept, a reminder that finds humorous iterations in Heine's situational comedy of linguistic confusions.

Heine's Modernity

Moving between cultural, national, and religious identities and challenging social, political, literary, and aesthetic conventions, Heine articulates a vision of modernity that would not be fully appreciated until New York Intellectuals and Weimar Jews in exile began to rally around a "transnational" Heine. Heine's approach to modernity lent him the "restlessness" that Jean-Luc Nancy recognizes as the defining moment in Hegel.[27] But Heine's restlessness was different, informed as it was by the cosmopolitan eye of an exile in Paris. The dialectic of Heine's restlessness was driven by a critical engagement with modernity that parted ways with Hegel at a critical point: Heine remained wary of a vision of modernity whose irresistibly universal perspective turned a blind eye to the singularity that had made it possible in the first place. Heine's unease with Hegel's dialectic as more than a discursive praxis and diagnostic tool distinguishes him from Hegel without compromising the emancipatory and philosophically critical aspect that Hegel's "restlessness" offers.[28]

Heine achieves this by turning to his Jewish difference as the point that makes it impossible to submit to Hegel's supersessionist embrace, the theological and teleological premises of which remained steeped in a notion of redemption that threatened to cancel the genuinely messianic force of a more inclusive emancipatory vision. Heine's recourse to the multiple sources of forgotten or repressed Jewish traditions and their often pointedly folkloristic allure emerges as a theoretically articulate, carefully calibrated critique of modernity's foundations in the religious and secular variations of "Western" cultural achievement. This recourse remains pointedly strategic and therefore functions critically in the precise meaning that Kant had proposed. Rather than a triumphant vision of restoration, Heine relies on the transformative notion of the messianic. Heine's comedic mode facilitates the project of imagining Jewish modernity as an autonomous and constitutive agent consistent with the project of "modernity" at large that, in his view, could only be a viable project in the plurality of diverse modernities whose various temporalities would be open to an emancipatory embrace of the simultaneity of the nonsimultaneous.

While Heine is among the first to follow Hegel in recognizing that modernity's claim to universality must be creatively anchored in historical particularity, he understood that the singularity of the particular could not be negotiated if it was not to be compromised. Hegel relied on Christianity as the paradigm for the spirit's way of reconciling the particular with the universal. For Heine, the desire for reconciliation and any other form of *Aufhebung* or sublation was precisely where the problem resided. For Heine, no tradition, religion, or culture was to be privileged over another. Rather, they were all to be considered in the context of their particular reciprocal relationships with the other traditions, religions, and cultures from which they distinguished themselves and which defined them differentially.[29]

Heine's approach to renegotiating modernity aims at more than just challenging literary genres, social norms, and disciplinary boundaries. He introduces the term *Modernität* in *The North Sea Part 3*, the third of his *Travel Pictures*, published in 1827. When the text was translated a few years later into French, it presumably introduced the term into French as well.[30] The second prose text in *Travel Pictures*, in which Heine innovatively and provocatively experimented by mixing prose and poetry, *The North Sea Part 3* scrutinizes early signs of the changing times leading up to the July Revolution of 1830, a period of intense conflict between the old and the new, where the "modern" is sometimes the old in new disguise and the "old" is the conduit and facilitator of the change and transformation that the radical desire for the "modern" can ironically threaten, if not undermine. For Heine, modernity is no stage, state, or period, but the name for the movement of the dialectic between old and new.

In Heine's text, the word "modernity" enters the world in a tellingly convoluted discussion that exemplifies the complicated dialectic of the phenomenon it seeks to grasp. For Heine, Napoleon is the character who captures, better than anyone else, the spirit of his time. A more precise understanding of Napoleon thus promises a better understanding of the meaning of modernity:

> But as this spirit of the age is not only revolutionary, but is formed by the antagonism of both sides—the revolutionary and the counterrevolutionary—so did Napoleon act not according to either alone, but according to the spirit of both principles, both efforts, which found in him their union. (L 2, 254)

> Da aber dieser Geist der Zeit nicht bloß revolutionär ist, sondern durch den Zusammenfluß beider Ansichten, der revolutionären und der contrerevolutionären, gebildet worden, so handelte Napoleon nie ganz revolutionär und nie ganz contrerevolutionär, sondern immer im Sinne beider Ansichten, beider Prinzipien, beider Bestrebungen, die in ihm ihre Vereinigung fanden. (B 2, 235)

However, in order to capture the rich and fluid phenomenon of Napoleon, we require a historiographical method that creatively responds to the challenge that the dialectic movement of this phenomenon represents. Heine addresses the question of how to understand modernity—the history of the now that is about to unfold—as the question of how to approach the problem of the history of the present, a problem he tackles by approaching the history that is yet to unfold. To this end, he addresses the expectations raised by a new book by the successful author of historical novels, Walter Scott. But Heine's particular interest in Scott's new book, a book, he points out, that he has not yet seen, is that despite the recent death of Scott's subject, Napoleon continues to represent a living history, a history whose consequences had not yet fully unfolded:

> It is a fortunate coincidence that Napoleon lived just in an age which had a remarkable inclination for history, for research, and for publication [Darstellung]. Owing to this cause, thanks to the memoirs of contemporaries, but few particulars of Napoleon's life have been withheld from us, and the number of histories which represent him as more or less allied to the rest of the world, increase every day. On this account the announcement of such a work by Scott awakens the most anxious [neugierigste] anticipation.[31]

> Es ist ein glückliches Zusammentreffen, daß Napoleon gerade zu einer Zeit gelebt hat, die ganz besonders viel Sinn hat für Geschichte, ihre Erforschung und Darstellung. Es werden uns daher, durch die Memoiren der Zeitgenossen, wenige Notizen über Napoleon vorenthalten werden, und täglich vergrößert sich die Zahl der Geschichtsbücher, die ihn mehr oder minder im Zusammenhang mit der übrigen Welt schildern wollen.

> Die Ankündigung eines solchen Buches aus Walter Scotts Feder erregt daher die neugierigste Erwartung.[32]

Precisely, Heine argues, because Walter Scott was so unlikely to embrace the revolutionary impulse in Napoleon, he would be more disposed to examine the counterrevolutionary features that inform Napoleon as well. While Byron would have seized on the revolutionary aspects, Scott's retrospective orientation would enable us to grasp the tug-of-war between modernity's unrelenting push and pull that an exclusively revolutionary outlook would be doomed to overlook. Scott's nostalgia enables him to comprehend the profound historical significance of the dialectic of "unpleasant modernity" (*unerfreuliche Modernität*, B 2, 236) to which Byron would remain oblivious, notwithstanding Heine's sympathies for Byron, whose German double he was considered early on.[33] Pointedly, Heine's discussion is based here on a speculation, that is, the question of how the difference between Scott's and Byron's approaches would play out in the face of live history. In other words, Heine stages the entry of expectation and its function for the writing of history as the moment where modernity emerges as the term for a new understanding of history and temporality.

Situating modernity's conflicted negotiation of the present at the intersection of what Reinhart Koselleck calls the horizon of experience and the horizon of expectation, modernity becomes the contested site for working out the antagonism between the old and the new.[34] On closer examination, the unpleasantness of this modernity turns out to be more complicated than it might have seemed at first glance. For Heine contrasts this "wide-spreading, unpleasant modernity" (*weite, unerfreuliche Modernität*) to the "comfortable narrow way of their ancestors" (L 2, 257, *behaglich enge Weise der Altvorderen,* B 2, 236).[35] The contrast of this juxtaposition leads to a dialectical reversal that simultaneously interconnects the binary scheme and switches the opposed pairs around, short-circuiting any quick and easy distinction. Modernity emerges as the moment when the antagonism between the old and the new becomes a dynamic constituting the present as the interface between past and future.

For Heine modernity means engagement and conflict rather than any overpowering, universal vision of grey, monotonous modernism. It is the clash between the contemporary and the noncontemporary, the forward and backward tension between "now" and "then": the contradiction between forces that seem to belong to the past even as they continue to define the present, and opposite forces that announce a new age whose outline can be glimpsed only by looking forward into a rearview mirror that reflects the past through visions of the future. Modernity is then the constellation of ever-new reconfigurations of the present mirrored in a vision of the future of the past and the past of the future, the ever-reconfigured constellation of the present at the interface of past and future. For Heine, this negotiation is a process whereby the simultaneity of the nonsimultaneous produces a contradiction that no longer calls for a final resolution or quiescence. Modernity is an open and open-ended project.

What Adorno identified as the "central philosophical theme and the central dialectical image" in Benjamin is the same concern we find at the heart of Heine's theorization of modernity: "The representation of the modern as the new, as the past and the eternally invariant in one"[36] (*die Darstellung der Moderne als des Neuen, des schon Vergangenen und des Immergleichen in Einem*).[37] Indeed, the late "Theses on History" and much of the *Arcades Project* read like a gloss on Heine's critical engagement with the challenge of rethinking time and temporality in the face of modernity:

> It's not that what is past casts light on what is present, or what is present its light on what is past; rather, image is that wherein what has been comes together in a flash with the now to form a constellation.[38]
>
> Nicht so ist es, dass das Vergangene sein Licht auf das Gegenwärtige oder das Gegenwärtige sein Licht auf das Vergangene wirft, sondern Bild ist dasjenige, worin das Gewesne mit dem Jetzt blitzhaft zu einer Konstellation zusammentritt.[39]

In identifying historical materialism's task of renouncing "the epic element in history" (*das epische Element der Geschichte*) in order to "blast the epoch out of the 'reified continuity of history'" (*sprengt die Epoche aus der "dinghaften Kontinuität der Geschichte" ab*),[40] Benjamin offers an apt description of Heine's mode of writing:

> Only dialectical images are genuine images (that is, not archaic); and the place where one encounters them is language.[41]
>
> Nur dialektische Bilder sind echte (d.h.: nicht archaische) Bilder; und der Ort, an dem man sie antrifft, ist die Sprache.[42]

We can grasp the rich complexity of Benjamin's critical appropriation of historical materialism more precisely if we attend to Heine's practice of a historical materialism *avant la lettre*—which Marx and Engels appropriated without always directly acknowledging their source, as Chapter 5 shows.

The often surprisingly striking affinity between Heine and Critical Theory bears significance not only for a better understanding of the prehistory of the Frankfurt School, it also allows for a more nuanced appreciation of Heine's approach to history.[43]

Repositioning Heine outside the canon of philology and contextualizing him in the history of Critical Theory sheds new light on the critical significance of literature as a form of critique that boldly reimagines modernity as the site for literary, social, and political renegotiation of culture and society.

Chapter 5, "Messiah in Golden Chains: Deferred Action and the Concept of History" thus explores Heine's often performative approach to rethinking history, time, and temporality. Exploring the various ways in which past and future inform each other as we seek to grasp the present, Heine brings out the present's transitory aspect as the fleeting moment of a modernity defined by the continuous experience of interruption and repetition. Heine not only offers an early form of the critique of historicism that Nietzsche will express a few decades later, his writing is also permeated with a sharp sense for historicity that anticipates historical materialism. At the same time, his keen sense for the effect of delay and deferral in the process of history anticipates what Simmel and Freud will call *Nachträglichkeit*.

Effects of deferred action recur in Heine's poetry and narrative fiction as well as in his writings on history and historiography—both as literary strategy and as their central theme. In contrast to Nietzsche and the Frankfurt School, where remnants of the trace of eschatological thinking linger, Heine retains an epistemologically critical angle. Heine's poetic and critical voice rejects any sort of ontology of history in what could be called, in analogy to Adorno's rejection of ontology of language, Critical Theory's rejection of ontology of history.

Heine's provocative embrace of pleasure and joy is subversive in the precise meaning of the word: it empowers to liberation from repressive regimes as such, that is, of body and matter over mind and spirit and vice versa. In a similar fashion, Benjamin, Adorno, Fromm, and Marcuse recognized the revolutionary force that pleasure and joy could set free; they shared Heine's view of the repressive character of asceticism to the same extent that Nietzsche had. Chapter 6, "The Comedy of Body and Mind: Emancipation and the Power of the Affects" examines how Heine and Critical Theory approach the relationship between body and mind. Heine's provocative advocacy for the body and matter—for a "rehabilitation of the flesh" and the life of the affects as well as his attention to the powerful dynamic of the unconscious—resonates deeply with Critical Theory's political and theoretical agenda for the complete recovery of the dignity of the bodily and material aspects of human existence. It is no coincidence that agreement on this point proves to be the linchpin and backbone of any critical thinking, an agreement that manifests itself in Heine and Adorno's shared embrace of Spinoza, which in Heine's case was proudly open, and in Adorno's case coyly covert. Spinoza's dual-aspect monism exposes the problematic character of the kind of theological-political commitments that both Heine and Critical Theory reject as ideologically suspect.

Approaching secularization as a process itself more profoundly tied up with religion than its champions realize, Heine examines the entanglement of what, following Spinoza, can be called the theological-political complex. Similar to Heine's creative use of Jewish tradition to contrast the theological-political implications of the dominant forms of secularization informed by the hegemonic constructions of modernity, Benjamin, Adorno, Horkheimer, Marcuse, and Fromm, among others, turn to Jewish tradition to suspend the discursive hold of organized religion in general and the institutionalized form of theological discourse informed by Christian-inflected forms of secularization in particular.

Chapter 7, "Myths of Enlightenment: Heine's Secularization Narratives" thus traces how secularization figures as a central concern for Heine and Critical Theory in theorizing modernity. For Heine, religion will not be driven one day to other pastures, as it were, by the light cast by reason on its path of secularization. Rather, Heine's narratives expose how religion, particularly in its institutionalized forms, is intrinsically a function of secularization. In order to exist, religion presupposes secularization because religion must lay claim to the secular in order to secure the divine and holy. Secularization is not a universal phenomenon. In other words, secularization itself is a theological concept contingent on the theological discourse that produces it. By exposing the theological character of secularization, Heine emphasizes the historically contingent character of modernity as a contested site of negotiation where there is a constant risk of enlightenment's relapse into myth. For Heine the post-secular is, strictly speaking, the condition produced by religion itself. We might be unable to simply opt out of religion, but critical independence does not require the abandonment of one's religious tradition so much as its creative renegotiation.

If the difference between Heine and Critical Theory is that Critical Theory lacks the boisterously liberating openness of Heine's humor, an allegorical reading of Heine's novella *The Rabbi of Bacherach* makes it clear that Critical Theory's endurance depends on its ability to reconcile skepticism, humor, self-irony, and the "haggadic" element as its most vital aspects. Chapter 8, "Another Abraham, Another Sarah: Heine's Frankfurt Shul in *The Rabbi of Bacherach*" thus concludes the book with a discussion of *The Rabbi of Bacherach*, a novella with an open-ended narrative trajectory underscored by its subtitle "a fragment"—a Romantic term suggesting a lack of completion open to future realization. Set in the late Middle Ages, Heine's story of Abraham and Sarah, the rabbi and rebbetzin of Bacherach on the River Rhine, offers an ingenious and playfully allegorical exploration of Judaism on the eve of modernity. While Abraham embodies the writ and legal wisdom of Jewish tradition, Sarah reflects the sovereign openness of love. Their marriage—the marriage between *Halacha* and *Aggadah*—illustrates that literal and allegorical gender balance is required if the life of tradition is to flourish. Yet something is missing in this marriage until Sarah opens her heart to welcome Isaac—the "prodigal son"—into their family. Tradition lives on, the story suggests, only by embracing its own antagonist inner tensions.

Heine's midrashic intervention opens the future by breaking off the narration at the resumption of the Passover meal the next day, thus restoring the Last Supper's function to its original meaning as a site of the transmission of living tradition rather than of martyrdom and sacrificial sanctification. If the name of Heine's double in the novella, Don Isaac, signifies the pleasure of laughter into which Sarah bursts when she hears God's messenger announce the unexpected arrival of a son, Heine's midrash suggests that Jewish tradition does not come to life until it opens its heart to the renegade, the heretic with the liberating laughter of joy and self-irony. This lesson does not hold true only for Abraham and Sarah as they encounter Isaac outside the Frankfurt Shul; the same can be said of any tradition, including that of the Frankfurt School and of Critical Theory more generally: theory, just like tradition, only has a chance where laughter born of pleasure and joy is welcomed in as the offspring that enables life. Heine's joyous comedy reminds us that tradition's most vital force is the pleasure it takes in the play of repetition and difference, continuity and change, or, in other words, the recognition that tradition itself consists in negotiating its identity through the difference it makes. Reading Heine with Critical Theory allows us to better appreciate Heine, but it also enables us to revisit, rethink, and reimagine Critical Theory as a project harboring the promise of liberation by embracing the pleasure of dissonance and alterity.

1

Displacement, Relocation, and the Dialectic of a Constellation: Heine, Critical Theory, and the New York Intellectuals

In 1908, Lev Davidovich Bronstein, a young Russian revolutionary who had a few years earlier assumed the name Trotsky, opened his article on the occasion of Tolstoy's eightieth birthday with the following comment:

> Tolstoy has passed his eightieth birthday and now stands before us like an enormous jagged cliff, moss-covered and from a different historical World.
>
> A remarkable thing! Not alone Karl Marx but, to cite a name from a field closer to Tolstoy's, Heinrich Heine as well appear to be contemporaries of ours.[1]

Trotsky's remark reflects the sentiment of generations of literary critics, intellectuals, revolutionary visionaries, and activists for whom Heine was still a contemporary whose striking literary voice continued to thrill with the same liberating thrust that had charmed his first contemporaries, from Schumann and Felix Mendelssohn to Marx and Engels, and unsettled admiring readers like Metternich.[2] But Heine's intellectual and literary presence has endured and developed a posthumous life of its own as his distinct voice continues to critically inform the literary, intellectual, and political discourse up to the present. It is not just that Heine's language, diction, and thinking have shaped contemporary linguistic sensitivities; he has also become a powerfully enduring presence in modern German culture and thought. Remarkably, Heine's impact was so profound and wide-reaching that it went well beyond the boundaries of linguistic spheres of influence. Around 1900, Alfred Schumacher noted in the *Manchester Quarterly* that no German poet, not even Goethe, had in that year an equally wide circle of readers throughout the globe.[3] By 1948, Heine was seen as a "citizen of the world"—at least as far as the anglophone world was concerned.[4]

In 1954, at the moment when the Cold War overshadowed debates about the course culture and politics were to take and the cultural identity of postwar America was being renegotiated, Sol Liptzin programmatically noted in the introduction to his book *The English Legend of Heine*:

> The English legend of Heine, from its origin in pre-Victorian days to its present configuration, is markedly different from the German legend and sheds light upon Heine and upon the English-speaking world which has assimilated him into its cultural pattern.
>
> Our Heine, citizen of the world, bears the contours of our day, contours that are no less valid or fascinating than those etched by our forebears in the many decades since he first appeared upon the literary horizon. Our Heine, as reshaped by us, may be exerting a significant influence upon the thinking and dreaming of the Occident in the years to come, even as the Heine of our fathers has influenced us in our eventful years. It is, therefore, of value to us to know that ever changing legend of Heinrich Heine.[5]

As we will see, this programmatic note was not as illusory as it might seem to today's readers. Indeed, the first decade after the end of Second World War saw an often intense engagement with Heine and his legacy that addressed the future cultural makeup of the postwar public sphere. This was a debate in which exponents of the Frankfurt School and New York Intellectuals met over a shared concern about the place and function of Jewish identity in modernity. If this encounter was brief, the shared concern reflected a remarkable convergence between American and German Jews at the juncture where Heine assumed paradigmatic significance for Americans and exiles who were negotiating Jewish identity as a part of the transnational identity they envisioned in a newly reconfigured world.

Since 1916, when Randolph Bourne published his article "The Jew and Trans-National America" in the December 1916 issue of *Menorah*, a journal published by the association of Jewish ivy league students of the same name, discussion concerning the promise of Jewish identity in enabling and enriching the concept of a transnational American identity had developed into a key concern, and it was no coincidence that Heine gained paradigmatic significance in this discussion as early as 1920.[6] This transnational context is key if we are to understand the fuller significance of Heine's role in the discussion of Jewish identity and modernity. The philosophically charged and theoretically sophisticated thrust of the Jewish negotiations of Heine emerges in this context as neither a European fixation nor an American invention but rather as a transatlantic project. Reflecting the displacement and relocation of Jewish lives in transit between the old and the new world, the discourse on Heine becomes a transnational affair that enables reflection on Jewish identity in a newly global perspective. This disconnect with the more nationally oriented project of German canon-building philology presents a creative friction in whose force field Heine assumes a differentially motivated liberating force.

This is the juncture at which Critical Theory emerges, itself a transatlantic formation whose European leg has for too long been overemphasized at the expense of acknowledging the critical importance of its other, "exilic" moment. It is not only that some of its most momentous contributions were worked out and written in exile in an American context, but that the experience of displacement and relocation plays a substantial role in the formation of Critical Theory itself, and not just in the way Heine figures in this formation process.

Examination of Heine's reception between the First World War and the early Cold War must therefore no longer limit its purview to Germany or to Europe, but must include a more global approach if it is to capture the larger picture of the role Heine played in the twentieth century. But entering the twentieth century, Heine faced the challenge of a fierce tug-of-war between a diverse array of audiences, from simple consumers to sophisticated connoisseurs, from literary critics on the left to state-salaried, tenured scholars on the right whose literary appreciation was determined by the agenda of the national canon-building project over which they presided. By the beginning of the twentieth century, a rigid dichotomy had split Heine asunder into a political and a lyrical voice. By pitting prose against poetry, subversive political writing against mellifluous and seemingly innocuous verse, the reception at the turn of the century had succeeded in neutralizing the critical impulse of what Heine's writing stood for: a continuous reminder of the deep link between aesthetics and politics.

The separation of the literary from the political, and the German from the Jewish aspect of Heine—as if such a separation were possible—rooted itself so deeply in the cultural unconscious that resistance to this great divide seemed to have become a lost cause. At the end of the nineteenth century, Heine had become popular as the foremost lyrical voice for romantic music. At the same time, he enjoyed notoriety as a critic whose mastery of subversive writing inspired the leftist intelligentsia. This split into a binary reception forced Heine into emigration from the canon of German literature as the literary scholars and historians who sought to enshrine him as a canonical figure succumbed to the Lorelei-like lure that assimilated Heine to the commitments of Goethe-centric philology. This move alienated the young, Jewish leftist intelligentsia from a Heine assimilated to a nationalist cultural politics that threatened to drown their revolutionary aspirations.

This splitting of Heine into the sublime romantic on the one hand, and the subversive critic on the other, thus reflected the pressures that defined the cultural, social, and political situation in the late nineteenth and early twentieth century. At the same time, the explosive force of Heine's emancipatory impulse was absorbed into the language and texture of Marx, Nietzsche, and Freud. Heine, in other words, was treated as if he had become an empty poetic shell whose living voice had to be hidden away as a transplant in order to live on.

Michael Löwy has argued that the generation of central European Jewish intellectuals from Martin Buber to Ernst Bloch, Gustav Landauer, and George Lukács—and that would also include, among many others, Franz Kafka, Franz Rosenzweig, Leo Löwenthal, Walter Benjamin, Max Horkheimer, and Theodor Adorno—shared a profound sense of elective affinity with a unique mix of German romanticism and revolutionary messianism.[7] Gershom Scholem's entries in his diaries during the First World War reflect this affinity and the often conflicted ambivalence that came with it in a paradigmatic manner. In his "95 Theses on Judaism and Zionism," Scholem noted this conflicted relationship, enigmatically asserting:

> 41) Jewish Romanticism means an illicit border transgression.
>
> 42) Romanticism is the only intellectual movement in history that has limited Judaism. The fact that it was unaware of this makes it demonic.
>
> 41) Jüdische Romantik bedeutet eine unerlaubte Grenzüberschreitung.
>
> 42) Die Romantik ist die einzige geistige Bewegung der Geschichte, die das Judentum limitiert hat. Daß sie dies nicht wußte, macht sie dämonisch.[8]

In a telling comment, Scholem states the same year: "Romanticism is a deducible constellation of the Messianic." ("Die Romantik ist eine deduzierbare Konstellation des Messianischen.")[9] Scholem's emphatic claim expresses this generation's shared sentiment that romanticism was not alien to Jewish thought and tradition but was, in fact, profoundly connected to it. While deeply connected to their unique version of romantic or, more precisely, post-romantic currents, Heine, the paramount figure who broke the ground for and modeled this constellation, remained curiously unacknowledged or, more precisely in the case of Scholem, resolutely ignored. But it was Heine's transformative engagement with romanticism that played a critical role in recovering the progressive and emancipatory potential hidden behind romanticism's conservative religious veneer. Not only this generation's language, diction, dreams, and aspirations, but also their particular form of articulating their conceptual and theoretical sensibilities will remain incomprehensible as long as Heine's critical role in setting the post-romantic agenda remains ignored; his intervention not only had a fundamental impact on the Central European Jewish generation at the turn of the century, it also played a seminal role in the formation of the turn-of-the-century generation of American Jewish intellectuals.

Leo Löwenthal, Max Horkheimer, and Heine in the Bronx

While tracing the various inflections of Heine's reception by this generation is a variegated proposition, we can distinguish a basic typology for the group of intellectuals associated with the Frankfurt School. Leo Löwenthal, for instance, argued in an essay that Jewish concerns were not only defining for Heine, but that it was these very aspects of his work that made Heine so significant for German culture, securing his universal relevance. As early as the 1920s, as he was going through a phase of strong Jewish self-identification, Löwenthal noted that for Heine, Judaism had become the symbol of liberation.[10] Two decades later, Löwenthal would repeat this point in the English translation of this Heine essay. Published in 1947 in *Commentary*, a journal that was at that time the progressive voice of the Jewish New York intellectuals, Löwenthal gave the English translation of his essay the striking title "Heine's Religion: *The Messianic Ideals of the Poet*." It concluded with the following statement, reflecting the degree to which the challenge presented by Heine remained for Löwenthal a conflict yet to be worked through:

> He [i.e. Heine] was a critic of capitalism, but he criticized it on spiritual rather than economic grounds. Judaism was for him a symbol of liberation. He was allowed to return to the symbol, but not to the reality the symbol stood for. He loved the symbol, though it made him suffer. He saw a sickness in Judaism, but he approved the sickness.[11]

As Martin Jay noted in a recent essay, Löwenthal remained convinced that "Heine's Jewish identity was central to his cosmopolitan, redemptive project."[12] The essay represents, as Thomas Wheatland points out in his account of the American period of the Institute for Social Research, "a powerfully crafted example of the kind of Jewish exploration that Elliot Cohen and the rest of the editorial board of *Commentary* were encouraging. The figure of Heinrich Heine functioned for Lowenthal as a symbol for the problems faced by the entire New York Intellectual community and by many German-Jewish exiles as well."[13] Wheatland argues that "through Heine [. . .] Lowenthal [was] able to discover a distinctly Jewish identity consistent with Critical Theory and the prewar political impulses that gathered the Horkheimer circle together [. . .] In the wake of the war, Heine stood as a symbol—perhaps all Jewish exiles could return home."[14]

While Löwenthal made this point openly, Max Horkheimer seemed to share it, though he remained more conflicted about openly addressing any sort of interest in, or affinity with, Heine. In 1935, when his secretary at Columbia University told him about her inability to come in for work the next day, a Sunday, Horkheimer inquired about the reason. She replied that she was planning to attend the wreath-laying ceremony at the Heine monument in the Bronx. Horkheimer responded with an impromptu speech on Heine that lasted one and a half hours. He asked her to return Monday with a report of what had been said at the monument. She returned Monday to report that at the event, a young speaker—a German Jewish Columbia undergraduate student—had mirrored Horkheimer's office speech in its vision that German culture was preserved by the very exiles it produced. At once, Horkheimer asked his secretary to find the young man. What followed was the final chapter of the Institute's history at Columbia, with Horkheimer hiring the speaker, Joseph B. Maier, as his last assistant in New York.[15]

Asked almost half a century later by his interviewer what he had said in that speech at the Heine monument in the Bronx, Maier recalled:

> What I said in that speech in front of the Heinrich-Heine monument was that we, the refugees, the German-Jewish immigrants, were the real, the genuine heirs of German philosophy and literature. If it weren't for us, this wonderful world, this party of humanity, as I thought of it, would be lost. It *was* our task and duty to preserve it in the language and in the spirit in which it was first conceived, a heritage, dear to *Mankind*. In two essays, one on the history of German philosophy and literature, and the other on the Romantic School, Heine conveyed the idea that the Germans anticipated in thought, in spirit, what the French had put into reality in the French Revolution—"*Liberté, égalité, et fratérnité*"—must be translated into the real world. German philosophy is an important concern to the whole human race and only our remotest descendants will be able to decide whether we are to be praised or blamed for having worked out our philosophy first and our revolution afterwards. I was convinced from day one that the Nazis were a threat to all of Western civilization. The world would be destroyed if we failed to stop them. So that was my linkage to the Frankfurt School and where one year later I married Alice, my young lady, with Heine's and Horkheimer's blessings.[16]

During this time, Maier also worked closely with Adorno, Marcuse, Fromm, Friedrich Pollock, and Löwenthal, among others. A few years later, at the German Jewish newspaper *Aufbau*, he also became a close collaborator with Hannah Arendt.[17]

But as far as Horkheimer is concerned, there is another crucial point to this story. Though Horkheimer seems to have embraced Heine as a Jewish writer and critic as well as a representative of German literature and culture's greatest achievements, he kept his enthusiastic impromptu advocacy at home. It apparently did not occur to him to take a cab to the Bronx to join the memorial celebration. In its more than comic aspect, this ambivalence sets in relief the eloquent advocacy he shied away from expressing in public.

In the third, February 1, 1935 issue of *Aufbau*, the new publication of the organization of the German-Jewish Club in New York that had just begun to appear in December 1934, the front page article announced the celebration at the Heine memorial. It underlined both the event's importance as a demonstration by the German Jewish emigrants who saw themselves as the legitimate heirs to the legacy of German culture and Heine's exemplary significance in this act of recovery. The article went on to explain that the German-Jewish Club had in January 1934 passed a resolution to commemorate the anniversary of Heine's death by organizing an annual wreath-laying ceremony. As the article notes, this amounted to a virtual rediscovery of the Bronx Heine monument, which had been practically unknown to many new arrivals from the most recent waves of German Jewish immigrants—a fact that was all the more surprising since in Germany, which was otherwise so memorial-saturated, there was not a single memorial for Heine.

New York's newest Jewish immigrants from German lands could thus relate especially well to Heine, or so *Aufbau* suggested, as the article's opening lines brought home the point of current emigrants' intimate ties with the past:

> The literature of the emigrants of the last two years is neither new nor unique. It had a great predecessor. That was the "young Germany" of the *Vormärz* [pre-March].[18]
>
> Die Emigrantenliteratur der letzten zwei Jahre ist weder erstmalig noch einmalig. Sie hatte einen grossen Vorläufer. Das war das "junge Deutschland" des Vormärz.

And in staccato style, the second paragraph explained:

> Heinrich Heine was the first Jewish emigrant literary figure of the German nation. He admired German culture but hated Prussianism. Because of this he had to go into exile.
>
> Heinrich Heine war der erste jüdische Emigrantenliterat deutscher Nation. Er verehrte das Deutschtum und hasste das Preussentum. Deshalb musste er ins Exil.

If the monument had, in 1899, been placed in a location defined by its marked lack of urban life, time had now caught up and the neighborhood surrounding the site of the monument in the Bronx had come to life with new urban development. As many Jews had moved into the neighborhood, the Heine monument contributed to a new feeling of home. Heine had become the figure who could make German Jewish emigrants feel at home so far away from home, because this was the city that uniquely offered their predecessor the home he never had. The *Aufbau* article left no doubt that the Heine monument's symbolical significance in making the newest wave of immigrants feel at home could barely be overestimated—for here, in their new exile, Heine himself was already at home.[19]

But Horkheimer's case was not an isolated one. A significant number of Weimar German Jewish intellectuals manifested an ambivalent mixture of embrace and rejection of Heine, and in an often highly conflicted manner. For them, Heine became the transferential object, the screen on which they projected the challenge of facing their own German Jewish experience.

A year later, in the run-up to the annual wreath-laying ceremony, a front-page article in *Aufbau* called Heine the Jewish prophet of the unholy Third Reich.[20] Its author, Erich de Jonge, underscored the "strikingly similar situation" (*verblüffend ähnliche Zustände*) that Heine was forced to confront compared to that of his own day. He went on to interpret comments made by Heine in his book *Ludwig Börne: A Memorial* as a prophecy with no less to say to readers in 1936 than to those of the nineteenth century. Yet these were times of turmoil, so it may come as no surprise that only four years later, in response to a brief note that *Aufbau* had printed on March 1, 1940, under the headline "Heine in New York," a reader observed that many readers might be oblivious to the monument in the Bronx.[21]

Adorno and Benjamin

Among the members of the Institute for Social Research, Adorno was the great exception. Going against the grain of conventional wisdom, he initially showed few or no anxieties at all about public displays of affection for Heine. Upon his return to Germany, however, he became careful in the face of what he would diagnose as expression of Germany's enduring trauma: the continuing denial and repression of Heine's significance, which he designated in the later and better known of his two Heine essays as the scar and the wound.

Indeed, one year after Löwenthal published the English translation of his clarion call for a proper appreciation of Heine's way of negotiating his Jewish identity, Adorno followed with his own call for a reappraisal of Heine, delivered in a lively and animated speech at the University of California in Los Angeles in December 1948. In this signal celebration of Heine as a trailblazing voice of modernity, Adorno articulated the project of Critical Theory he would later give expression to in *Negative Dialectics* and the *Aesthetic Theory*. Whereas Lukács's Heine essay of 1935 (reprinted in 1951 in his *Deutsche Realisten des 19. Jahrhunderts*) had omitted any reference to Heine's Jewish background, themes, or concerns, Adorno does not shy away from these, although he does pointedly resist any reduction of Heine to his Jewish identity. Instead, Heine's Jewishness becomes—as in Löwenthal—the very foundation of his universal significance. While Adorno's cheerful West Coast Heine essay of 1948/9 has received little or no attention and is curiously absent from Heine and Adorno research, it calls for a reexamination not just of the standard narratives on Heine but also of those on Adorno, and not just with regard to his relationship to Heine.[22] The essay also sheds a different light on Adorno's later, much more famous and remarkably subdued German Heine essay that was first broadcast over the radio and published in 1956—on the centennial anniversary of Heine's death—and then included in volume 1 of *Notes on Literature* in 1958.

While it is generally accepted that Adorno's 1956 essay "Heine the Wound" presents Critical Theory's quasi-official dismissal of Heine, a closer examination of both essays suggests that we attend to their strategically and tactically cautious, if resolute, pleas for recognition of the critical thrust that powers Heine's writing. First published in 1985 in volume 20.2, the last volume of Adorno's collected works, the 1948 essay on Heine was largely ignored and has of late received only limited attention. But appreciation of the essay's critical significance remains a desideratum.[23] Delivered at the moment of what was, according to Wheatland, the crucial encounter between the Columbia branch of the Frankfurt Institute for Social Research and the New York Jewish intellectuals affiliated with *Commentary*, Adorno's Californian talk intervened in the challenging question of Jewish self-definition that both groups faced as attempts to define American culture and identity were renewed in the postwar period.[24]

For now, let us simply note that Adorno not only reflects on Heine's critical significance in a differentiated and sophisticated manner, but also openly acknowledges Heine's importance for Critical Theory as a whole. Yet while Marcuse's concepts of repressive tolerance and of the affirmative character of culture, and his theory of desublimation resonate well with Heine, as do Ernst Bloch's notions of the simultaneity of the nonsimultaneous and of the emancipatory power of dreams—to name just a few of the notions Heine had so eloquently pioneered—neither Marcuse nor Bloch reflect on Heine as a source of their inspiration.[25] In similar fashion, Siegfried Kracauer—whose micrological gaze was turned to the minutiae of modern life—remains silent when it comes to appreciating the great but hidden figure who anticipated critique by attention to minute detail as the condition for rethinking the project of modernity. By 1948, Adorno had already broken with the marginalization of Heine's critical voice his canonization entailed, as Chapter 3 will show.

By the middle of the last century, Heine had been so thoroughly internalized, and at the same time silenced, that even the anxiously self-reliant Hannah Arendt was unable to read Heine as anything other than a shlemiel who had submitted to the dictates of assimilation. It comes as no surprise then that the distant cousin of her ex-husband Günther Stern,

Walter Benjamin, hardly strayed from the path taken by his cohort. For Benjamin, Heine largely remained a stranger, as Benjamin claimed that he was utterly unfamiliar with Heine. But this mask of the "unfamiliar" soon falls, revealing its "*unheimlich*" origins. Benjamin's early resistance to Heine, with whom he shares so many concerns and ideas that are crucial to both, may not have been accidental. Benjamin was not only a distant relative of Heine, but the family tradition had it that as a small girl, Benjamin's grandmother had been dandled on the poet's knees.[26] Benjamin's grandmother on Heine's lap: I think we can now understand why Benjamin came to Heine only late in life, as his biographers Eiland and Jennings note. Though not despite his family relation to Heine, as they claim, but *because* of it.[27]

If Heine appears to be absent in Benjamin, a closer look shows that he nonetheless occupies an illuminatingly marginal place in Benjamin's landmark study "On Some Motifs in Baudelaire," the essay that argues for Baudelaire's paradigmatic significance for theorizing modernity. Baudelaire was himself a great admirer and defender of Heine, who is often considered as key inspirational figure for French symbolism.[28] Celebrating Baudelaire meant also embracing Heine's poetically innovative approach to modernity, which in Germany had received little recognition and been of little import, if the historians of German literature were to be believed; but it had had a palpably formative impact on nineteenth-century French poetry, Benjamin pointedly suggested, if only indirectly. In the opening paragraph of "On Some Motifs in Baudelaire," Benjamin turns to the fact that Baudelaire was the last lyric poet to achieve mainstream success, adding in parentheses that in Germany, Heine's *Book of Songs* represents the "threshold."[29] This incomplete reference is how Benjamin includes Heine in the genealogy of Baudelaire; tellingly, the term "threshold" serves in Benjamin's own writing as an important signifier for figurations of the suppressed whose uncanny staying power signals the double function of in and out as well as the centrality of the marginal.[30]

For Benjamin, Heine may indeed have represented an existential challenge so great that he could respond only by ignoring it, for it pursued him as what Arendt described as a hidden, and at the same time familial, tradition. Benjamin's studied neglect of Heine became an issue for friends like Werner Kraft and Adorno, who felt the urge to point out interesting affinities with Heine that could have been of interest to Benjamin. And indeed, there is a series of themes, concerns, and ideas that Benjamin shares with Heine and that help us read them together in productive ways. While their affinity will be pursued in more detail throughout this book, a shorthand summary of their relationship might read as follows: Benjamin's relation with Heine assumes truly allegorical, and not just symbolic, proportions; if Heine serves many of the exponents of early Critical Theory as the transferential interface to address, repress, or otherwise negotiate their Jewishness, Benjamin's quite literal family connection makes kinship and affinity in this allegorical constellation a doorway whose gatekeeper has become the canonical tradition itself.

In his essay on Benjamin's ancestors and relations written in 1981, shortly before his death in 1982, Scholem notes: "In Benjamin's family the tradition was alive that the paternal grandmother was related to Heine, but nobody knew what the exact relationship was."[31] It was Scholem who, in one of his last essays, provided the solution to this question. However, it is precisely the family tradition's open question that made it so suggestively *un/heimlich*.

Benjamin therefore might not be the key to Heine, but by refusing to be it, he might be like the gatekeeper in Kafka's "Before the Law" who both marks out and blocks the point of entry. In this way, we might consider the canonical Benjamin as the gatekeeper of one of Critical Theory's most important entry or connecting points, especially when it comes not just to Heine, but to its difficult and often vexed relationship to Jewish tradition: an open doorway that critics have, in their partial reading of Benjamin's gesture, refused to enter.

As a result, Heine's own critical significance often seems to be in danger of eclipse. But it is the very fact of this nexus—this doorway—between what is inside and outside the tradition of Critical Theory that poses the challenge of "reappraisal" that Adorno had already begun in 1948. For it is the finer nuances of German Jewish sensibilities—to which much of Frankfurt School scholarship has remained oblivious—that inform the early days of Critical Theory.

For the associates of the Frankfurt School, Heine presents the problem and challenge, but also the promise of the possibility of coming to terms with themselves, with their aspirations, expectations, and dreams, grounded in their own identity as Germans and Jews. Heine helped them see that it was the very embrace of their own particularity that carried the promise of setting them free to envision universal emancipation: a vision grounded in the recognition of their own genealogical nexus—that doorway between the different, as Benjamin suggests, in which denial marks the passageway where such truths are so often found.

But if Heine's legacy seemed to assume its full critical momentum in the twentieth century only in places like New York and Los Angeles, the location scarcely seemed accidental. Heine had an enthusiastic early reception in the United States in the second half of the nineteenth century with the achievement of two major milestones: the publication of the first German edition of his collected works in America as well as the completed translation of a large body of his collected works.[32] By the time the wave of Jewish exiles from Europe arrived in the 1930s, Heine was already firmly entrenched on American soil, especially with regard to his Jewish reception. At this point in time there existed, besides the complete edition of Heine's works in seven volumes published in Philadelphia from 1856 to 1867,[33] an almost complete edition of Heine's writings translated into English by Charles Godfrey Leland, as well as two translations by the American Jewish authors Emma Lazarus's 1881 translation *Poems and Ballads of Heinrich Heine* and the congenial translation of Heine's poetry by Louis Untermeyer, who was later known as the "American Heine."[34] In addition, a nearly complete Yiddish translation of Heine's works in eight volumes appeared in New York in 1918 under the title *Di verk fun Haynrikh Hayne*, edited by Nachman Syrkin, an effort that involved Yiddish poets associated with the avant-garde group "Di Yunge" (The Young Ones). The name of the group linked the New York Yiddish literary movement with the movement of the "Young Germany" that was intimately associated with Heine as its guiding spirit.[35]

Adolph S. Oko

At roughly the same time, Heine began to play a crucial role for the group of Jewish students around the newly founded journal *Menorah*, which was to become one of the leading intellectual Jewish publications in the anglophone world and the training ground for a group of young New York intellectuals who would become editors of *Commentary*, the new publication of the American Jewish Committee, in 1945.[36]

In 1920, under the pseudonym S. Baruch—a sign of the writer's affinity for Spinoza—Adolph S. Oko argued that to celebrate the anniversary of *Menorah* also meant commemorating the hundredth anniversary of the Verein für Cultur und Wissenschaft der Juden, the association of young Jewish intellectuals that sought to establish Judaism as a legitimate subject of academic inquiry. Remarkably, Oko's article "One Hundred Years Ago: A 'Menorah' Anniversary" foregrounded Heine's significance for contemporary American Jewish intellectual life by focusing on the way he brought his creativity to bear on the spiritual renewal of Jewish life.[37] Born in 1883 in Russia, Oko was educated in Germany and went to the United States in 1902. From 1906 to 1933 he served as librarian of the Hebrew Union College, transforming the college library to a rich collection of Judaica. He was a Spinoza scholar, actively involved in the *Societas Spinozana*. Keeping low public exposure, Oko was an intellectual who preferred to work behind the scenes. It is characteristic for the elusiveness of his work that his literary opus magnum is the posthumously published *Spinoza Bibliography* that continues to be of invaluable significance for the study of the history of Spinoza reception.[38] The essay on Heine belongs to the few exceptions of original contributions of his own that Oko published, albeit under pseudonym, and expression of his other passion besides Spinoza: Heine.[39]

Discussing Heine in the context of the "*Menorah*-like" Verein für Cultur und Wissenschaft der Juden,[40] Oko elegantly dealt with the question of Heine's Jewishness, pointing out that the Verein's president, Eduard Gans, had insisted on the election of Heine as a member. For Oko, Heine's work in the Verein had exemplary significance and it is precisely Heine's refusal to "treat Judaism as a kind of modernized Pietism"[41] that demonstrated, for Oko, Heine's enduring importance. But what made Heine's modernity possible, he suggests, was that his creative and progressive approach to Judaism was matched by an intellectual power that allowed him to see the connections between Jewish concerns and other realms. Precisely because Heine's outlook was universal—with a critical difference—he was able, Oko argues, to embrace modernity from an independently Jewish point of view:

> Heine, besides being a great poet, fascinated by the eternal riddle of existence, was also a great man of letters, who coined thought into language so terse and so vivid as to become part and parcel of the intellectual currency of the nineteenth century. (21)

With striking perceptiveness, Oko tore both Heine's opponents and his "frenemies," as we might say today, to intellectual shreds, with the panache for which the New York Intellectuals were famous:

> Few poets throughout the ages, and few, if any, thinkers of the nineteenth century had such deep things to say. He had perhaps the greatest message for this great century. But he was—like his great "cousin" Jesus of Nazareth—a spendthrift who, while delivering his message, dropped so much by the way. Our natural enemies, the anti-Semites, brand him therefore as "Jew"; while our unnatural friends, the philo-Semites, lay stress on his "cynicism." (21)

Later that year, another author in the same volume of *Menorah* called Heine "the greatest modern poet of the Hebrew race."[42]

If Heine had become the emblem of the modern Jewish poet, intellectual, and exile who had already arrived intellectually in the Bronx, ready to welcome the European refugees in the 1930s, his paradigmatic significance intensified as Jewish intellectuals in New York began to lay claim to their own critical voice. Heine was not only the case study but also the challenge and provocation, spurring American Jews and newly arrived exiles to negotiate their identity both self-critically and self-consciously, as he had done a century earlier. Heine's memorial in the Bronx—the historically removed, uncanny, *heimlich* source of inspiration—became the symbol of a struggle that defined not just the debate about the literary role of Jews in America, but equally about their cultural, social, and political roles.

Heine was therefore also an important figure for the readers of *Aufbau*, New York's German-Jewish newspaper, from its inception in 1934 through the turmoil of the Second World War. He functioned as a reassuring figure whose memory renewed hopes and instilled confidence for cultural survival. Heine, the exemplary German poet and European intellectual, thus emerged in the 1940s as the critical agent for negotiating Jewish identity during the

Cold War. The politics of cultural containment in this period crystallized perfectly in the new appraisals of Heine, who now appeared as a figure capable of resisting assimilation and the demands to submit to the imperial fantasies of postwar America.

In 1943, Oko who had that year become the editor of the *Contemporary Jewish Record*—the official publication of the American Jewish Committee and the precursor of *Commentary*—published in the journal's pages a choice selection of Heine's writings on Jews and the Jewish tradition. He opened his introductory remarks to the selection "Of Judaism and Jews" with the following words:

> Heinrich Heine (1797–1856) is not dead. The world has not yet settled its account with him, nor he with the world. In him and around him come to light all the problems of today, political, social and moral.[43]

Whereas the introductory remarks went on to concede that "Heine also wrote things which are irreconcilable with those culled here" and that the article featured "only the positive [while] the negative was left out," the critical point of the anonymous article is that Heine's "intuitive" acuity had produced an "exacting inquiry" that continued to pose the questions Jews face today independently of scholarly correctness (551). During his brief tenure, Oko transformed the *Record* into a more intellectual forum,[44] and it might well have been with this article that Heine returned to the center of critical attention in the debates to come, with Hannah Arendt as the first to pick up the baton after Oko's death in 1944.

In a moving obituary of Oko in *Aufbau*, Arendt notes that for Oko—"the last of the great Spinoza scholars"—the *Contemporary Jewish Record* had become "more and more his personal work" that "might have made the *Record* a genuine center of contemporary Jewish productivity."[45] An increasingly rare voice of integrity, Arendt continued, "everything he wrote turned beneath his pen into fragments" (230). However, Arendt reminded her readers, the scattered remnants of this intellectual has left traces that deserve our undiminished attention:

> In the few sketches he published [. . .] is found such a precious, concentrated stylistic talent, such a mastery of succinctness and significance, that one asks oneself whether those whom the barbarity of the age strikes dumb are precisely those with the most to say." (230)

Hannah Arendt

Hannah Arendt's 1944 essay "The Jew as Pariah: A Hidden Tradition" brought this critical significance of Jewish identity to attention early on. The piece was classic Arendt: an unsparing examination of the costs of assimilation and the perils of forsaking cultural difference and submitting to cultural hegemony in ways fatal for both the individual and culture at large. Her analysis of Heine's poetic playfulness as a pointed program of cultural politics cast Heine as anything but an assimilationist who sold out his Jewish identity for a mess of European cultural pottage. For Arendt, Heine was an author whose play with assimilation's lure could enable us to reclaim the liberating impulse of the Jewish imagination nestled at the heart of German culture's hidden tradition. Arendt recognized Heine as an uncompromising proponent of an exhilaratingly open approach to the Jewish and German experience, one that enacts the simultaneity of the entwined cultural and linguistic traditions as a hallmark of modernity's promise of universal emancipation. Arendt's Heine stood for a West that would no longer seek to erase the singularity of the particular, but celebrate it as one of the infinite modes in which the universal might find form and voice. Arendt leaves no doubt that her approach is anything but nostalgic, critically engaging with the current situation she and her contemporaries faced in the United States in 1944. Heine's bold intermixing of Jewish and German experiences demonstrated that culture's most powerfully liberating impulse would always trump the assimilationist injunction to repress difference. For insisting on such an injunction reflected, as Arendt notes, a fatal failure to recognize the critical significance of cultural self-determination:

> In a manner least expected, he confirmed the queer notion so widely entertained by the early Prussian liberals that once the Jew was emancipated he would become more human, more free and less prejudiced than other men. That this notion involved a gross exaggeration is obvious. In its political implications, too, it was so lacking in elementary understanding as to appeal only to those Jews who imagined—as do so many today—that Jews could exist as "pure human beings" outside the range of peoples and nations. Heine was not deceived by this nonsense of "world-citizenship." He knew that separate peoples are needed to focus the genius of poets and artists; and he had no time for academic pipe-dreams. Just because he refused to give up his allegiance to a people of pariahs and schlemihls, just because he remained consistently attached to them, he takes his place among the most uncompromising of Europe's fighters for freedom.[46]

It was precisely Heine's provocative inscription of the emancipatory moment of Jewish experience at the heart of the German literature he created that constituted Heine's legacy, Arendt insists, and then goes on to summarize the enduring significance of that legacy:

> Of all the poets of his time Heine was the one with the most character. And just because German bourgeois society had none of its own, and feared the explosive force of his, it concocted the slanderous legend of his characterlessness. Those who spread this legend, and who hoped thereby

> to dismiss Heine from serious consideration, included many Jewish journalists.[47] They were averse to adopting the line he had suggested; they did not want to become Germans and Jews in one, because they feared that they would thereby lose their positions in the social order of German Jewry. For Heine's attitude, if only as a poet, was that by achieving emancipation the Jewish people had achieved a genuine freedom. He simply ignored the condition which had characterized emancipation everywhere in Europe—namely, that the Jew might only become a man when he ceased to be a Jew. Because he held this position he was able to do what so few of his contemporaries could not—to speak the language of a free man and sing the songs of a natural one. (ibid.)

Arendt therefore read Heine's "schlemihl"—rather than follow the American Yiddish spelling she opts for the German that shadows Chamisso's protagonist Peter Schlemihl—as a celebration of cultural difference that reclaims the hidden power of tradition's repressed origins. Her model serves as a pointed argument that Jews in America will make a difference—just like everybody else—only as long as they remain uncompromisingly true to the multiple origins of their many traditions and the experiences that shape them. This represents, for Arendt, the challenge of modernity.[48]

If Arendt's choice of the *pariah* and the *schlemihl*—the Yiddish shlemiel she marked with the German spelling—might pose problems of their own as they seemed to suggest a quick and easy reduction to sociological typecasting, they at the time signaled her resolutely critical move to reclaim difference in a critical way: as the category in the political sphere that, against the grain of Cold War cultural politics, could preserve the emancipatory vision of freedom. As vulnerable as Arendt's approach to political theory might have been given that her terms showed weary signs of obsolescence, her insistent stance on difference as a key constituent of freedom distinguished her reading of Heine as a challenging intervention in Cold War cultural politics and made it difficult to ignore. For Arendt, Heine's advocacy of the pariah and the shlemiel as agents of difference drove the point home that it was precisely a marginalized position that would facilitate realization of a free society. This, if anything, represented the continuing critical mission of Jewish emancipation in modernity. The resonance of Heine's literary voice had therefore not come to an end in a Europe that no longer existed—Arendt's reading made clear—but kept its enduring relevance as an articulate vision of a free world in the face of the homogenizing pressures of Cold War politics:

> Confronted with the natural order of things, in which all is equally good, the fabricated order of society, with its manifold classes and ranks, must needs appear a comic, hopeless attempt of creation to throw down the gauntlet to its creator. It is no longer the outcast pariah who appears the schlemihl, but those who live in the ordered ranks of society and

> who have exchanged the generous gifts of nature for the idols of social privilege and prejudice. (103)

Arendt's response simultaneously addressed a sentiment that was by that time widely shared by German and American Jewish intellectuals in the United States.

The Heine Debates in *Commentary*

However, a young critic from Palestine who had emigrated from Prague in 1938 took a rather different approach. In his article "From Mendelssohn to Kafka: The Jewish Man of Letters in Germany," published in *Commentary* in April 1947, his sweeping survey was constructed around the idea that German Jewish literary production culminated in Kafka, whom he called "the absolute figure of modern man."[49] This view precariously painted Kafka into a modernist corner of rarefied universalism from which there seemed to be no escape. This critic then threw down the gauntlet by asserting Kafka's stature as the deracinated modernist par excellence. Alongside such a towering Kafka there seemed to be no room for Heine, or so this article suggested. But Heine was also taken to task for his allegedly haphazard poetry's display of "the dissolution of artistic form," and of a style that was "scarcely the result of conscious purpose" (346). Heinz Politzer, the author of the piece, left no room for doubt: in his project of turning Kafka into the epitome of high modernism, Heine had become the fall guy, the persona non grata to be sacrificed on the altar of a revisionist view of the German Jewish experience.[50] In Heine, Politzer declared, "the German language had never really taken root": "The music of these stanzas is the consummate shaping of a consummate shapelessness." But worse: "The uncertainty of the modern European mind shows in Heine's verse," an uncertainty, Politzer went on, that consisted "in the alienation of the spirit from life" (346).

For Politzer, Heine's was a false universalism consisting in the following error:

> The need to be extraordinary forced Heine to become a European poet before becoming essentially a German poet. (346)

Germany's political sphere, however, was "too restricted, for Heine to overcome the contradiction between his German and his Jewish natures. He did not break down the barriers between the two, he jumped over them" (346), as Politzer polemically noted. Yet it was precisely by "jumping over them" rather than breaking them down that Heine remained true to the respective specificity and difference they represented.

Remarkably, it was the editor of *Commentary* himself who, in a programmatic editorial piece published in the next issue of May 1, 1947, signaled his differences with Politzer. In his essay "Jewish Culture in America: Some Speculations by an Editor," Elliot Cohen, the chief editor, laid out the pointedly progressive and inclusive vision he had for his journal and American Judaism more generally. His point was to remind his readers of the paradigmatic role American Judaism was set to play:

> We must be hospitable to all the diverse cultural elements of all the various Jewish groups within our community.[51]

Against any sort of exclusionary politics, Cohen spelled out the vision that reflected Oko's imprint. As editor of the *Contemporary Jewish Record* during its transformative years, Oko had prepared the transition to *Commentary* as the journal that would succeed the *American Jewish Record* as the new venue for intellectual debate in the public sphere.[52] Now, Cohen's comments carried on Oko's particular emphasis on Spinoza and Heine as the harbingers of Jewish modernity:

> We will excommunicate nobody. We will include also the heretic, the rebel, and the "alienated"; we remember the long line of those, Spinoza and Heine and the rest, who enriched us from outside the community—and there will be others. Necessarily and desirably, our Jewish culture will have "plural sources."[53]

Cohen concluded his "speculations" on a note that deserves attention for its resolute clear-sightedness, which highlighted the imperative to attend to a vision of Jewish culture that would creatively engage the challenges of modernity rather than submit to modernism by assimilation. The challenge was not whether or not to agree with modernism or remain stuck in some anachronistic limbo, but to embrace modernity's rich fabric of differences and to embrace them as one's own. His comments made it clear that the evocation of Spinoza and Heine was no coincidence:

> The question, "Should we have a Jewish culture in America?" is already academic. Man cannot live without culture, nor will he. Nature abhors that particular kind of vacuum. The choice that lies before us is not whether we will have a Jewish culture or not in America—we have one today. The question is whether we shall have a first-rate culture or a tenth-rate one. The question is whether we shall have a Jewish culture conceived and nurtured in imitativeness, apologetics, nationalist separatism, and mediocrity, or whether we shall have a culture that we respect and that enhances our self-respect.[54]

Cohen's call did not go unheard. Löwenthal, whose essay exposed the problematic bias of Politzer's uncharitable reading as intent on erasing the conflict at the heart of modernity and ascribing the conflict instead to those who diagnosed it, was just one of a number of critics who would challenge Politzer's essay. Published four months later in August, Löwenthal's "Heine's Religion: The Messianic Ideals of the Poet" can be read as a resolute and caustic response that, as we have seen, made the case for a more inclusive reading of Heine's cultural politics. As if in retort, Politzer returned a year later to the pages of *Commentary* to provocatively argue in a short book review that Heine's *Rabbi of Bacherach* "is no masterpiece, not even a truncated one."[55] If Salomon Maimon's autobiography, which Politzer reviewed here as well, was "a quest for truth, we find [in Heine] a quest for expediency, instead of the laugh of derision, a casual irony" (288). Reading Kafka with Politzer would however require ignoring the liberating force of the translinguistic perspective that Kafka so strikingly shares with Heine and which David Suchoff's recent study, *Kafka's Jewish Languages: The Hidden Openness of Tradition*, so eloquently brings to the fore as Kafka's postnational impulse.[56]

The same year that saw Politzer's review, Adorno began his reappraisal of Heine, while Hal Draper began the work of translating Heine's poetry (D xv). An outspoken Marxist, Draper later went on to play a role in the Free Speech Movement at Berkeley. In the 1940s in New York he was part of the Jewish New York intellectual scene, where he divided his time between his Marxist commitments and the project of translating *The Complete Poems of Heinrich Heine*, the current standard English translation of Heine's poetic works, published in 1982.

A year later, in 1949, another critic joined the fray when Martin Greenberg, an associate of *Commentary*, published his thoughtful essay entitled "Heinrich Heine: Flight and Return." Written between the publication of Politzer's essay and Greenberg's intervention, Adorno also issued his call for a reappraisal of Heine, which resonates well with Greenberg's. In his essay Greenberg exposed "The Fallacy of Being Only a Human Being," as the subtitle formulated it.[57] Greenberg framed his argument as a trenchant critique of Sartre's "Portrait of the Inauthentic Jew," which had been featured in English translation in the pages of *Commentary* a few months earlier. Heine's very life and work, Greenberg argued, demonstrated Sartre's distinction between the authentic and the inauthentic Jew to be a false one, prefiguring Derrida's analysis by several decades.[58]

Through analysis of Heine's case, Greenberg shows that Sartre's distinction commits a fatal error that speaks to the very issue at the center of the debate around Heine then swirling in the pages of *Commentary*. For Jewish intellectuals in America, Heine had become the case in point for discussing the place, role, and identity of Jews in the new vision of America that was being renegotiated while the cultural Cold War properly took hold. David Daiches expressed this sentiment in a striking manner when he concluded his review of Israel Tabak's *Judaic Lore in Heine* half a year later in the October 1949 edition of *Commentary* with the following remark:

> Heine saw Jewish thought as a part of the Western tradition, and concentrated on those aspects of it which could best be absorbed by that tradition. In doing so, he unconsciously posed the kind of problem that contributors to *Commentary* have been concerning themselves with during the last few months.[59]

Tabak himself had made a point of Heine's importance just at the moment his book was going to print, when he noted the timely significance of "Heine's messianic quest"[60] in the preface to his study dated Baltimore, December 1947:

> When about a hundred years ago Heine's writings were banned in Germany, he was hailed with enthusiasm in America, and an uncensored edition of his German works was printed in Philadelphia (John Weik 1855–7). In our time again when Heine's books were consigned to the flames in his native land, free scholars in this country have been diligently delving into his thought, holding him out, as it were, as the champion of the new freedom which mankind is hoping today.[61]

While Heine might have given cause for being seen as inauthentic, it was his very escape or "flight" from Judaism, along with the "return" he enacted, that exposed the construction of authenticity as a profoundly questionable project in itself, as Greenberg noted:

> Heine's example is one, I think, that reveals how purely formal and analytic Sartre's categories are, how little they obtain in "existence" itself. Heine was not, nor is there any Jew—or any person—entirely authentic or inauthentic. You are not confronted with a clear-cut choice between the two, as Sartre would seem to argue.[62]

The reason, Greenberg continues, is less a problem with the inauthentic than with the claim to authenticity, a descriptor that presupposes a state or form of existence that can no longer be considered viable, if it ever could have been:

> You are inauthentic, in this world, before you are aware of the possibility of being otherwise. (And yet you cannot deny your own inauthentic past, for that is a type of inauthenticity too. There are Jews who change their names from Siegfried to Yitzhak, and who, in thus attempting to deny themselves, such as they were, are as inauthentic as they were in the first.) (231)

If the desire of being otherwise undermines the very logic of authenticity, it also liberates us from the dictate of being "othered" by a universalism that depends on a hegemonic erasure of the specificity of the singular elements of which we are comprised:

> Officially, the modern world considers you of the Jewish "persuasion." A free agent, you have been "persuaded" to be a Jew, and are free, as part of your Rights of Man, to be "unpersuaded," as was Heine for a time. This is the lie with which you begin to live. Here, of course, Sartre is correct. You cannot choose not to be a Jew, you can only choose to be an authentic or inauthentic Jew. But in the same breath Sartre is wrong. You cannot choose to be authentic or inauthentic; Jew or Gentile, you can only choose not to be inauthentic any longer. And in that lies Heine's greatness as a Jew. (321)

Between Arendt's intervention in her "The Jew as Pariah" in 1944, with its bold statement of the central challenge that Heine posed to Jewish intellectuals, and Greenberg's critique of Sartre via Heine, Heine had become the critical lever against the pressures that the Cold War politics of containment posed, and not just for Jews. As Adorno's earlier essay remained unpublished for more than three decades, Heine's significance for Critical Theory easily went undetected. And even after its publication, it eluded wider recognition. A similar delay occurred with the publication of *The Complete Poems of Heinrich Heine*. Hal Draper had begun the translation in 1948, but the project was not finished until the 1970s and did not appear until 1982. All these efforts share a history of delay that led to an erasure of the specific historical juncture at which they were produced and of the way they throw into relief the decisive role that Heine played for a full century: from the middle of the nineteenth century until the late 1940s, and for negotiating not only German and Jewish but also American identity.

I think we are now in a better position to understand how Heine had become a "wound": not just in Germany, but in a similar way also in America. The forgetting of Heine and the resistance to his rediscovery were so powerful not because Heine was unknown on the American continent but, on the contrary, precisely because he had once been welcomed so enthusiastically by progressive and often revolutionary-minded German, German Jewish, Sephardi Jewish (like Emma Lazarus), and Yiddish-speaking members of American society: voices that the postwar era had so effectively silenced, if not merely contained, and whose memory has been completely erased.

It is in the course of this history, then, that the Heine monument in the Bronx has become a symbol and symptom for the role that all memorials in some way play: they reach out to us from a past to which we seek to confine them. Their aesthetically challenging sight is a reminder of the unfinished past we often prefer to pass over in order not to be reminded of the scars they represent. As the screen memory of a trauma that might reach further than just the memory of a presence that once was there but has now become a haunting absence, the monument in the Bronx stands as a monumental reminder of the once so lively and stimulating debates the postwar cultural politics so effectively succeeded in containing. But the fact that Heine arrived in America so early on and was welcomed by his German, English, and Yiddish readers—who read, recited, sang, celebrated, and commemorated him as an enduring voice in all their languages—only to then be so powerfully forgotten and repressed, suggests that Heine's critical significance can only be fully appreciated if we attend to the full force of the powerful but subliminal role Heine plays and continues to play, if often only as an absent presence, in Critical Theory.

2

Heine's Readers: Marx, Nietzsche, and Freud

Tracing resonances of Heine in Marx, Nietzsche, and Freud—three of his most attentive readers—will help bring out some of the deeper critical aspects in Heine. But examining how Marx, Nietzsche, and Freud read Heine also sheds light on key aspects of their own thought. These three readers' distinct temperaments, concerns, and agendas present us with three different readings that not only reflect the particularity of each of their approaches, but exemplify in each case the particular significance Heine assumes for their respective critical projects. Marx, Nietzsche, and Freud all turn to Heine as a formative resource.

Marx

Marx was Heine's contemporary and for a short and intense period his associate, brother-in-arms, and close interlocutor. Marx not only appreciated Heine's literary virtuosity, he was also inspired and ready to put Heine's poetry to immediate use by giving it a new venue in the *Rheinische Zeitung* he edited. Marx had already been impressed by his earlier exposure to Heine's writings, and their stylistic and rhetorical influence is evident in the young Marx's writings from the early 1840s. But Heine did not serve Marx just as an arsenal for tropes and effective syntagmatic constructions; he also evoked in Marx a response with more significant conceptual and theoretical implications. This connection and its formative role for the young Marx has been downplayed—if not completely ignored—by critics for reasons of party politics. Toeing the party line, they have sought to cordon off Marx from any sort of dependence on, or association with, anything that could be perceived as bourgeois contamination—or could not but appear as such to a hardline Marxist perception. In the wake of 1989 and the various permutations of Marxism that have emerged in the East and West, we have reached a point where we can revisit the formative scenes of theory formation in the early Marx in less constrained ways, and with a more open attitude to the multiple sources of inspiration on which Marx was able to draw.[1]

While Heine's stylistic trademark features such as chiasm, contrast, dissonance, bathos, and irony dripping to the point of caustic sarcasm recur prominently in Marx, it is Heine's critical stance against the distorting and deceptive effects of conceptual thinking and his comedic exposure of conceptual thinking's complicity in ideological purposes that Marx may have found most congenial. For Marx, Heine's style was not just paradigmatic for articulating his ideas, it also had crucial significance for the formation of his critical project. Just as Heine would identify his ultimate purpose as that of a freedom fighter, Marx understood from Heine that the most powerful means of engaging oppressive forces is a critique with an irresistible performative force. Style for Marx had a critical significance not just because it communicated his vision to his readers but also because its affective charge could empower both writer and reader in the struggle for emancipation and liberation. Marx's style, in other words, took its cue from Heine's ability to capture complex situations in a language replete with striking imagery and tropes that made it possible to express, reflect, and theorize the problems and issues that for so long had remained taboo and beyond the reach of previous forms of critique.

Heine's strategy of engagement by exposure strikes the reader with its comedy and humor, producing literary scenes with an irresistible motivating force. Condensed into snapshots whose radical moments of surprise shock the reader through comedy and laughter into recognition, Heine's writing triggers cognitive relief as his writing skirts, undermines, and exposes censorship, language politics, and containment. Heine's scenes, images, and play with tropes function subversively as a dazzling display of provocative thought-images that spotlight the deeper social and political dynamics of the scenes they enact. Marx's inspiring and sharp-edged diction with its occasional sudden changes to a fast, staccato-like style of formulaic brevity releases the firepower of a dynamics that mobilizes the reader's affects. The emancipatory energy of his writing anticipates and at the same motivates the emancipatory move it already realizes or ushers in, announcing it through its literary force as a speech act whose performativity presents an act of intervention.

Marx's description of the function of critique sheds illuminating light on Heine's writing as a literary mode committed to involving and engaging the readers rather than simply enlightening or educating them. Heine involves the reader through the drama of the affects, and Marx's writing is likewise not an epistemologically neutral body of texts but one that, through its dramatic energy, confronts the reader with his and her own complicity in cognitive repression. Marx's description of the function of critique as one of making the "petrified social relations dance by the singing of their tune"[2] captures the provocative, subversive, and liberating dynamics of Heine's poetics: a form of critique that in Marx's description is always "*hand-to-hand* combat" (30). Most importantly, Marx's point that "critique is no longer an *end in itself* but simply a *means*," and therefore no longer just a scholarly pastime but a move toward enabling new forms of praxis (30), embraces Heine's vision of the social and aesthetic dimensions as reciprocally intertwined. It is no coincidence that Marx's account of the task of critique profoundly resonates with Heine's literary practice and its implicit theoretical commitments, for Marx composed the passages just quoted during the period from the end of 1843 to January 1844, at the very moment when he met Heine in Paris and they became close collaborators and friends.[3] By that time Marx had already come to appreciate Heine's work, and while the personal encounter may have sparked buoyant intensification, Marx was already intimately familiar both with Heine's writing style, his ideas, and concepts as well as the social, political, and cultural critique they voiced. Marx's senior by two decades, Heine had come to prominence as the head of the vanguard of critical voices in Germany since the 1820s. The German and Austrian authorities had taken note of him, and he was feared and admired by Metternich for the power of his style—as Heine himself proudly liked to point out.[4]

Many of Heine's critical insights in exposing the consequences of the social conditions created by the political, economic, cultural, and religious regimes of the times recur in Marx. Heine's critical eye for how these regimes are ultimately socially produced, historically conditioned, and therefore contingent and open to change and reinvention allowed him to read and present scenes, situations, and experiences of everyday life in their minutiae allegorically as manifestations of the larger social arrangements that define the social condition. In Heine, the reality of social, cultural, and intellectual life is grounded in an economic regime that in turn is understood to be historically—and this means, for Heine, materially—produced and therefore always contingent on the vicissitudes of life. Heine's critical attention to the material conditions of social existence and their manifestations in political, cultural, and religious life manifests as a programmatic concern no later than his *Travel Pictures* of the mid-1820s, but arguably constitutes a critical concern even in his earliest work.

On the basis of his post-romantic, post-metaphysical attitude, Heine developed a strong grasp of the significance of the material conditions of social existence early on. But given his theoretical makeup, based on his particular adoption of a Spinozistically informed perspective, his materialist stance remained pointedly distanced from the radicalized forms of materialism of his time and their reductionist stance with regard to the materiality of life. Rather, relying on Spinoza's dual-aspect monism, body and mind, spirit and matter remain irreducible, but relate to each other as two sides of the same coin and only together amount to a functional whole. Heine's approach to analyzing social and cultural conditions with recourse to their material conditions as their defining moment prepared the ground for what Marx would develop into his method of historical materialism. If Hegel's history of emerging consciousness was critically challenged and subverted by Heine's complementary counternarrative of a history of unconsciousness where the underside of the world appeared with the return of the repressed, Marx gave this turn eloquent and programmatic expression when he noted that "in direct contrast to German philosophy, which descends from heaven to earth," the task had since become that of ascending "from earth to heaven."[5]

Marx's formulation that "the production of ideas, of conceptions, of consciousness is directly interwoven with the material activity and the material relationships of men" (111) echoes the narrative strategies Heine had explored since the days of the *Travel Pictures* and later elevated to a theoretically explicit and stringent narrative in the intellectual history presented in his *On the History of Religion and Philosophy in Germany*. As we will look at these texts in the coming chapters, it suffices for the purpose of these introductory remarks to note that Heine's writing offered Marx not just a wealth of stylistic and rhetorical features on which to model his writing, but in equal measure a conceptually and theoretically engaging alternative to the dominant schools of thought.

I will not argue any point of influence in what follows, but simply highlight the often striking correspondence between Heine and Marx, for it not only sheds light on the literary and poetic qualities of Marx, but also reflects in turn the conceptually and theoretically critical impetus in Heine's writing. Common to both authors' critical approaches is a way of exposing the ideological hold that has petrified social and political conditions into a repressive regime that uses its power to naturalize a system of ruthless exploitation.

In the *Harz Journey*, Heine's inaugural installment of the *Travel Pictures* published in 1826—a decade and a half prior to his encounter with Marx—the narrator takes us on a visit underground to the silver mines at Klausthal, only to find that the production of shiny silver thalers is based on a dirty, risky, and laborious process of extraction curiously associated with the exploitation of prostitution and a blindly submissive loyalty to royalty. Entering the mines, the narrator notes:

> Even the putting on of the dark convict-dress awakens very peculiar sensations. Then one must clamber down on all fours, the dark hole is so *very* dark, and Lord only knows how long the ladder may be! [. . .] I first entered the Caroline, the dirtiest and most disagreeable of that name with whom I ever had the pleasure of becoming acquainted. The rounds of the ladders were covered with wet mud. And from one ladder we descended to another with the guide ever in advance, continually assuring us that there is no danger so long as we hold firmly to the rounds and do not look at our feet, and that we must not for our lives tread on the side

> plank, where the buzzing barrel-rope runs, and where two weeks ago a careless man was knocked down, unfortunately breaking his neck by the fall. (L 2, 82f.)

> Es gibt schon eine eigene Empfindung, daß man sich ausziehen und die dunkle Delinquententracht anziehen muß. Und nun soll man auf allen Vieren hinab klettern, und das dunkle Loch ist so dunkel, und Gott weiß, wie lang die Leiter sein mag. [. . .] Ich war zuerst in die Carolina gestiegen. Das ist die schmutzigste und unerfreulichste Carolina, die ich je kennen gelernt habe. Die Leitersprossen sind kotig naß. Und von einer Leiter zur andern gehts hinab, und der Steiger voran, und dieser beteuert immer: es sei gar nicht gefährlich, nur müsse man sich mit den Händen fest an den Sprossen halten, und nicht nach den Füßen sehen, und nicht schwindlicht werden, und nur bei Leibe nicht auf das Seitenbrett treten, wo jetzt das schnurrende Tonnenseil heraufgeht, und wo, vor vierzehn Tagen, ein unvorsichtiger Mensch hinunter gestürzt und leider den Hals gebrochen. (B 2, 115f.)

Making his way over to Dorothea, the other, cleaner mine with more air to breathe, the narrator's guide shares the story of the Duke of Cambridge who brought his entire entourage on a visit to his mines, concluding the event with a dinner down in the entrails of Dorothea, where he and his company took their seats at a long wooden table, with the Duke presiding over the festivities on a big chair made of ore that had been especially made for this occasion. As the miner reports this event, animated "with fire" as he recounts all the glamorous details of this royal visit, he concludes his account by describing

> how the dear, delighted fat Duke had drained many healths, and what a number of miners (himself especially) would cheerfully die for the dear, fat Duke, and for the whole house of Hanover. (L 2, 85)

> wie der vergnügte, liebe, dicke Herzog sehr viele Gesundheiten ausgetrunken habe, und wie viele Bergleute, und er selbst ganz besonders, sich gern würde totschlagen lassen für den lieben, dicken Herzog und das ganze Haus Hannover. (B 2, 117)

While the narrator seems to be sentimentally reminiscing and praising the loyalty of the German people, such unsuspecting allegiance is pushed to the point where a naïve reading is no longer possible:

> I see loyalty thus manifested in all its natural simplicity. It is such a beautiful sentiment! And such a purely German sentiment! Other people may be more intelligent and wittier, and more agreeable, but none are so faithful as the real German race. Did I not know that fidelity is as old as the world, I would believe that a German had invented it. German fidelity is

> no modern "yours very truly," or "I remain your humble servant." In your courts, ye German princes, ye should cause to be sung, and sung again, the old ballad of *The trusty Eckhart and the base Burgund* who slew Eckhart's seven children, and still found him faithful. Ye have the truest people in the world, and ye err when ye deem that the old, intelligent, trusty hound has suddenly gone mad, and snaps at your sacred calves! (L 2, 85f.)
>
> Innig rührt es mich jedesmal, wenn ich sehe, wie sich dieses Gefühl der Untertanstreue in seinen einfachen Naturlauten ausspricht. Es ist ein so schönes Gefühl! Und es ist ein so wahrhaft deutsches Gefühl! Andere Völker mögen gewandter sein, und witziger und ergötzlicher, aber keines ist so treu, wie das deutsche Volk. Wüßte ich nicht, daß Treue so alt ist, wie die Welt, so würde ich glauben, ein deutsches Herz habe sie erfunden. Deutsche Treue! Sie ist keine moderne Adressenfloskel. An Euren Höfen, Ihr deutschen Fürsten, sollte man singen und wieder singen das Lied von dem getreuen Eckart und dem bösen Burgund, der ihm die lieben Kinder töten lassen, und ihn alsbald doch noch immer treu befunden hat. Ihr habt das treueste Volk, und Ihr irrt, wenn Ihr glaubt, der alte, verständige, treue Hund sei plötzlich toll geworden, und schnappe nach Euren geheiligten Waden. (B 2, 117f.)

If money emerges as a commodity produced by a process marked by labor and pain, the sparkling brilliance of the silver coins effectively seems to blind the untrained eye by eclipsing the darker side of the conditions of the mode of their production. Before the narrator enters the mines, he learns at the mint office how money is made and reminds the readers that his lot has been limited to watching the process of making money rather than making any himself:

> With feelings in which comic reverence was blended with emotion, I beheld the new-born shining dollars, took one as it came fresh from the stamp in my hand, and said to it, "Young Dollar! what a destiny awaits thee! what a cause wilt thou be of good and of evil! How thou wilt protect vice and patch up virtue! How thou wilt be beloved and accursed! how thou wilt aid in debauchery, pandering, lying, and murdering! how thou wilt restlessly roll along through clean and dirty hands for centuries, until, finally laden with trespasses and weary with sin, thou wilt be gathered again unto thine own, in the bosom of an Abraham, who will melt thee down and purify thee, and form thee into a new and better being. (L 2, 80f.)
>
> Mit einem Gefühle, worin gar komisch Ehrfurcht und Rührung gemischt waren, betrachtete ich die neugebornen Taler, nahm einen, der eben vom Prägstocke kam, in die Hand, und sprach zu ihm: junger Taler! Welche Schicksale erwarten dich! Wie viel Gutes und wie viel Böses wirst du

> stiften! Wie wirst du das Laster beschützen und die Tugend flicken, wie wirst du geliebt und dann wieder verwünscht werden! wie wirst du schwelgen, kuppeln, lügen und morden helfen! wie wirst rastlos umherirren, durch reine und schmutzige Hände, jahrhundertelang, bis du endlich, schuldbeladen und sündenmüd, versammelt wirst zu den Deinen im Schoße Abrahams, der dich einschmelzt und läutert und umbildet zu einem neuen besseren Sein. (B 2, 115)

Like Jews wandering in exile and abjection, carrying the Christian projection of debt, guilt, and sin, money serves as a universal carrier of value at the expense of the erasure of the dirty secret of its origins. The shine of its sparkling mint condition, as the narrator comments in his address to the thaler, or dollar. as Leland translates it, blinds the eye to the filth from which it is extracted. Just as the naive aspiration has humankind one day united in Abraham's bosom, money's aspiration is to be cleansed by being melted, refined, and transformed into a new and better existence. Upon closer examination, however, the religious inflection of this address highlights how society's casting of the Jew as the blank silver coin stamps the Jew like money in the image of a theological and simultaneously economic vision that turns a blind eye to the mechanism of repressive guilt on which it runs.

Preluding this sentiment upon entering the town of Klausthal, Heine plays with the incompatibility of catechism and mathematics, pointing out that

> the multiplication table contrasted with the Holy Trinity on the last page of the catechism, as it at once occurred to me that by this means the minds of the children might, even in their earliest years, be led to the most sinful scepticism. We Prussians are more intelligent, and, in our zeal for converting those heathens who are familiar with arithmetic, take good care not to print the multiplication table behind the catechism. (L 2, 78f.)
>
> das Einmaleins, welches doch mit der heiligen Dreiheitslehre bedenklich kollidiert, im Katechismus selbst, und zwar auf dem letzten Blatt desselben, abgedruckt ist, und die Kinder dadurch schon frühzeitig zu sündhaftem Zweifeln verleitet werden können. Da sind wir im Preußischen viel klüger, und bei unserem Eifer zur Bekehrung jener Leute, die sich so gut aufs Rechnen verstehen, hüten wir uns wohl, das Einmaleins hinter dem Katechismus abdrucken zu lassen. (B 2, 113f.)

If the career of a freshly minted thaler appears in the bright light of a theology of redemption that can acknowledge it only as the bearer of its own displaced indebtedness to an unavowed guilt, the journey into the pit's entrails as the dirty underside of the birth scene of money brings home in a more obvious way the point of what Marx will call the moment of original sin: the quid pro quo of the explanandum for its explanation.[6] Heine's description of his descent into the pit reminds us that the dirty secret of the production of money is tied to the social and political conditions subliminally reproduced in the process of the production of the ore and its processing into silver and, eventually, money. This mode of production, Heine's description reiterates, produces along with the radiance of the precious metal also the dirt that adheres to the operation. The image of the busily whirring ropes on which the buckets are dropped down to extract the ore suggests that the forms of the human costs of risk, danger, and exploitation involved are inseparably linked to its modes of production, which in turn render possible the social and political realities that it serves.[7]

A few years later, in 1832, a year after his arrival in Paris, Heine described the Paris stock exchange as the "great temple of marble, where Périer is adored like a God and his word like an oracle."[8]

> I vex myself every time I enter the Bourse, the beautiful edifice of marble, built in the noblest Greek style, and consecrated to the most contemptible business to swindling in the public funds. It is the most beautiful building in Paris. Napoleon erected it, and he also built in the same style and proportions a temple to Glory. Unfortunately, the temple to Glory is as yet unfinished; the Bourbons changed it to a church, and dedicated it to the repentant Magdalen (*La Madeleine*). But the Bourse is perfect in its completed splendour, and to its influence we may ascribe the fact that its nobler rival, the Temple of Fame, is still unfinished and still remains, as if in disgraceful derision, dedicated to the repentant Magdalen. (L 7, 230)

> Ich ärgere mich jedesmal, wenn ich die Börse betrete, das schöne Marmorhaus, erbaut im edelsten griechischen Stile, und geweiht dem nichtswürdigsten Geschäfte, dem Staatspapierenschacher. Es ist das schönste Gebäude von Paris; Napoleon hat es bauen lassen. In demselben Maßstabe ließ er einen Tempel des Ruhms bauen. Ach, der Tempel des Ruhms ist nicht fertig geworden; die Bourbonen verwandelten ihn in eine Kirche, und weihten diese der reuigen Magdalene; aber die Börse steht fertig in ihrem vollendetsten Glanze und ihrem Einfluße ist es wohl zuzuschreiben, daß ihre edlere Nebenbuhlerin, der Tempel des Ruhms, noch immer unvollendet und noch immer, in schmählichster Verhöhnung, der reuigen Magdalene geweiht bleibt. (B3, 192f.)

While the repurposing of the temple of Glory or fame (*Ruhm*) for the penitent Magdalene functions as a reverse form of secularization, it highlights the function of the stock exchange as its secularized correlate. Heine's account of the subordination of the glory of secular power to the grip of the church—and a penitent Magdalene at that—suggests with provocative innuendo that the splendor of the stock exchange over its "nobler rival, the Temple of Fame" comes at the expense of subjecting fame—as symbol of human achievement—to domination by the church, an arrangement that suggests that the instrument of finance capitalism seems to be curiously in cahoots with religion. As the big-moneyed pimps of the new finance economy shamefully mock penitent Magdalene, they rely on the state control of the small-time harlots who threaten to steal the limelight. As Heine notes, continuing the thread of his account:

> Here, in the vast space of the high-arched hall, here it is that the swindlers in public funds, with all their repulsive faces and disagreeable screams sweep here and there, like the tossing of a sea of egotistic greed, and where, amid the wild billows of human beings, the great bankers dart up, snapping and devouring like sharks one monster preying on another; and where, in the gallery, like birds of prey watching on a cliff, even speculating ladies may be seen. Yet here it is that the interests are at home which in this our time decide peace and war. (L 7, 230f.)

> Hier, in dem ungeheuren Raume der hochgewölbten Börsenhalle, hier ist es, wo der Staatspapierenschacher, mit allen seinen grellen Gestalten und Mißtönen, wogend und brausend sich bewegt, wie ein Meer des Eigennutzes, wo aus den wüsten Menschenwellen die großen Bankiers gleich Haifischen hervorschnappen, wo ein Ungetüm das andere verschlingt, und wo oben auf der Galerie, gleich lauernden Raubvögeln auf einer Meerklippe, sogar spekulierende Damen bemerkbar sind. Hier ist es jedoch, wo die Interessen wohnen, die in dieser Zeit über Krieg und Frieden entscheiden. (B 3, 193)

The stock exchange as the scene of the seat of the rule and power of the emerging new order of finance capitalism shows that while sharks and sirens might make a killing, they too are subject to the hydraulic laws of the flow of money,[9] while the logic of capital is what guides the interests that decide over war and peace, life and death. This is why the stock exchange is so important. Heine explains:

> The rate of state papers and of discount is of course a political thermometer. (L 7, 231)

> Der Kurs der Staatspapiere und des Diskontos ist freilich ein politischer Thermometer. (B 3, 193)

Like frogs forecasting the weather, stockjobbers are focused only on the facts, that is, expectations of political change or stability:

> Neither existence nor non-existence, but peace or disturbance is the great question of the Bourse. According to this, the rate of discount regulates itself. (L 7, 233)

> Weder Sein noch Nichtsein, sondern Ruhe oder Unruhe, ist die große Frage der Börse. Danach richtet sich auch der Diskonto. (194)

The transition to a world governed by the desire for stability changes the rules of engagement in radical ways, where the anticipated movement of capital dictates political interests rather than the other way around. While Germany's freshly minted silver thalers might still be stuck in a mode of production that reflects the theological-political regime of the ancien régime, the finance system in Paris, the capital of the world's monetary flow, follows the modern regime over which Rothschild presides as the chief financier, having taken over the reins from the rulers who now owe their sovereignty to him:

> In restless times money is uneasy; it retreats into the coffers of the rich as into a citadel, remains retired, and the rate of interest rises (*der Diskonto steigt*). In peaceful times money becomes free from care and confiding; offers itself cheaply, shows itself publicly, and is very affable—discount is low. By which we see that an old louis d'or has more intelligence than any man, and can best tell of coming war or peace. (L 7, 233f.)
>
> In unruhiger Zeit ist das Geld ängstlich, zieht sich in die Kisten der Reichen, wie eine Festung, zurück, hält sich eingezogen; der Diskonto steigt. In ruhiger Zeit wird das Geld wieder sorglos, bietet sich preis, zeigt sich öffentlich, ist sehr herablassend; der Diskonto ist niedrig. So ein alter Louisdor hat mehr Verstand als ein Mensch, und weiß am besten, ob es Krieg oder Frieden gibt. (B 3, 194)

A decade later, in his report from Paris of March 31, 1841, Heine calls Rothschild the best political thermometer, not to say weather forecaster (L 8, 230; B 5, 355). Just like Marx, Heine is fascinated by the fact that finance capitalism has a revolutionizing effect that reinvents politics in its own image. While Rothschild may seem like a far cry from being the liberator of the world, his authority, Heine reminds his readers, has the power to command kings, emperors, and popes alike.[10] If the revolutionary way capitalism transforms space and time through the steam machines on water and railways, it is owed to the financing that makes such rapid modernization possible. Just like Marx's later famous formulation "all that is solid melts into air,"[11] Heine's comments bring home the liberating and empowering, as well as problematically dictatorial, effects of this new order of emerging finance capitalism. Money is the new principle of the revolutionizing force that treats everybody's cash with equal interest:

> For gold is the God of our time and Rothschild is his prophet. (L 8, 231)
>
> Denn das Geld ist der Gott unserer Zeit und Rothschild ist sein Prophet. (B 5, 355)

A decade earlier, in *Die Romantische Schule*, and with a wary eye turned to the Middle Ages, Heine had asked:

> Does the religion of to-day consist in the monetisation of the Deity, or the deification of money? (L 6, 49)
>
> Besteht nun die heutige Religion in der Geldwerdung Gottes oder in der Gottwerdung des Geldes? (B 3, 472)

Heine's claim that the Middle Ages built everything on faith in blood while the modern day has laid its foundations on money resonates suggestively with Marx's conception of money as the expression of congealed labor extracted, through alienation, with the blood and sweat of the worker's labor power. The sublimation from blood distilled into the silver and gold hosts of the modern-day Eucharist resonates suggestively with Marx's vision of the bloodsucking process of the production of value from the early *Economic and Philosophic Manuscripts of 1844* to *Capital*. In paradigmatic fashion, Heine's observations as a newspaper correspondent in 1830s Paris prelude Marx's recognition of the theological underside that informs the theorization of political economy:

> Does the religion of to-day consist in the monetisation of the Deity, or the deification of money? Enough, the people believe in money only; it is the coined metal, the silver and golden pyxes, in which they think that virtue lies; gold is the beginning and end of all their works, and when they have a great building to erect they take care that a few coins of different kinds are placed in a capsule under the foundation-stone. (L 6, 49)
>
> Besteht nun die heutige Religion in der Geldwerdung Gottes oder in der Gottwerdung des Geldes? Genug, die Leute glauben nur an Geld; nur dem gemünztem Metall, den silbernen und goldenen Hostien, schreiben sie eine Wunderkraft zu; das Geld ist der Anfang und das Ende aller ihrer Werke; und wenn sie ein Gebäude zu errichten haben, so tragen sie große Sorge, daß unter dem Grundstein einige Geldstücke, eine Kapsel mit allerlei Münzen, gelegt werden. (B 3, 472)

And he continues the next paragraph by juxtaposing but at the same time subliminally linking faith in blood with faith in money, society's new or, more precisely, condensed and bottled form of lifeblood:

> Yes, just as in the Middle Age [*sic*] all things, all buildings, including the whole edifice of Church and State, were based on the belief in blood, so all our institutions of the present day rest on the faith in money, and in money alone. That was superstition, this is clear current egoism. (L 6, 49f.)

> Ja, wie im Mittelalter Alles, die einzelnen Bauwerke ebenso wie das ganze Staats- und Kirchengebäude, auf den Glauben an Blut beruhte, so beruhen alle unsere heutigen Institutionen auf den Glauben an Geld, auf wirkliches Geld. Jenes war Aberglauben, doch dieses ist der bare Egoismus. (B 3, 472)

In his most outspoken political commentary on Rothschild, in *Ludwig Börne: A Memorial*, published in 1840, Heine returns to the significance of Rothschild for the process of modernization:

> There are no stronger promoters of the revolution than the Rothschilds, and what may sound stranger yet: these Rothschilds, these bankers of kings, these princely pursemasters, whose existence could be most seriously threatened by the overthrow of the system of European states, nevertheless carry in their hearts the consciousness of their revolutionary mission. This is especially the case with the man who is known by the unassuming name of Baron James and in whom now, since the death of his illustrious brother of England, the whole political significance of the house Rothschild resides. This Nero of finance, who has built his golden palace in the Rue Lafitte, and from there rules the stock markets as the absolute imperator, he is, like his predecessor in his time, the Roman Nero, ultimately a violent destroyer of the privileged patriciate and founder of the new democracy.[12]
>
> Es gibt keine stärkere Beförderer der Revolution als eben die Rothschilde … und was noch befremdlicher klingen mag: diese Rothschilde, die Banquiers der Könige, diese fürstlichen Seckelmeister, deren Existenz durch einen Umsturz des europäischen Staatensystems in die ernsthaftesten Gefahren geraten dürfte, sie tragen dennoch im Gemüthe das Bewußtsein ihrer revolutionären Sendung. Namentlich ist dieses der Fall bei dem Manne, der unter dem scheinlosen Namen Baron James bekannt ist, und in welchem sich jetzt, nach dem Tode seines erlauchten Bruders von England, die ganze politische Bedeutung des Hauses Rothschild resümiert. Dieser Nero der Finanz, der sich in der Rue Laffitte seinen goldenen Palast erbauet hat, und von dort aus als unumschränkter Imperator die Börsen beherrscht, er ist, wie weiland sein Vorgänger, der römische Nero, am Ende ein gewaltsamer Zerstörer des bevorrechteten Patrizierthums und Begründer der neuen Demokratie. (B 4, 28)

Beyond the good and evil of ideological blindness, the sharp-edged sword of the logic of finance capital severs the deepest roots of the old social order as it transforms the world from the bottom up:

> [I] see in Rothschild one of the greatest revolutionaries who have founded modern democracy. Richelieu, Robespierre, and Rothschild are for me

three terrorist names, and they signify the gradual destruction of the old aristocracy. Richelieu, Robespierre, and Rothschild are the three most terrible levellers of Europe. (S 20)

> [I]ch sehe in Rothschild einen der größten Revolutionäre, welcher die modern Demokratie begründeten. Richelieu, Robespierre und Rothschild sind für mich drei terroristische Namen, und sie bedeuten die graduelle Vernichtung der alten Aristokratie. Richelieu, Robespierre und Rothschild sind die drei furchtbarsten Nivelleurs Europas. (29)

Heine keenly perceives how the tremendous, revolutionary consequences of the rise of the house of Rothschild are not a derailment of the emerging forces of modernization but rather a result of the very logic of modernity. As we will see, it is the regime of finance capitalism that will put the engine of modern industrialization on track.[13] While Richelieu effectively destroyed the aristocracy to make way for the absolute sovereignty of the court, and Robespierre gave it the coup de grace, they left landed property intact.

> Then came Rothschild and destroyed the supremacy of the land by raising the system of government bonds to the highest power, thereby mobilizing the great properties and revenues, and, so to speak, endowed money with the former privileges of land. (S 20)

> Da kam Rothschild, und zerstörte die Oberherrschaft des Bodens, indem er das Staatspapierensystem zur höchsten Macht erhob, dadurch die großen Besitztümer und Einkünfte mobilisierte, und gleichsam das Geld mit den ehemaligen Vorrechten des Bodens belehnte. (29f.)

Welcoming the momentous consequences the Rothschilds helped usher in, Heine reminds us that they, too, are just a function of the power of money, which subjects even its masters and representatives to the dictate of its iron logic and the lure of the transitory glory it bestows:

> Money is more fluid than water, breezier than air, and we can forgive the impertinences of today's finance nobility when we consider its transience. It melts away and evaporates before you know it. (S 20)

> Geld ist flüssiger als Wasser, windiger als Luft, und dem jetzigen Geldadel verzeiht man gern seine Impertinenzen, wenn man seine Vergänglichkeit bedenkt ... er zerrinnt und verdunstet, ehe man sich dessen versieht. (30)

Money is not only liquid and subject to the laws of hydraulics, as Georg Simmel will observe, it is also shifty and shady (*windig*), that is, devoid of any moral pretense, a brute force of nature.

As a consequence, Heine understands modernization and large-scale industrialization to be a direct function of the modus operandi of finance capital. It is only due to the large-scale scheme of financing that mass transportation by steam machines and engine-driven trains is able to transform the world in shock-like manner. In his May 5, 1843, report from Paris, Heine compared the railways to the discovery of America, the invention of the powder, and book printing, heralding the railways as another "providential event" ushering in a new era:

> What marvellous changes must now enter into our methods of perception and action. Even the elementary ideas of space and time are tottering; for by the railway space is annihilated, and only time remains. Oh, that we had money enough to kill the latter properly! (L 8, 368f.)
>
> Welche Veränderungen müssen jetzt eintreten in unsrer Anschauungsweise und in unsern Vorstellungen! Sogar Die Elementarbegriffe von Raum und Zeit sind schwankend geworden. Durch die Eisenbahn wird der Raum getötet, und es bleibt uns nur noch die Zeit übrig. Hätten wir nur Geld genug, um auch letztere anständig zu töten! (B 5, 449)

Observing how space and time are shrinking and revolutionizing not just traveling but the exchange of ideas and commodities as well, bringing hitherto isolated regions into an interconnected world, Heine describes the financing schemes that bring his beloved linden trees and the North Sea, along with the "mountains and forests of all countries," to the doors of Paris citizens (L 8, 369; B 5, 449). When Heine is later confined to bedridden existence, it will be the books of German libraries that he will command to assuage his condition by steamboat and train—by busily exploring these fastest and most convenient means of transportation, which he had personally enjoyed just a few years earlier when he traveled to Germany by both.[14]

Heine's writing serves as a constant reminder of the imperative to attend to the material conditions that inform modern life. As a result, Marx's famous statement regarding the turn from a consciousness-based approach to one grounded in a critical reflection on the material conditions also serves as an apposite description of the critical impetus that informs Heine's programmatic new writing style:

> The mode of production of material life conditions the general process of social, political and intellectual life. It is not the consciousness of men that determines their existence, but their social existence that determines their consciousness. (Preface to *A Contribution to the Critique of Political Economy* in Marx, *Selected Writings*, 211)
>
> Die Produktionsweise des materiellen Lebens bedingt den sozialen, politischen und geistigen Lebensprozess überhaupt. Es ist nicht das Bewußtsein der Menschen, das ihr Sein, sondern umgekehrt ihr

gesellschaftliches Sein, das ihr Bewußtsein bestimmt. (Preface to *Zur Kritik der Politischen Ökonomie* [1859] MEW vol. 13, 8f.)

If Heine's anti-Hegelian thrust is undeniable, he also prepares the way for Marx. Language, style, diction, tone, and the sharp-edged, unforgiving sophistication of Heine's striking bluntness anticipate not only many features considered typical of Marx, but also the grounds for the critical rethinking of the theoretical foundations both Heine and Marx challenge. Indeed, Heine's voice accompanies Marx's thinking through all of his writings. Citations begin to appear with steady frequency in 1837, when the then 19-year-old Marx cites Heine in a letter to his father.[15] As Paul Lafargue, Marx's son-in-law observed: "He knew Heine and Goethe by heart and often quoted them in his conversations."[16] Heine citations run through Marx's newspaper articles like a basso continuo.[17] Heine also makes it into the central theoretical writings—though, as we have seen, rarely with explicit reference (his role in *The Eighteenth Brumaire of Louis Bonaparte* of 1852 will be discussed in Chapter 5). Heine also appears in the pages of volume 1 of *Capital*, where an extended footnote on Jeremy Bentham ends on the following note:

> Had I the courage of my friend, Heinrich Heine, I should call Mr. Jeremy a genius in the way of bourgeois stupidity.[18]
>
> Wenn ich die Courage meines Freundes H. Heine hätte, würde ich Herrn Jeremias ein Genie in der bürgerlichen Dummheit nennen. (MEW 23, 637)

Interestingly, Heine makes it into *Capital* not as a poet, for a turn of phrase or a stylistic feature, but for his intellectual uprightness, sharp judgment and blunt directness. But more importantly, the citation credits Heine upon closer examination with another quality: the ability to expose ideological consciousness when he sees it. Heine comes to stand here as the paragon of the weapon of critique that demystifies dogmatically sedimented forms of rationality as it reveals their vacuous recourse to a reason reduced to ideology.

The relationship between Heine and Marx was intense and enduring, as the passage in *Capital* shows. But Marx could occasionally also show his ambivalent feelings for what was otherwise one of his intellectually closest and most engaging friends. In an attempt to gloss over a critical remark that Heine had published about him, Marx referred to Heine in a letter to Engels as "the old dog."[19] Yet as Klaus Briegleb suggests, the passage might reveal more about Marx's frustration with criticism than about Heine, for whom dogs were no odious affair.[20] But as late as 1849—writing in the *Neue Rheinische Zeitung*, whose editor he was at the time—that is, even after the political differences between himself and Heine had become clear, Marx had no reservations about calling Heine "one of the greatest minds."[21]

Nietzsche

> It was Heinrich Heine who gave me the most perfect idea of what a lyrical poet could be. In vain do I search through all the kingdoms of antiquity or of modern times for anything to resemble his sweet and passionate music. He possessed that divine wickedness, without which perfection itself becomes unthinkable to me,—I estimate the value of men, of races, according to the extent to which they are unable to conceive of a god who has not a dash of satyr in him. And with what mastery he wields his native tongue! One day it will be said of Heine and me that we were by far the greatest artists of the German language that have ever existed, and that we left all the efforts that mere Germans made in this language an incalculable distance behind us.[22]

> Den höchsten Begriff vom Lyriker hat mir Heinrich Heine gegeben. Ich suche umsonst in allen Reichen der Jahrtausende nach einer gleich süßen und leidenschaftlichen Musik. Er besass jene göttliche Bosheit, ohne die ich mir das Vollkommne nicht zu denken vermag,—ich schätze den Werth von Menschen, von Rassen darnach ab, wie nothwendig sie den Gott nicht abgetrennt vom Satyr zu verstehen wissen.—Und wie er das Deutsche handhabt! Man wird einmal sagen, dass Heine und ich bei weitem die ersten Artisten der deutschen Sprache gewesen sind—in einer unausrechenbaren Entfernung von Allem, was blosse Deutsche mit ihr gemacht haben.[23]

Nietzsche's praise of Heine as an exemplary stylist and ironist singled him out as an exile, master provocateur, and Jew with the stinging fervor of a gadfly, but Heine's importance for Nietzsche was more than just literary. As Adorno aptly put it:

> Nietzsche not only expressed his adoration for Heine but shows the latter's influence in the nervous flexibility of his style and the climate of irony as a medium of subjective expression which permeates his whole work. (Adorno, 20.2, 441)[24]

The depth of his elective affinity went deep. An early critic called Heine the propaedeutic to Nietzsche and Nietzsche the key to Heine.[25] There was of course Nietzsche's refined attention to prose and (not just) poetry as modes of writing requiring a sophisticated understanding of the function of rhythm and sound as well as the dynamics of the affects. If Marx appreciated the strikingly combative and engaging force of Heine's writing, Nietzsche found its treacherously pleasing but at the same time undercutting flow particularly worthy of emulation, as well as the manner in which Heine employed the principle of free association to bring out the deeper connections among apparently disparate issues and concerns. But in extolling Heine's literary prowess, Nietzsche downplayed the further reaching and deeper significance Heine had for the development of his thought. Nietzsche's keen desire for originality may have prevented him from recognizing Heine not just for his paradigmatic style and vanguard role as one of the first modern European intellectuals, free spirits, and culture critics of his time, but also for his critical impact as a scrutinizing critic of philosophy more generally.[26]

It was not until the 1880s that Nietzsche returned to the early appreciation for Heine he had confessed in passing in his early twenties.[27] In the 1870s, Nietzsche interestingly associated Heine with Hegel, whom he declares to be his stylistic opposite:

> Hegel's and Heine's influence! The latter destroys the sense for uniformly colored style and prefers the clown's mantle. His ideas, his images, his observations, his words don't fit together, but he virtuosically masters all sorts of styles in order to toss them together. In Hegel there is the most useless grey, in Heine a scintillating, electric play with colors which assaults the eyes just as terribly as Hegel's grey. Just imagine everything as mimic in Hegel and Heine. Hegel is a *factor* [creator, maker], Heine a farceur.
>
> Die Wirkungen Hegels und Heine's! Letzterer zerstört das Gefühl für einheitliche Farbe des Stils und liebt die Hans Wurst Jacke. Seine Einfälle, seine Bilder, seine Beobachtungen, seine Worte passen nicht zueinander, er beherrscht als Virtuose aber alle Stilarten, um sie nun durcheinander zu werfen. Bei Hegel ist das nichtswürdigste Grau, bei Heine das Schimmern der elektrischen Farbenspiele, die die Augen eben fürchterlich angreifen, wie auch jenes Grau. Denkt euch nur alles mimisch, bei Hegel und Heine. Jener ein factor, dieser ein farceur. (KSA 7, 595 from 1873; cf. also the almost identical entry KSA 8, 281 from spring 1876)

Nietzsche's more positive appreciation of irony in *Human All Too Human* (1878) part 1, §252 marks a turn that will allow for a more generous appreciation of Heine as well:

> Everything human deserves to be viewed ironically so far as its origin is concerned: that is why irony is so superfluous in the world.[28]
>
> Alles Menschliche verdient in Hinsicht auf seine Entstehung die ironische Betrachtung: deshalb ist die Ironie in der Welt so überflüssig. (KSA 2, 210)

Within two years, Nietzsche transitioned from his initially more reluctant attitude toward Heine—who, in Nietzsche's eyes, seemed incapable of true feeling (KSA 7, 657)—to seeing him as a man to be praised for his purity: "H. Heine hat etwas Reines." ("H. Heine has something pure." KSA 9, 326). By spring 1885, Nietzsche had moved to a full endorsement of Heine:

> Germany has produced only one poet besides Goethe: this is Heinrich Heine—and in addition he is a Jew [. . .] he had the most refined instinct for the blue flower called "German," but also for the grey donkey called "German." The Parisians claim furthermore that he, along with two other non-Parisians, represents the quintessence of Parisian esprit.
>
> Deutschland hat nur Einen Dichter hervorgebracht, außer Goethe: das ist Heinrich Heine—und der ist noch dazu ein Jude. [. . .] er hatte den feinsten Instinkt für die blaue Blume "deutsch", freilich auch für den grauen Esel "deutsch." Die Pariser behaupten außerdem, daß er mit 2 anderen Nicht-Parisern die Quintessenz des Pariser Geistes darstelle. (KSA 11, 472)[29]

And in 1887 Nietzsche noted that "the pinnacle of modern poetry ha[d] been reached by two brother-geniuses, Heinrich Heine and Alfred de Musset" (KSA 12, 475). While Nietzsche in the first half of 1888 remained ambivalent enough about Heine to write a comment pairing him and Wagner as "the two greatest impostors Germany has given Europe" (KSA 13, 500), in the second half of that year Nietzsche offered his most illuminating comments. In the summer of 1888 he notes:

> Heine had enough of a sense of taste to not take the Germans seriously; instead, the Germans took him seriously and Schumann set him to music—to Schumannish music! All refined maidens sing "Oh, You are like a flower."—Today, it is considered a crime in Germany that Heine had a sense of taste—that he laughed: for today the Germans take themselves desperately seriously.
>
> Heine hatte Geschmack genug, um die Deutschen nicht ernst nehmen zu können; dafür haben ihn die Deutschen ernst genommen, und Schumann hat ihn in Musik gesetzt—in Schumannsche Musik! "Du bist wie eine Blume" singen alle höheren Jungfrauen.—Heute macht man Heine in Deutschland ein Verbrechen daraus, Geschmack gehabt zu haben—*gelacht* zu haben: die Deutschen nämlich nehmen sich heute verzweifelt ernst. (KSA 13, 533)

The same year, Nietzsche referred to Heine in *Twilight of the Idols*, along with Goethe, Hegel, and Schopenhauer, as "a *European* event" (*ein* europäisches *Ereigniss*, KSA 6, 125). But the turning point for Nietzsche may well have been the increasing attacks under which Heine had come from a mounting nationalism. Outraged at the lack of solidarity with Heine, on July 20, 1888, Nietzsche wrote to Richard Avenarius, the editor of the new journal *Der*

Kunstwart, in response to a series of polemical articles attacking Heine in its first volume. In this letter, Nietzsche moves to a full-hearted, unqualified embrace of Heine and takes a jab at Victor Hehn, the author of *Gedanken über Goethe* (1887). This book, which was reviewed in the volume, had declared Heine an inferior writer unworthy of comparison to Goethe:

> That I was really upset—because of the *betrayal of H. Heine*, just at this moment when a cursed wind of German chauvinism is blowing [. . .] In Turin, I read the book by bloody Hehn thinking that this gentleman must be oblivious to the fact that the cultural worth of an artist or thinker to his people has nothing to do with his worth per se—and that the Germans may for instance owe more to Lessing and Heine than they owe to Goethe, for instance—they had greater need of them. This says nothing against Goethe (on the contrary)—but it does say something *against* the wretchedness and ingratitude with which they are now inveighing against Lessing and Heine. I am used to the different manner in which Heine is treated in France: where for instance the Goncourt brothers honor him by presenting him together with Abbé Galiani and the Prince de Ligne as the most sublime manifestation of Parisian esprit (—three foreigners! remarkable!).
>
> daß ich wirklich verstimmt war—durch das *Preisgeben H. Heine's*; gerade jetzt, wo ein verfluchter Wind von Deutschthümelei bläst [. . .] Ich habe in Turin eigens das Buch des verfluchten Hehn darauf hin gelesen: diesem Herrn [. . .] mag es wohl nicht in den Kopf gekommen sein, daß der Cultur-Werth eines Künstlers oder Denkers in Hinsicht auf sein Volk noch ganz und gar nicht mit seinem Werth an sich zusammenfällt—und daß z. B. die Deutschen Lessing und Heine mehr verdanken dürfen, als sie z.B. Goethe verdanken—sie haben sie nöthiger gehabt. Das sagt nichts gegen Goethe (im Gegentheil)—aber es sagt Etwas *gegen* die Miserabilität und Undankbarkeit die jetzt gegen Lessing und Heine eifert. Ich bin an die Andere Art gewöhnt, mit der Heines Andenken in Frankreich behandelt wird: wo ihm z.B. die Goncourts die Ehre ehrweisen, zusammen mit dem Abbé Galiani und dem Prince de Ligne die sublimste Form des esprit Parisien darzustellen (—drei Ausländer! merkwürdig!).[30]

By the end of the year, Nietzsche had added to *Ecce Homo* the paragraph about Heine quoted at the beginning of this section.[31] In a letter he sent to Jean Bourdeau along with two of his last books as evidence, *Beyond Good and Evil* and *Twilight of the Idols*, Nietzsche wrote on December 17, 1888: "I count cheerfulness [*Heiterkeit*] among the proofs of my philosophy."[32]

If Nietzsche's early fragment on "Truth and Lie in an Extra-Moral Sense" had brought out the critical significance of dance and lightness, he only later moved to a programmatic embrace of the critical power of laughter, comedy, and irony.[33] This move correlates interestingly with Nietzsche's turn to

Heine as a paradigmatic literary voice he felt increasingly more comfortable embracing. Nietzsche's move to a full appreciation of Heine's outspoken critical thrust and liberating artistic sovereignty allowed him to take on philosophy directly and on aesthetic terms. Nietzsche also shares Heine's playful approach to language and his intuition regarding the fundamental role of language in the process of knowledge production, including the constitutive role of metaphors as the fulcrum of this process. Heine's language games resound in Nietzsche's seemingly jumpy and associative, but always pointedly suggestive and resourceful style and diction. A closer look at Nietzsche's "Truth and Lie in an Extra-Moral Sense" brings to light some of the underlying affinities that connect Nietzsche to Heine.[34] This short text mirrors Heine's approach to language and the play of metaphors as a shifty yet empowering movement that enables critical thinking. Nietzsche's theory of the formation and function of concepts as a dance-like movement of and in-between metaphorical complexes thus reflects Heine's poetics in suggestive manner.[35] The insight that concepts are never completely pure or detached from the contingent movements that inhere in the linguistic dimension that determines them as the upshots of negotiations of ultimately metaphorical relations is shared not only by Heine and Nietzsche, it is also of central critical importance to Critical Theory.

Heine's critical exposure of the dark underbelly of intellectual history and culture, the incapacitating epistemological limits of reason and the power of the concept, and the defining role of the affects; his keen sense for the non-teleological nature of history; and his use of genealogy as an alternative model for examining the role of the past as a function of the present: these all reverberate in Nietzsche and go to the core of his critical project. Nietzsche's distinctions between the Hellenes and Nazarenes, the Apollonian and Dionysian; his way of presenting the history as well as the social and cultural functions of Christianity; his notion of *ressentiment*, critique of philosophy, and his approach to rethinking history all take their cue from Heine's interventions. Thomas Mann, one of the first to note Heine's significance for Nietzsche, wrote in 1908: "His psychology of the type of the Nazarene anticipates Nietzsche."[36]

Nietzsche was not only a strikingly perceptive reader of Heine the poet—and perceptively aware of Heine's seminal impact on contemporary French poetry—but was also familiar with such controversial and unpopular books as Heine's *Börne: A Memorial*. As early as between the end of 1870 and April 1871, Nietzsche noted a line from this text for a future epigraph (*Motto*): "The great Pan is dead" (*der große Pan ist todt*).[37] This phrase occurs in a passage preceding Heine's lamentation of the death of Pan, in which he outlines some ideas on what Nietzsche will call the genealogy of morality. *Börne: A Memorial* is also the book in which Heine first introduced the distinction between the Hellenes and Nazarenes, which Nietzsche would go on to productively appropriate; and it also served as a source text for Nietzsche's notion of the *ressentiment*.

In the late "The Gods in Exile" (*Götter im Exil*), Heine introduces Dionysus as a disguised but life-affirming deity powerfully present in modernity. Wrapped in a monk's cloth, ancient pagan life is allowed to go on, if only in the domesticated form of the nocturnal return of the repressed, while during the day it submits to the religious regime of Christian authority. Heine's story suggests that Christian life and its forms of spiritualized religion continue to be defined by the pagan forces that help sustain it, albeit surreptitiously. In "The Gods in Exile," the abbot (*Superior*) of a Franciscan monastery turns out to be the latter-day incarnation of the Greek god Dionysus, who by day denies his pagan nocturnal life to a startled fisherman. The fisherman later recognizes the god as the judge presiding over the religious court to which he reports the nocturnal Dionysian activities, only to learn that the holy court is run by the very pagan deity the court is supposed to outlaw.[38]

Heine's renegotiation of Apollo and Dionysus, and particularly his approach to what he envisions as a constitutive relationship between the two as the foundation of poetic and cultural production, serves as seminal inspiration for Nietzsche's approach to Greek culture and for the idea of its origin in the creative tension between the two principles the gods respectively personify. From the early days of Heine's career as a poet, Apollo had played a key role in his attempts to negotiate his role and reinvent himself as a modern German Jewish poet.

"Der Apollogott" and his Dionysian brother

In a late poem (after 1844) dedicated to his brother Max, Heine notes:

> And if you are full of Bacchus,
> You are rhyming songs like Apollo.
>
> Und wenn du des Bachus voll
> Reimst du Lieder wie Apoll.[39]

If Bacchus is reduced here to a metonym for a generous consumption of wine or alcohol more generally, the intimate connection between Dionysus and Apollo is only the more starkly borne out. Heine composed "Der Apollogott" during the same period. He positioned it exactly in the middle of the "Historien," the first part of the tripartite *Romanzero*. If we leave out the twenty-page-long "Vitzliputzli"—Heine's sharp critique of Mexico's conquest, exploitation, and colonization, which dwarfs all the other poems in this part—the position of "Der Apollogott" in the anthology corresponds symmetrically with that of "Jehuda ben Halevy," which he placed at the center of part 3.[40] Both articulate alternative genealogical filiations of the Jewish poet Heine while playfully reimagining him in the image and counterimage of Apollo.

"Der Apollogott" is a bold and provocatively subversive travesty of Apollo—played by a Dionysian understudy. As this poem's staging on the Rhine's waterways turns out to be a Jewish masquerade, it does so by way of turning into a Dionysian bacchanal. The Rhine, which in the Lorelei poem ("Ich weiss nicht, was soll es bedeuten") represents the demise of speculative idealism's high aspirations by the demands of nature's reality, serves here, too, as the subversive interspace of intercultural mobility. Aesthetics is no longer projected elusively onto an imagined vision on high, as the Lorelei poem had suggested, but rather drawn down to, and onto, the waterways: the in-between of an abyssal space devoid of any grounds for founding narratives, an interspace that can only be imagined as a function of ever-new creative connections on the move.[41]

The transient nature of this in-between no-man's-land points to the ever-fluid and open plasticity of creation to which art and poetry (particularly in their Jewish instantiations) are subject. The groundless and transitory nature of the situation on the boat expresses in physical terms the undulating movement performed by the Apollonian-Dionysian back-and-forth in the staging of the Apollonian in the guise of the subversively Dionysian poetic persona. Remarkably, out of this masquerade of staging an Apollo in Dionysian guise there arises a distinctly Jewish voice, or—or vice versa—it is through the Jewish voice that the Apollonian-Dionysian play makes its entry:

A blond-haired swain stands fair and bold
Under the streaming banner;
His purple cloak is worked with gold,
Cut in the antique manner.

Like marbled forms, nine women lie
There at his feet reclining;
Their tunic robes are girdled high,
Their slender bodies entwining.

[. . .]

I am the god of music, I,
Beloved by lads and lasses;
My temple under Grecian sky
Stood on Mount Parnassus. (D 581)

Ein schön blondgelockter Fant
Steht in des Schiffes Mitte;
Sein goldgesticktes Purpurgewand
Ist von antikem Schnitte.

Zu seinen Füßen liegen da
Neun marmorschöne Weiber;

Die hochgeschürzte Tunika
Umschließt die schlanken Leiber.

[. . .]

Ich bin der Gott der Musika,
Verehrt in allen Landen;
Mein Tempel hat in Gräcia,
Auf Mont-Parnaß gestanden. (B 6.1, 32f.)

In search of this enthralling singer, a young nun has left her convent:

Have you seen Apollo? Have you?
See, he wears a scarlet mantle;
Sweet he sings, and plays the lyre,
And he is my darling idol.

Habt ihr nicht gesehn Apollo?
Einen roten Mantel trägt er,
Lieblich singt er, spielt die Leier,
Und er ist mein holder Abgott.

But nobody stops to answer her questions until she encounters "a shabby oldster," who answers:

Have I seen him? What a question!
Sure I've seen him, seen him often.
Why, it was at Amsterdam,
In the German synagogue.

There he was the leading cantor,
And was known as Rabbi Faibisch,
Which means Phoebus in High German—
But he's certainly not my idol.

Scarlet mantle? Yes, it's scarlet,
That I know; vermilion really.
By the yard it costs eight florins,
And it's not quite paid for yet.

I'm a good friend of his father,
Moses Yitscher—circumciser
For the Portuguese, and also
Just as good at clipping sovereigns.

His old mother is a cousin
Of my brother-in-law; she deals in
Sour pickles at the market
And in secondhand old trousers.

Ob ich ihn gesehn habe?
Ja, ich habe ihn gesehen
Oft genug zu Amsterdam,
In der deutschen Synagoge.

Denn er war Vorsänger dorten,
Und da hieß er Rabbi Faibisch,
Was auf Hochdeutsch heißt Apollo—
Doch mein Abgott ist er nicht.

Roter Mantel? Auch den roten
Mantel kenn ich. Echter Scharlach,
Kostet acht Florin die Elle,
Und ist noch nicht ganz bezahlt.

Seinen Vater Moses Jitscher
Kenn ich gut. Vorhautabschneider
Ist er bei den Portugiesen.
Er beschnitt auch Souveräne.

Seine Mutter ist Cousine
Meines Schwagers, und sie handelt
Auf der Gracht mit sauern Gurken
Und mit abgelebten Hosen.

The son, however, is no good:

And he's one of those freethinkers—
Gobbled pork, and lost his post,
And he knocked about the country
With a bunch of painted players.

In the stalls and at the markets
He played clowns and merry-andrews,
Holofernes, and King David—
It's the last got most applauded.

For he sang the psalms of David
In the king's own mother language
With the tremolando quavers
Of the niggun's old tradition. (D 581–3)

Auch ein Freigeist ist er, aß
Schweinefleisch, verlor sein Amt,
Und zog herum im Lande
Mit geschminkten Komödianten.

In den Buden, auf den Märkten,
Spielte er den Pickelhering,

Holofernes, König David,
Diesen mit dem besten Beifall.

Denn des Königs eigne Lieder
Sang er in des Königs eigner
Muttersprache, tremulierend,
In des Nigens alter Weise. (B 6.1, 35)

In this scene, the multiple origins of art can no longer be clearly distinguished from one another: the performance unfolds on a boat afloat on the Rhine somewhere between an Amsterdam pleasure house and some more respectable German destination upriver in the heartland of German poetry. Triangulating between Apollo and the Dionysian force that arises from the travesty of Apollo—in a pointedly dissonant manner—the Jewish poet finds his own voice genealogically linked to Apollo and at the same time liberated thanks to recourse to its Dionysian roots. The comedically farcical nature of the performance takes on all its uncanny undertones as it liberates them to open articulation. With its tableau-like staging of the Apollo impersonator surrounded by priestesses of love recruited from an Amsterdam brothel, the poem presents the reader with a love boat whose bacchanal-like art party offers a tongue-in-cheek glimpse of the numerous contemporary paintings of Apollo and the muses that, to the more discerning eye (and sense of humor), are more suggestive of orgies than of the solemn celebrations of art they purport to be.[42] At least that is what the poem's concluding stanzas suggest—which, in a fashion typical of Heine, end on a contrapuntal inversion that comes off with the effect of a thunderbolt:

From the Amsterdam casino
He took certain wenches lately,
And he's trouping with these Muses
Round about, as an Apollo.

There's a fat one in the bevy
Grunts and squeals to beat the band;
From her jumbo laurel headdress
She is called the big Green Sow. (D 583)

Aus dem Amsterdamer Spielhuis
Zog er jüngst etwelche Dirnen,
Und mit diesen Musen zieht er
Jetzt herum als ein Apollo.

Eine dicke ist darunter,
Die vorzüglich quikt und grünzelt;
Ob dem großen Lorbeerkopfputz
Nennt man sie die grüne Sau. (B 6.1, 36)

Nietzsche's *Birth of Tragedy* located the origin of art in the creative tension between the irreducibly linked, mutually interdependent Apollonian and Dionysian principles, a tension-ridden relationship that produces the dissonant sparks he identifies as the hallmark of true art:

> Dionysos speaks the language of Apollo, but finally it is Apollo who speaks that of Dionysos. At which point the supreme goal of tragedy, and indeed of all art, is attained.[43]
>
> Dionysus redet die Sprache des Apoll, Apollo aber schliesslich die Sprache des Dionysus: womit das höchste Ziel der Tragödie und der Kunst überhaupt erreicht ist.[44]

It is significant that Nietzsche calls this a *Bruderbund* or fraternal union (ibid.), a familial relation that comes into play when Phoebus Apollo turns out to be Faibisch, the Jewish cantor whose variation of the Yiddish name Feyvl comically evokes the Greek *phoibos*, Apollo's epithet as the God of the sun and of light. This alternate genealogy plays on, if not with, the Aramaic some critics call the Yiddish of the Second Temple period, that is, a Jewish appropriation of the seemingly original Greek that assimilates the fantasy of Winckelmann's Greek aesthetics of "noble simplicity and quiet grandeur" (*stille Einfalt und edle Grösse*) into a self-conscious Jewish genealogical substitution for the Greek Phoebus. Heine's poem "Apollogott" turns the River Rhine into a counterimage that sets free the silenced repressed and gives expression to its liberating power.

For only in its corruption and dissonant cacophony can the name of the Greek god be invoked in modernity, as Nietzsche seems to agree:

> At this point we need to take a bold run-up and vault into a metaphysics of art, as I repeat my earlier sentence that only as an aesthetic phenomenon do existence and the world appear justified; which means that tragic myth in particular must convince us that even the ugly and disharmonious is an artistic game which the Will, in the eternal fullness of its delight, plays with itself. Yet this difficult, primal phenomenon of Dionysiac art can be grasped in a uniquely intelligible and direct way in the wonderful significance of *musical dissonance*; as indeed music generally is the only thing which, when set alongside the world, can illustrate what is meant by the justification of the world as an aesthetic phenomenon. The pleasure engendered by the tragic myth comes from the same homeland as our pleasurable sensation of dissonance in music. The Dionysiac, with the primal pleasure it perceives even in pain, is the common womb from which both music and the tragic myth are born.[45]
>
> Hier nun wird es nötig, uns mit einem kühnen Anlauf in eine Metaphysik der Kunst hinein zu schwingen, indem ich den früheren Satz wiederhole, dass nur als ein aesthetisches Phänomen das Dasein der Welt gerechtfertigt

> erscheint: in welchem Sinne uns gerade der tragische Mythus zu überzeugen hat, dass selbst das Hässliche und Disharmonische ein künstlerisches Spiel ist, welches der Wille, in der ewigen Fülle seiner Lust, mit sich selbst spielt. Dieses schwer zu fassende Urphänomen der dionysischen Kunst wird aber auf directem Wege einzig verständlich und unmittelbar erfasst in der wunderbaren Bedeutung *musikalischen Dissonanz*: wie überhaupt die Musik, neben die Welt hingestellt, allein einen Begriff davon geben kann, was unter der Rechtfertigung der Welt al seines aesthetischen Phänonems zu verstehen ist. Die Lust, die der tragische Mythus erzeugt, hat eine gleiche Heimat, wie die lustvolle Empfindung der Dissonanz in der Musik. Das Dionysische, mit seiner selbst am Schmerz percipirten Urlust, ist der gemeinsame Geburtsschoos der Musik und des tragischen Mythus. (KSA 1, 152)

While Heine's puckish performance of a renegade cantor in the guise of Apollo surrounded by a circle of whorish muses might be provocative and iconoclastic, the poem also displays a curiously deep form of experience of the primal joy of giving voice to Jewish pain, and one which resonates profoundly, if surprisingly, with Nietzsche's "metaphysics of art" and his justification of aesthetics—as if it had taken its cue from the deep pain channeled by Heine's *Romanzero*.[46]

Hellenes, Nazarenes, and the Origins of Ressentiment

If Heine's memorial portrait of Ludwig Börne—once his idol and alter ego, but eventually his fiercest opponent—serves as an object lesson on their differences, it also offers an exploration of what Nietzsche will come to call *ressentiment*. As Walter Kaufmann aptly notes in describing the relationship between Börne and Goethe, which became the case study for understanding *ressentiment*: "Heine's analysis of the little Nazarene's hatred of the great Greek is the psychology of *ressentiment*, *in nuce*."[47] Expressing his admiration for this book by Heine, Thomas Mann noted in 1908: "Of his [Heine's] works I have long loved the book on Börne most [. . .] His psychology of the Nazarene type anticipates Nietzsche. [. . .] And incidentally, this book contains the most ingenious [*genialste*] German prose prior to Nietzsche."[48]

While Heine's intervention concerning the distinction between Hellenes and Nazarenes became decisive for Nietzsche, Matthew Arnold, and others, Nietzsche's appreciation of the provocative iconoclasm of Heine's approach in exposing the problematic implications of the discourse on the Hellenes and Nazarenes, and Heine's dialectic use of the distinction, seems unique.[49] We can easily see why Heine's painstaking critique of parochialism and resentment resonated so deeply with Nietzsche if we examine a passage that appears toward the end of Heine's Börne book in which the virulence of *ressentiment* is captured in an image that will echo throughout Nietzsche's *Genealogy of Morality* and later texts. Heine's description, which we will encounter again in a different context in book 5 of *Ludwig Börne: A Monument*, anticipates Nietzsche's comments on the pathology of *ressentiment* in illuminating fashion. Heine talks here about how the erection of an obelisk stolen from Egypt by Napoleon and transplanted to the square of Louis XVI had encountered an unexpected obstacle:

> In the place where the great stone had lain before being set up they found some little scorpions that probably came from some scorpion eggs that had been brought from Egypt in the packing of the obelisk and were hatched here in Paris by the heat of the sun. At the sight of these scorpions the *badauds* cried genuine bloody murder, and they cursed the great stone to which France now owed the poisonous scorpions, a new plague on the land from which children and children's children would suffer. (S 120f.)
>
> Auf der Stelle, wo der große Stein gelegen, ehe man ihn aufrichtete, fand man einige kleine Skorpionen, wahrscheinlich entsprungen aus etwelchen Skorpioneneiern, die in der Emballage des Obelisken aus Egypten mitgebracht und hier zu Paris von der Sonnenhitze ausgebrütet wurden. Über diese Skorpionen erhuben nun die Badauds ein wahres Zetergeschrei, und sie verfluchten den großen Stein, dem Frankreich jetzt die giftigen Skorpionen verdanke, eine neue Landplage, woran noch Kinder und Kindeskinder leiden würden . . .. (B 4, 139)

Just as these unhatched creatures accompany the material object that symbolizes the culture of an ancient civilization now subdued, the "spiritual obelisks" carry the same danger:

> During the erection of great spiritual obelisks, too, all kinds of scorpions can appear, petty little poisonous beasts that perhaps also originate in Egypt and soon will die and be forgotten, while the great monument stands sublimely and indestructibly, admired by our latest descendants. (S 121)
>
> Auch bei der Aufrichtung großer Geistesobelisken können allerlei Skorpionen zum Vorschein kommen, kleinliche Gifttierchen, die vielleicht ebenfalls aus Egypten stammen und bald sterben und vergessen werden, während das große Monument erhaben und unzerstörbar stehen bleibt, bewundert von den spätesten Enkeln. (B 4, 139)

In introducing the notion of *ressentiment*, Nietzsche models his discussion closely on Heine's description. Just as high civilizations, with their supreme culture, give birth to the *ressentiment* that accompanies all acts of cultural production, the little poisonous beasts hatched in the full daylight of modern

Parisian life serve as a painful reminder that culture's repressive character remains inescapable.

> The beginning of the slaves' revolt in morality occurs when *ressentiment* itself turns creative and gives birth to values: the *ressentiment* of those beings who, being denied the proper response of action, compensate for it only with imaginary revenge.[50]

> Der Sklavenaufstand in der Moral beginnt damit, dass das Ressentiment selbst schöpferisch wird und Werthe gebiert: das Ressentiment solcher Wesen, denen die eigentliche Reaktion, die der That versagt ist, die sich nur durch eine imaginäre Rache schadlos halten. (KSA 5, 270)

Creeping out from under the weight of the highest moral achievements of civilization, *ressentiment* hatches under the moral pressure to send forth venom as a by-product of morality's highest aspirations. In the continuation of paragraph 10 of section one of *Genealogy of Morality*, Nietzsche addresses the delayed reaction of the venom, which need not manifest itself immediately (or at all) but might operate undetected over long periods of time as it pervades the body and mind, irreversibly changing the character of human beings. The "race of such men of *ressentiment*," Nietzsche argues, evolves to higher intelligence—"will inevitably end up cleverer" (23; *wird nothwendig endlich klüger*, KSA 5, 273)—whereby *ressentiment* becomes something of a "condition of existence" (*Existenzbedingung*). Heine's description of the scorpions creeping out from under the obelisk and crawling into the Parisians' imagination resonates with Nietzsche's theory of the internalization of *ressentiment* as described in *Genealogy of Morality*: a physiological indisposition that dangerously affects the will, a kind of toxic reaction that exposes the pathology of an ultimately life-threatening and self-destructive morality. Heine's diagnosis of Börne's hypocrisy as the rotten worm at the heart of his bourgeois values or, more precisely, as the poisonous scorpion posthumously creeping out from behind those values, returns in Nietzsche's exposure of the lie of the ascetic ideals in the third and final essay of *Genealogy of Morality*. Heine's unforgivingly acute portrait of Börne describes the physiognomy of his period in a way that also articulates a program of cultural critique that addresses many of the same concerns that would become central for Nietzsche—for whom Heine's analysis of the ideological function of morality would of course prove nothing less than paradigmatic.

History, Counterhistory, and Genealogical Thinking

Whereas Heine pointedly emphasizes the social dimension of his project, Nietzsche seems to privilege the individual. Yet, contrary to appearances,

Nietzsche's staunchly individualist focus relies on theorizing the social conditioning of the individual in a way that takes a hint from—and emulates—many of Heine's various counternarratives and genealogies. Resonances in style, diction, and mode of expression are thus more than just coincidental and reflect Nietzsche's deeper family resemblance with Heine, including shared, far-reaching insights into the workings of language and its formative role for thinking as well as an intense passion for the expression of freedom and self-articulation.

Nietzsche's critique of historicism and his pointedly revisionist approach to history display a critical interest in the contingent but always constitutive role of social history in forming the individual down to his and her most intimate psychological constitution. Read with Nietzsche in mind, Heine appears as the underlying subtext that grounds Nietzsche's form of argument, often down to its minutest details of expression and imagery. Nietzsche's groundbreaking appropriation of Heine's renegotiation of history through counternarrative and his reimagining of alternative genealogies becomes a paradigmatic form of critical intervention for Benjamin, Adorno, Foucault, Derrida, and others. If it was Nietzsche who gave genealogical thinking its seminal form, in doing so he relied on Heine's critical rethinking of the concept of history.

Heine's keen sense of the simultaneity of the past, present, and future and of their recurrence—which we will examine in Chapter 5—returns in Nietzsche's concept of eternal recurrence. Both Heine and Nietzsche view the notion of the return of the same as the reminder that while human existence is defined by the social conditions that define history, history is not a simple linear function of progress. Rather, the unpredictability of regress and repetition make it impossible to conceptualize history simply in terms of a linear development and unidirectional progress. The sense that the fragile conditions of human existence rest on a history whose progress as such remains precarious, reversible, and always open to contingency, rendering the blithe optimism in steady progress often associated with unreconstructed notions of Enlightenment unsustainable, is a central concern not only for Heine and Nietzsche, it is also close to the heart of Critical Theory. If the particular critical inflection of this issue in Benjamin, Adorno, and others may surprise us, attention to its particular "Frankfurt" iteration allows us to rethink its role in Nietzsche by revisiting its genealogical filiation in Heine, as Chapter 5 will show.

Nietzsche's approach to secularization similarly follows Heine's cues, down to his eulogy on God, theology, and his views on the history of religion in general. While Jean Paul, Ludwig Feuerbach, and others played groundbreaking roles in laying to rest religion and theology and preparing for the burial of God, it is Heine's initiative that Nietzsche reflects in tone, diction, and much of his argument. Nietzsche's notorious aphorism "The Madman" (KSA 3, 482–4), which has assumed signal status, betrays upon closer examination telling stylistic vestiges that point to Heine's striking, pithy writing. From the madman's opening slapstick quest for God with a lantern in his hands to the aphorism's concluding line—which notes that churches are nothing but God's crypts and tombs—Heine's irreverently emancipatory laughter resonates throughout Nietzsche's aphorism.[51]

Freud

While Marx's and Nietzsche's engagement with Heine played a decisive role in the formation of their thought, Heine's traces in Freud demonstrate a continuous engagement with Heine that goes at least as deep, and is perhaps even more profound, because it builds in some respects on Marx's and Nietzsche's work. More decisively, in Freud, Heine's is a sustained and continuous, lifelong presence that proved a reliable source text for psychoanalysis. Heine is quasi-omnipresent in Freud not just on the level of language, thought, and theorizing, but on a very personal level as well. More than just an informant on the forms of knowledge that psychoanalysis pursues in its strenuous work of step-by-step disclosure and recovery, Heine figures as an inspiring though distant family relation to whom Freud sees himself linked not only electively but also by his and his wife's genealogical affiliation. In some ways, Heine had always already been where Freud wanted to go—and their relationship is therefore tinged with ambivalence despite its moments of open identification.[52]

In Freud's *Interpretation of Dreams*, his entry ticket to the European world of letters and culture at large, Heine makes a striking appearance staged in three acts that attest both to his central role as well as to Freud's ambivalent resistance to acknowledging Heine, an ambivalence that accentuates Heine's significance in the face of Freud's tendency to obscure it. We might view this playful referencing of Heine as a subliminal reenactment of the drama of this relationship. For this comedy of Freud's resistant recognition of Heine tracks and rehearses the dynamics of the struggle that defines the psychoanalytic process of the release of the repressed. The curtains open on a particular scene: the site where Freud reluctantly welcomes Heine into the *Interpretation of Dreams*.

In the *Interpretation of Dreams*, Heine first appears in a footnote clarifying the operation of dream-work. Here Freud explains the transformation of latent content into manifest form by way of analogy to a similar method Heine employs in exposing the object of his critique by travesty. Set in the margin and apart from the text, the footnote names Heine as the purveyor of an example that demonstrates how dream-work and fiction proceed in similar ways:

> The dream-work is thus parodying the thought that has been presented to it as something ridiculous, by the method of creating something ridiculous in connection with that thought. Heine adopted the same line

> when he wanted to ridicule some wretched verses written by the King of Bavaria. He did so in still more wretched ones.[53]

> Die Traumarbeit parodiert also den ihr als lächerlich bezeichneten Gedanken, indem sie etwas Lächerliches in Beziehung mit ihm erschafft. So ähnlich verfährt Heine, wenn er die schlechten Verse des Bayerkönigs verspotten will. Er tut es in noch schlechteren.[54]

Freud's comments are followed by an excerpt from Heine's poetry:

> This Ludwig's a poet of renown;
> When he sings one of his lays, he
> Has Apollo begging, on his knees:
> "Stop, stop! You're driving me crazy!" (D 539)

> Herr Ludwig ist ein großer Poet,
> Und singt er, so stürzt Apollo
> Vor ihm auf die Kniee und bittet und fleht:
> Halt ein, ich werde sonst toll, o. (B 4, 459)

The second time Freud refers simply to "the poet" (*der Dichter*) as the source for a passage he paraphrases. To a turn-of-the-century reader, the reference to Heine would have been obvious.[55] And indeed, Heine's description of the "German professor" mending the holes in the universe with patches and rags is a perfect example of Freud's concept of "secondary elaboration" of the dream-work.[56] Heine has entered the text as "the poet"—a distinction, albeit under erasure of his name—reflecting the ambivalence of the reference. While Freud has Heine side with himself against the rationalizing philosopher, Freud's use of the epithet "the poet" iterates performatively the meaning of "secondary elaboration" in patching up the lacuna that stands in as a blind reference to Heine as the author of the poem to which it refers. The third act of this little drama of recognition finally culminates in citing "the poet" verse for verse in the main body of the text. Freud's reluctant yet insistent induction of Heine into the text builds up to the last and most provocative of the passages that, as Stéphane Mosès's reading has shown, demonstrates Freud's intimate identification with Heine.[57]

The poem—Freud cites it in full—goes:

> Seldom did you understand me,
> Nor I you, in all the past;
> Only when in filth we land, we
> Understand each other fast. (D 107)

> Selten habt ihr mich verstanden,
> Selten auch verstand ich Euch,
> Nur wenn wir im Kot uns fanden,
> So verstanden wir uns gleich. (B 1, 145)[58]

In quoting the poem, Freud sets the first "verstanden" and "Kot" apart typographically to direct the reader's attention to the two words, as Mosès notes. In his careful contextualization of the poem's function in Freud's text, Mosès points out how the returning "revenant" in Freud's dream suggests a form of identification with Heine in which the "revenant" returns, but also haunts Freud's consciousness. While both Freud and Heine play with the multiple meanings of "verstehen" (understand), that is, the verb's cognitive, affective, but also social connotations, they also share the insight that it is only in the state of abjection—in sharing the knowledge and place of dirt and sexuality—that understanding, cognitively and emotionally, is possible. As Mosès shows, the language and the framework of associations that Heine's poem offers helps Freud work out some of the implications of the dream. Heine's cycle "Die Heimkehr" rehearses the theme of returning too late—when his love has already been married off to somebody else—and the theme of understanding and its lack, including being or not being understood emotionally. Freud's specific context and meaning may be different, but the play with the double meaning of cognitive and emotional understanding is the same: a theme that Freud is able to address with (and through) Heine as his fellow traveler on the trail of the human psyche. In this way, Heine is not "the poet" who surfaces coincidentally; rather, he is deeply inscribed in Freud's text as a crucial interlocutor.

Gerhard Höhn has pointed out the remarkable correlation between Heine's and Freud's respective literary techniques of distortion and dissimulation, what Heine calls smuggle or contraband and what Freud calls displacement.[59] A few years later, after the publication of the *Interpretation of Dreams* and after having worked out the fundamentals of psychoanalysis, Freud allowed Heine a more overt and prominent role in his 1905 study *Der Witz und seine Beziehung zum Unbewussten* (*The Joke and its Relation to the Unconscious*). He returned to Heine again in a more indirect way at the end of his life, in his last book, *Moses and Monotheism*.

In *The Joke and its Relation to the Unconscious*, Freud is willing to give Heine special credit as a spirited wit and author of great examples of comedic and revealing jokes. But it is as if Heine's exposure in the limelight came at the price of his reduction to the minor role of a supporting character who appears only on the scene of the preconscious, so that the starring role of exponent of the unconscious could be left uncontested to Freud alone. If this overt inclusion of Heine as an expert humorist puts him openly in an important position, it is at the same time carefully limited to avoid the risk of exposing Heine's profound affinities with Freud's way of theorizing the unconscious, the critical function of censorship, association, the return of the repressed, and other themes that recur in Heine and seem to prelude many aspects of Freud's approach.

But Heine's identification with wit, and with Jewish wit in particular, offers a helpful pointer for addressing the Jewish dimension of Freud's identification. Indeed, it is only with Freud that Heine's Jewish dimension receives open and explicit attention. Nietzsche addressed it, but for the almost exclusively negative purpose of rubbing against the Christian presumptuousness of hegemonic German culture. In Marx, it was toned down practically to the level of silence. It is only with Freud that the Jewish aspects of Heine's (and Freud's) identity come to the fore as an undeniable, and undeniably productive, source and resource. Sander Gilman's felicitous suggestion that "Heine's text functions for Freud as his rhetorical double," performing as it were "a dialogue with the voice of the Jew within," makes it possible to appreciate the critical role that Freud ascribes to Heine. But the full extent of Heine's ultimately liberating function—anticipated in the deferral of his appearance in *The Interpretation of Dreams*—comes into view only if we qualify Gilman's corollary claim that Heine serves as "the sign of the double bind of being both the authoritative voice of the observer and the ever suspect voice of the patient" representing, as Gilman's formulation has it, "one of the voices of the signs and symptoms of their disease from which they both suffered, their Jewishness."[60]

Gilman's assertion seems to be profoundly at odds with the very impulse and thrust of Freud's joke book, which—with steadily and self-consciously pointed recourse to Heine—argues that the pleasure in jokes (*Lust des Witzes*) is a product of the spared effort of inhibition, as Freud so trenchantly sums up his findings.[61] As we will see, Freud is anything but afraid of sharing his identification with Heine with the reader and even takes pleasure in sharing a private anecdote disclosing his family relations with Heine with a wider audience, a gesture Freud was more than aware could only provoke the anti-Semitic sentiments of much of the reading public. But let us first look at Heine's role in Freud's text as the key purveyor of literary, but also biographical examples of the most refined art of jokes—Freud's chief exhibit, as Louis Untermeyer notes.[62] In Freud's book, Heine becomes, as it were, the gold standard, the classic and most accomplished master of that wit which is—as Freud has no qualms about intimating—of the Jewish variety.

At the center of Freud's discussion stands Heine's coinage "familionär," a condensation of "familial" and "millionaire"—and its overdetermined affective charge. For Freud, this example of wittily subversive word creation takes on paradigmatic stature as it highlights the liberating power of the joke as a "psychic power factor."[63] Freud presents numerous examples from Heine's prose and poetry as paradigmatic object lessons on what is at stake in jokes. While for Freud, the way jokes work shares much with the way dreams work, and the analysis of symptoms offers insights that help in the examination of the function of jokes, Freud does not locate the dynamics of jokes in the unconscious but rather in the preconscious. As a consequence, Heine on the one hand gets generous credit for his role as a literary guide to understanding jokes. On the other hand, by associating Heine exclusively with the literary art of the joke, Freud reduces Heine's importance to the analysis of the preconscious, thereby distracting from, and obstructing acknowledgement of, Heine's potentially more extensive role in his understanding of the unconscious.

Emphasizing Heine's significance as expert wit led to de-emphasizing his contribution to the field of Freud's jealously guarded claim to originality: the discovery and exploration of the unconscious. If the notion of the preconscious—as distinct from the unconscious—was the result of a distinction introduced by Freud, it seemed to enable Freud to declare the preconscious a domain in its own right, detached from the unconscious. Against the functional interconnection that would have the preconscious theorized as a function of the distinction between the conscious and the unconscious, Freud thus curiously attributed to Heine competence with regard to a subdistinction functionally contingent on the master distinction. This would direct attention away from the deeper convergence between Heine and his own project of the discovery and exploration of the unconscious as a continent in its own right, and present Freud's work as untainted by any literary or other artistic form of imagination. This may have served Freud's desire for respectability and legitimation as a scientist, but it came at the cost of obscuring the profound nexus of psychoanalysis with the arts and particularly with the creative resources of literary imagination.

Freud's acknowledgment of Heine as source for understanding the preconscious thus contributed to obscuring Heine's critical significance for Critical Theory, for which Freud had become the gateway when it came to theorizing the critical potential of imagination, literary form, and artistic creation. In reducing Heine to a talent of wit whose sharp, intuitive sense for the intricate functioning of the preconscious can serve as a guide to the psychodynamic economy of jokes, Freud at the same time limited Heine's critical role in discovering the dynamics of the unconscious in general as a formative factor that defines thought, imagination, and action in ways that foreshadow the intuitions of the exponents of the Frankfurt School. As a consequence, Freud's shrouding of Heine's critical significance effaced the specifically Jewish genealogy of Freud's discovery of psychoanalysis by associating the Jewish nexus exclusively with wit and jokes and thus separating the broader implications that Heine had suggested from his name and his particular form of Jewish comedy.

But if—as if to undermine and challenge this genealogical construction, which to Freud seemed more like a family romance, and in order to accommodate his desire for originality—Freud restricted Heine to the role of auxiliary support for theorizing the preconscious, in doing so he illustrates the deeper significance of Heine's pun "*familionär*" ("famillionaire")—which serves throughout the book as the central paradigm for theorizing jokes—with a family anecdote whose overdetermined character calls out for attention. Placed in the middle part of the book, that is, section B of sections A, B, and C, this anecdote opens Chapter 5 "The Motives of the Joke: The Joke as Social Instance." Returning, as he so often does, to Heine's "famillionaire," Freud here takes up the comical character who introduces the witty coinage "famillionaire." The figure of Hirsch-Hyazinth, Freud argues, is nothing but a "self-parody" of Heine himself. This argument allows him to suggest that hiding behind the ironic presentation of Salomon Rothschild who, as Hirsch-Hyazinth's account has it, treats poor Hirsch-Hyazinth so "famillionairely," is Heine's answer to his own humiliating treatment by another Salomon, his uncle Salomon Heine, one of Germany's wealthiest bankers at the time, whose relation with Heine was profoundly conflicted. For Heine, Freud reminds us, was the poor relation whose desire to marry his rich uncle's daughter had been so disappointingly thwarted that it became one of the key themes in Heine's poetic production and especially in the cycle "*Die Heimkehr*" ("Homecoming") from which Freud quotes not just in the joke book but, as we have already seen, as early as in *The Interpretation of Dreams*. The biographical connection now suggests that "what in the mouth of Hirsch-Hyazinth seemed just a joke, shows a background of serious bitterness" once we read the joke as Heine's revenge for his rejection by his uncle Salomon's daughter and their family's humiliating treatment of him as a poor relation. At this point Freud shares

> a story told by an old aunt of my own, who had married into the Heine family, how one day, when she was an attractive young woman, she found sitting next her at the family dinner-table a person who struck her as uninviting and whom the rest of the company treated contemptuously. She herself felt no reason to be any less affable towards him.[64] It was only many years later that she realized that this negligent and neglected cousin had been the poet Heinrich Heine.[65]

> [die] Erzählung einer eigenen alten Tante, die durch Heirat in die Familie Heine gekommen war, daß sie eines Tages als schöne junge Frau einen Sitznachbar an der Familientafel fand, der ihr unappetitlich schien und gegen den die anderen sich geringschätzig benahmen. Sie fühlte sich nicht veranlaßt, herablassender gegen ihn zu sein; erst viele Jahre später erkannte sie, daß der nachlässige und vernachlässigte Vetter der Dichter Heinrich Heine gewesen war. (133)

While, as Stéphane Mosès's reading demonstrated, it was precisely the "gross" factor (*unappetitlich*) that drew Freud to Heine and allowed him to appreciate their profound affinity, that is, as the citation of Heine's poem in *The Interpretation of Dreams* suggests, their shared insight that it is in the dirt where the hidden dynamics of the psyche reveal themselves, Freud relives the discomfort of the emotions that his aunt had experienced as he repeats the gesture toward Heine, leaving to his "poor" relation the crumbs of the preconscious while reserving for himself the more exquisite pleasure of discovering the unconscious.

Two decades later, in what is arguably Freud's principal work on religion, *The Future of an Illusion*, Heine returns at a central moment concluding the penultimate section of the book. Here Freud cites Heine's endorsement of Freud's own Voltairean turn toward cultivating our garden here on earth while leaving speculation about heaven to others. Heine's clarion call from his most prominent revolutionary plea for freedom of thought, *Germany: A Wintertale*, signals Freud's pointed send-off of any form of theological thinking. According to Freud's description of liberation from the hold of religious subjugation, turning away from every expectation of a transcendent existence sets human life free to embrace the here and now:

> By withdrawing their expectations from the other world and concentrating all their liberated energies into their life on earth, they will probably succeed in achieving a state of things in which life will become tolerable for everyone and civilization no longer oppressive to anyone. Then, with one of our fellow-unbelievers, they will be able to say without regret:[66]
>
> Den Himmel überlassen wir
> Den Engeln und den Spatzen.[67]
>
> Dadurch, daß er [man] seine Erwartungen vom Jenseits abzieht und alle freigewordenen Kräfte auf das irdische Leben konzentriert, wird er wahrscheinlich erreichen können, daß das Leben für alle erträglich wird und die Kultur keinen mehr erdrückt. Dann wird er ohne Bedauern mit einem unserer Unglaubensgenossen sagen dürfen:
>
> Den Himmel überlassen wir,
> Den Engeln und den Spatzen.[68]

Following Heine's strikingly disenchanting move of secularizing heaven into sky, the angelic into the animal, and the spiritual into the embodied corporeality of sparrows, Freud openly identifies here with Heine as his "fellow unbeliever" (*Unglaubensgenosse*)—a term that Heine had introduced and Freud had referenced in his joke book as an exemplary play on words whose array of connotations for Heine is further discussed in Chapter 6.[69]

As Freud notes,

> Negative particles make very neat allusions possible at the cost of slight alterations. (SE 8, 76)
>
> Die Negationspartikeln ermöglichen sehr schöne Anspielungen mit geringen Abänderungskosten. (SA 4, 75)

In Freud's case, such allusions include—besides the Jewish, secular, religious-critical, and humor connection he shared with his favorite poet—also his close affinity with Heine's notion of imagination and his intuitive grasp of the dynamic power of the unconscious. "*Unser Unglaubensgenosse*" thus alludes to the rich connotations that, besides pointing to their shared Jewish background and experience, also express their shared attitudes with regard to religion and the limits of reason, the role of imagination and the dynamics of the affects; resemblances that run deep enough for Freud to give literary acknowledgement to his actual family relation to Heine as well as to their shared critical irreverence.

A few years after the publication of *The Future of an Illusion*, in *Civilization and Its Discontents*, Heine makes a stunning appearance in support of the existence of a powerful, underlying force of aggression that, according to Freud, informs the love of one's neighbor. This citation deserves attention for its source:

> A great imaginative writer may permit himself to give expression—jokingly, at all events—to psychological truths that are severely proscribed. Thus Heine confesses: "Mine is a most peaceable disposition. My wishes are: a humble cottage with a thatched roof, but a good bed, good food, the freshest milk and butter, flowers before my window, and a few fine trees before my door; and if God wants to make my happiness complete, he will grant me the joy of seeing some six or seven of my enemies hanging from those trees. Before their death I shall, moved in my heart, forgive them all the wrong they did me in their lifetime. One must, it is true, forgive one's enemies—but not before they have been hanged." (Gedanken und Einfälle [Section I].)[70]

> Ein großer Dichter darf sich gestatten, schwer verpönte psychologische Wahrheiten wenigstens scherzend zum Ausdruck zu bringen. So gesteht H. Heine: "Ich habe die friedlichste Gesinnung. Meine Wünsche sind: eine bescheidene Hütte, ein Strohdach, aber ein gutes Bett, gutes Essen, Milch und Butter, sehr frisch, vor dem Fenster Blumen, vor der Tür einige schöne Bäume, und wenn der liebe Gott mich ganz glücklich machen will, läßt er mich die Freude erleben, daß an diesen Bäumen etwa sechs bis sieben meiner Feinde aufgehängt werden. Mit gerührtem Herzen werde ich ihnen vor ihrem Tode alle Unbill verzeihen, die sie mir im Leben zugefügt—ja, man muß seinen Feinden verzeihen, aber nicht früher, als bis sie gehenkt werden." (Heine, Gedanken und Einfälle.)[71]

Freud relies thus not only on Heine's poetry and notoriously cutting prose, but in this case also on his posthumously published notes and reflections. But Freud also finds reference texts not only in Heine's notebooks but also in his posthumously published poetry.[72] In his 1932 essay "The Acquisition and Control of Fire," Freud does not shy away from citing a rhyming scatological joke of Heine's mocking the silliness of teleological thinking. To illustrate how deep—and low—their fellowship in unfaith goes, Freud quotes from Heine's posthumously published poem "Contribution to Teleology" ("*Zur Teleologie*"):

> What one needs to piss, thereby
> Also serves to multiply. (D 802)

> Was dem Menschen dient zum Seichen,
> Damit schafft er seinesgleichen. (B 6.1, 304)[73]

Heine makes a final appearance in *Moses and Monotheism*, but it is a deeper connection with Heine—which goes unnamed in the book—whose link with the central concern of Freud's last study is crucial for a critical understanding of both Freud and Heine. Freud's explorations of *Nachträglichkeit*, deferred action, and the function of the messianic resonate with Heine's rendition of the story of the Messiah in golden chains and its role in Heine's exploration of the concept of history and the critical role of deferred action. These will be discussed in more detail in Chapter 5.

Heine's Legacy and its Continuing Significance

From Marx to Nietzsche to Freud, the momentum of Heine's legacy continued to unfold into an ever-thriving afterlife that informed their respective trajectories in profound ways. Aspects of the critical thrust of Heine's project shaped Marx, Nietzsche, and Freud to such a degree that failure to acknowledge Heine's critical role displaces and distorts our understanding of the dynamics of their respective projects. Moreover, such a lacuna deprives us of an important historical context of reception by which the three "masters of suspicion" are linked. Read with Heine, however, the projects of Marx, Nietzsche, and Freud come into focus as communicating and intersecting, a confluence that produces in its wake a cumulative effect. As the constellation of their thought crystallizes into a force of its own, Heine becomes increasingly important. By the time this constellation fully emerged in Critical Theory, Heine had been completely incorporated as an inseparable but also indistinguishable part of the project. Ironically, the force of this transmission has assimilated the critical thrust of Heine's legacy to such a degree that his own distinct contributions are no longer recognized in their own right. The work of recovery allows us, however, to trace the genealogical connections that link Heine to the historical origins of Critical Theory in Marx, Nietzsche, and Freud and Heine's enduring relevance to their projects as they assume formative significance for the Critical Theory of the Frankfurt School.

3

Heine's Dissonant Aesthetics

Heine can be sharp, pointed, shrill, and occasionally loud, racy, rowdy, and of course always provocative—the epitome of what might appear as literary chutzpah. His writing—his narrative prose, poetry, as well as his critical writings—is a study in the art of critical play with contrast.[1] However, the dynamics his writing evokes produce more than just the effects of contrast. Rather, he uses contrast to create an often strident dissonance with a strikingly emancipatory thrust. While contrast serves in Heine as a constitutive feature, it is only by attending to the dissonance it produces that we can bring into sharper relief the critical role Heine's dissonant aesthetics played for Adorno.

Contrast, Dissonance, and Disenchantment

The many examples of irony and wit that Heine so generously lavishes on his readers in his expert studies in contrast are only too familiar: from poems that open with hyper-romantic charm only to conclude on a deflating note of sober debunking to subversively disenchanting prose shot through with contrapuntal irony. Ernst Simon has noted perceptively that Max Weber's term of disenchantment can be traced to Heine.[2] And it is certainly no coincidence that disenchantment is a key stylistic feature of Heine's dissonant aesthetics. In fact, Heine's use of disenchantment creates a dynamic between contrasts that produces, poetically and aesthetically, the effect of a dissonant clash of expectations that has become the hallmark of Heine's aesthetics.

Let me illustrate this with a poem in which the critical interplay of contrast, disenchantment, and dissonance—hammered home by Heine's paradigmatic and virtuoso use of the punch line—creates a lingering effect:

Upon the shore, a maiden
Sighs with a troubled frown;

She seems so sorrow-laden
To see the sun go down.

Don't let the old thing grieve you,
Look up and smile, my dear;
For, though in front he may leave you,
He'll rise again in the rear.[3]

Das Fräulein stand am Meere
Und seufzte lang und bang,
Es rührte sie so sehre
Der Sonnenuntergang.

"Mein Fräulein! Sein Sie munter,
Das ist ein altes Stück;
Hier vorne geht sie unter
Und kehrt von hinten zurück.[4]

Read as a pure study in contrast, the poem artfully performs the aesthetics of contrast by articulating the disunity of *Weltzerrissenheit* and giving voice to the painful fragmentation that rends the world and the poet's heart (B 2, 405). However, such a reading would be culturally pessimistic and require dampening, if not muting and ignoring, the buoyantly joyful impulse the poem expresses when read with its accent on the emancipatory note that the movement of disenchantment sets free.

It is only when we attend to the particular effect of the dissonance to which the poem gives voice that the critical thrust of Heine's poetics comes into full view. But of course this implies that "critical" is understood here to mean more than simply "negative," "destructive," or "skeptical." Rather, "critical" suggests here a self-reflexive turn to addressing the conditions of the possibility of one's own position and perspective. And indeed, in Heine's prose and poetry, the critical function of poetics serves an essential, constitutive purpose. On such a reading, however, the seemingly circular, cyclical, and repetitive movement—of the sun in the case of this poem—does not reiterate the fixed and unchangeable state of nature and the incorrigibly narrow-minded perspective of human vision. Rather, the poem's dissonant momentum ushers the reader beyond every sort of standoff in contrast to a turn in understanding, mood, and vision, as its dissonance sets us free to hear with new ears, see with new eyes, or, to quote Heine, to tune in to "a newer song, a better song."[5]

Similarly, the famous—or should we say infamous?—poem "Lorelei" generates an atmospheric force field of contrasts between a high up there and a down here situated between a rock and the hard place of the treacherous currents of the River Rhine. Here as well, the contrasts seem to have the effect of projecting the nostalgic fatalism of a culturally conservative outlook. However, the haunting dissonance arising from the shades of halftones cautions the reader and listener against succumbing to this fatalism, which the poem exposes as a treacherous and fatal lure. Instead of lamenting the boatman's destiny, the poem suggests that the illusion that charms and dooms the boatman to run aground is a thin veneer that decomposes the moment the spell is broken or, more precisely, spelled out. In "Lorelei," harmony is the phantasmagoric desire that invokes the siren-like apparition. But the poem suggests that this desire—so utterly removed from all reality—functions as a smoke screen whose deceptive consequences take a murderous turn.

The enduring effect of this lingering dissonance is a stark reminder of the consequences of purchasing harmony at the cost of silencing the dissonant—a silencing that costs the lives of those who succumb to the siren's seductive call. The high-strung idealism that has the boatman fixate his gaze on a vision high above—or rather his own projection of it—separates the ideal from the material conditions of life down here on earth and wreaks havoc for those who mistake the denial of dissonance for harmony and the rarefied and the ethereal for beauty. Idealist attempts to subjugate nature to a fantasy regime of harmony, the poem reminds us, inevitably fail in the face of nature's refusal:

I do not know why this confronts me,
This sadness, this echo of pain;
A curious legend still haunts me,
Still haunts and obsesses' my brain:

The air is cool and it darkles;
Softly the Rhine flows by.
The mountain peak still sparkles
In the fading flush of the sky.

And on one peak, half-dreaming
She sits, enthroned and fair;
Like a goddess, dazzling and gleaming,
She combs her golden hair.

With a golden comb she is combing
Her hair as she sings a song
A song that, heard through the gloaming,
Is magically sweet and strong.

The boatman has heard it has bound him;
In the throes of a strange, wild love.
He is blind to the reefs that surround him;
He sees but the vision above.

And lo, the wild waters are springing—
The boat and the boatman are gone . . .

And this, with her poignant singing,
The Loreley has done.[6]

Ich weiß nicht, was soll es bedeuten,
Daß ich so traurig bin;
Ein Märchen aus alten Zeiten,
Das kommt mir nicht aus dem Sinn.

Die Luft ist kühl, und es dunkelt,
Und ruhig fließt der Rhein;
Der Gipfel des Berges funkelt
In Abendsonnenschein.

Die schönste Jungfrau sitzet
Dort oben wunderbar,
Ihr goldenes Geschmeide blitzet,
Sie kämmt ihr goldenes Haar.

Sie kämmt es mit goldenem Kamme
Und singt ein Lied dabei;
Das hat eine wundersame,
Gewaltige Melodei.

Den Schiffer im kleinen Schiffe
Ergreift es mit wildem Weh;
Er schaut nicht die Felsenriffe,
Er schaut nur hinauf in die Höh'.

Ich glaube, die Wellen verschlingen
Am Ende Schiffer und Kahn;
Und das hat mit ihrem Singen
Die Lorelei getan. (B 1, 107)

The poem exposes the treacherous logic of national border constructions[7]—for building a nation on a mythological rock is a dangerous proposition that will land you in treacherous waters. And shifting responsibility from human agency to a mythologized scheme of nature, the poem further suggests, is doomed to fail. Devolving responsibility for one's actions in the present onto a mythical past gives rise to a fictional destiny that functions as the secularized version of a divine regime of preestablished harmony; the phantasmagoric force of this regime functions just like the mirage of the Lorelei, acting as the culprit for human failure. In the poem "Lorelei," the performance of contrasts creates the jarring effect of a dissonance that is difficult, if not altogether impossible, to shake off. It lingers to produce a piercing final note—a striking fermata that is critically different from the classical concepts of the beautiful and the sublime that it challenges, subverts, and—to stay within the poem's imagery—literally submerges. Poignantly dissonant, the poem signals a distinctly post-romantic take on harmony as that which has been irretrievably lost but, in being lost, announces—once the tragic has been recognized as farce—the very hope for liberation from secularized regimes of repression and the displacement of human agency.

The lure of "Lorelei" is its dissonant turn signaling disenchantment with regard to the schemes of social and political order. The aesthetically entrancing appeal derives from the unsettling impulse that drives the poem beneath its façade of resignation and submission to the social, political, and aesthetic orders the poem so subtly undermines or, more precisely, runs aground.

Heine had introduced the notion of disenchantment in his early tragedy "Almansor," which he composed between 1820 and 1821. There the term appears in the phrase "a single word of disenchantment" (*ein einziges Entzaubrungswort*), a play on "magic word" (*Zauberwort*) that reverses its effect, undoing the spell. Heine's drama not only anticipates Max Weber's use, it also captures the particular critical use the concept will later assume in Horkheimer and Adorno's *Dialectic of Enlightenment*. In the play, the "single word of disenchantment" dissolves the oppressive veil of magic that blinds the protagonists. Breaking the spell of the seductive powers of this magic, the play figures disenchantment as a dialectical move. As the protagonist Almansor points out "coldly and gloomily" while "reeling as if in a dream," as the stage directions put it:

> Old fairy tales tell us of golden castles
> Where harps ring out and lovely maidens dance,
> And servants smartly flit about, and jasmine,
> Myrtle, and roses shed their fragrance—
> And yet one magic word of disenchantment
> Makes all the splendor vanish in a twinkling
> And only crumbling ruins are left standing
> With croaking night birds round a marshy fen.
> So too have I, with but a single word,
> Snapped the enchantment on the blossoming world. (D 218)
>
> In alten Märchen gibt es goldne Schlösser,
> Wo Harfen klingen, schöne Jungfraun tanzen,
> Und schmucke Diener blitzen, und Jasmin
> Und Myrt und Rosen ihren Duft verbreiten—
> Und doch ein einziges Entzaubrungswort
> Macht all die Herrlichkeit im Nu zerstieben,
> Und übrig bleibt nur alter Trümmerschutt,
> Und krächzend Nachtgevögel und Morast.
> So hab' auch ich mit einem einzgen Worte
> Die ganze blühende Natur entzaubert. (B 1, 318)

For Heine, just as for Adorno and Horkheimer, disenchantment is not (just) a sociological process but an emancipatory move that fulfills a key critical epistemic function: its articulation of the dissonant breaks myth and magic by releasing what would otherwise be silenced, suppressed, and contained. Rather than just displaying loss and nostalgia, it spells out the forward looking promise of emancipation. For both Heine and Adorno, disenchantment is the emancipatory speech act through which the word breaks up the phantasmagoric hold of enchantment.

The Critical Function of Dissonance in Adorno

While turning now to Adorno will enable us to grasp Heine's dissonant aesthetics in conceptually more precise terms, our introductory remarks about Heine have already pointed us toward Adorno. To bring out the fuller implications of the function of dissonance in Heine, a look at the central function of dissonance in Adorno—and not just in his aesthetics—will prove instrumental. In Adorno, dissonance informs the critical project as a whole; his style of writing and thinking reflects a sophisticated praxis of giving eloquent expression to the dissonant. For Adorno, then, dissonance (in a Heinean sense) plays a central part in articulating critique. Critique is the form of discontent that articulates difference by way of reclaiming the dissonant as the moment of truth. After a discussion of the function of dissonance in Adorno, we will turn to the two interventions Adorno dedicated to reappraising Heine. Attention to Adorno's attempt to explore his affinities with Heine will yield not only a more nuanced understanding of Adorno's aesthetics and his critical thought in general, but also a more finely tuned reading of Heine.

Dissonance serves a key role in the shaping of Adorno's particular style of writing and thinking. Its musical aspects have not been lost on his readers. But they are more than accidental gimmicks. They function as prompts or clues, guiding the reader through the twists and turns of a tightly constructed alternation between movement and standstill. Dissonance is the effect of a dialectic that is pointedly negative. As such, dissonance has not just an aesthetic but also a decisive, epistemologically critical function. It is the crucial moment where aesthetics and epistemology critically intersect. The social, political, and epistemological aspects of the critical function of dissonance are irreducibly interlinked with the aesthetic; this is a nexus that had already informed Heine's poetics and one that resonates profoundly with Adorno.

In his *Aesthetic Theory*, Adorno states: "Dissonance is the truth about harmony."[8] As Adorno unfolds this thought, the challenge of harmony is that according to its own claims, it must remain, in absolute terms, out of reach. What it aspires to is only realized where its impossibility and its failure are made part of its own aesthetic program. This can happen, for instance, when mature artists achieve such mastery that they are able to embrace their own insufficiency with a sovereign attitude and express, in their "late style," the force of "the historical suspension of aesthetic harmony altogether."[9] At this point, as it were, the artist may realize his or her inadequacy to be an intrinsically necessary and therefore critical failure. Or, as Adorno argues with an eye toward Kafka and Beckett—the foremost figures of his late, that is, posthumously published, *Aesthetic Theory*—the rehearsal of this inadequacy of the aesthetic becomes the subject, content, and message of art itself.[10] In other words, as Adorno's notorious definition of art goes: while art requires philosophy for its interpretation, to say about it what it cannot say about itself, this can only be said by art by not saying it.[11]

Adorno introduces dissonance as a programmatic notion in 1962 in the title of his book *Dissonanzen: Musik in der verwalteten Welt* (*Dissonances: Music in the Administered World*) on the function of music in modern society. Dissonance is of course first of all a musical term. But the dissonant is ubiquitous in Adorno's thinking, which he conceives as a praxis that exposes, critiques, protests, and resists. It signals a pointed departure from the traditional privileging of the scopic regime and of the fine arts as the paradigm for setting the agenda of the discourse on art and aesthetics. For Adorno, the theorist of the prohibition of images whose aniconic impulse informs the project of rethinking the role and function of art in principal terms, dissonance comes into view as a liberating praxis of critique that offers an alternative to the primacy of vision. It allows us to practice and reimagine aesthetics against the normative pressure exerted by the classical concepts of beauty, harmony, perfection, and the desire for other forms that offer a facile promise of redemption.

In this book, dissonance refers to the role music might play for critical resistance "in the administered world." Adorno offers little in the way of a sustained examination of the notion of dissonance per se. Rather, he brings the term into play paradigmatically in theorizing the function and role of music and art more generally. His use of dissonance as a critical notion stakes out the playing field of a negative dialectic that recognizes how the dissonant is not a lack, but a catalyzing, liberating mode of articulating the deeper truth of disagreement, dissidence, protest, and resistance in response to the assertive, affirmative, and compliant mode that silences the protest against exclusion, mutilation, and repression.

In his essay "On the Fetish Character in Music"—initially published in 1938—Adorno addresses dissonance as "what refuses to trust the deception of existing harmony" (*Dissonanz, die dem Trug der bestehenden Harmonie den Glauben verweigert*).[12] In developing the dialectics of asceticism and the problem of "enjoying art"—a rather curious understanding of how art works, as he notes (19)—Adorno spells out his ideas on art programmatically and with a critical edge that resonates suggestively with Heine's writing praxis as well as with Heine's theorizing about the function and role of art:

> Kunst verzeichnet negativ eben jene Glücksmöglichkeit, welcher die bloß partielle positive Vorwegnahme des Glücks heute verderblich entgegensteht. Alle "leichte" und angenehme Kunst ist scheinhaft und verlogen geworden: was in Genußkategorien ästhetisch auftritt, kann nicht mehr genossen werden, und die promesse du bonheur, als welche man einmal Kunst definiert hat, ist nirgends mehr zu finden, als wo dem falschen Glück die Maske heruntergerissen wird. (GS 14, 18f.)

> Art records negatively just that possibility of happiness which the only partially positive anticipation of happiness ruinously confronts today. All "light" and pleasant art has become illusory and mendacious. What makes its appearance aesthetically in the pleasure categories can no longer give pleasure, and the *promesse du bonheur*, once the definition of art, can no longer be found except where the mask has been torn from the countenance of false happiness.[13]

As the aesthetic category that enables this kind of unmasking of false happiness, dissonance assumes a critical function in art but points at the same time beyond aesthetics. Mandating a critical praxis and a praxis of critique—aesthetics as the continuation of critique by other means, to vary the Kantian Clausewitz—aesthetics pushes its praxis against the limits. This move then means that critique is no longer relegated to the outside of aesthetics, politics, philosophy, and culture more generally, but situated squarely at the heart of art's immanent constitution. For Adorno, as for Heine, dissonance is no longer to be marginalized as extraneous, but rather to be recognized as a constituent part of social existence. Both Heine and Adorno view dissonance as key to the articulation of the human voice and the production of art. And here is the seemingly odd turn that Adorno shares with Heine: happiness requires not just consonance, stasis, and tranquility, but also dissonance, movement, and transitory moments of excitement.[14]

In posing the question of happiness and the conditions of its possibility, Adorno links dissonance and its aesthetic import to one of the biggest challenges of rethinking the problem of harmony: the mind-body problem, the deep-seated dichotomy that so profoundly informs modern philosophy and culture. The moment of overcoming the repressive regime that the dichotomy of mind and body represents—Adorno's *Negative Dialectics* argues—is also the moment of liberation and emancipation that carries the promise of redemption. Only once the body is acknowledged will the mind (*Geist*) reconcile with the body and become what it otherwise promises to be, as he notes in the concluding lines of part 2 of *Negative Dialectics*, "Concepts and Categories":

> Erst dem gestillten leibhaften Drang versöhnte sich der Geist und würde, was er so lange nur verheißt, wie er im Bann der materiellen Bedingungen die Befriedigung der materiellen Bedürfnisse verweigert.[15]

The English translation unfortunately reflects in its wording something of the repressive character Adorno seeks to expose and which he of course rejects:

> Only if the physical urge were quenched would the spirit be reconciled and would become that which it only promises while the spell of material conditions will not let it satisfy material needs.[16]

Dissonance then is a reminder that body and mind will not reconcile until the material conditions are met in such a way that the oppression of mind over body, or of body over mind, no longer distorts our lives. Adorno's point that the redemptive moment is marked by proper attention to material needs finds its most articulate expression in Heine's unwavering insistence that behind all these questions looms what he calls the "great soup question" (*die große Suppenfrage*, B 1, 340), that is, the question of the underlying material conditions and their attendant social and political arrangements. The way in which Heine reiterates this point signals the critical use of dissonance in his writing. The dissonant, we could say, is the theoretical *and* aesthetic manifestation of the need to give voice to critique.

We have now outlined the function of the dissonant as more than just the voice of disagreement, discontent, and dissatisfaction. Rather, dissonance returns the repressed as the moment of the truth of harmony. Remarkably, Adorno does not only find a certain agreement and affinity with Heine's approach to dissonance; he makes dissonance the central aesthetic category for understanding Heine, first in his 1949 essay "Toward a Reappraisal of Heine" and a few years later in 1956 in "*Die Wunde Heine*" ("Heine the Wound"). Marginal as they might seem, both Heine essays testify to the central role Adorno's reading of Heine played in the development of his aesthetic theory and his critical thought in general.

A Californian Perspective

Written in English in 1949 at a time when Adorno had begun to divide his time between California and Frankfurt, "Toward a Reappraisal of Heine" is a meditation on returning "home" to Germany, but addressed to an American audience. Heine is, after all, the great poet of the *Buch der Lieder* with its canonical yet also profoundly stirring cycle of poems "Die Heimkehr," which address homecoming as an experience of utter ambivalence, a traumatic and at the same time utopian proposition. In the context of Adorno's trajectory of literary production, this meditation takes place just a couple of years after the completion of *Dialectic of Enlightenment* and *Minima Moralia* and thus falls into the period in which he was preparing his first publication in Germany since the war, his *Philosophie der neuen Musik* (*Philosophy of*

New Music) of 1949. If *Philosophie der neuen Musik* articulates Adorno's attempt to return Critical Theory to Germany, it also served as a reflection on the resistance that awaited those who would return. At this juncture it was clear that the dissonances that would unsettle his audience would be so unbearable because they concerned their own situation:

> The dissonances that frighten them speak of their own situation; for this reason only are those dissonances intolerable to them.[17]
>
> Die Dissonanzen, die sie schrecken, reden von ihrem eigenen Zustand: einzig darum sind sie ihnen unerträglich.[18]

For Adorno, Heine occupied an interesting position somewhere between the opposition of high art and popular art that, he argued, Schoenberg and Stravinsky, respectively, represented. As Adorno noted in 1948/9,

> The history of the German *Kunstlied* is unthinkable without Heine.[19]

For Adorno there is no doubt that Heine's poetry was instrumental for the development of nineteenth-century German music and that without him, none of the "boldest and most advanced musical ventures of the period" including those by Schubert, Mendelssohn, and Schumann would have been possible (ibid.). Heine serves, as it were, as a predecessor of the opposition between Schoenberg and Stravinsky—and in many ways Heine's *Ludwig Börne: A Memorial* operates on a distinction between Heine and Börne that speaks to the critical concerns of Adorno's juxtaposition of Schoenberg and Stravinsky. For Adorno, Heine serves as the invisible *tertium comparationis* whose critical agenda shares the crucial concerns that drive the *Philosophy of New Music*. Read in this context, Adorno's explanation of why dissonance causes discomfort is repeated point for point in the two Heine essays of 1949 and 1956. And the book's conclusion connects to the heart of both the Heine essays and the later *Aesthetic Theory*, and shows the central role the idea of dissonance was playing for Adorno as early as 1948/9. Two decades later, the dissonance Adorno found paradigmatically prefigured in Heine will assume key significance in the *Aesthetic Theory* and become a defining feature of Critical Theory in general.

> Perhaps that art alone would be authentic that would be liberated from the idea of authenticity itself, of being thus and not otherwise.[20]
>
> Vielleicht wäre authentisch erst die Kunst, die der Idee von Authentizität selber, des so und nicht anders Seins, sich entledigt hätte.[21]

Much of what Adorno has to say about Heine relates to exactly this issue, that is, the (then contemporary) rampant return of the claim that Heine was inauthentic. Adorno's point, however—that Heine's seeming triteness might not express Heine's own shallowness so much as the objective deprivation of the reified world he sought to expose—is intimately connected to the recognition Adorno shares with Heine that authenticity has long been lost in modernity, if it ever existed in the first place. The "deep ambivalence toward the intrinsic nature of Heine's poetry itself," Adorno notes, is thus caused less by Heine himself than by the particular turns taken by his reception:

> Some kind of uneasiness seems to prevail wherever Heine's spirit manifests itself, comparable to the *malaise* that sometimes arises in the presence of people who are resented as aggressive, overly self-conscious and tactless—just because these very qualities strike a chord in the souls of those who react against them. In other words, something disquieting and unsolved remains in the phenomenon of Heine, and his supposed obsolescence as a poet is at least partly a means to repress this discomfort rather than to cope with it consciously. (GS 20.2, 442)

Critical of nationalistic pressure to exclude Heine from a German literary canon characterized by an obsession with linguistic purity, Adorno notes:

> Those qualities of Heine's which account superficially for this uneasiness are generally explained by his Jewishness. But this procedure seems to be dubious. (442f.)

Recourse to Heine's Jewishness in this context is not just dubious but also deeply suspect, Adorno notes, "due to the projective mechanisms on the part of the indignant" (443). Instead of seeing Heine's Jewishness as a constraint, however, Adorno argues that it might have enabled him to take a more universal stand than others precisely because his identification with the German tradition was less than consummate:

> Granted that Heine actually possesses some of those qualities, it would be more pertinent to understand what they mean than merely to point them out. This can be done only by an attempt to derive the characteristics of Heine's poetry from those historical dynamics in which he was involved, not by being satisfied with the private and accidental qualities of his descent. The role of the latter was probably confined to enabling him to give voice to universal experiences of his epoch, without the restrictions brought to bear upon those more completely identified with German tradition than he was. (443)

But in case he had not already made it completely clear that he has no time for any sort of nationalist agenda or national linguistic ontology, Adorno continues:

> Moreover, while there is no doubt about the existence of Jewish traits not only in Heine's psychological make-up but also in his poetic imagery, his

> medium, the German language, makes it almost impossible to disentangle them from non-Jewish elements. If one is not satisfied with simply referring to Jewish subject matters like those of the *Hebräische Melodien*, one would have to enter into an interminable process of linguistic analysis in which very frequently what appears to be Jewish may actually be due to that self-alienation of poetic language as such which took place in the era of early industrialism. It would be fallacious to attribute to Heine the Jew what actually characterizes his work as one of the early manifestations of the invasion of poetry by journalistic mass communication. (443)

In addition to expressing a very different view on the interplay of the German and Jewish aspects of Heine's identity and commitments, Adorno also argues that Heine is theoretically significant in a way that is continuous with the dialectical force of Marxist thought. Adorno takes great care to get the latter point across without using any terminology that might have been incriminating in the United States of the period:

> He expressed, through the material of his art, what the great social theorists of his era formulated on a discursive level: that only those take the Utopian dream seriously who try to make it become real and enter into a dialectical process with reality, while those who maintain the dream world in its aloofness are liable to surrender to the very reality from which they try to get away. (445)

This is no coincidence. For Adorno recognizes Heine as the "first 'modern' German poet" because his poetry directly addresses conflict as defining not just the world outside, but also his own subjectivity. But most importantly—and this is the decisive aspect of Heine's modernity according to Adorno—Heine's poetry does not merely talk about conflict. Rather, conflict is inscribed it in the very form of his writing:

> Heine is the first "modern" German poet in as much as he is the first one expressive of conflict not only with the outer world but also within himself, the first who does not merely bespeak such conflict but gives evidence of it through every nuance of his form. (448)

Turning away from the formal impositions of a grand classical style and toward everyday experience, Heine embraced the lower-class folk song whose uncouth bluntness deflates any kind of high idealist pretention. But here, too, Heine is insistently dialectical, or so Adorno argues. Whereas earlier romanticism had raised poetry "beyond the level of the private," Heine reclaimed the paradigmatically critical significance of the private for the public. With this move, his poetry opted out of what had been a constitutive feature of the reactionary romantic discourse of the time and its imaginary of a communal national spirit. Instead, Adorno notes, Heine

> made use of the looseness and flexibility of rhythm and tone of the folk song so as to make it befit highly individualized, differentiated psychological impulses. What was once a device of creating the "semblance of the well-known," of social objectivity, was put by him into the service of radical subjectivism. (447)

Irony, Heine's other critical feature, brings the dialectics of subjectivity to a head, exposing subjectivity through the very subjective means it employs. Here, too, Adorno notes Heine's resolute departure from romanticism in terms of irony, "changing completely its function" (447). For Heine's use of irony does not elevate it to a meta-reflection for the purpose of hyper-idealism, but marks the pointed impossibility of its claims and of poetry itself (447):

> Through irony, the impossibility of poetry becomes its own subject matter. But if Heine ever proved to be a genius, it was in this respect. He did not content himself with the abstract negativism of revoking poetry by poetry itself but forged this revocation into a means of expression. (448)

As Adorno understands it, the subtlety of Heine's irony consists in its ability not just to negate and undermine the reader's expectations, but at the same time to deal a theoretically decisive blow. Often reduced to a merely self-destructive move of self-abnegation and self-ridicule, the dissonant thrust in Heine's use of irony emerges as a profoundly critical force:

> When he ends, as he frequently does, a poem with a joke, a pun or a grimace, he does so not merely in order to suggest that he does not really believe in the poetic anymore, but reveals the underlying antagonism of the poetic subject itself. Heine's irony is more than mere sabotage of his own poetry. Rather, this sabotage obtains the meaning of overcoming a problematic state of the mind by giving voice to it. (448)

In *Minima Moralia*, Adorno had noted that in Heine, the process of lyrical subjectification should not be seen to be in simple contradiction to the commercial aspects of poetry. Rather, "the saleable is itself the subjectivity administered by its own subjectivity."[22] But if Adorno's discussion of Heine's irony in *Minima Moralia* had been hesitant, now, a year or two later, in "Toward a Reappraisal of Heine," where he examines more closely the specific form of subjectification in Heine, it becomes a feature Adorno can embrace with a more sanguine tone. Adorno now finds the process of subjectification critically reflected in Heine as his poetry stages subjectification as inseparably bound up with the progress of self-reification. However, as the desire for enacting the autonomy of art deteriorates into commercialism, Heine's saving grace is that his poetry performs this movement with shameless honesty. In extending the reification of everything into commercially available, marketable, exchangeable, and sellable goods, Heine's candid move to follow through with poetry is now no longer just a questionable submission to the forces of the commodification of all social relations ("all that is solid melts into air"[23]). Instead, the possibility comes into view of understanding this as its very critique:

> A decisive re-evaluation of Heine could not content itself with "salvaging" certain phases of his work from the wreckage of a poetry that flirts with mass production. This could amount to no more than half-hearted apologetics and historical appreciation. The ultimate aim should be, instead, to save those very aspects of Heine which lay him open to attack and which are identical with the trauma represented by Heine throughout the history of the modern mind. (450)

But understanding the dialectics of the rejection of Heine, Adorno suggests, requires giving more careful attention to the particular nexus of objective reasons for Heine's break with the norms of classical aesthetics on the one hand, and to the subjective resistance to the pleasure of aesthetics' emancipation on the other:

> For the indignation about Heine's brilliant cheapness is always tainted by bad conscience. It is as if Heine, through the unabashed configuration of romanticism and journalism, had revealed basic changes in the presuppositions of responsible lyrical poetry itself which are otherwise not recognized and overcompensated by the passionate and stubborn claim to the monumentality and dignity of poetry. (450)

But the rejection of Heine is more than just an indictment of those who mistake his aesthetic radicalism for the symptom it so mercilessly exposes; it is, rather, the very effect of the challenge his writing presents in exposing the discomfort of a subjectivity that is experienced as so profoundly threatening precisely because it is so radically subjective. The refusal to acknowledge Heine's as a genuine form of poetry in all its various, vituperative manifestations serves Adorno as an objective index of the radically innovative thrust of Heine's art: its aggressive refusal reveals the truth of art itself.

Capturing the dissonant aesthetics of Heine's poetry as the effect of a subjectification so extreme that it dialectically turns into objectification, Adorno suggests that in Heine, the dialectic of subject and object is figured as a critical rather than a legitimating process. Heine's attention to the preponderance of the object is then the very opposite of submission. It is a critical gesture that exposes the social forces of the powers that be. In a nutshell, Adorno's reading of Heine articulates the dialectical movement at the heart of the *Aesthetic Theory* two decades later:

> The *malaise* that emanates from his verses, their somewhat shocklike and scandalous effect, is that of an art heralding its own impossibility. (450)

In a surprise move, Adorno goes here so far as to enlist even Karl Kraus for the purpose of buttressing the case of Heine's irrefutable significance.[24] If Kraus and his consequences had the effect of distorting the image of Heine for generations of German readers, Adorno, in a provocative counterstrike, suggests that it was no one other than Heine who did, in fact, meet the criteria that Kraus had set out for a form of literature that would stand the test of time:

> Heine may well claim for himself that he is able to do what his posthumous arch enemy Karl Kraus once postulated: "to listen to the noises of the day as though they were the chords of eternity." (451)

In a dialectical move, Adorno argues that upon closer reflection it was precisely Heine who delivered what Kraus demanded but was too blind to appreciate in his predecessor:

> Heine was a great poet not in spite of his journalism but through by conserving, in snapshots, as it were, the moment when poetry was transformed into journalism. His verses preserve an almost archaic freshness in as much as they summon authentically and for the first time archetypes of the modern world. (451)

In a further move, Adorno succeeds in smuggling Critical Theory's cherished contraband theorem of the nexus between fascism and capitalism into the text—that anyone who talks about fascism must also talk about capitalism.[25] This point appears in a diplomatic and carefully worded formulation in the penultimate paragraph of the essay, and while it may at first appear apologetic, it in fact articulates the pointed culture critique that—from *Minima Moralia* to *Negative Dialectics*—constitutes Adorno's critical impetus. In a dialectical turnaround, Adorno argues that what might be construed as Heine's weakest point, his prioritizing of individual subjectivity and therefore his political unreliability or "hedonistic individualism," might well be his most significant critical legacy:

> It has even to be admitted that there was a reactionary and nationalistic German streak in him, in spite of his satirical poetic narrative on Germany. While he was anti-feudalistic, he doubtlessly was, on account of his hedonistic individualism, afraid of the rising proletariat. One generation ago, such facets of his ideology looked simply like compromises with the existent, and Heine certainly was not beyond such temptation. However, his supposed lack of political faith and conviction has revealed in the meantime some different implications. (451)

Circumspectly formulated, Adorno's carefully coded phrasing gives his argument a fresh force of conviction as he continues:

> His skepticism against what might be called the ideals of Jacobinism was not merely reactionary but he had sensed in these ideals traces of puritanic coldness and regressive egalitarianism. His self-ironical tenacity with regard to the romantic heritage is at least partly due to the fact that he was unwilling to subscribe completely to a trend of civilization the barbaric consummation of which he foresaw. (451f.)

In a finale-like move, Adorno concludes on a note that stunningly aligns Heine's view of history with that of Critical Theory:

> In one of his poems he has reached full consciousness of the dialectics of progress. [. . .] After stating, against Schiller, that he never liked the predatory and domineering Homeric gods, he deplores in almost Nietzsche-like words, that they were dethroned by Christianism. Then he continues, in Untermeyer's translation, as follows:
>
> For even though, ye ancient deities,
> When you joined in the furious combats of mortals,
> You always fought on the side of the victor;
> Now you will see that man is greater than you.
> For I stand here in the combat of gods
> And fight on for you, the vanquished. (452)[26]

The bottom line of this is no longer the kind of Promethean rebellion that defined the poetic protest of the young Goethe. Rather, Heine's protest is less triumphant and more enduring. As Adorno concludes his "reappraisal" of Heine, the programmatic diction of his statement references a final, striking constellation: the legacy of Benjamin's theses on the concept of history and what emerges here as an intimate affinity with his predecessor Heine:

> What survives in Heine seems to be an inherent appeal to continue to fight for the vanquished and to resist the merciless judgment of history. (452)

Returning "Home": Heine the Wound

While Adorno's Californian reappraisal of Heine brought out a forward-looking reading of Heine in close alliance with the project of Critical Theory as Adorno envisioned it—a vision that Adorno suggested was well in tune with a good part of that among his Los Angeles audience and the readers he hoped to reach—in his 1956 radio talk, which was published two years later in 1958, he addressed a very different audience under very different cultural and political conditions. The hopeful, forward-looking vision now modulated into a stern tone on the evacuated place that Heine's absence—or the curious role of his precarious presence—occupied in divided postwar Germany.

Certainly, the elements of Heine's emancipatory vision that Adorno had enumerated in 1948/9 were not entirely ignored, but their explosive force was put under wraps and kept in latency. Nevertheless, the German iteration of Adorno's reappraisal of Heine suggested a new emphasis on the work of mourning. However, "Heine the Wound" was not meant to mourn Heine nor did Adorno present Heine as a "wound." Rather, the essay speaks to the loss of the liberating force of Heine's legacy, which a traumatized Germany was no longer able to experience as its own. The trauma that Adorno calls "Heine the Wound"—the wound that Heine inflicted—did not imply a failure on Heine's part, as the culture discourse was quick to assume. Rather, the essay exposed the wounded nature of this discourse itself, the open wound this discourse enacted and acted out and which was propagated, in an act of selective reading, by some of Adorno's most enthusiastic students as well as the apparatus of German Studies. Exponents of both mistook the essay for an occasion to act out their ambivalent attitudes toward Heine while appearing to sail under the flag of Critical Theory. But while steadfastly following the cultural critique of the Frankfurt School seemed to promise absolution from the guilt complex the postwar generation confronted, intellectual mimesis would not always save its progressively minded followers from betraying the emancipatory program of dialectical critique Adorno resolutely sought to implement.

A consciously targeted strategic performance, this radio talk and its later published iteration constituted an intervention whose dissonant aesthetics challenged, provoked, and troubled the muddy waters of Germany's postwar culture industry and its inability to deal with the painful legacy of its disconcertingly unreconstructed Heine reception. Distorted and paralyzed to the point of pathological denial, Germany's deeply conflicted relationship to one of its most seminal literary figures had, after the Shoah, become a paradigmatic demonstration of just how far the trauma of collective guilt could go, or so it seemed. A century after Heine's death in Paris in an exile that had increasingly become one imposed by the German powers that be, Heine seemed even less welcome "at home" posthumously. But this time he was not only kept at arm's length by the resistance of the authorities, he was also rejected by the literary public and by intellectuals to whom just decades earlier he had been a household name. The diverse readers from all kinds of backgrounds who had once embraced him as their own were gone.

The essay's title "Heine the Wound" sounds a dissonant chord that presents a provocation that has been difficult to assimilate. The entry for *Wunde* (wound) in Grimm's Dictionary cites among the examples it lists the following lines from Heine's poem "Die Grenadiere" (The Soldiers), about Napoleon's soldiers who return defeated from battle:

> "Alas," cried one, half-choked with tears,
> "Once more my old wound is burning."[27]

> Der eine sprach: Wie weh wird mir,
> Wie brennt meine alte Wunde![28]

Certainly, Heine's "wound" is also the wound of those who repress or censor Heine even after the Second World War and the Shoah. Or, as Gerhard Höhn succinctly put it, "the 'knife in the wound' was simply mistaken for the 'internal scissors of self-censorship.'"[29] The strident power of the image of the wound touched a nerve with a degree of apparently enduring irritation. The irritation derives from the displacement that the exposure of the wound makes manifest. While Adorno makes occasional use of the technical term trauma, the recurrence of the word "wound" makes it clear that Adorno does not wish to reduce the phenomenon of rejection, repression, and denial to a merely psychological phenomenon. Rather, by referring to this phenomenon as a wound, Adorno brings home the somatic and broader material conditions that constitute it. As Adorno concludes his essay, Heine the wound will only heal in a society that has achieved reconciliation.[30]

The word wound has critical significance for Adorno. Unlike the term trauma, "wound" also occurs at critical junctures in *Minima Moralia* and the *Aesthetic Theory*, and not just in the reflections on how to work through the Shoah.[31] The central reference to the notion of the wound for our purposes, however, can be found in the last of the fragmentary notes in the appendix to the *Dialectic of Enlightenment*. This concluding fragmentary note is entitled "On the Genesis of Stupidity."[32] For, as Adorno notes, stupidity is nothing but a scar or "Wundmal."[33] At the point "where pleasure has been struck or foreclosed," there develops an unnoticeable scar, a small hardening where the surface becomes numb. "Such scars produce deformations." Stupidity is produced, Adorno writes, not just from questions that are foreclosed in advance, but also from imitation that is frowned upon and from the forbidden need to cry, as the *Dialectic of Enlightenment* suggests:

> And not only the forbidden question but the suppressed imitation, the forbidden weeping or the forbidden reckless game, can give rise to such scars. Like the genera within the series of fauna, the intellectual gradations within the human species, indeed, the blind spots within the same individual, mark the points where hope has come to a halt and in their ossification bear witness to what holds all living things in thrall.[34]

> Und nicht bloss die verbotene Frage, auch die verpönte Nachahmung, das verbotene Weinen, das verbotene waghalsige Spiel, können zu solchen Narben führen. Wie die Arten der Tierreihe, so bezeichnen die geistigen Stufen in demselben Individuum Stationen auf denen die Hoffnung zum Stillstand kam, und die in ihrer Versteinerung bezeugen, daß alles Lebendige unter einem Bann steht.[35]

But hope, Adorno's "Heine the Wound" reminds its readers despite its seeming shortcomings, is precisely what Heine keeps alive against all odds and ire. Seemingly inflicted from without, the scar—*Wundmal*, or sign of a wound—is a hardened wound, a reaction formation that excludes what irritates. Calling it a wound opens and liquidates hardened positions, exposing the process of reaction formation and playing at the same time with the double aspect of trauma for victim and perpetrator. For Adorno, then, the image of the wound serves a critical purpose. It is a dialectical image.

As Katya Garloff has suggested, Adorno's intervention was carefully inserted at the site of the wound and with a surgical purpose.[36] But instead of intervening in a way that would reenact the wound itself, the essay offers an expository tracing according to the idea of a procedure, the other connotation of the title of Adorno's later collection of essays, *Eingriffe* (*Interventions*). While the theory of mimesis figures centrally in the earlier *Dialectic of Enlightenment*, which Adorno had coauthored with Horkheimer, his own *Minima Moralia* offered a more differentiated approach to mimesis. Adorno's renewed turn to Heine after the release of *Dialectic of Enlightenment* enabled him to revise the theory of mimesis and its quasi-archetypical figuration in Odysseus. With Heine—no double of Odysseus, but his outspoken Jewish Other—the mimetic function of poetry in the age of commodification changes; and, while minute, this change offers a moment of agency that Odysseus's more primeval praxis of mimesis did not yet permit. Adorno grants this agency to Heine in explicit terms. This differentiation of the theory of mimesis points forward to the *Aesthetic Theory* as well as *Negative Dialectics*, a dialectic whose emancipatory features the Odysseus of the *Dialectic of Enlightenment* did not yet anticipate. For Adorno, Heine is Odysseus but with a difference, and the next logical step toward the formulation of his *Aesthetic Theory*.

In Adorno—even in his densely coded Heine essay of 1956/8—the critical force of the liberating aspect of Heine's poetics of dissonance is never lost. At least not for a discerning reader like Höhn who, at the time of the publication of his 1985 essay on Adorno's "Heine the Wound," could not yet have known of Adorno's earlier engagement with Heine, as it was only published later that year in the concluding volume of Adorno's collected writings.[37] As Höhn puts it, both Heine and Adorno were driven by the "daemon" of negative critique and both were practitioners of dissonance.[38]

However, the later essay also has revisionary moments, as if the postwar hope of moving forward with Heine had now, in 1950s Germany, come to a halt. The prospects for what in California had seemed possible—an appreciation of Heine's dissonant aesthetics as a hallmark of the emancipatory promise of critique—had now become dim, or so it seemed. While Adorno's 1948/9 talk had presented Heine as going in the opposite direction to that of Baudelaire (GS 20.2, 446), now, in 1950s Germany, Adorno seemed to suggest that Heine did not go far enough in Baudelaire's direction. In postwar Germany, it seemed, Heine could no longer be seen as having summoned "authentically and for the first time archetypes of the modern world" (451). That had now become the prerogative of Baudelaire only. Still, Heine was not to blame, Adorno maintained. But those who came after felt ashamed about what seemed to be an inadequacy on Heine's part, a shame that had been noted but now seemed acceptable.[39] But this shame turns out to be yet another projection, as Heine's dialectical play between romanticism and the Enlightenment radically suggests:

> Heine the advocate of enlightenment unmasked Heine the Romantic, who had been living off the fortune of autonomy, and brought the commodity character of his art, previously latent, to the fore. He has not been forgiven for that.[40]
>
> Dem Romantiker Heine, der vom Glück der Autonomie zehrte, hat der Aufklärer Heine die Maske heruntergerissen. Das hat man ihm nicht verziehen. (GS 11, 97)

But the rage that perceives the secret of its own humiliation only through the recognition of the failure of the Other fixates—with sadistic certainty, as Adorno notes—on the other's weakest point, which in Heine's case, he adds, is the failure of Jewish emancipation.[41] From this arises a relationship to language that is very different from that of those who claim to be its native speakers. The language of those who cannot claim to own it displays a fluency and taken-for-grantedness that easily communicates because it is used like an instrument rather than a secure property:

> Only someone who is not actually inside the language can manipulate it like an instrument.[42]
>
> Nur der verfügt über die Sprache wie ein Instrument, der in Wahrheit nicht in ihr ist. (98)

Those completely at home in their language would be caught up in the dialectics of language and the polished linguistic form would dissipate. However, for the subject that uses language like a depleted object, language remains foreign. In a dialectical move similar to that of the 1948/9 essay, Adorno suggests now in 1956/8, in a Germany under reconstruction, that it was precisely the insidious claim that Heine's language reflected the acquired taste of assimilated Jews, assumed from a position of what many held to be a form of linguistic alienation, that facilitated Heine's most accomplished writing. While the earlier essay conceived in a sunnier California had argued that Heine's universalist vision arose precisely from his lack of commitment to the German nationalism whose zealots sought to exclude him from the canon of German literature, Adorno now developed a linguistic version of the argument that responded critically to the language politics of the German postwar situation. Just like Heine, Adorno too found himself challenged by an exclusionary linguistic nationalism whose claim to linguistic organicism seemed to run counter to his most cherished critical views about language. For Adorno, as he also argued elsewhere, language was not to be mistaken for a construct defined by organic growth or even "Bildung."[43] What many read to be Adorno's criticism of Heine was thus, upon closer examination, praise and recommendation of a poet pointedly removed from the view that language held an organic key to truth. The powerfully emancipatory moment of Heine's scandalous instrumentalization of the German language consisted, according to Adorno, in his irreversible move of liberating his prose and poetry from the repressive strictures of an idealism that had long become suspect. Adorno's circumspectly expressed point could easily be overlooked, but critical attention is drawn precisely to the dialectical move at the heart of his analysis:

> His lack of resistance to words that are in fashion is the excessive mimetic zeal of the person who is excluded. Assimilatory language is the language of unsuccessful identification.[44]
>
> Seine Widerstandslosigkeit gegenüber dem kurrenten Wort ist der nachahmende Übereifer des Ausgeschlossenen. Die assimilatorische Sprache ist die von mißlungener Identifikation. (98)

For Adorno, then, to be excluded and marked as a person who assimilates has critical significance because such a person fails to successfully identify, but in failing marks difference all the more poignantly. But Heine does not stop here, as Adorno notes, but takes this "failure" to the next level. Heine thus forges this inadequacy—the "lack of language of his language"[45] ("Sprachlosigkeit seiner Sprache," 98)—into a way of expressing a break with the repressive, hegemonic demands his language seeks to expose.

In a last turn, Adorno then goes on to praise, as the very means to Heine's success, what others merely deemed to be a form of degenerate virtuosity:

> So great was the virtuosity of this man, who imitated language as if he were playing on a keyboard, that he raised even the inadequacy of his language to the medium of one to whom it was granted to say what he suffered. Failure, reversing itself, is transformed into success.[46]
>
> So groß war die Virtuosität dessen, der die Sprache gleichwie auf einer Klaviatur nachspielte, daß er noch die Unzulänglichkeit seines Worts zum Medium dessen erhöhte, dem gegeben war zu sagen, was er leidet. Mißlingen schlägt um ins Gelungene. (98)

In other words, Heine's poetry owes its striking power to the unashamed enactment of its own failure. Because Heine faces his own limits, he is spared the hubris and eventual fall to which flawless, aestheticized, and therefore eventually ideologically instrumentalized art would be subject. In this final turn of the argument, Heine's art proves itself because it does fulfill the mission of giving voice to the suffering the artist experiences. The Goethean expression "to say what one has suffered" assumes here the critical meaning Adorno recognizes in *Negative Dialectics* as the ultimate task not just of art, but of philosophy and critical thinking in general:

> The need to lend a voice to suffering is a condition of truth. (ND, 17f.)
>
> Das Bedürfnis, Leiden beredt werden zu lassen, ist Bedingung aller Wahrheit." (GS, 6, 29)

In a surprising but suggestive comparison, Adorno points to Gustav Mahler rather than to composers such as Schumann, Schubert, and Mendelssohn, who put Heine's songs to music. It is by way of a comparison with the music of Mahler and reflection on how the fragility of the banal and the derivative expresses a more powerful reality and releases the wild force of lamentation that Heine's character reveals itself.[47] The shrill change between major and minor keys and the wild movements of Mahler's orchestra have unfettered the music of Heine's verses:

> In the mouth of a stranger, what is old and familiar takes on an extravagant and exaggerated quality, and precisely that is the truth. The figures of this truth are the aesthetic breaks; it foregoes the immediacy of rounded, fulfilled language.[48]
>
> Das Altbekannte nimmt im Munde des Fremden etwas Maßloses, Übertriebenes an, und das eben ist die Wahrheit. Ihre Chiffren sind die ästhetischen Risse: sie versagt sich der Unmittelbarkeit runder erfüllter Sprache. (GS 11, 99)

While dissonance plays a central role in Adorno's appreciation of Heine, Adorno's approach to aesthetics and Heine's particular role in it can help us attend to the critical function of dissonance as a constitutive feature of Heine's writing, both in his fiction and poetry as well as his critical writings.

In *Minima Moralia*, Adorno remarked that "German words of foreign derivation are the Jews of language"[49] ("Fremdwörter sind die Juden der Sprache").[50] And in his essay "Words from Abroad," published in 1959, one year after the publication of "Heine the Wound," he seemed to single out one such Jew who had gone into exile never to return—except in his words, which seemed to many to have become foreign even in the place where they had created the most modern German that ever was:

> By acknowledging itself as a token, the foreign word reminds us bluntly that all real language has something of the token in it. It makes itself

language's scapegoat, the bearer of the dissonance that language has to give form to and not merely prettify.[51]

Das Fremdwort mahnt kraß daran, dass alle wirkliche Sprache etwas von der Spielmarke hat, indem es sich selber als Spielmarke einbekennt. Es macht sich zum Sündenbock der Sprache, zum Träger der Dissonanz, die von ihr zu gestalten ist, nicht zuzuschmücken. (GS, vol. 11, 221)

Heine's Dissonant Voices

If we now return to Heine's own texts—not that we ever really left them—we will be able to register dissonance as the underlying principle of this Jewish "Protestant" author's work. For Heine's dissonant aesthetics amounts to a consistent and programmatic praxis in his writing, an aesthetics whose dissonant thrust advances in bold new terms. With Heine, poetics assumes the form of an insistently critical engagement that reimagines critique as a praxis for social and political change. More than just a rhetorical exercise allied with the universal fight for liberation and emancipation, this praxis takes the form of a dissonant aesthetics that understands itself self-consciously as a critical feature in this fight. In other words, Heine's dissonant aesthetics realizes in and through its performative intervention the emancipatory move it announces, that is, it initiates with its performance the social and political change it advocates. As a result, Heine emerges as one of the critical thinkers who grasps and explores the depths of the constitutive link between the aesthetic and the political. For Heine, the insight that the aesthetic *is* the political and the political *is* the aesthetic is a fact that in modernity can no longer be ignored.

Let us now turn to some of the key passages in Heine's inaugural *Travel Pictures*, and especially the *Travel Pictures'* opening part, *The Harz Journey*, Heine's striking entry onto the literary scene and a work of enduring significance. *The Harz Journey* is an object lesson in contrasts, a comedic and pleasurable tour de force on the play with contrastive elements. A hybrid of literary genres that mixes prose, poetry, and scathing social, political, and cultural commentary, the text's compositional principle is to constantly shift between contrasting elements in form and content—insofar as the latter distinction can even be upheld in the face of its performative decomoposition.

Famously, *The Harz Journey* opens with a salvo of contrasts that runs the gamut of distinctions between city and country, culture and nature, high and low; a proliferating, puckish staging—and more precisely, upstaging—of the academic aspirations of the university city of Göttingen. After opening with a satirical poem of four stanzas that produces a firework of contrasts between the pretentious urban civilization of Göttingen and the majestic nature of the Harz mountain range, home of the Brocken, which dwarfs the petty aspirations of the human lot, the text jumps to an equally capricious and whimsical prose that continues firing off more lists of contrasts (L 2, 58–60; B 2, 103f.). Arranging poetry and prose in a sudden and unmediated back-and-forth demonstrates how the formal switch between poetry and prose does not contain but rather releases the contrasts into a proliferation of dissonances.

Structured by the sequence of day and night, the succession of time creates a pattern of contrasts that rotates between waking life and a nighttime in which dreams and spectral apparitions return the repressed and the remnants of the day to the surface. In consequence, however, the poetic function of the play of opposites suggests more than just an aesthetics of contrasts.

Let us examine the moments when dissonance assumes vocal expression, during the narrator's first nighttime dream following a day brimming with contrasting descriptions of social and intellectual life—or a dismal lack thereof—in Göttingen. In the midst of a narrative animated if not driven by a succession of fireworks of dazzling contrasts, the text's opening scene performs a very literal instance of dissonance, and this time a divine one. With the appearance of "mighty Themis" (*die gewaltige Themis*), the Greek goddess of law and justice, in the university library's law room, Heine introduces a primal scene of the vocalization of dissonance that reverberates through all his writing: a critical basso continuo that comes through loud and clear. Surrounded by the faculty of the law school along with prominent exponents of the historical tradition of legal thought, Themis, towering over this nocturnal assembly, breaks into a tremendous lamentation whose overpowering sound blasts "in gigantic tones of terrible agony" ("in einem Tone des entsetzlichsten Riesenschmerzes") befitting a goddess of the Titan race:

> Silence! Silence! I hear the voice of the loved Prometheus. Mocking cunning and brute force are chaining the Innocent One to the rock of martyrdom, and all your prattling and quarrelling will not allay his wounds or break his fetters! (L 2, 70)

> Schweigt! schweigt! ich höre die Stimme des teuren Prometheus, die höhnende Kraft und die stumme Gewalt schmieden den Schuldlosen an den Marterfelsen, und all Euer Geschwätz und Gezänke kann nicht seine Wunden kühlen und seine Fesseln zerbrechen! (B 2, 109f.)

In this inaugural dream vision, Heine, a recent graduate of the University of Göttingen's law school, mobilizes the principle of law itself to express a profoundly heartfelt critique of a jurisprudence that has ceded its theory and praxis to the pettiness of the academic apparatus and become forgetful of its raison d'être. More than just an expression of abject misery, suffering, and pain, the comedic staging of the Titan goddess amid an army of quibbling legal scholars gives voice to a dissonance that exposes the very challenge of expressing dissonance—a task haunted by false loudness and silence—as one that can perhaps only be met with the help of divine intervention. This primal scene of strident dissonance reminds us that the voicing of discontent, critique, and protest does not happen in a silent, soundproof vacuum but is always the function of a context defined by a secondary discourse that threatens to cancel and assimilate the voice it claims to represent. Impotent to act itself, this secondary discourse remains ephemeral, irrelevant noise that threatens to drown out the very voices for which it advocates. As a consequence, Themis reclaims the only means by which the voice—threatened with silencing and abnegation even, and especially by those who claim to be its advocates—can make itself heard: as clear and undeniable dissonance.

As pandemonium breaks out, the whole assembly of dream figures begins to wail as if rattled by fear of death. As the law library hall collapses, the narrator escapes to the library's history room, ending up in the corner where the paintings of the Apollo Belvedere and the Medicean Venus hang side by side. As he finds comfort at the feet of Venus, he hears Phoebus Apollo playing on his lyre the sweetest melodies like a heavenly blessing. It is with this reassuring dream music still in his ears that the narrator awakes to a new day (L 2, 70f.; B 2, 110). The crucial link between dissonance and the art of Apollo will return and Heine will develop this theme further and with special emphasis in the poem "Der Apollogott," written over two decades later.[52] But the genealogical link suggested by the escape to the library's historical room announces a theme that will henceforth inform Heine's poetic imagination.

On a lighter note, another voicing of dissonance can be heard when, on one of the following nights, the Kantian dyed-in-the-wool rationalist Saul Ascher makes an appearance as a ghost in another dream, vigorously arguing—as a ghost—that ghosts don't exist, a performative self-contradiction that does more damage than just putting a damper on the Kantian claim to reason. But the most articulate poetic rendering of pointed dissonance occurs in the middle of the text's poetic centerpiece where, in the guise of spiritual poetry, Heine enunciates his call for the rehabilitation of flesh. The lyrical celebration of the rebellious and audibly dissonant materialism at the center of *The Harz Journey* does not only mock religious and religiously oppressive idealism, the irreverently provocative lyrics voice a dissonance that suggests an alternative vision, or to stay with the image, an alternative tune—one that is enabled through dissonance rather than merely contrast.[53] For while contrast simply juxtaposes opposites, dissonance marks uncompromising resistance against the dominant and repressive power of affirmation as it gives voice to the articulation of difference (while contrast can only portray contraries and oppositions).

I would like to conclude this chapter by returning to a poem whose dissonant pitch has too easily been reduced to an indictment of Heine's lewd sense of comedy while its aesthetically more profound implications have remained largely unexplored. The discussion of "Der Apollogott" in Chapter 2 highlighted a striking resonance of Heine's dissonant aesthetics with Nietzsche's conception of the profound interrelation of the Apollonian and Dionysian as a fundamental tension whose catalyzing force enables cultural creativity. Read with Nietzsche's theory of the deep connection between the Apollonian and Dionysian in mind, whose genealogical filiation is clearly associated with Heine, Heine's poem gains sharper contours as an enactment of the relationship between the Apollonian and the Dionysian as a site for negotiating the underlying tension that defines all cultural creation.

Published in 1851 in *Romanzero*, "Der Apollogott" belongs to Heine's last large collection of poems, a volume that defined the poetic legacy of Heine's late period. A strident celebration of dissonance in excess, the lyrics accentuate the constitutive significance of dissonance for the subversively liberating creation of art. Traveling between cultures, artistic traditions, and superimposed identities, this latter-day God Apollo—or Dionysus for that matter—and his motley crew testify to the critical significance of hybridity as the creative force that enables and drives art. With Nietzsche's conception of the birth of tragedy and culture in general, Heine's dissonant aesthetics assumed paradigmatic significance for theorizing the function of culture in modernity.

Dissonance is the moment that enables and defines art and its emancipatory power. Against the pressures to submit to harmony and compliance, dissonance first of all reclaims the insight that without it, no harmony is possible in the first place. And second, that such harmony is not a mindless surrender to a consonance that feigns identity. Resonating with Nietzsche and Adorno, Heine's dissonant aesthetics enriches the dynamics of harmony by comprehending that dissonance is the enabling and empowering principle of creativity, openness, and innovation.

In his dissonant aesthetics, Heine prefigures Adorno's recognition that dissonance holds out the promise of liberation from the canon of harmony and beauty whose repressive features it calls by name. Heine's shlemiel does not represent the problematic form of assimilation, as Hannah Arendt claimed. Rather, he embodies precisely the critique of assimilation as an imposed model. Heine's shlemiel, a liberatingly puckish figure, represents the disarming, liberating moment of chutzpah in the face of the dictates of a heteronomous doctrine of art whose pretense of harmony and beauty signals repression rather than the freedom, emancipation, and self-realization it must deny. For Heine, just as for Adorno, dissonance carries the promise of liberation as it expresses the hope for a poetics of emancipation whose critical force sets free to sound—and that means to imagine, think, write, and act—*differently*. If Heine and Adorno seem unlikely partners, their shared commitment to the empowering function of dissonance suggests a resonance that requires our critical attention if we are to understand the genealogical filiations that connect Adorno's theory and praxis to Heine's subversively emancipatory dissonant aesthetics.

4

The Signifying Lizard: Language, Sign, and Play

As Heine's language became paradigmatic for both politically activist and poetically symbolist writers, the bifurcation of his reception as either a politically or an aesthetically significant trailblazer divided his audience into two opposite camps. The more resolutely Heine would challenge the separation of prose from poetry, the aesthetic from the social and political spheres, the more the binary logic he sought to expose took hold in his readers, who were largely resistant to broader critical commitments. When Schiller envisioned the aesthetic mission of literature as opening up the emancipatory resources of the literary imagination, it did not take long for his project of aesthetic education to be assimilated into the bourgeois agenda of enforcing the divide between the social realities of politics and the aesthetic pleasure of literature Schiller had sought to break down. Similarly, Heine sought to critically address the problem of the division between politics and aesthetics, but the reception of his writings reproduced the very division created by the nineteenth-century capitalist modes of production in the literary market place he had sought to challenge. As a result, Heine's critical resistance against the separation of politics and aesthetics was ignored while the distinction between his "literary" and "political" writings continued to rely on an aesthetics whose ideological commitments Heine had so provocatively sought to expose from the moment he entered the literary scene.

Continuous reflection on the nature and function of language was a defining feature of romantic writing. Responding to the self-reflective attitude of romanticism and its culmination in romantic irony as the defining feature of this self-reflective turn, Heine gives irony a pointedly post-romantic edge. But besides his explicit staging of the problem of language, signification, the use of concepts, and textual creations that sometimes assume the cutting edge of proto-surrealist forms, Heine's approach to language harbors behind its slapstick comedy a deeper, critical impulse that exposes the problematic implications of the expectations of the romantics and other idealists unwilling to recognize the subversive force of the free play of language at the heart of the process of signification.

Ignoring the underlying play with—and of—language would make it difficult if not altogether impossible to account for a poem like "On Wings of Songs" (*Auf Flügeln des Gesanges*) or hum or sing along to the tune accompanying this poem, set to the irresistibly ethereal music of Felix Mendelssohn; a poem that thrives, as so many of Heine's texts do, on the deferral of sense and signification. Yet, while the poem's lure rests on the subtle play of dissonance and delay that highlights the displacement of meaning as the site of its production, the poem articulates its "message" by exposing the process of signification. The poem thus performatively reiterates the play that defines the precarious process of signification as the enactment of its deferral as it ends, in Draper's translation, with the stanza:

> Oh, let us lie down by it [the river],
> Where the moon on the palm tree beams;
> And drink deep of love and quiet
> And dream our happy dreams. (D 54)

In Untermeyer's rendering:

> O, that we two were by it!
> Beneath a palm by the stream.
> To drink in love and quiet,
> And dream a peaceful dream.[1]

> Dort wollen wir niedersinken
> Unter dem Palmenbaum,
> Und Liebe und Ruhe trinken,
> Und träumen seligen Traum. (B 1, 78)

The move of deferral and doubling up—the poetic doubling up of the dream dreaming the dream—returns the reader, singer, and listener to the curious scene where, by taking language to its limits on the wings of song, the exposure of language stages the process of signification as that moment of deferral whose liberating impulse sets free the excess of nonsense that serves as the hidden dynamic force that creates meaning. Rather than transporting the reader, singer, and listener to a realm of magical identity between language and the world, the poem transforms the search for meaning into the process of signification itself, the scene where signification becomes legible in its movement in and through language: a play of differance, that is, deferral and delay:

On wings of song, my darling,
I'll carry you off, and we'll go
Where the plains of the Ganges are calling,
To the sweetest place I know.

Red flowers are twinning and plaiting
There in the still moonlight:
The lotus flowers are awaiting
Their sisters acolyte.

The violets whisper caresses
And gaze to the stars on high;
The rose in secret confesses
Her sweet-scented tales with a sigh.

Around them, listening and blushing,
Dance gentle, subtle gazelles;
And in the distance rushing
The holy river swells.

Oh, let us lie down by it [the river],
Where the moon on the palm tree beams;
And drink deep of love and quiet
And dream our happy dreams. (D 54)

Auf Flügeln des Gesanges,
Herzliebchen, trag ich dich fort,
Fort nach den Fluren des Ganges,
Dort weiß ich den schönsten Ort;

Dort liegt ein rotblühender Garten
Im stillen Mondenschein,
Die Lotosblumen erwarten
Ihr trautes Schwesterlein.

Die Veilchen kichern und kosen,
Und schaun nach den Sternen empor,
Heimlich erzählen die Rosen
Sich duftende Märchen ins Ohr.

Es hüpfen herbei und lauschen
Die frommen, klugen Gazelln,
Und in der Ferne rauschen
Des heilgen Stromes Welln.

Dort wollen wir niedersinken
Unter dem Palmenbaum,
Und Liebe und Ruhe trinken,
Und träumen seligen Traum. (B 1, 78)

As the poem comes full circle, the self-referential turn makes this dream a dream of dreaming its dream. However, this does not lead to a collapse, but highlights the process of signification as producing meaning exactly at the point where transparence and the moment of self-reflection on the precarious project of the production of meaning come to the fore as deferral and delay. Rather than aestheticizing, the poem performs a turn that points beyond every kind of instrumentalization in the service of a program of *l'art pour l'art*; while it suggestively seems to approximate the latter, it falls short of endorsing it. Instead, the poem hovers on the edge of an unstable irony that—self-referentially and self-reflectively—levitates in the creative space between meaning and suspense. It thereby produces a poetic momentum that brings home the point—as the poem plays with an exotic backdrop that resolutely stages the impossibility of coming to rest, not to mention to any form of "home"—that where there is no play and suspense of signification, there is no meaning. For any attempt to bring the poem's movement of deferral and displacement to a halt arrests the process of the production of meaning. We could say that Heine's poetic turn from talking about flowers to flowers conversing with each other signals a departure from the conventions of poetry that reconstitutes the level playing field of language and brings out the precariousness of the expectation that signification is stable, secure, and unequivocal. But language is no mere aesthetic effect. The poem's lingering, utopian dream of love and desire reminds us that there is always a social and political dimension to the process of signification. As a consequence, the poem can be understood simultaneously as a love poem and a subversive political commentary. The ambiguity of this double aspect accentuates the spectrum of meaning the poem opens up in the seemingly exclusive binary between the individual and society.

Irony, then, is not a matter of choice or style but a constitutive moment at the heart of the play that produces languages and literary forms; be they poetry, prose, or Heine's often preferred hybrids that combine prosaic and poetic features into new literary forms. This self-conscious and playful reflection on the constitutive feature of the ironic moment accounts for the critical thrust that gives Heine's writing its fluidity and lightness and at the same time its programmatic purpose.

If, for Heine, the use of language is not a neutral affair but a matter determined by the context and the purpose for which it is engaged, signification takes its cue from the subject position of the speaker. *Who* speaks is as important for Heine as *what* they say, and especially if the subject position is anything but clear, as for instance in the case of Dr. Saul Ascher in *The Harz Journey*—or rather his ghost, who makes an appearance in the narrator's dream only to refute the existence of ghosts. What exactly is the logic of a speech act performed by a ghost of seemingly dubious ontological status, a ghost who furthermore categorically denies the existence of his own kind? In this vein, Heine again and again makes clear that signification occurs in between interlocutors and that it is the reader or listener who ultimately must fill in the meaning by responding to the author. Heine's mockery of German censorship exemplifies this point graphically. For the critical theorist, the passage that follows is not just funny, it also poses some critical questions concerning the ambiguity of meaning:

> The German censors of the press – – – – – – – – – – – – – –
> –
> –
> –
> – – – – – – – – – – – – – – – blockheads – – – – – – – – – – –
> –
> –
> – – – – – – – — – – – – – – – – – (L 2, 334)
>
> Die deutschen Zensoren – – – – – – – – – – – – – – – – – – –
> –
> –
> –
> –
> –
> – – – – – – – – – – – – – Dummköpfe – – – – – – – – – – – – – –
> –
> –
> –
> – – – – – – – – – – – – (B 2, 283)

While the intended meaning appears to be quite obvious, the question immediately arises as to where exactly to locate it. Of course, the site where meaning crystallizes resides in the moment of reading, that is, interpretation. It is as if Heine were poking fun at Richelieu, who was known to have claimed that two words put on paper were enough for him to convict anybody of anything he wished. The critical point of the passage is that the trap snaps in the reader's mind, making the transgression the reader's and censor's rather than the author's. As a consequence, the censors find themselves confronted with the fact that there is nobody more suspect than themselves. While Heine occasionally uses this schema and scheme of writing to dupe censorship, it also poses a more profound question. The desire to fixate on meaning produces a hermeneutic snare that transfixes meaning at the expense of the play of language necessary for creating the conditions of meaning in the first place. Meaning, in other words, always comes at the cost of a reduction of complexity, erasing the moment of poetic excess that informs language and makes signification possible.

For Heine, similarly to Goethe, irony is less a technical rhetorical device than a structural, constitutive feature of language itself. Heine's post-romantic attitude embraces irony as a self-consciously critical mode that makes humorous and comedic slippage the condition that opens, rather than closes, the scene where the production of meaning plays out its movement. Irony is thus for Heine less an aesthetic flavor or added feature but an underlying condition necessary for the dynamics of the metaphorical movement that defines the operation of language.

Goethe and the Frankfurt School of Language

In a striking passage in *Ludwig Börne: A Memorial*, Heine points out that the dialect spoken in a particular place does not distinguish its users as Jews or non-Jews, but rather as linguistically coequal agents of a shared linguistic community. With the citation of parts of the passage in the Grimm dictionary of the German language under the entry "mauscheln," the passage has assumed canonical significance.[2] David Suchoff has called attention to the critical significance this passage bears for the way dialects function when read in its full context.[3] In describing Frankfurt, the city of Börne but also of Goethe, Heine includes an account of the Frankfurt stock exchange as the place where German and Jewish traders meet to conduct business:

> Here the noble class of businessmen assembles, and engages in wheeling and dealing with its mosaic accent [*mauscheln*]. What those of us from Northern Germany actually call *Mauscheln* is nothing other than the actual spoken language of the Frankfurt region, and it is spoken splendidly by the uncircumcised and circumcised alike. Börne spoke the jargon poorly, although he, like Goethe, could never fully disown this native dialect. I have noticed that people from Frankfurt who have kept their distance from any sort of business concerns, were in the end able to unlearn this Frankfurt accent that we in Northern German, as I've said, call *Mauscheln*.[4]
>
> Hier versammelt sich der edle Handelsstand und schachert und mauschelt . . . Was wir nämlich in Norddeutschland Mauscheln nennen, ist nichts anders als die eigentliche Frankfurter Landessprache, und sie wird von der unbeschnittenen Population eben so vortrefflich gesprochen, wie von der beschnittenen. Börne sprach diesen Jargon sehr schlecht, obgleich er, eben so wie Goethe, den heimatlichen Dialekt, nie ganz verleugnen konnte. Ich habe bemerkt, daß Frankfurter, die sich von allen Handelsinteressen entfernt hielten, am Ende jene Frankfurter Aussprache, die wir, wie gesagt, in Norddeutschland Mauscheln nennen, ganz verlernten. (B 4, 24)

Here the stock exchange, where "the city's golden vein flows" (*hier fließt die goldene Ader der Stadt*, 24) becomes, as Suchoff notes, "an extended metaphor for the treasure of Goethe's literary voice."[5] The linguistic family relations no longer separate "Jargon," "Mauscheln," or "Judeo-German," as Yiddish was called at the time, from the other German dialects, but suggest a contiguity and linguistic interrelatedness that renders disavowal of the Jewish dialect's status as a coequal dialect of the German language impossible. Or as Paul Mendes-Flohr has noted in another context: High German had become a Jewish dialect.[6]

Heine's innocuously jocular comment thus carries profound implications for the status of German as a canonized dialect, the status of Goethe, and the inseparable linguistic entanglement of the German and Jewish experience. More generally, the passage is a critical reflection on canonization and what makes a canon. If—as we will see in the section after the next—Heine could comically claim a nobler linguistic affiliation with German than the Olympian godhead of the German Parnassus could with Frankfurt as his native city, Heine's—and, for that matter, as we will see, Goethe's—refusal of all ontologically privileged pretense signals a radically critical intervention in the discourse of the philosophy of language of the time. Goethe had never considered himself—or anybody else for that matter—as master of their "own" language.

In making Goethe the "Mauschler" that Börne refused to be, and a better "Mauschler" than Börne at that, Heine not only exposed the tribal, anthropological foundation of linguistic theory but also pointed to the more profound relationship between Goethe and himself. Playing on the double meaning of "bad" in this context, Heine's comment that Börne spoke the "jargon" very badly while Goethe never lost it signals a gesture of deeper familial association by way of disassociation with Börne, the radical champion of Goethe's opponents. That the relationship to one's mother tongue was not a matter of uncontested inheritance was well understood by the grandmaster of canonical High German.[7] In his essay "Deutsche Sprache" (1817), Goethe gives voice to concerns that align in striking affinity with Heine. In response to the surge of parochialism he sees taking hold of the Germans, Goethe musters the multiple multilingual origins that inform German cultural production and the development of the German language. In a striking aside, the uncontested ruler of the German Olympus notes:

> Unfortunately one does not consider that one often writes poetry in one's own mother tongue as if it were a foreign one.
>
> Leider bedenkt man nicht, daß man in seiner Muttersprache oft ebenso dichtet, als wenn es eine fremde wäre.[8]

Oblivious to what they have received from other nations and continue to receive daily, the time will come when the Germans will ask how their ancestors succeeded in taking German to the heights of independence it now enjoys (268). In the roundabout way typical of Goethe's late style, he eloquently expresses his concerns with regard to the project of language purification:

> To purify and at the same time to enrich the mother tongue is the business of the best minds; purification without enrichment turns out to often be mindless; for nothing is more convenient than disregarding content when attending to expression. The ingenious man shapes the stuff words are made of without worrying what substance it consists of, the mindless can well speak purely for he has nothing to say.
>
> Die Muttersprache zugleich reinigen und bereichern ist das Geschäft der besten Köpfe; Reinigung ohne Bereicherung erweist sich öfters geistlos: denn es ist nichts bequemer, als von dem Inhalt absehen und auf den Ausdruck passen. Der geistreiche Mensch knetet seinen Wortstoff, ohne sich zu bekümmern, aus was für Elementen er bestehe, der geistlose hat gut rein sprechen, da er nichts zu sagen hat. (269)

Remarkably, Goethe's remarks are framed by a discussion of an essay by a Swiss author, Karl Ruckstuhl, "Von der Ausbildung der Teutschen Sprache, in Beziehung auf neue, dafür angestellte Bemühungen," which had appeared in the journal *Nemesis*.[9] In other words, Goethe gives voice to his concerns not only in the words of another or, to be more precise, through the mouth of another but, to stay with the image Goethe employs, "through a foreign mouth" ("durch fremden Mund," 265). While it may take a Swiss to appreciate the multiple foreign sources of the multilingual origins of the German language, Goethe is keen to remind his audience that recognition of the internal differences of the German language is just as inseparably bound up with the drawing of a nation's external boundaries as it is with the consciousness of a single speaker such as himself.

The stuff that words are made of thus comes from many different sources, and it is precisely the linguistic traffic across borders that fosters intellectual, cultural, and linguistic growth.[10] Contrary to the expectations of linguistic nationalism, the desire for a purified language will only lead to an atrophy of language's inspiring richness. Heine's renegotiation of Goethe's linguistic genealogy reinvents the canon as a linguistically and culturally open meeting point—"a stock exchange"—of the multiple origins of language, culture, tradition, and identity. Heine's Goethe is a paradigm of open and cross-fertilizing exchange with an approach to language that is ironic in the profound sense of the critical philosophical tradition. Heine produces a Goethe whose language, style, and literary significance recovers the exhilaratingly liberating force that defined Goethe's literary project all along, but which many of his contemporary readers, from the reactionary champions of national renewal to the liberals such as Börne, were no longer prepared to appreciate. But with Heine, who presented himself as the legitimate successor of the ruler of the German Olympus, Goethe became newly accessible to an approach to literature and culture that returned agency to the individual by rejecting all normative expectations to submit to a nationalist or any other form of nation-building agenda.

Heine's creative use of language as an ever-moving force of shifting signifiers foreshadows Nietzsche's description in his fragment "On Truth and Lie in a Non-Moral Sense."[11] But it also highlights the affinity with Goethe's light touch concerning language, a light touch whose profound commitment to tracing irony as what enables language to produce meaning has a liberating significance for Heine. As Goethe's reflections on language demonstrate, his critical concerns not only aligned well with Heine, Heine also allows us to read Goethe differently. While it is often seen as proof of a noncommittal attitude, Goethe's seemingly aloof approach to language features an irony that does not submit to "resignation" but, on the contrary, realizes language's play as the process of signification that makes it possible in the first place.

The Signifying Lizard

If Heine suggests that the question "What is language?" is inseparably linked to the question "What is human?"—which, in turn, is inseparably tied up with problematizing the distinction between Jews and non-Jews—language emerges, just like human nature, as a function of difference rather than a stable, self-identical reference. That this is not just the case for human beings and animals is demonstrated by Heine's staging of inanimate objects' relationship to language.

In the opening scene of the *Travel Pictures*' last installment on Italy, *The City of Lucca*, the beauty of the landscape inspires the narrator to appreciate that nature has its own history, one that is "an altogether different Natural History from that which is taught in schools" (L 3, 244; B 2, 477). An encounter with an old lizard whose reptilian nature qualifies his species as among the oldest denizens of the world illustrates the possibility of a different take on the history of nature.[12] A tongue-in-cheek answer to German idealism, the talking lizard's account of the history of nature brings out the theology-ridden assumptions that inform the philosophy of language and hermeneutics that define romanticism:

> The lizards have told me that there is a legend among the stones that God will yet become a stone to redeem them from their torpid motionless condition. One lizard was, however, of the opinion that this stone-incarnation will not take place until God shall have changed himself into every variety of animal and plant, and have redeemed them.
>
> But few stones have feeling, and they only breathe in the moonlight; but these few which realise their condition are fearfully miserable. The trees are better off; they can weep. But animals are the most favoured, for they can speak, each after its manner, and man the best of all. At some future time, after all the world has been redeemed, then all created things will speak, as in those primeval times of which poets sing. (L 3, 245f.)

> Die Eidechsen haben mir erzählt, es gehe eine Sage unter den Steinen, daß Gott einst Stein werden wolle, um sie aus ihrer Starrheit zu erlösen. Eine alte Eidechse meinte aber, diese Steinwerdung würde nur dann stattfinden, wenn Gott bereits in alle Tier- und Pflanzenarten sich verwandelt und sie erlöst habe.
> Nur wenige Steine haben Gefühl, und nur im Mondschein atmen sie. Aber diese wenige Steine, die ihren Zustand fühlen, sind schrecklich elend. Die Bäume sind viel besser daran, sie können weinen. Die Tiere aber sind am meisten begünstigt, denn sie können sprechen, jedes nach seiner Art und die Menschen am besten. Einst, wenn die ganze Welt erlöst ist, werden alle anderen Erschaffnisse ebenfalls sprechen können, wie in jenen uralten Zeiten, wovon die Dichter singen. (B 2, 477f.)

For those readers on which the irony might be lost, Heine makes it clear that the lizards are, after all, an "ironic species" (478). The conversation with the old lizard brings out the species' irony further as the animal proceeds to expound the limits of the human mind. Not only do the roots of language reach deeper than the surface of human consciousness, the lizard explains, thought itself springs from sources so deep beneath the surface of the conscious mind that lizards have a better grasp on it than humans. What the human mind likes to call thinking, the old lizard points out, is just what affects the mind accidentally:

> No human being *thinks*; only once in a while something occurs to a man, or comes into his head, and these altogether unintentional accidents they call thoughts, while the stringing them together they call thinking. (L 3, 250)

> Kein Mensch denkt, es fällt nur dann und wann den Menschen etwas ein, solche ganz unverschuldete Einfälle nennen sie Gedanken, und das Aneinanderreihen derselben nennen sie Denken. (B 2, 480)

Reiterating the critique of Hegel and Schelling he had just expressed, the old lizard goes on:

> But in my name you may deny it; no man thinks, no philosopher thinks, neither Schelling nor Hegel thinks; and as for all their philosophy, it is empty air and water, like the clouds of heaven. I have seen myriads of such clouds, proud and confident, sweeping their course above me, and the next morning's sun dissolved them again into their primeval nothingness. (L 3, 250f.)

> Aber in meinem Namen können Sie es wiedersagen: kein Mensch denkt, kein Philosoph denkt, weder Schelling noch Hegel denkt, und was gar ihre Philosophie betrifft, so ist sie eitel Luft und Wasser, wie die Wolken des

> Himmels; ich habe schon unzählige solcher Wolken, stolz und sicher, über mich hin ziehen sehen, und die nächste Morgensonne hat sie aufgelöst in ihr ursprüngliches Nichts;—[. . .]. (B 2, 480)

There is only one true philosophy, the lizard continues after the dash (omitted in Leland's translation), concluding his discourse:

> There is but *one* true philosophy, and that is written in eternal hieroglyphs on my tail. (L 3, 251)
>
> —es gibt nur eine einzige wahre Philosophie, und diese steht, in ewigen Hieroglyphen, auf meinem eigenen Schwanze. (480)

With these words, the lizard turns away, displaying the "most singular characters, which in variegated significance spread at length over his entire tail" (*die wunderlichsten Charaktere, die sich in bunter Bedeutsamkeit bis über den ganzen Schwanz hinabzogen*) as he slowly wriggles away (ibid.). The lizard's capricious comments, comedic as they might seem, address a philosophically more profound point. Claiming to carry the truth on his own tail, the lizard critic and philosopher flaunts a perfect identity of sign and signified that the wildest speculations of romanticism and German idealism could only dream of. With the lizard's tail dancing into rational thinking's sunset, Heine's allegory of allegory struts its ironic edge. A living sign, the semiotic solipsist exemplifies how deeply philosophy of language, semiotics, and discursive thought are caught up with each other. The natural sign that poses as a hieroglyph enacts the problem of the status and function of the sign. While romanticism and German idealism yearn for the identity of signifier and signified, the lizard's claim to represent the only true philosophy points to the fatal failure of the self-absorbed absolutizing of thought. The signifier that speaks and explains itself—how could that be a sign that represents? The lizard's curious logic acts out the romantic desire to solve the problem of the dead sign by substituting it with the fantasy of a living sign/signifier. Yet, the sign that speaks remains the captive of its own tautology. Certainly, the lizard is right in making his otherwise false claim. For him, the truth appearing on his tail cannot be anything else but the "*one* true philosophy" because the sign itself cannot reflect on its own claim. For it is nothing but a sign, a mere signifier, albeit one that speaks: "There is but *one* true philosophy, and that is written in eternal hieroglyphs on my own tail" (L 251; B 2, 480); a rather dubious claim even according to the lizard's own views.

All the talkative sign can do is to refer to its tail and to the "eternal hieroglyphs" supposedly written on it. Whether the pattern on his tail constitutes a form of signage is another question. But how could a symbol, a signifier, impress itself upon an individual living creature who furthermore claims membership of the most ancient and primeval species there is? And even if it were so, who would the reader be? The lizard short-circuits the logic of his own claims by turning them on his tail. But does that mean he can actually read his own tail? And if he indeed could read it, would he understand? Would he not have to realize that the identity of signifier and signified exists only in dreams and fairy tales, where signs can speak? Would not a speaking sign like the one he claims to represent bring the very process of the play of signification to a halt, effectively rendering it impossible? In other words, aspiring to the identity of signifier and signified undermines the very possibility of the process of signification and the play of meaning. The unsuspecting lizard expresses a critique of Schelling and Hegel that runs deeper than a willfully simple-minded comedy of the absurd. As the lizard acts out the short-circuit produced by the desire to align the process of signification with a German idealist agenda, Heine highlights the problematic nature of the assumptions that inform Schelling, Hegel, and German idealism more generally as they remain oblivious of the fundamental role of language for thought and philosophy.

In a provocative turn, Heine's allegoric play with the hieroglyph reworks romantic and idealist conceptions of hermeneutics into a theory of "depth hermeneutics" that attends to the unconscious as the driving force of human consciousness and, consequently, of language and thought.[13] A compromise formation of contradictory tendencies, writing is the site where the clash between the unconscious and the conscious gains articulation. In Heine, the shining brightness of daylight thoughts and the discursive clarity of concepts are pitted against the dark obscurity of dreams and fantastic imagery, reminding the reader of an ever-different world, inaccessible to the powers of reason alone. Poetic language, as a semiotic system formed on the basis of a historical repository of experienced illnesses, as Altenhofer puts it,[14] knows of a world suppressed and submerged by conscious thinking, whose discursive system of concepts lacks the power to fully grasp what it suppresses.

Ten years later, in *Ludwig Börne: A Memorial*, Heine returns to the hieroglyphs as the sign language of the repressed. In this book, the metaphorical use of an Egyptian obelisk transplanted to a Paris square serves more than one purpose. In a cruel joke on Börne and his ilk, Heine notes that just as the erection of an obelisk may entail the release of scorpions caught up in the process of packing and shipping the artifact from Egypt to modern-day France, the formation of great cultural obelisks (*Geistesobelisken*) may also allow "petty little poisonous beasts" (*kleinliche Gifttierchen*) to break loose. While this passage, like the book as a whole, might appear to serve the sole purpose of settling the score with the recently deceased Börne, it serves as a reminder that the history of cultural monuments and their hieroglyphic inscription is not a thing of the past, but one that reaches deep into the present it keeps under its spell: an ever-present history that reclaims history's repressed as the refuse that returns as history's most present feature (S 121; B 4, 139).

While the writing of the past may have become illegible, the neglected past returns, as the eggs of the scorpions buried under the obelisks will one day hatch and release their contents. Just like such a return from the past, the message buried in the hieroglyphs yet awaits its recovery:

> Who will decipher this voice of prehistory, these ancient hieroglyphs? Perhaps they do not contain a curse but a prescription for the wounds of our time! Oh, if one could read them! (S 121)
>
> Wer enträtselt diese Stimme der Vorzeit, diese uralten Hieroglyphen? Sie enthalten vielleicht keinen Fluch, sondern ein Rezept für die Wunde unserer Zeit! O wer lesen könnte! (B 4, 140)

The inscription on the obelisk transplanted to the Square Louis XVI and waiting to be deciphered by those who know how to read it gives visual expression to the poet's challenge to express what refuses containment in conceptually determinate speech:

> In garish picture-writing my dream shows me the great suffering that I would gladly conceal from myself and that I hardly dare to utter in the sober conceptual sounds of the bright day. (S 123)
>
> In greller Bilderschrift zeigt mir der Traum das große Leid, das ich mir gern verhehlen möchte, und das ich kaum auszusprechen wage in den nüchternen Begriffslauten des hellen Tages. (B 4, 141)

This pictorial script represents the coded form into which culture and tradition have locked the contentious forces of life's antagonisms. The poet's task, the passage suggests, consists in articulating what eludes the regime of discursive reason. As formations of the submerged consciousness, the relics and ruins of the past have become hieroglyphs of a language we no longer understand. Reading them as palimpsests whose different layers of inscriptions indicate an excess of meaning beyond the narrow scope of rationality's comprehension, Heine performs his writing as a reading that liberates the subversive power writing contains from its hieroglyphic petrification.[15]

The philosopher lizard on the road to Lucca is more than just a parodic impersonation of Schelling's philosophy in the guise of reptilian ossification. This talking hieroglyph, representing speech-endowed nature and thus serving as an eloquent reminder of pantheism's anti-idealist truth, exposes German idealism and romanticism's misguided yearning for the ultimate form of identity between the signifier and the signified. For signs cannot speak or else they would not be signs, and if they could, what they say would constitute an act of signifying but could never pass as the signified it signifies. What would a sign that could talk look like, what would it say, what could it say? It would be a sign with consciousness, a self-conscious agent. But would that still be a sign? Can any speaking subject be a sign other than metonymically?

Far from short-circuiting language completely and collapsing meaning into mere nonsense, the blithe lizard lecturer carries, at this crucial junction of the *Travel Pictures*, a critical message: meaning lies inextricably buried in the sign, and the sign, as a consequence, calls for ever-new acts of reading. For signs can proliferate meaning only if—just like the signs the lizard claims to carry on his tail—they refer to embodied experience. Ironically, the reptilian informant signals not just the seeming agelessness and timelessness of time immemorial but also reminds the reader—as the lizard speaks—that speech, signification, and the production of meaning are always figured in and through temporality. They are a function of time that reaches deep into the dynamics of the unconscious.

A second aspect of the lizard's message is that the comedic enactment of the identity of signifier and signified demonstrates—counter to the lizard's claim—that the site of the production of meaning is in the act of the performance rather than a text that could be booked,[16] fixed, and carried on one's tail. The talking lizard is thus more than just a vaudeville sideshow. The lizard's performance reminds us that while consciousness may play a key role in the production of meaning, there is more to it. As the other of the unconscious, consciousness remains inseparably tied to the reptilian, that is, to the ossified animal roots from which it springs.

While the philosopher's stone—if ever found—may not speak, the hieroglyphs on the lizard's tail tell an altogether different story. They "speak," but only for those who know how to read, that is, interpret them. As an encoded, enigmatic, silent sign—that is albeit suggestively brimming with meaning—that awaits hermeneutic redemption, the hieroglyphs work as Heine's telling metaphor for allegory. Heine's lizard performatively anticipates Benjamin's discussion of allegory in his *Origin of German Tragic Drama* (*Ursprung des bürgerlichen Trauerspiels*):

> Allegory [. . .] is not a playful illustrative technique, but a form of expression, just as speech [language] is expression, and, indeed just as writing is.[17]
>
> Allegorie [. . .] ist nicht spielerische Bildertechnik, sondern Ausdruck, so wie Sprache Ausdruck ist, ja so wie Schrift.[18]

The pulsating dialectics that in Benjamin drives the semiotic movement of allegory is prefigured in Heine's shuttle-like movement between the ever-continuous projection of images and their equally perpetual revocation, an oscillation that results in the release of a free play of language. Benjamin's comment that allegory presents to the eye of the spectator the Hippocratic face of history as petrified primal landscape (343) helps flesh out the radical critique of philosophy in Heine's seemingly absurd proliferation of the play of allegory.

In the light of Benjamin's comments on allegory, the curious connection between history and natural philosophy that the lizard invokes appears as the precise moment of critical decomposition where allegory arises:

> It is by virtue of a strange combination of nature and history that the allegorical mode of expression is born.[19]
>
> Mit einer sonderbaren Verschränkung von Natur und Geschichte tritt der allegorische Ausdruck selbst in die Welt.[20]

In the tradition from the Renaissance to the nineteenth century, hieroglyphs served as symbols of the mystical approach to philosophy of nature and its claim to access the esoteric truth of the absolute. Hieroglyphs were the images of divine ideas. As the allegorical gaze transforms everything into pulsating writing—represented as fragments, ruins, and runes—thus bringing home the deep-seated antinomies of the allegorical, the illusion of totality fades away. As Benjamin concludes:

> For the *eidos* disappears [extinguishes], the simile ceases to exist [dies away], and the cosmos it contained shrivels up.[21]
>
> Denn das Eidos verlischt, das Gleichnis geht ein, der Kosmos darinnen vertrocknet. (Benjamin, 352)

Heine's lizard—not quite biting his tail—suggests that the *eidos* is a self-feeding illusion that the allegorical fixity of concepts dissolves. An allegory of allegory, the lizard—Heine's *Eidechs*—appears as the *eidos* in retreat.

Monkeys Might Understand but Choose Not to Speak

Lizards are not the only animals that are able to speak. In the case of monkeys, however, the issue is less their ability to speak than their refusal to do so, and not for any lack of intelligence. Quite to the contrary, they enjoy a kind of wisdom humans often seem to lack. In a passage in his late "Memoirs" written in his "mattress grave," as he called his confinement to his bed, Heine mentions—in the context of a discussion about the gradual transition between dialects from one language to another—monkeys who refuse to talk. His father, he notes, spoke the Hanover dialect, a dialect that to this day is considered the clearest, cleanest, and grammatically most correct use of German. While Heine calls his father's linguistic background "a great advantage for me" (B 6.1, 582), he suggests that this has nothing to do with any pretense of purity but is owing simply to the agreeable sounds associated with this dialect. Heine even grants the possibility that "it might be true that our own German language, as patriotic linguists in the Netherlands have claimed, is but a corrupted Dutch" (ibid.). But he does not do so without mocking Dutch and the dialect spoken in his native city Düsseldorf:

> In the language of the people of Düsseldorf one can already recognize the frog's squawking of the Dutch swamps.
>
> In der Sprache der Düsseldorfer merkt man schon einen Übergang in das Froschgequäke der holländischen Sümpfe. (B 6.1, 582)

As the transition from human to animal speech seems gradual, the remark describing German as corrupted Dutch is followed by the citation of an unnamed zoologist's opinion—not just any zoologist's opinion, for that matter, but a "cosmopolitan" zoologist's who, according to Heine's memoirs, declared the ape humankind's ancestor and maintained that humans are merely developed, even overdeveloped, apes. To this Heine adds:

> If the monkeys could speak they probably would claim that humans are merely degenerated monkeys and that humanity is a corrupted monkeydom in analogy to the opinion of the Dutch that the German language is a corrupted Dutch.
>
> Wenn die Affen sprechen könnten, sie würden wahrscheinlich behaupten, daß die Menschen nur ausgeartete Affen seien, daß die Menschheit ein verdorbenes Affentum, wie nach der Meinung der Holländer die deutsche Sprache ein verdorbenes Holländisch ist. (ibid.)

The resonance with the report to an academy delivered by Kafka's character Rotpeter highlights Heine's approach to language as a phenomenon that defies categories of origin and purity. Heine continues:

> I say if monkeys could talk, although I am not convinced of their inability to do so. The negroes on the Senegal assert unswervingly that monkeys are just as much human beings as we are, except smarter, since they abstain from talking in order to avoid being recognized as human beings and forced to work.
>
> Ich sage, wenn die Affen sprechen könnten, obgleich ich von solchem Unvermögen des Sprechens nicht überzeugt bin. Die Neger am Senegal versichern steif und fest, die Affen seien Menschen ganz wie wir, jedoch klüger, indem sie sich des Sprechens enthalten um nicht als Menschen anerkannt und zum Arbeiten gezwungen zu werden. (ibid.)

Challenging the absurd implications of all the claims of origin-thinking, Heine's questioning of language as an exclusively human gift deflates the ontologically exclusive status ascribed to human language and reimagines it as a feature of natural history. In highlighting the instrumental aspect of language as a means of exploitation, Heine is doing more than just making a witty aside. Language, he suggests, is anything but an innocent ability, gift, or means. It is a part and an expression of the social relations it represents. In a similar way, Marx and Engels suggest in *German Ideology* that the nexus between language and the material conditions of social relations, including the division of labor, is at the heart of the production of language:

> Language like consciousness only arises from the need and necessity of traffic of relationships with other men.[22]
>
> Die Sprache entsteht, wie das Bewusstsein, erst aus dem Bedürfnis, der Notdurft des Verkehrs mit andern Menschen.[23]

Similarly, Heine's point concerning the monkeys' refusal to submit to the protocol of human language and communication—and therefore to exploitation—addresses the same concern with language in a pointedly post-idealist and post-romantic manner.

As he continues his journey on the road to the city of Lucca, the narrator encounters an eagle, that proud bird of prey that in *Germany, a Winter's Tale* will serve as an ominous emblem of Prussian oppression. But here, gliding free and lighthearted under the Italian sun, the king of the skies is a reminder of the heroic ages when Jupiter reigned and Napoleon was the promise of liberation. At the sight of the eagle, the narrator imagines the bird addressing him a way that traverses the distinction between humans and birds:

> "What sort of a bird art *thou*? Knowest thou not that I am as much of a king as I was in those heroic days when I bore Jupiter's thunders and adorned Napoleon's banners?" (L 3, 254)
>
> "Was bist Du für ein Vogel? Weißt du wohl, daß ich noch immer ein König bin, eben so gut wie in jenen Heldenzeiten, als ich Jupiters Blitze trug und Napoleons Fahnen schmückte?" (B 2, 482f.)

The imagined monologue continues as the eagle asks the narrator:

> "Art thou a learned parrot, who hast learned the old songs all by heart, and pedantically repeats them? Or a sulky turtle-dove, who feels beautifully and coos miserably? Or an almanack nightingale? Or a gander who has seen better days, and whose ancestors saved the Capitol? Or an altogether servile farmyard cock, around whose neck, out of irony, men hang my image in miniature, the emblem of bold flight, and who for that

> reason spreads himself, and struts as though he himself were a veritable eagle?" (L 3, 254f.)
>
> "Bist du etwa ein gelehrter Papagoi,[24] der die alten Lieder auswendig gelernt hat und pedantisch nachplappert? Oder eine vermüffte Turteltaube, die schön fühlt und miserabel gurrt? Oder eine Almanachsnachtigall? Oder ein abgestandener Gänserich, dessen Vorfahren das Kapitol gerettet! Oder gar ein serviler Haushahn, dem man, aus Ironie, das Emblem des kühnen Fliegens, nämlich mein Miniaturbild um den Hals gehängt hat, und der sich deshalb so mächtig spreizt, als wäre er nun selbst ein Adler?" (B 2, 483)[25]

If Heine, the self-declared nightingale of German literature, had called himself at an earlier point in a punning poem a *Gimpel* (a bullfinch but also a fool), the odd bird making its appearance here is a *Papagoy*—a parrot of a particular kind: an exotic bird who evokes with his linguistic difference the Jewish beak that mocks the gravitas of the eagle.[26] While the aviary in the passage above includes a motley group of established literary creatures such as the *Turteltaube*, *Almanachsnachtigall*, *Gänserich*, and *Haushahn*,[27] the *Papagoy* stands out as the literary newcomer. Neither parvenu nor pariah—to follow Hannah Arendt's distinction[28]—the odd bird poses a challenge to conventional taxonomies. With the appearance of the *Papagoy*, the narrative recalls an earlier scene in the "Baths of Lucca," the prequel to *The City of Lucca*, in which the bird had been introduced as a particular kind of zoological subject. There, Hirsch-Hyazinth offers the following reflection:

> What is man? He goes walking with pleasure out of the Altona Gate and on the Hamburg Hill, and there he sees the sights, the lions, the birds, the poll-parrots [Papagoyim], the monkeys, the great folks, and he takes a turn on the flying horses, or gets electrified, and then thinks how jolly he'd be if he was only in a place a thousand miles off, in Italy, where the oranges and lemons are a-growing! What is man? When he's before the Altona Gate he wants to be in Italy, and when he's in Italy he wants to be back again before the Altona Gate. (L 3, 140)
>
> Was ist der Mensch! Man geht vergnügt vor dem Altonaer Tore, auf dem Hamburger Berg, spazieren, und besieht dort die Merkwürdigkeiten, die Löwen, die Gevögel, die Papagoyim, die Affen, die ausgezeichneten Menschen, und man läßt sich Karussel fahren oder elektrisieren, und man denkt was würde ich erst für Vergnügen haben an einem Orte, der noch zweihundert Meilen von Hamburg weiter entfernt ist, in dem Lande wo die Zitronen und Orangen wachsen, in Italien! Was ist der Mensch! Ist er vor dem Altonaer Tore, so möchte er gern in Italien sein, und ist er in Italien, so möchte er wieder vor dem Altonaer Tore sein! (B 2, 402)

Turning mankind's possibly oldest question around and into its own answer, Hirsch-Hyazinth plays the double agent of the self-ironically assimilated

Jew who cannot help but remain true to his roots.[29] Hirsch-Hyazinth, in many ways Heine's double, reminds us that the one who posed the serious question concerning human nature was also the one who is half human and half animal. The half-woman, half-human sphinx is often depicted with wings in nineteenth-century representations. If the sphinx was the one to pose the consequential question that Oedipus knew how to answer, Heine's passage turns the intertextual reference around in a comedic twist: the question/answer "what is man," which in Heine's variation substitutes the question mark with an exclamation point, becomes the question to which the motley mix of lions, birds, "*Papagoyim*," monkeys, and humans hold the answer.

The biblical and Greek resonances make this passage even more saliently comic. Psalm 8:5 and its question—"Who is man that you think of him?"—and Sophocles's chorus' enigmatic verdict in *Antigone*—"Terrible is man!"—endow the question with the sublime gravitas of the heritage of Europe's great traditions only to turn the spotlight on a menagerie of animals and humans that renders the desire for a stable distinction between them only the more dubious. At this point, then, Jews, non-Jews, and other animals become indistinguishably marked as linguistic riddles that challenge and expose all ontological assumptions concerning the nature of language as ludicrous.

Mingling among humans and other animals, the "*Papagoyim*" promenading with their families in the Hamburg park suggest that the desire for "*goyim naches*" submits to the need of the false pretense that assimilation requires as it seeks to erase the rich diversity of species that makes life possible. Appearing out of the blue in the Italian sky and a thousand miles away from Hamburg, the eagle's questioning of the traveler's nature, couched in seemingly zoological terms, turns out to be the very Jewish question that the German eagle, in its Prussian or any other form, would never cease to pose. But the eagle's question calls at the same time for a different and more empowering interpretation: the eagle's singling out of the "*Papagoy*" might also be the birdcall that spells the promise—and announcement of the consummation—of emancipation as the final recognition of the voice of difference.

Ticking Watches and the Beat of Drums

It is not just nature that talks in Heine; man-made objects such as drums and watches also have a language of their own. The speaking lizard's is just one of the challenges to conventional notions of language the narrator encounters in the *Travel Pictures*. An earlier installment, *Ideas. Book Le Grand*, had already introduced the reader to the foreign languages spoken in Heine's hometown by traveling back in time to the Düsseldorf of his childhood. Taking us back to his school days and the one exceptional day when school was closed—for the welcome celebration in honor of Napoleon's entering the city—Latin, Greek, Hebrew, and German are mentioned as making up the core subjects instilled at school (B 2, 266; L 2, 306.). But it is Heine's pocket watch that has greater success in picking up Hebrew, for the reason that it gets more exposure to the holy language than its owner. For the watch, he confides, had

> a much more intimate intercourse with pawnbrokers than I, and in consequence acquired many Jewish habits; for instance, it would not go on Saturday. (L 2, 309)

> viel intimen Umgang mit Pfänderverleihern [. . .], und dadurch manche jüdische Sitte annahm—z.B. des Sonnabends ging sie nicht. (B 2, 268)

The watch had another odd feature: it would practice grammar, an exercise the narrator witnessed during sleepless nights as the watch conjugated verbs:

> *katal, katalta, katalti—kittel, kittalta, kittalti—pokat, pokadeti—pikat—pik—pik—*. (L 2, 310; B 2, 268)

Conjugating verbs such as to kill, criticize, order, and command, Heine's pocket watch converses in a Hebrew that is both grammatically correct, mechanical, and to the point. Keeping Heine company during his sleepless nights, the watch gives voice to the unconscious that keeps him up and communicates by what he hears. If the lizard in *The City of Lucca* will suggest a few years later that the question of the exact site of language and signification is a problem whose fundamental challenge philosophers have not even begun to comprehend, the talking pocket watch comments on the temporal aspects of the problem of the dislocation of the site of the production of meaning or, in other words, the question of where exactly in space and time language is situated.

The stakes of this question are raised a few pages later with the introduction of a French drum major whose drum is his principal instrument of communication with the narrator. Assigned quarters with Heine's family, the Frenchman and his drum engage in a conversation with the young Heine who, at this time, was a schoolboy. Between the drum major's French and Heine's German, the drum assumes the role of the medium of translation. While his efforts to translate between German and French cost Heine some painful disciplinary consequences at school, the soldier's drumming is represented as a more effective and most consequential learning experience:

> We must know the spirit of a language, and this is best learned by drumming. Parbleu! how much do I not owe to the French drummer who was so long quartered in our house, who looked like the devil, and yet had the good heart of an angel, and who above all this drummed so divinely! (L 2, 314)

> Man muß den Geist der Sprache kennen, und diesen lernt man am besten durch Trommeln. Parbleu! Wie viel verdanke ich nicht dem französischen Tambour, der so lange bei uns in Quartier lag, und wie ein Teufel aussah, und doch von Herzen so engelgut war, und so ganz vorzüglich trommelte. (270f.)

After all, beating the drum's hide is always preferable to collecting beatings of one's own, as Heine was quick to learn when his attempt to render the German word for faith (*Glaube*) as *crédit* ran afoul of his teacher's finer philological sensibilities. While at school this resulted in a rain of beatings pouring down on his back, the lesson was duly learnt. Every time the word "*la religion*" is mentioned, Heine's back cringes in anticipation of another generous helping and his cheeks turn red with shame, but "*le crédit*" nonetheless stands him in better stead than "*la religion*" (L 2, 312f.; B 2, 270). While having one's own skin beaten will always leave behind a lesson for life, substituting a drum hide seems a more advantageous approach. This is especially true when it comes to mastering the great ideas of modern times, in which this approach to language acquisition is basically "the best method to learn" (L 2, 315; B 2, 271). However, the drum major Le Grand occasionally gets so caught up in his teaching of history and drumming the battles of Austerlitz, Jena, Eylau, and Wagram that he eventually brings the drumming to an ear-splitting crescendo that nearly shatters Heine's eardrums:

> Monsieur Le Grand drummed so that I nearly burst my own sheepskin. (L 2, 320)
>
> Monsieur Le Grand trommelte, daß fast mein eigenes Trommelfell dadurch zerrissen wurde. (B 2, 274)

One or the other, skin or hide, always gets a beating. And what else does hitting a drum imply than eventually getting at the eardrums? The image of the drum as medium also figures the process of knowledge's translation and transmission by way of a language that allows understanding precisely because it exemplifies that signification works by way of indirection. This also underscores the underlying political dimension of the episode of the bracing French drum major. Freedom, equality, civil society, and democracy all rely on forms of language that reflect meaning as an emancipatory social practice of self-determination. If the beat and tune make the music, the social and political practice is interlinked with the linguistic dimension of the production of meaning. For meaning to occur they need to come together. The drum episode brings home this point loud and clear.

Rallying the troops, the drum sets the beat and the process of signification in motion. The production of meaning, then, is neither dictated nor determined by the drum, but set in motion by the social-political processes it engenders. Heine's lowly infantry drum major is no leader or commander, but a historical witness and ordinary observer who marches as part of the army of liberation. Marching in the line that writes history at eye level, the drum major reflects the way meaning is mediated through the concert of communal negotiation.

Heine stages meaning and signification as performative acts. As a result, meaning and the process of signification are figured as dynamic. Linked to the social-political context, they are not fixed inventory that can simply be called up, but defined by the work of interpretation. Meaning emerges not by a purely hermeneutic act of exegesis, but through performance. Signification is an act of praxis. Heine's talking animals, objects, and humans playfully illustrate that language is less humankind's exclusive prerogative as a species so much as a function of the use to which human beings put it. And precisely this pragmatic outlook gives poetry and fiction their critical importance. If the recourse to imagination proves to be critical for staging language and signification as performative acts, Heine's insistent performance of the performative act as a speech act brings home the decisive link between language, sign, and play.

Displaced Philology and the Language of the Other

At the end of *Florentine Nights*, Heine offers a striking illustration of the problems that define the desire for pristine linguistic origins, the problems of translation, interpretation, and authenticity. In a story that traces the paradoxical structure of narration as an act of continuous deferral, the question of the identity of the central figure, Laurence, turns out to be nothing but an irresolvable enigma. Laurence's identity is defined precisely by the impossibility of clear origins, genealogy, and meaning. Instead of resolving the question of her identity, the narrative suggests that Laurence serves as a marker of alterity that can only be expressed through the translation and interpretation of a self that can only be addressed as the displaced loss of an origin that is always already appropriated by the other.

In a radically post-romantic gesture that outdoes romanticism by pushing it to the brink, Heine's triply mediated narrative explodes the desire for foundational narratives to reveal an act that appropriates the other's voice. In this passage, the narrator tells the story that Laurence tells him about her own origins. Heine's inversion of philological desire suggests that all origin narratives are but some sort of ventriloquism: a capture and re-projection of the other's voice, which at the same time challenges every claim to linguistic or cultural priority.[30] In this respect, the voice of the other, as Heine points out, will always be considered deadly, a bursting forth from the "tomb" and "thieves" of a foundational tradition that lives by stealing, then imitating the other's voice.[31]

Laurence is an image of the other's centrality to linguistic and national traditions: prematurely buried, but nonetheless multiply mediated and very much alive. Having survived the quasi-philological impulse, she is considered dead, then saved, only to be exploited in a narrative that suggests the robbery and burial of foreign voices is the very process by which a living tradition is formed. Laurence says as much to the narrator of the thieves who discovered her in her untimely grave, and who brought her to the "great ventriloquist," husband of the dealer in stolen goods who becomes her surrogate father. This ventriloquist or "*Bauchredner*" at the same time comes into view as the text's ultimate, but ultimately problematic, source of authority for an origin accessible only by way of translation and interpretation. As a result, he can only gesture toward the moment of displacement that constitutes the moment of linguistic creation. In Heine's tale, the "great ventriloquist" gives voice to the family romance of a philology that establishes its authority by throwing its voice. The project he represents speaks for the other, and sustains itself from stolen goods:

> While the great ventriloquist was alive, and when he was discontented with me as often happened he always cried: "Cursed Death-Child, I wish I had never taken you from the grave." As he was of great skill in his calling, he could so modulate his voice as to make any one think that it came from the ground, and so he would make me believe that it was the voice of my dead mother who related her story. He could have well known[32] the terrible tale, for he had once been a servant of the Count my father. (L 1, 86f.)
>
> Als der große Bauchredner noch lebte und nicht selten mit mir unzufrieden war, rief er immer: verwünschtes Totenkind, ich wollt ich hätte dich nie aus dem Grabe geholt! Ein geschickter Bauchredner wie er war, konnte er seine Stimme so modulieren, daß man glauben mußte sie käme aus der Erde hervor, und er machte mir dann weis, das sei die Stimme meiner verstorbenen Mutter, die mir ihre Schicksale erzähle. Er konnte sie wohl kennen, diese furchtbaren Schicksale, denn er war einst Kammerdiener des Grafen. (B 1, 611)

Heine's exposure of the problem of claiming that a language has an origin or that a voice has authenticity, and of the inextricable intertwinement of death, theft, the gift of life, origin, and tradition, underscores that the inventions of genealogies of mother tongues might be the last place one should try to anchor a philology that can only be addressed as fundamentally displaced.

Exile and displacement play a crucially central role in Heine and they figure throughout his writing. But the story of Laurence the mercurial and elusive dancer stands out as a pointed reminder that exile and displacement are the result of a process of social and political expropriation that legitimates itself with narratives of linguistic origins and authenticity that silence others by ventriloquizing their voices. When Heine arrived in Paris, his first theoretically ambitious project was his *On the History of Religion and Philosophy in Germany*, a book that would not only become the first work of intellectual history as we know it, but also a sophisticated study of the dynamics of intellectual movement and exchange, a virtuoso study of displacement, the return of the repressed, and what Derrida would call "hauntology."[33] The upshot of Heine's work was to show how Germany's and Europe's greatest cultural and intellectual achievements are the products of a continuous movement of displacement.

As has often been observed, and in a pointed countermove to Madame de Staël's counterrevolutionary agenda, Heine put the spotlight on the larger European nexus that undergirds the emergence of modern national cultures and particularities. This change was driven not so much by national linguistic features but, more profoundly, by the particular development of political, religious, and larger cultural forces, which in turn determined linguistic habits, practices, and forms. In other words, the origin of language is for Heine always already a scene of displacement, appropriation, transformation, and substitution; movements that define the interplay of tradition and innovation that constitutes language-making.

Like Adorno, Heine refused to submit to any scheme of *Sprachontologie* or ontology of language. And what Adorno said about language is something he found confirmation for in his reading of Heine:

> No language, not even the old vernacular language, is organic and natural [. . .] but every victory of the advanced, civilizatory linguistic element contains as a precipitate something of the injustice done to the older and weaker element.[34]

No Idea: The Nonconceptual

If Heine's writing reflects playfully on language and signification from a post-romantic view, his critical reserve is matched by an equally pointed stance with regard to Hegel's concept of the idea and the labor of the concept. Heine's satirical exposure of Hegel's notion of the idea as an unwitting comedy of philosophy runs through much of *The Harz Journey* and comes to a head in *Ideas: Book Le Grand*. Provocatively, the title pits the notion of ideas against the lowly drum major Monsieur Le Grand who is the very opposite of grandiosity: a down-to-earth foot soldier in the struggle for universal freedom and equality.[35] The account of his percussionist language instruction, earlier discussed,[36] is—after a short interlude of two very brief chapters—followed by a satirical digression concerning scholarly erudition, writing, the composition of books, and the nature of ideas. If Heine's treatment of ideas comes off as a bit of a cavalier summary, it certainly gets its point across with utmost clarity. The passage cites the supposed table of contents of a scholarly work the narrator announces as his forthcoming opus. Notice that the chapter where this passage occurs follows Chapter 12, which contains Heine's treatment of the German censors shot through with a plethora of dashes cited above. Here is the table of contents:

> I. Of ideas.
> A. Of ideas in general.
> a. Of reasonable ideas.
> b. Of unreasonable ideas.
> α. Of ordinary ideas.
> β. Of ideas covered with green leather. (L 2, 341)[37]

> I. Von den Ideen.
> A. Von den Ideen im allgemeinen.
> a) Von den vernünftigen Idee.
> b) Von den unvernünftigen Ideen.
> α. Von gewöhnlichen Ideen.
> β. Von den Ideen, die mit grünem Leder überzogen sind. (B 2, 287)

Critical of Hegel's concept of the idea since his early days as a student in Berlin when he followed Hegel's lectures, Heine's mocking citational play pokes fun at the methodological havoc that looms behind the schematism of Hegelian thought. Wary of the totalizing impulse of Hegel's concept of the idea, Heine gives voice to the concern to resist obliteration of the singular and particular. The rudimentary setup of the distinctions that inform the logic of the imaginary table of content highlights the way in which the particular and singular are displaced and obliterated from the start. The absence of the particular and its comedic return in the form of a book bound in green leather comments on the restrictive manner in which the particular and singular are marginalized. For Heine, the worry that Hegel's concept of the idea eliminates the concerns of real life assumed existential urgency. In a letter of May 23, 1823, to Moses Moser, Heine's closest friend during his Berlin time, he reports the following dream:

> I saw a crowd of people laughing at me, even small children laughed at the sight of me, and I ran ashamed with anger to you, my dear Moser, and you opened your arms as a friend and comforted me and said I should not be upset, for I am just an idea. And in order to demonstrate to me that I was just an idea you hastily reached for Hegel's *Logic* and showed me a confused passage there, and Gans knocked at the window,—but I ran around the room enraged, screaming: I am no idea and don't know anything about any idea and never in my whole life have had any idea—It was a horrible dream and I remember that Gans screamed even louder and on his shoulders sat the little Markus who added the appropriate citations screaming in an uncannily hoarse voice and smiling in such a dreadfully friendly manner that I woke up from fear.

> Ich sah eine Menge Menschen die mich auslachten, so gar kleine Kinder lachten über mich, und ich lief schämend vor Ärger zu Dir, mein guter Moser, und Du öffnetest mir Deine Freundes Arme, und sprachest mir Trost ein, und sagtest mir ich solle mir nichts zu Gemüthe führen, denn ich sey ja nur eine Idee, und um mir zu beweisen daß ich nur eine Idee sey, griffest Du hastig nach Hegels Logik und zeigtest mir eine konfuse Stelle darin, und Gans klopfte ans Fenster,—ich aber sprang wütend im Zimmer herum und schrie: ich bin keine Idee und weiß nichts von einer Idee und hab mein Lebtag keine Idee gehabt—Es war ein schauderhafter Traum, ich erinnere mich Gans schrie noch lauter, und auf seiner Schulter saß der kleine Markus und schrie mit unheimlich heiserer Stimme die Zitaten hinzu und lächelte auf eine so gräßlich freundliche Weise daß ich vor Angst aufwachte. (HSA 20, 86)

If this dream seems to make some striking insinuations about the role Hegel came to play for Heine's friends at the Verein für Cultur und Wissenschaft der Juden, the dream (whether actually dreamt or imagined) serves as more than just a parody of the idea as a disembodied thought, lifeless notion, and all-comprising movement of thinking. It expresses anxiety in the face of the destructive power of a universalist frame of mind demanding complete erasure of the singularity of the particular. For Heine, the seductive power of Hegel's lure consists in the tyrannical hegemony of an overreaching universalism to which Hegel sought to submit all that exists. While for Heine the particular refuses subjection to the rule of repression, he views the move of Hegel's thought as a dangerous attempt to recommit to the resignation to the status quo from which it promises delivery.

But what then is an idea, or rather, the idea of an idea, the narrator in *Ideas. Book Le Grand* wonders, and not without a critically Spinozist twist that opens the doorway to an epistemologically critical move that suggests a challenge to Hegel on his own terms.[38] In a quick aside, Heine's text goes through a sampling of examples that highlight the pointedly nonphilosophical use of the word idea—or else perhaps a critically philosophical use with a Spinozist inflection, depending on the view of the observer:

> Madame, have you, on the whole, an idea of an idea? What is an idea? "There are some good ideas in the build of this coat," said my tailor to me, as he with earnest attention gazed on the overcoat which dates in its origin from my Berlin dandy days, and from which a respectable quiet dressing-gown is now to be manufactured. My washerwoman complains that the Reverend Mr. S—has been putting "ideas" into the head of her daughter, which have made her foolish and unreasonable. (L 2, 341)

> Madame, haben Sie überhaupt eine Idee von einer Idee? Was ist eine Idee? "Es liegen einige gute Ideen in diesem Rock", sagte mein Schneider, indem er mit ernster Anerkennung den Oberrock betrachtete, der sich

> noch aus meinen berlinisch eleganten Tagen herschreibt, und woraus jetzt ein ehrsamer Schlafrock gemacht werden sollte. Meine Wäscherin klagt: "der Pastor S. habe ihrer Tochter Ideen in den Kopf gesetzt, und sie sei dadurch unklug geworden und wolle keine Vernunft mehr annehmen." (B 2, 288)

If Heine's implied answer to the question "What is an idea?" is "No idea," his answer speaks to the epistemological conundrum of the question as his examples highlight some of the issues that haunt the concept. This sartorial take exemplifies the dynamic movement of the idea as a possibly latent force that is connected to history—in this case, the Berlin days when Hegel's ideas fell on fertile ground. But with the development from social outfit to tired robe de chambre or dressing gown (*Schlafrock*), the example also insinuates a downhill tendency of even such grand ideas as come with the promise of a great career, such as that of a Berlin overcoat. Like overcoats, ideas are a kind of passe-partout. Their one-fits-all size clothes the subject in the fashion of the day. But the idea/coat turned robe de chambre is also doomed to retire to the privacy of domestic life where, reduced to serving in the comfort of one's home, it has nevertheless now been put to an honorable use, albeit exclusively in the privacy of one's home. If the idea's fashionable aspects touch on the idea's historical dynamics, the feisty washerwoman's complaint highlights the question of the status, nature, and function of ideas. What exactly the relationship between ideas and reason consists in then becomes a question that still needs sorting out. If the washerwoman's comments directly engage with Hegel's famous pronouncement that "what is rational is actual and what is actual is rational,"[39] she uncannily suggests that ideas and reason might be mutually exclusive, as the ideas put into her daughter's head by the pastor illustrate that they have made her foolish. The coachman seems to be of the same opinion. Asked to define an idea, he replies:

> "Nu, Nu,—an idea is an idea!—an idea is any d—d nonsense that a man gets into his head." (L 2, 342)
>
> "Nu, nu, eine Idee ist eine Idee! eine Idee ist alles dumme Zeug, was man sich einbildet." (288)

Heine's take on the idea serendipitously navigates the pitfalls of nonsense. While we might agree with him that he is no idea, his ideas about ideas might be quite to the point. Beneath its apparent tomfoolery, Heine's comedy touches on a critical nerve with a surgical sharpness that bypasses the pain only to cut deeper. Ideas, it becomes clear, are not necessarily the solution to the problems in philosophy and life, but are themselves part of the problem. Ideas are thus less the site where the dialectics between the reasonable and the foolish are resolved so much as where they are given the possibility to come to the fore in the first place. Heine, it turns out, was then not necessarily the least of Hegel's students, but he understood a thing or two about the dialectics of reason and the nature of ideas. Albeit no Hegelian, and resolutely so, his critique of Hegel avails itself of the critical grounds that Hegel offers in order to move beyond the philosopher's limits, thereby displaying a distinctly post-Hegelian outlook. If Heine's movement of freely associative argumentation is everything but rigorous dialectics, his satirically lighthearted frolicking outlines an alternative whose pointedly and freely associative dialectics eludes the problems of the deadlocked iron grip of rigorous dialectics. Heine's play with the idea of the idea resonates with the critical concerns articulated by Benjamin, Adorno, and the general thrust of the Frankfurt School it anticipates in its most critical aspects.

If scholarly pursuits such as composing academic books are a pastime that might bring out the more foolish undersides of reason, writing about foolish fellow beings will always occupy the mind. Foolishness, satire, and reason feed off each other, sometimes to a degree that makes it difficult to keep them apart. In *Ideas. Book Le Grand*, Heine's travesty of pedantic scholarship and its citation mania bring foolishness and reason into focus as two sides of the same coin.

Unless the limits of reason are taken seriously, Heine's comedy of fools suggests, reason is necessarily doomed to fail and turn into its opposite. The distinction between reason and foolishness is always tentative and unstable. Concepts might be based on sharp distinctions, but because of this they go only as far as the attention that is given to their limited range. For Heine, the process of conceptualization is never complete, but always leaves behind a remainder of what Adorno will call the nonconceptual. Much of Heine's energy is dedicated to elaborating those aspects of thought that resist conceptualization but are not therefore any less legitimate; while reason may label them as irrational, foolishness highlights them as reason's waste products. If there is no such thing as pure reason or pure foolishness, but only unstable compromise formations, the concept of reason itself—or, for that matter, of foolishness—is itself a problematic proposition that produces its own nonconceptual remnant as well as the problem of nonidentity.[40] If ideas and concepts—bound in volumes of green leather—belong to the subspecies of unreasonable ideas, then what a book fails to contain is what resists assimilation to a discourse whose rationality has failed the nonconceptual and whose concepts must therefore be lacking.

Again and again, Heine's writing suggests that relying on concepts must fail. The higher the stakes driving the concepts and ideas such as freedom, equality, truth, and history, the more pointedly Heine exposes the resistance of the nonconceptual. In Heine, just as in Adorno and Benjamin, there is no concept without the shadow of its nonconceptual remainder. Heine's writing is the scene where the continuous conflict between the conceptual and the nonconceptual becomes the site for negotiating the terms of modernity. Rather than halting the process of modernity, the dialectics plays itself out as the very struggle that enables rather than limits the emancipatory move to reimagining modernity on terms that no longer exclude the nonconceptual. In Heine, therefore, the remnant that resists, the rest that remains as a result of the push to the concept, is never presented as purely negative, but constitutes the site where the emancipatory impulse resists unconditional surrender to the concept. This is the reason why all the negativity of Heine's sharp-edged criticism, all his radically critical attitude, never suggests any form of submission to nihilism or defeatism. Instead, if hope has any empowering function in Heine, it is here: not in the nonconceptual per se but in the empowering experience of the joy of embracing the nonconceptual as the promise of a vision that points critically beyond the conceptual. This is the moment where the power of critical thinking resides in Heine with its most liberating thrust.

The borders between the conceptual and the nonconceptual are fluid and unstable. They therefore call for ever-new renegotiation. The question, for instance, of the distinction between reason and foolishness is not just a matter of the concept of reason alone, it also concerns the nonconceptual that the conceptual seeks to shut out. In the case of reason, its other includes not just unreason as lack of reason, but also faith and religion, among others. Faith and religion, in other words, do not creep up because of their exclusion from reason; they come into view as what has been driving the construction of reason and its opposite—as foolishness—all along. Reason and its concept are thus a function of theological-political power relations. But how else can this issue be addressed if not in the only terms left to a critique unwilling to settle for those that reiterate the status quo? Yet those terms are the terms of the losing party, the minority, which in this case is the party of the fools. And while they are anything but stable, the fools are, in turn, a product of the discourse of reason as controlled by the party of reason. Chapter XV of *Ideas. Book Le Grand* is a case study in openly acting out this predicament. How do you argue with reason when you are denied a part in it, how do you justify your difference with reason when it is denied to you? And how do you argue for religious difference when religious difference is declared from a supersessionist perspective to be a form of religious insufficiency, deviance, and defiance?[41]

In Heine's account, the picaresque adventures of the quid pro quo between reason and foolishness expose the theological-political coding that informs the underside of the concept of reason and hence the relationship between the conceptual and the nonconceptual. Caught between the rock of reason and the hard place of Jewish tradition, the narrator finds himself out in the conceptual cold. For while the narrator's aspiration is to belong to the party of reason, the party of the fools recognize him as a renegade fool just the way the party of reason does,

> and as a monkey is more ridiculous the more he resembles man, so are these fools more laughable the more reasonably they behave. (L 2, 357)

> und wie der Affe um so lächerlicher wird, je mehr er sich dem Menschen ähnlich zeigt, so werden auch jene Narren desto lächerlicher, je vernünftiger sie sich gebärden. (B 2, 298)

The vicious circle is mercilessly fatal: the more the fool aspires to reason, the more he shows his foolishness. But if this is true, what is left for reason? Doesn't the logic of this dialectics of difference ultimately lead to a breakdown? As Heine pushes it to its extreme, the logic of reason will eventually reveal itself as theologically informed and, to be more precise, by the particularity of a specifically Christian-inflected theology. So while the fools display a particular animus against the narrator—whom they see as an apostate—the party of reason also refuses to accept this renegade fool as one of its own:

> It is true that my party do not regard me as one of themselves, and often laugh at me in their sleeves. I know that right well, though I pretend not to observe it. But my heart bleeds within me, and when I am alone, then my tears flow. I know right well that my position is a false one, that all I do is folly to the wise and a torment to the fools. (L 2, 358)

> Es ist wahr, jene halten mich nicht für ihres Gleichen und mir gilt oft ihr heimliches Gekicher. Ich weiß es sehr gut, aber ich laß mir nichts merken. Mein Herz blutet dann innerlich, und wenn ich allein bin, fließen drob meine Tränen. Ich weiß es sehr gut, meine Stellung ist unnatürlich; alles was ich tue, ist den Vernünftigen eine Torheit und den Narren ein Greuel. (B 2, 298)

Between the chattiness of lizards and the silence of monkeys arises a play of signification. Language signifies, and signification calls for meaning, because its sense is always precarious, unstable, and problematic. But for Heine this challenge also grounds language's critical force. Language—human, animal, vegetal, and mineral—is not a privileged attribute from above, but the complex social act of negotiation that, ever nimble and fluid, gives voice to the precarious intersubjective relation of the interlocutors, their conversation, and the operation of literature. Heine's comedy of linguistic signification provocatively enacts and acts out critical concerns that resurface in Nietzsche, Freud, Benjamin, and Adorno at the moment when ontologies of language—as Adorno reminds us—are no longer an option. In returning the critical role of the play of language to the heart of writing, Heine articulates this insight "prosaically" and "poetically" as the critical force that drives the "language games" of his literary production.

5

Messiah in Golden Chains: Deferred Action and the Concept of History

Marx famously opens his *The Eighteenth Brumaire of Louis Bonaparte* with a trenchant aperçu that has become a notorious bon mot:

> Hegel remarks somewhere that all facts and personages of great importance in world history occur, as it were, twice. He forgot to add: the first time as tragedy, the second as farce.[1]
>
> Hegel bemerkt irgendwo, daß alle großen weltgeschichtlichen Tatsachen und Personen sich sozusagen zweimal wiederholen. Er hat vergessen hinzuzufügen: das eine Mal als Tragödie, das andere Mal als Farce.[2]

Highlighting the predicament of modernity with striking perspicacity, the idea that history is the tragedy of repetition turned into a farce has become a powerfully suggestive metaphor for the plight of the modern condition. Yet no passage can be found in Hegel that would suggest itself as a source for this remark. Marx's second paragraph offers some clues, however:

> Men make their own history, but they do not make it just as they please; they do not make it under circumstances chosen by themselves, but under circumstances directly encountered, given and transmitted from the past. The tradition of all the dead generations weighs like a nightmare on the brain of the living. And just when they seemed engaged in revolutionizing themselves and things, in creating something that has never yet existed, precisely in such periods of revolutionary crisis they anxiously conjure up the spirits of the past to their service and borrow from them names, battle-cries and costumes in order to present the new scene of world history in this time-honoured disguise and this borrowed language.[3]

> Die Menschen machen ihre eigene Geschichte, aber sie machen sie nicht aus freien Stücken, nicht unter selbstgewählten, sondern unter unmittelbar vorgefundenen, gegeben und überlieferten Umständen. Die Tradition aller toten Geschlechter lastet wie ein Alp auf dem Gehirne der Lebenden. Und wenn sie eben damit beschäftigt scheinen, sich und die Dinge umzuwälzen, noch nicht Dagewesenes zu schaffen, gerade in solchen Epochen revolutionärer Krise beschwören sie ängstlich die Geister der Vergangenheit zu ihrem Dienste herauf, entlehnen ihnen Namen, Schlachtparole, Kostüm, um in dieser altehrwürdigen Verkleidung und mit dieser erborgten Sprache die neue Weltgeschichtsszene aufzuführen.[4]

The Hegelian resonances are indisputable. But so are the self-referential gestures that echo Marx's early essay "Toward a Critique of Hegel's Philosophy of Right," written in the brief and intense period in Paris when Marx saw Heine almost daily. There, Marx notes,

> The modern *Ancien Régime* is merely the *comedian* in a world whose real heroes are dead. History is thorough and goes through many phases as it conducts an old form to the grave. The final phase of a world-historical form is *comedy*. The Greek gods, already tragically and mortally wounded in Aeschylus' *Prometheus Bound*, had to die again comically in Lucian's dialogues. Why this course of history? So that mankind may part from its past *happily* [heiter].[5]
>
> Das moderne *ancient régime* ist nur mehr der *Komödiant* einer Weltordnung, deren *wirkliche Helden* gestorben sind. Die Geschichte ist gründlich und macht viele Phasen durch, wenn sie eine alte Gestalt zu Grabe trägt. Die letzte Phase einer weltgeschichtlichen Gestalt ist ihre *Komödie*. Die Götter Griechenlands, die schon einmal tragisch zu Tode verwundet waren im gefesselten Prometheus des Äschylus, mußten noch einmal komisch sterben in den Gesprächen Lucians. Warum dieser Gang der Geschichte? Damit die Menschheit *heiter* von ihrer Vergangenheit scheide.[6]

The fresh and irreverent tone and the light and humorous touch of irony point to another source who stands out as an insubordinate commentator on Hegel's approach to history; a voice that responds to Hegel's best insights with a subtle, yet critical difference that takes pleasure in redescribing history against the grain of the Hegelian scheme it calls into question. The cheeky resonance of Heine's voice is hard to ignore both in Marx's early "Toward a Critique of Hegel's Philosophy of Right" and the opening passage of his later *The Eighteenth Brumaire*.[7] But the particular twist of Heine's subtle yet theoretically suggestive appropriation of the Greek theater custom—performances traditionally concluded with a comedy—should not be taken too lightly. It is no coincidence that Marx ends the opening section of *The Eighteenth Brumaire* with an explicit homage to Heine by directly quoting a character from Heine's political poetry, the failed freedom fighter Krapülinski.[8] For it was Heine who had observed that history, as it were, imitates art by following the performance sequence of Greek drama:

> After tragedy comes the farce. (OH 87)
>
> Nach der Tragödie kommt die Farce. (B 3, 604)

Marx's critique of history and of the historicist mimicry that haunts the nineteenth century follows in style and content the critical attitude Heine had expressed not only in *On the History of Religion and Philosophy*, where the comment on tragedy followed by farce is to be found.[9] This critique is also already prominent in Heine's early prose and poetry, starting with his *Travel Pictures*. Heine's first suggestive articulation of this idea appears in a passage in the *Travel Pictures' Ideas. Book Le Grand*, where he cites and then expands on Napoleon's dictum "Du sublime au ridicule il n'y a qu'un pas." (L 2, 332). It is difficult to ignore the resonances of Heine's rich comedic imagery in Marx:

> After the departure of the heroes, the clowns and graciosos enter with their baubles and lashes, and after the bloody scenes of the Revolution there came waddling on the stage the fat Bourbons, with their stale jokes and tender "legitimate" *bon mots*, and the old noblesse with their starved laughter hopped merrily before them, while behind all swept the pious Capuchins with candles, cross, and banners of the Church. Yes, even in the highest pathos of the World Tragedy bits of fun slip in. It may be that the desperate republican, who, like a Brutus, plunged a knife to his heart, first smelt it to see whether some one had not split a herring with it—and on this great stage of the world all passes exactly the same as on our beggarly boards [*Lumpenbrettern*]. On it, too, there are tipsy heroes, kings who forget their parts, scenes which obstinately stay up in the air, prompters' voices sounding above everything, *danseuses* who create astonishing effects with their leg-poetry, and, above all, costumes, which are and ever will be the main thing. And high in heaven, in the first row of the boxes, sit the lovely angels, and keep their lorgnettes on us poor sinners comedianising here down below, and the blessed Lord himself sits seriously in his splendid seat, and, perhaps, finds it dull, or calculates that this theatre cannot be kept up much longer because this one gets too high a salary, and that one too little, and that they altogether play far too indifferently [schlecht]. (L 332f.)
>
> Nach dem Abgang der Helden kommen die Clowns und Graziosos mit ihren Narrenkolben und Pritschen, nach den blutigen Revolutionsszenen und Kaiseraktionen kommen wieder herangewatschelt die dicken Bourbonen mit ihren alten und abgestandenen Späßchen und

> zartlegitimen Bonmots, und graziöse hüpft herbei die alte Noblesse mit ihrem verhungerten Lächeln, und hintendrein wallen die frommen Kapuzen mit Lichtern, Kreuzen und Kirchenfahnen;—sogar in das höchste Pathos der Welttragödie pflegen sich komische Züge einzuschleichen, der verzweifelnde Republikaner, der sich wie ein Brutus das Messer ins Herz stieß, hat vielleicht zuvor daran gerochen, ob auch kein Hering damit geschnitten worden, und auf dieser großen Weltbühne geht es auch außerdem ganz wie auf unseren Lumpenbrettern, auch auf ihr gibt es besoffene Helden, Könige, die ihre Rolle vergessen, Kulissen, die hängen geblieben, hervorschallende Souffleurstimmen, Tänzerinnen, die mit ihrer Lendenpoesie Effekt machen, Costümes, die als Hauptsache glänzen— Und im Himmel oben, im ersten Range, sitzen unterdessen die lieben Engelein und lorgnieren uns Komödianten hier unten, und der liebe Gott sitzt ernsthaft in seiner großen Loge, und langweilt sich vielleicht, oder rechnet nach, daß dieses Theater sich nicht lange mehr halten kann, weil der eine zu viel Gage und der andere zu wenig bekommt, und alle viel zu schlecht spielen. (B 2, 282f.)

But while Marx, following Hegel's conception of the tragic, submits to Hegel's privileging of tragedy over comedy and imposes a normative vision, Heine exposes this vision as ultimately repressive.[10]

Marx's striking formulation of tragedy's repetition as farce brings out the illuminating power of Heine's critical vision. But Marx does so only by oblique reference to the source, presenting Hegel as the stand-in for a stance critical of Hegel. While Marx's irony may have been lost on many readers, a closer examination of his programmatic opening statement reveals it to be more than just a rhetorical flourish. Echoing the voice of Heine's writings of the 1830s and 1840s, Marx takes up a trope that Heine revisits again and again. Whereas ancient Greece saw the performance of tragedy normally followed by a comedy, Heine's comic formulation articulates a critique of history that turns the traditional order of the performance into a political comment. Instead of reinforcing the normative expectation of the tragic, Heine replaces the tragic with the comic in a way that does not just provide comic relief, but turns the tragic upside down, exposing its ultimately comic underside. In Heine, this turn is not a final move but a continuous movement of back-and-forth; a dialectic that does not reach a final end but defies any fixation or ultimate historical goal beyond its own emancipatory thrust. Heine's view of history remains always tentative, reflective. Heine articulates an early critical approach to historical materialism that foreshadows the crucial elements of critique that return in Marx, Nietzsche, Freud, Benjamin, Adorno, and Foucault. Heine's poetry and prose display a highly developed sense and sensibility for issues of time, temporality, genealogy, and the various modes that inform historiography, such as repetition, return, and, most profoundly, *Nachträglichkeit*, that is, the phenomenon in which aftereffect, deferred action, and fiction are revealed as constitutive conditions for the writing of history. Foucault's notion of genealogy as the archeology of the present, Benjamin's rich reflections on the dialectical relationship of the past, present, and future, or what he calls the messianic,[11] Bloch's notion of the simultaneity of the nonsimultaenous,[12] Nietzsche's notions of the eternal return of the same, and Freud's and Simmel's nearly simultaneous discussions of *Nachträglichkeit* are linked just as intimately to Heine as Marx's notion of history as the farcical return of the tragic and its attendant "hauntology," to borrow a term from Derrida that felicitously describes a central aspect of Heine's poetics and theorizing of history.[13]

Just as Marx's, Nietzsche's, Freud's, and Critical Theory's preoccupation with the past serves the purpose of a radically critical renegotiation of the terms of modernity, Heine approaches history as the condition for rethinking the present through the future and the past by looking back from an anticipated future. In the early 1830s, Heine articulates his critical view on history in *The Romantic School* and *On the History of Religion and Philosophy in Germany*, offering a sort of counterhistory in which he not only revisits and reimagines the dominant narratives but also critically exposes many of the problematic assumptions that inform conventional historiography.

Taking a critical stand against the historical school and the dominant approach to history, Heine exposes the darker aspects of the underside of history and the received opinions that inform it. Heine articulates his critique of history in his poetic and fictional writing as well, including, from the very start, critical reflections on the desire for history. As Hayden White notes, "Heine anticipated Nietzsche's attack, in the 1870s, on all forms of academic historiography."[14]

While history might occasionally appear to be nothing but a "a comfortless, endless game of reproduction" (*trostlos ewiges Wiederholungsspiel*), as Heine puts it in the *Journey from Munich to Genoa* (L 3, 123; B 2, 388), the *Travel Pictures*' sustained critical reflection is laced with meta-historical comments reminding the reader that any form of history is based on a narrative's storyline that requires the creative component of fiction. In *The North Sea, Part 3*, the third of the *Travel Pictures*, Heine offers a fitting image for the ever-changing perspectives we bring to the understanding of history, that is, the way we deal with the past, present, and future, and the irreducible way in which they interconnect. In a passage addressing why the abundant richness of the larger-than-life figure Goethe exceeds not only the understanding of his contemporaries but will never be exhausted by any one particular age, Heine also speaks to the reason why every attempt to write history necessarily remains a work in progress, and why history needs to be reimagined and written anew by every generation:

> Later times will also, in addition to this ability of plastic perception, feeling, and thinking, discover much in Goethe of which we have as yet no shadow of an idea. The works of the soul [Geist] are immutably firm,

> but criticism is somewhat volatile; she is born of the views of the age, is significant only for it, and if she herself is not of a sect which involves artistic value, as, for example, that of Schlegel, she passes with her time to the grave. (L 2, 230f.)
>
> Spätere Zeiten werden, außer jenem Vermögen des plastischen Anschauens, Fühlens und Denkens noch vieles in Goethe entdecken, wovon wir jetzt keine Ahnung haben. Die Werke des Geistes sind ewig forstbestehend, aber die Kritik ist etwas Wandelbares, sie geht hervor aus den Ansichten der Zeit, hat für diese ihre Bedeutung, und wenn sie nicht selbst kunstwertlicher Art ist, wie z.B. die Schlegelsche, so geht sie mit ihrer Zeit zu Grabe. (B 2, 221)

There can be no closure as far as the narrative presentation of history is concerned. Rather, history and its presentation form an open-ended process that requires continual renegotiation of its terms. Every stage of history denotes a process in movement rather than a moment of final closure and stasis. Heine captures this dynamic most eloquently in concluding the passage quoted above:

> Every age when it gets new ideas, gets with them new eyes, and sees much that is new in the old efforts of mind that have preceded it. (L 2, 231)
>
> Jedes Zeitalter, wenn es neue Ideen bekömmt, bekömmt auch neue Augen, und sieht gar viel Neues in den alten Geisteswerken. (B 2, 221)

Life's dynamics of unceasing change prompt the historical perspective to change as well. Even and especially a figure like Goethe, who seems to transcend the conditions of his time, calls for an understanding that grasps history as itself a historically contingent mode of reasoning that cannot ignore its own historically defined conditions. Crucially, this continuous need for adjustment presents a chance rather than a limit. This empowering moment is—Heine suggests—what enables the terms of history to be renegotiated. In other words, history consists to a certain degree in this renegotiation and reimagining of its own terms. This self-reflective feature is the key to the emancipatory force that drives Heine's project of rethinking history against the restorative forms of nineteenth-century historicism.

Historical Materialism

When Benjamin mounted his critique of historicism in his essay "Eduard Fuchs, Collector and Historian," he did so by radically rethinking historical materialism.[15]

Quoting from a letter Engels wrote to Franz Mehring in 1893, Benjamin sets the stage to unfold the terms of historical materialism as a critical project. In this exercise Benjamin brings out the revolutionary thrust of Marx and Engels's dialectical approach to history that he had already found expressed in Marx's earliest studies of Feuerbach.[16] While Benjamin's intervention might be considered a resolute renegotiation of the terms of historical materialism,[17] it does so by recovering critical motives that inform Marx and Engels's thinking. Benjamin's programmatic appropriation of historical materialism as a constructivist project of critical experience not only reopens the discussion on the nature of historical materialism, it does so by acknowledging key features that Marx and Engels found in Heine.

In his review of Marx's *A Contribution to the Critique of Political Economy* in 1859, Engels called the book the birth of the materialist conception of history, citing the now classic passage in the preface that leads up to the famous formulation:

> It is not the consciousness that determines life, but their social existence that determines their consciousness.[18]
>
> Es ist nicht das Bewußstein der Menschen, das ihr Sein, sondern umgekehrt ihr gesellschaftliches Sein, das ihr Bewußtstein bestimmt. (MEW 13, 9)[19]

However, it was not until 1892 that Engels overcame initial misgivings concerning the terminology and introduced "historical materialism" as a term for the materialist conception of history. Two years prior to embracing the term, Engels articulated concerns that are central for a proper understanding of what exactly the critical project of historical materialism meant for him. In a letter to Conrad Schmidt in 1890, Engels expressed reservations with regard to this "phrase," since "materialist" had become a buzzword enthusiastically appropriated by uncritical critics to conceal their ignorance:

> But our conception of history is above all a guide to study, not a lever for construction after the manner of the Hegelian. All history must be studied afresh, the conditions of existence of the different formations of society must be examined individually before the attempt is made to deduce them from the political, civil law, aesthetic, philosophic, religious, etc., views corresponding to them. [. . .] But instead of this too many of the younger Germans simply make use of the phrase historical materialism (and *everything* can be turned into a phrase) only in order to get their own relatively scanty historical knowledge—for economic history is still as yet in its swaddling clothes!—constructed into a neat system as quickly as possible, and they then deem themselves something very tremendous.[20]
>
> Unsere Geschichtsauffassung aber ist vor allem eine Anleitung beim Studium, kein Hebel zur Konstruktion à la Hegelianertum. Die ganze Geschichte muß neu studiert werden, die Daseinsbedingungen der verschiedenen Gesellschaftsformationen müssen im einzelnen

> untersucht werden, ehe man versucht, die politischen, privatrechtlichen, ästhetischen, philosophischen, religiösen, etc. Anschauungsweisen, die ihnen entsprechen, aus ihnen abzuleiten [. . .] Statt dessen aber dient die Phrase des historischen Materialismus (man kann eben alles zur Phrase machen) nur zu vielen jüngeren Deutschen nur dazu, ihre eignen relative dürftigen historischen Kenntnisse—die ökonomische Geschichte liegt ja noch in den Windeln!—schleunigst systematisch zurechtkonstruieren und sich dann sehr gewaltig vorzukommen.[21]

Engels's reminder of the distinctly non-Hegelian approach to a yet largely unknown and uncharted territory—"for economic history is still as yet in swaddling clothes!"—bears critically on how he understood historical materialism in distinct contrast to classical "materialist" and "idealist" conceptions of history. Two years later, in 1892, Engels seemed ready to embrace historical materialism as a term; for while it met with rejection among his English readers, this rejection, Engels argued, illustrated the dynamics he associated with a critically materialist conception of history.[22]

A few years earlier, in *Ludwig Feuerbach and the End of Classical German Philosophy*, Engels had addressed Feuerbach as the key figure for the formation of Marx's materialist approach. In the appendix, Engels had published Marx's 1845 theses on Feuerbach, thus highlighting the central pushing away from Feuerbach Marx achieved in the years leading up to 1848.[23]

For Marx, so the narrative went, Feuerbach had become the escape route from the Hegelian vortex. By crossing the "Feuerbach," or purgatorial creek of fire, Marx managed to push beyond Hegel to the safe grounds of materialism. Once arrived, he was able to toss old Feuerbach—who was himself still stuck in idealism—and move on.

While Engels's narrative featured Feuerbach as the decisive catalyst of Marx's departure from Hegel and breakthrough to a modern materialist conception of history, his opening gambit complicates the lineage he is about to present with an acknowledgement that draws Heine into its ambit:

> But what neither the government nor the liberals saw was seen at least by one man as early as 1833, and this man was indeed none other than Heinrich Heine.[24]
>
> Was aber weder die Regierungen noch die Liberalen sahen, das sah bereits 1833 wenigstens ein Mann, und der hieß allerdings Heinrich Heine. (MEW 21, 265)

Leaving it at this brief allusion and returning to Feuerbach, Engels invites his readers to listen for the echoes of Heine's *On the History of Religion and Philosophy in Germany* that reverberate in his text. And Heine's traces are indeed difficult to ignore, as Hermann Braun and Joachim Müller have reminded us.[25]

Returning to Marx's *A Contribution to the Critique of Political Economy*—to which Engels thus traces the beginnings of historical materialism—we can now appreciate the biographical detail Marx shares with his readers a few lines before the often cited passage stating that "the mode of production of material life conditions the general process of social, political and intellectual life" and that it is thus "social existence that determines [people's] consciousness." Here Marx indicates that it was in Paris that he had begun to turn his primary focus to the study of the "mode of production of material life conditions" (MEW 13, 8f.),[26] that is, during a particularly productive and intense yet short period marked by almost daily encounters with Heine. Marx and Engels's overt and covert references to Heine suggest that the analysis Heine first presented in *On the History of Religion and Philosophy in Germany* and continued to reiterate in his critical prose, fiction, and poetry—which Marx and Engels knew intimately—was a crucial and acknowledged source text for historical materialism.

Constellation and Counterhistories

Wary of the temptation to reduce history to linear, causality-driven, and teleological schemes, Heine argues for a more nuanced approach that heeds the nonlinear and complex forms of reciprocal relations that inform the temporality of history. History defies reduction to simple sequencing and—as Heine's Hebrew-speaking pocket watch we encountered in the previous chapter so eloquently highlighted—temporality resists reduction to mere chronological patterns. Heine's counterhistories emphasize the non-teleological character of historical action in a way that undermines intentionalism and unsettles the practices of historicism.[27] In *The Romantic School*, Heine observes:

> In the world's history every event is not the direct result of another; all events rather exert a mutual influence. (L 5, 255)
>
> In der Weltgeschichte ist nicht jedes Ereignis die unmittelbare Folge eines anderen, alle Ereignisse bedingen sich vielmehr wechselseitig. (B 3, 370)

This of course poses a direct challenge to any attempt at conceptualizing history. History eludes the grip of the concept as it proliferates into a plurality of histories and, more precisely, counterhistories that make up the anarchically brimming life from which historians seek to rarify their story lines. *The Romantic School* hammers home the point that while we need historical explanations to make sense of the world, the narrative-making involved in writing (literary) history is a creative act. While it is the creative moment of fiction that makes meaning possible, fiction at the same time reveals its literary-historical origin as a product of the historical condition that generates it. If *The Romantic School* is thus Heine's answer to the challenge of writing literary history critically, he does not address the conditions of its possibility until late in Part 3 of Book 3:

> It is a difficult matter to write the history of Literature as Natural History. In both we occupy ourselves with the most striking phenomena. But as in a small glass of water there is a whole world of marvelous beings [Tierchen] which manifest the omnipotence of God as much as do the largest animals [Bestien], so the smallest Almanac of the Muses reveals a multitude of poetlings who are to the eye of the calm investigator as interesting as the largest elephants of literature. God is great! (L 6, 36)
>
> Die Geschichte der Literatur ist eben so schwierig zu schreiben wie die Naturgeschichte. Dort wie hier hält man sich an die besonders hervortretende Erscheinungen. Aber wie in einem kleinen Wasserglas eine ganze Welt wunderlicher Tierchen enthalten ist, die eben so sehr von der Allmacht Gottes zeugen, wie die größten Bestien: so enthält der kleinste Musenalmanach zuweilen eine Unzahl Dichterlinge, die dem stillen Forscher eben so interessant, wie die größten Elefanten der Literatur. Gott ist groß! (B 3, 465)

Ironically, Heine continues that indeed literary historians are prone to present their subject matter neatly classified just like a well-kept zoo:

> Most literary historians really give us a history like a well-arranged menagerie, and show us in their separate cages epic mamma-lians, lyrical-aerial bird-poets, dramatic water-fowl of watery verse, prosaic amphibia who write land and sea novels, comical odd-fish, and so on. (L 6, 36)
>
> Die meisten Literaturhistoriker geben uns wirklich eine Literaturgeschichte wie eine wohlgeordnete Menagerie, und immer besonders abgesperrt, zeigen sie uns epische Säugedichter, lyrische Luftdichter, dramatische Wasserdichter, prosaische Amphibien, die sowohl Land- wie Seeromane schreiben, humoristische Mollusken usw. (B 3, 465f.)

The zoological-literary comedy exposes the (literary) historian's dilemma of always already being committed to a system of classification he or she therefore cannot examine critically but on which it remains contingent. In contrast to a method that relies on a dubious taxonomy such as that cited above, Heine distinguishes those critics who proceed strictly historically:

> Others, on the contrary, treat such history practically, and begin with the primitive feelings of man, which developed themselves in various ages, and finally assumed artistic form; that is, they begin *ab ovo,* like the

historian who opened the tale of the Trojan War with the egg of Leda. Wherein they—like him—act foolishly. (L 6, 37)

> Andere, im Gegenteil treiben die Literaturgeschichte pragmatisch, beginnen mit den ursprünglichen Menschheitsgefühlen, die sich in den verschiedenen Epochen ausgebildet und endlich eine Kunstform angenommen; sie beginnen ab ovo wie der Geschichtschreiber, der den trojanischen Krieg mit der Erzählung vom Ei der Leda eröffnet. Und wie dieser handeln sie törigt. (B 3, 466)

Both approaches, the systematic and the chronological, Heine points out, have their difficulties explaining change and development. The mere succession of time does not account for change and development or, we can add, continuity. But does discontinuity then define history? Any sort of classification or taxonomy is confronted with the challenge of accounting for the interplay of the dialectics between succession and simultaneity, continuity and discontinuity. The comedy of the two ways to do literary history highlights the madness of mutual exclusion that informs their respective methods. They both remain blind to the underlying aporia at the heart of history writing: the challenge to consider continuity and discontinuity, stasis and dynamics as constituents of the aftereffect we call history. Coming strikingly close to an idealist view in the Hegelian vein, Heine notes:

> Great deeds [Fakta], like great books, do not spring from such trifles—they are the result of necessity, they are connected with the course of the sun, moon, and stars, and originate perhaps in their influence on the earth. Deeds [Fakta] are the results of ideas; but how does it come that at certain times certain ideas make themselves so preponderant that they shape the whole of human beings, their drivings and strivings, their thinking and writing, and in the strangest manner. (L 6, 37)

> Die großen Fakta und die großen Bücher entstehen nicht aus Geringfügigkeiten, sondern sie sind notwendig, sie hängen zusammen mit den Kreisläufen von Sonne, Mond und Sterne, und sie entstehen vielleicht durch deren Influenz auf die Erde. Die Fakta sind nur die Resultate der Ideen; . . . aber wie kommt es, daß zu gewißen Zeiten sich gewisse Ideen so gewaltig geltend machen, daß sie das ganze Leben der Menschen, ihr Tichten und Trachten, ihr Denken und Schreiben, aufs wunderbarste umgestalten? (B 3, 466)

But Heine is no idealist, nor a Hegelian for that matter. Rather, his approach preludes a key notion at the heart of Benjamin's and Adorno's historical materialism. Heine makes it clear that the forces that reshape human life are not driven by ideas themselves—for ideas have no power in themselves, but gain force only to the degree that they reflect, that is, express, the power of the dynamics of the affects that determine people's actions. This notion—close to Spinoza's conception of the function and life of ideas[28]—points beyond the dichotomous distinction between idealist and materialist explanation of cultural production and of history. Heine's point is that the power of ideas is derived not from any isolated pure act of thinking, but rests instead on a complex nexus of material conditions in which ideas gain life as the products of a process that creates "the great facts and the great books." This process defies idealist and materialist explanations as it calls for a model that comprehends life as the sum total of the function of the infinitely complex interplay of the material conditions that determine life, down to our most personal actions and the way we think. It is at this point in his discussion that Heine introduces a notion that will assume critical significance in Benjamin and Adorno:

> Perhaps it is time to write a literary astrology, and in it explain the appearance of certain ideas or of certain books wherein these reveal themselves, according to the constellations of heavenly bodies. (L 6, 37f.)[29]
>
> Es ist vielleicht an der Zeit eine literarische Astrologie zu schreiben und die Erscheinung gewisser Ideen, oder gewisser Bücher worin diese sich offenbaren, aus der Konstellation der Gestirne zu erklären. (B 3, 466)

Presented in Heine's seemingly haphazard style, the passage is more than just a parodic exposure of the ill-conceived methods of literary criticism.[30] As is so often the case, Heine's humorous approach to theory presents a crucial aspect of the way he reimagines critical thought. Similar to Benjamin and Adorno, Heine signals unease when it comes to establishing an alternative to flawed methodical thinking. For any theoretically sound approach must remain critical and abstain from any sort of ultimately dogmatic impulse to make normative for its own method. If we return one more time to the sentence that precedes Heine's introduction of the term "constellation," we can now read the triad of "sun, moon, and stars" in its critically enriched context:

> Great deeds [Fakta], like great books, do not spring from such trifles—they are the result of necessity, they are connected with the course of the sun, moon, and stars, and originate perhaps in their influence on the earth. (L 6, 37)
>
> Die großen Fakta und die großen Bücher entstehen nicht aus Geringfügigkeiten, sondern sie sind notwendig, sie hängen zusammen mit den Kreisläufen von Sonne, Mond und Sterne, und sie entstehen vielleicht durch deren Influenz auf die Erde. (B 3, 466)

Turning away from scientific pretense, the passage calls for a more nuanced paradigm for understanding the rich dynamics of intellectual history and, by implication, of history in general. Teasingly couched in hyperbolically metaphysical language, the passage gives voice to a critical concern regarding the relationship between facts and ideas, the nexus of their genesis, and the role of their dynamic interaction. Given the particular modulation in this consciously post-romantic account of the "Romantic School," the "sun, moon, and stars" (*Sonne, Mond und Sterne*)—the poetic triad of heavenly bodies that rule the universe—evoke a poetic vision of the universal causality of nature all the way down to the sublunar regions down here on earth. Resonating with the poetic, starry-eyed idealism of romantic imagination, the triad at the same time evokes the sober notion of an all-inclusive nature, suggesting in an affectively mediated way that all that exists is interconnected, down to the way we think, feel, and experience, but with a complexity that might evade straightforward conceptual grasp.

The kind of "literary astrology" that Heine suggests is then more than a playful way of escaping the deadlock of the determinist approaches to history that ruled in his time. If the critical cue of the play with concepts the passage sets in motion is attended to, the figure of the constellation emerges as an alternative theoretical model for reconceiving and reimagining history as the product of an open-ended interplay of social forces. *The Romantic School* is Heine's attempt to demonstrate the cognitive promise of this form of critical history writing. *On the History of Religion and Philosophy*, which Heine wrote after *The Romantic School,* does this by fleshing out the implications of such a rethinking of history in more detail. We will examine some of the critical aspects of this text in Chapter 7.

After History: The View from the Prompter's Box

After completing the two texts, Heine published them as companion pieces. An 1833 draft of an introduction to *On the History of Religion and Philosophy in Germany* examines the three models of historiography current at the time. In a short outline from the same period, with the title "Different Views of History" (*Verschiedenartige Geschichtsauffassung*), Heine opposed the dreary "fatalist" outlook (DHA 3, 301) that considered life an eternally recurring cycle of the repetition of the same (DHA 3, 301) to a brighter, messianic outlook that views history as the stepping stone

> to a higher, God-like state of humanity, whose moral and political struggles will finally lead to the holiest peace, the purest fraternization, and the most eternal happiness.

> zu einem höheren gottähnlichen Zustande des Menschengeschlechts, dessen sittliche und politische Kämpfe endlich den heiligsten Frieden, die reinste Verbrüderung, und die ewigste Glückseligkeit zur Folge haben. (DHA 3, 301)

However, neither of these perspectives agrees with our "most vital feelings of life" (*lebendigsten Lebensgefühlen*, DHA 3, 302). The sketch cautions against devaluating the present as a mere means to the purpose of a distant future (DHA 3, 302).[31] As Heine formulates it:

> We feel our importance too much to wish to settle for seeing ourselves as but a means to a purpose.
>
> Wir fühlen uns wichtiger gestimmt, als daß wir uns nur als Mittel zu einem Zwecke betrachten möchten. (DHA 3, 302)

He continues:

> It seems to us generally as if means and ends were merely conventional concepts which man projects into nature and history, but of which the creator had no knowledge, since every creature has its purpose in itself and every event has itself as condition and everything, like the world itself, exists and happens for its own sake.
>
> Es will uns überhaupt bedünken, als seyen Zweck und Mittel nur konvenzionelle Begriffe, die der Mensch in die Natur und in die Geschichte hineingrübelt, von denen aber der Schöpfer nichts wußte, indem jedes Erschaffniß sich selbst bezweckt und jedes Ereigniß sich selbst bedingt, und Alles, wie die Welt selbst, seiner selbst Willen da ist und geschieht. (DHA 3, 302)

Just as Nietzsche reminds us in "On the Advantage and Disadvantage of History for Life" that understanding history is not a purely objective affair, but one that implies social and moral considerations of a normative order, Heine concludes with a change of register:

> Life is neither end nor means: life is a right. Life wants to assert this right against rigidifying death, against the past, and this assertion is the revolution.
>
> Das Leben ist weder Zweck noch Mittel; das Leben ist ein Recht. Das Leben will dieses Recht geltend machen gegen den erstarrenden Tod, gegen die Vergangenheit, und dieses Geltendmachen ist die Revoluzion. (DHA 3, 302)

Over and against the past and a preconceived future, the present—"life"—affirms itself as a right, and a right to revolution at that. It is only through this forward-moving impulse that history comes into view as potentially meaningful: as the site for negotiating a different present with the help of an emancipatory notion of life devoid of teleological instrumentalization. Concluding this sketch, Heine gives this idea a turn that sheds a striking light on the need to ground history in the present:

> *Le pain est le droit du people*, says Saint-Just and that is the greatest word that has been spoken during the whole revolution.
>
> Le pain est le droit du people, sagt Saint-Just, und das ist das größte Wort, das in der ganzen Revoluzion gesprochen worden. (DHA 3, 302)

If farce follows tragedy, Heine's draft introduction to *On the History of Religion and Philosophy in Germany* suggests that farce is followed by the comedy of historiography.[32] In a little parable, he describes the three views on history in terms of the different points of view in a theater: the view from the audience, the view from the prompter's box, and the view from backstage, where the mechanism of the ropes sheds light on the material conditions of the production. While none of these perspectives alone can account for the theatrical effect as a whole, Heine suggests that the three ways of looking at history remain incommensurable. The cyclical, idealist, and materialist aspects that stand in entrenched opposition to each other attest to the irreducible theological-political differences that challenge any attempt at making sense of history. Seen as forms of fatalism, spiritualism, and skepticism, the three perspectives evince ideological commitments that are grounded in one or another kind of belief. This scene, in which three conflicting parties are all proven false, is reminiscent of Lessing's *Nathan the Wise*, where the story of the three rings demonstrates how the stances of Judaism, Christianity, and Islam are equally problematic. The lesson of Heine's fable, in which mice mistake the theater for the world, is that those who do so remain oblivious to the fact that history, too, is always the performance of an interpretation of a performance according to the viewpoint it chooses. Impatient with the blinding effects of this scenario, the draft of the introduction concludes:

> No, humankind does not revolve pointlessly in bleak circles with all its thoughts and feelings; there is development and progress, and one who actively works for it is no fool. Neither is everything in this world illusion and lie, nor are material interests all-powerful; matter obeys spirit, and if the spirit demands it, even the liar will sacrifice himself for truth, and the rogue himself for right. Nor is God as pure spirit separated from the world, in a particular box called heaven; no, God is all there is.
>
> Nein, die Menschheit dreht sich nicht zwecklos in öden Kreisen mit allen ihren Gedanken und Gefühlen; es gibt Entwicklung und Fortschritt, und wer dafür tätig wirkt, ist kein Tor. Auch ist nicht alles Schein und Lüge in der Welt, und die materiellen Interessen sind nicht alleinherrschend; die Materie gehorcht dem Geiste, und wenn der Geist es verlangt, opfert sich sogar der Lügner für die Wahrheit und der Schelm für das Recht. Auch ist Gott nicht als reiner Geist abgeschieden von der Welt, in einem besonderen Kasten, welcher Himmel heißt; nein, Gott ist alles was da ist. (DHA 8, 446)

Taking the three partial viewpoints to the level of a more expansive vision of history as the battleground of emancipation, Heine addresses the critical need to rethink the terms in which history is negotiated. History, as this fragmentary look at the conditions of historiography indicates, is less a concept than a mirror that reflects the way we look at the world. Provocatively Spinozist, Heine renders the dichotomy between matter and spirit obsolete. While the ideas of development and progress carry the promise of breaking free from the grinding cycle of history's absurdities, historical movement follows a vision of emancipation rather than the dictate of a fixed teleological scheme. In other words, while things might not be what they seem, there is no logic according to which they could be forced to march to the tune of history, Hegel-style. With God defined as all that exists, Heine has shot down all claims to meta- or extra-historical knowledge.

With no exit from history, however, we are freer and more self-determined than when caged-in and bound by teleological suppression. Because all we have are the histories we tell and imagine, reimagining history becomes a crucial and necessary task. For it is a hermeneutic exercise that searches for sense by producing it through narrative. Telling history is a performance that is contingent on the plurality of the narratives it produces. For Heine, telling histories is thus always a retelling, a reinvention, a revisiting of the terms on which we rely when telling ourselves the stories we use to make sense of history.

The Terror of Deferred Action and the Problem of Representation: Heine on Delaroche's History Paintings

In the summer of 1831, Heine arrived in Paris, the capital of modernity he would so enthusiastically embrace as his new home. His first text from Paris, which explored the challenges posed by any attempt to understand history, took the form of a newspaper report about the first art exhibition after the 1830 July Revolution (the revolution was the signal event of the postrevolutionary era and the one that had drawn Heine to Paris). For Heine, visiting the salon at the Louvre where the postrevolutionary art was on display was itself a historical event worthy of public contemplation. The Louvre exhibition was for him an expression of the historical moment of 1831, a moment when the repression of the past, and its uncanny return in the form of repetition with a difference, produced the tragedy of the belatedness of the farce that follows tragedy.

"French Painters" (*Französische Maler*) revisits the issue of the representation of history and the present as a struggle to locate the ever-elusive now.[33] For Heine—as his discussion of contemporary French painting shows—understanding history is a function of deferred action and as such it is challenged by the paradox that all forms of representation are a kind of repetition and at the same time an expression of the impossibility of presenting the past, or present for that matter. The insight into this loss and its compensation by way of repetition assumes the paradoxical feature of a melancholy contemplation that figures the terror of the uncanny on which it fixates. But upon closer examination, Heine suggests, the tragic outlook figures as a repetition of the tragic whose repression of the difference that drives it cannot contain its farcical underbelly. This enigmatic function of representation is explored in its various aspects in Heine's discussion of art's "writing of history in colors" (B 3, 57) by examining a particularly extreme moment: the instant that separates life from death, the moment of anticipation of the end of horror. As Heine's discussion is modeled on the afterward of deferred action, his art historical discourse represents a critical exercise in addressing deferral and displacement as decisive aspects of the experience and representation of temporality.

Lessing's *Laocoon: An Essay on the Limits of Painting and Poetry* offered an exploration of the different forms of representation in art. It addresses the crucial difference between how temporality figures in visual as opposed to linguistic art forms in a way that highlights what is at stake in Heine's discussion. Lessing's choice of the sculpture of Laocoon and his sons in the deadly embrace of the snakes addresses the issue of art and temporality in a manner that paradigmatically figures the nexus between terror and representation.[34] In order to plumb this nexus and its critical function in Heine, it will be helpful to briefly discuss Lessing's approach to addressing the nexus between terror and representation as it informs his crucial distinction between visual and linguistic representation. This will enable us to appreciate the significance of Heine's approach to dealing with the representation of history and terror and the import his approach has for theorizing the question of temporality.

To recall Lessing's argument: while visual arts such as drawing, painting, and sculpture are limited to exclusively spatial forms of expression, literary representation follows the temporality that drives the consecutive nature of language. Artists are therefore confronted with the necessity to make up their mind: either they avail themselves of linguistic forms of signification that track action in time and are then defined by the temporality of discursive forms of signification, or they give shape to visual representation. Visual representation, however, can do so only by arresting the flow of time, which means giving it spatial form, translating time into stasis in space. Representation, Lessing reminds us, entails the displacement either of space or of time, one at the expense of the other. In focusing on the statue of Laocoon, Lessing introduces an example that links and literally—or rather, visually—entangles representation and terror in an inextricable knot.

Lessing thus highlights the particular structure of anticipatory delay, the transfixion of the before/after relation, what he calls the "pregnant moment" where visual art arrests action in order to produce the desired artistic effect of mimetic representation transfixing time in a moment of mimicry. But if the visual arts can represent only by acts of containment, by mimicking the moment of terror through substitutions that stand in for what they cannot represent but can only invoke by means of a supplementary displacement that expresses its paradoxical predicament through the figure of infinite displacement, then literary representation proceeds subject to the order of temporality by enacting the performance of delay and deferral. In contrast to the visual arts, however, literary modes of representation mediate action through endless chains of metaphorical substitution that play back the terror they seek to represent through the recursive loop of narrative delay. But while Lessing's *Laocoon* examines the bifurcation of visual and linguistic modes of expression, it also highlights the underlying nexus between terror and representation.

Yet the problem of representing terror and its particular form of temporality is not just a challenge that confronts painting and poetry with their specific limits; it raises the question of representation and temporality as such. It is a problem so challenging that Hegel's *Phenomenology of Spirit* resorts to equating the unspeakable terror of execution to the frighteningly evacuated image of "cutting off a head of cabbage or swallowing a mouthful of water."[35] Hegel's point, of course, is that it is precisely this empty, formulaic, vacated, and vacuous moment, in all its absurd depletion, which presents the very absence of meaning that produces the *horror vacui*, the terrifying horror of nothingness. The sheer challenge of representing terror poses, then, a fundamental challenge, and not just for art, poetry, and philosophy. For if we take the limits of representation seriously, the problem of political representation—which can never be excluded from any discussion of representation—must never be ignored.

Hegel's discussion of terror in the chapter of the *Phenomenology of Spirit* titled "Absolute Freedom and Terror" highlights the challenges of comprehending the relationship between terror and representation and the question of temporality. From the opening chapter of the *Phenomenology*, Hegel makes it clear that there is no such thing as an immediate, unmediated sense-certainty, but that all reality is always already mediated. The dialectic of 'now' and 'here' turns right from the start into a game of "fort"/"da"—as Freud will call it—suggesting that a phenomenologically nuanced approach is required for reflecting what cannot be grasped in any immediacy, but only by considering the play of deferral and displacement that defines the function of terror. In other words, we need to theorize terror in a way that critically reflects terror's intimate relationship with representation without getting tangled up in terror's insidious play with representation. Such a critical engagement with terror requires a careful examination of terror's elusive illusoriness, the phantasmagoric dynamics that inform its representational game and result in a fatal form of epistemological hostage-taking. In order to avoid the trap of representational complicity by mimesis and succeed in exposing and annulling the unrelenting violence of terror's death grip, critical understanding must reflect the play of representation with a difference.

Heine's description of his visit to the 1831 Paris art exhibition is an exacting study of the dialectics of displacement and delay at the center of terror. His translation of the experience of his visit to the Louvre's art gallery into a narrative also involves a translation of the visual representation of painting into language, and of one painting in particular that is central to this critical task. This act of translation performs a reflection on the function of temporality as the fulcrum not just of history but also of historical reflection and the theorizing of history. It is here, on the occasion of his visit to the Louvre's art exhibition, that Heine has us return to a scene of trauma, a scene that reflects the problem of how to capture the moment of historical time, the moment of history as a moment with its own temporality that extends to the temporality in which history and time itself are contemplated.

The nexus of history, trauma, and loss comes into focus as a paradigmatic interface as Heine turns to painting to talk about history, politics, and more directly about the present and the concerns, fears, and anxieties banned, displaced, and repressed from public discourse only to hauntingly resurface in the realm of contemporary art. Exploring contemporary art's representation of the return of the repressed, Heine brings home the point that terror and the experience of the temporal structure of history more generally rely on the effect of deferred action's afterward.

Heine's staging of his intervention as a report by an art critic appropriates the genre playfully, and with the lightness of self-reflective irony. The play of displacement and delay the text rehearses spell out the strategic positionality at the interstice between painting and poetry, image and language, that is, between mutually exclusive forms of representation whose juxtaposition reflects the spatio-temporal difference that constitutes the phenomenon of temporality. Heine's account articulates the insight that the experience of temporality and its radicalized form in the guise of terror is a function and effect of displacement and delay, as is representation itself.

Historically, terror has become associated with the French Revolution, the decapitation of the king and the unleashing of the killing frenzy of the Grande Terreur. The large-scale execution and mass deaths had immense and catastrophic consequences that brought about a profound crisis concerning the question of representation in art, literature, philosophy, and politics, and the challenge to deal with the consequences in everyday life. Once terror had reared its ugly head, it became clear that it would not disappear anytime soon. Having thus taken root in modern consciousness, it profoundly shaped social relations down to their most intimate aspects. The question then became how to confront, present, and represent terror without giving way to its repetition by way of its representation: how to escape and put a stop to the ubiquitous undertow of its effects.[36]

Heine's description of Paul Delaroche's 1831 painting *Cromwell and the Corpse of Charles I* offers an elucidating contemplation on this challenge.

It is through the discussion of this painting that Heine reflects on the role of temporality in terror and the problem of representation by way of negotiating a reading of the painting at the interface of the translation between the visual and the linguistic presentation of representation or, if you wish, representation of presentation. Heine thus contributes to the question of (re)presentation with an incisive reflection on its dialectics.

Introducing Paul Delaroche to his readers as the "ringleader" of a new group of historical painters, Heine notes that Delaroche's import does not relate so much to history itself but to the question how to represent history, how to visualize its "spirit" in writing history with colors:

> This painter has no preference for the past itself, but rather for its representation, for making its spirit visible, for historiography in color.[37]
>
> Dieser Maler hat keine Vorliebe für die Vergangenheit selbst, sondern für ihre Darstellung, für ihre Veranschaulichung ihres Geistes, für Geschichtschreibung mit Farben. (B 3, 57)

At the exhibition, Delaroche had arranged the paintings in a particular order: *Cromwell and the Corpse of Charles I* was framed by three other paintings with historical subjects. Heine organizes his discussion of the paintings starting with *The State Barge of Cardinal Richelieu on the Rhone River* (1829), followed by *Cardinal Mazarin on His Death Bed* (1830) and *The Children of King Edward Imprisoned in the Tower* (1830).[38] Concluding with *Cromwell and the Corpse of Charles I*, he turns to the theme of terror in a subtle but indirect manner, first discussing the two figures of the death-dealing and death-awaiting deputies of French sovereignty and then deflecting the gaze across the channel and back in time, focusing on two traumatic moments in England's past.

The subject that has come to haunt France and the rest of Europe in the wake of the 1830 July Revolution comes to the fore as a result of history experienced through the belated aftershocks of the events whose traumatic effects consciousness can only assimilate by way of repressed memory, that is, by way of displacement and, as Freud will later point out, the reaction formation of symptoms and dream-work. If we look at the paintings as an arrangement, Heine suggests that they constitute a narrative whose plotline mirrors a cross-channel reflection that brings out the underlying common theme of the sovereign's precarious existence in a state of exception in which his life and death hang in the balance and have become reduced to the pure contingency of time.

The first painting presents Cardinal Richelieu, Louis XIII's chief minister, in his state barge: the fearsome but now moribund cardinal is traveling deathbound with two captives in tow, who will be decapitated upon arrival (Figure 1). The second painting features Richelieu's protégé and successor Cardinal Mazarin in the lonesome solitude of the second in power, awaiting

FIGURE 1 *The State Barge of Cardinal Richelieu on the Rhône, Paul Delaroche, 1829. Oil on canvas, Wallace Collection, London, Great Britain.*

FIGURE 2 *Cardinal Mazarin's Last Sickness, Paul Delaroche, 1830. Oil on canvas. Wallace Collection, London, Great Britain.*

death amidst the hustle and bustle of ostentatious, vacuous life at court (Figure 2). With the third painting, the scene changes across the channel to England, and more precisely to the Tower of London and almost 350 years back in time, showing King Edward's two young sons awaiting execution by Richard III (Figure 3). The stage is thus set for the fourth painting, which Heine announces with the words:

FIGURE 3 *Edward V and the Duke of York in the Tower, Paul Delaroche, 1831. Oil on canvas, Wallace Collection, London, Great Britain.*

> It is the scene from that horrific tragedy, which has now been translated into French as well, and which has cost so many tears on both sides of the Channel, and which also moves the German viewer so deeply. (146)
>
> Es ist eine Szene aus jener entsetzlichen Tragödie, die auch ins Französische übersetzt worden ist und so viele Tränen gekostet hat, diesseits und jenseits des Kanals, und die auch den deutschen Zuschauer so tief erschüttert. (B 3, 60)

It is the emblematic portrayal of Cromwell with the body of his opponent stretched out in its coffin, the defunct Charles I (Figure 4). Powerfully reminiscent of the regicide of Louis XVI and its iconic significance for the postrevolutionary imaginary, the painting becomes in Heine's discussion the symptomatic site for negotiating the post-traumatic aftershock that haunted Europe in the aftermath of the July Revolution when another Charles, Charles X, came to power as the exponent of the new bourgeoisie. While the act of contemplating the painting solicits a critical political reflection on the present by way of a reflection on a past that is at the same time both traumatically actualized and removed, Heine reminds his readers—not

FIGURE 4 *Cromwell opens the coffin of King Charles I. (1625–1649). Paul Delaroche, canvas, painted 1831, Musée des Beaux-Arts de Nîmes, France.*

without irony—that Louis XVI compares unfavorably to Charles I. But while Louis XVI may have been no match for his executioners, Heine argues, Charles I certainly stands, or rather lies here stretched out, as a stark reminder of the paradoxical ways of terror; only to add, again with the utmost iconoclastic irony, that while Louis XVI was no Charles, Napoleon was no Cromwell (150; B 3, 65). And where exactly would Charles X and his time fit into this equation? That is of course the eloquently silent question here.

Unlike Napoleon, who spent his nights running enraged about the halls of the Tuileries to finally emerge the next morning pale and exhausted at the council meeting, Cromwell's insomnia, Heine notes, had a different reason:

> If Cromwell was also unable to sleep peacefully at night and anxiously ran about in Whitehall, it was not, as pious gentlemen thought, the ghost of a bloody king that pursued him, but a fear of the physical avengers of his guilt; he feared the real daggers of his enemies, and for that reason he always wore armor under his jerkin and grew more and more suspicious; and finally, when the pamphlet appeared, *To Kill Is Not to Murder*, Oliver Cromwell never smiled again. (150)

> Wenn Cromwell ebenfalls nicht ruhig schlafen konnte und des Nachts ängstlich in Whitehall umherlief, so war es nicht, wie fromme Kavaliere meinten, ein blutiges Königsgespenst, was ihn verfolgte, sondern die Furcht vor den leiblichen Rächern seiner Schuld: er füchtete die materiellen Dolche der Feinde, und deshalb trug er unter dem Wams immer einen Harnisch, und er wurde immer mißtrauischer, und endlich gar, als das Büchlein erschien: "Töten ist kein Mord", da hat Oliver Cromwell nie mehr gelächelt. (65f.)

The terror's haunting presence catches up with the Puritan revolutionary, Heine suggests here so vividly, not owing to any metaphysical force, but in a pointedly materialist manner with the return of the repressed. What goes around comes around. The primal scene of terror here is not the scene of the murder but the way the agent of terror returns to behold his victim.

History as the repetition of itself in descending cadence turns the historically later instance into an iteration of the earlier one and makes any iteration into a genetically derivative after-event: the farce that follows the tragedy. Following tragedy is by definition a tragedy turned farce, reduced to the iteration of a model it can only mimic.

Heine's critical point in examining the painting as a study of the relationship between the defunct body of Charles I and his seemingly vigorous nemesis and visitor Cromwell suggests the uncanny legacy that terror carries for its victims as well as its perpetrators. The public's main concern, Heine notes, was with reading Cromwell's thoughts as he faced the open coffin with the body:

> The viewers of Cromwell seemed most preoccupied with deciphering his thoughts at the coffin of the dead Charles. (151)
>
> Was die Beschauer des Cromwell am meisten beschäftigte, war die Entzifferung seiner Gedanken bei dem Sarge des toten Karl. (66)

At this point questions of belatedness and deferred action announce themselves as a problem of representation tied up with the question of reading and legibility. Or, to put it otherwise, the question of reading and legibility emerges as a problem defined by the afterward of belatedness and the deferred action of history:

> History reports this scene according to two different legends. According to the one, Cromwell had the coffin opened at night, by torchlight, and stood before it for a long while, his body paralyzed and his face contorted, like a mute stone figure. According to the other legend, he opened the coffin by day, calmly looked upon the corpse and spoke the words: "He was a strong built man, and he could have lived much longer." In my opinion, Delaroche has this more democratic legend in mind. (151)

> Die Geschichte berichtet diese Szene nach zwei verschiedenen Sagen. Nach der einen habe Cromwell des Nachts, bei Fackelschein, sich den Sarg öffnen lassen, und erstarrten Leibs und verzerrten Angesichts sei er lange davor stehen geblieben, wie ein stummes Steinbild. Nach einer anderen öffnete er den Sarg bei Tage, betrachtete ruhig den Leichnam und sprach die Worte: "Es war ein starkgebauter Mann, und er hätte noch lange Leben können." Nach meiner Ansicht hat Delaroche diese demokratischere Legende im Sinn gehabt. (66)

Notice that for Heine "democratic" and certainly "more democratic" is anything but a reassuring attribute, at least not necessarily. And so Heine continues:

> The face of his Cromwell clearly expresses no astonishment or bewilderment or any other turmoil of the soul; on the contrary, what stuns the viewer is the awful, terrifying calm in the man's face. There it stands, the firmly anchored, earth-rooted figure, "as brutal as a fact," powerful without pathos, demonically natural, wonderfully vulgar, an outlaw and yet immune, and there he looks upon his work, almost like a lumberjack who has just felled an oak. (151)
>
> Im Gesichte seines Cromwells ist durchaus kein Erstaunen oder Verwundern oder sonstiger Seelensturm ausgedrückt; im Gegenteil, den Beschauer erschüttert diese grauenhafte, entsetzliche Ruhe im Gesichte des Mannes. Da steht sie, die gefestete, erdsichere Gestalt, "brutal wie eine Tatsache," gewaltig ohne Pathos, dämonisch natürlich, wunderbar ordinär, verfemt und zugleich gefeit, und da betrachtet sie ihr Werk, fast wie ein Holzhacker, der eben eine Eiche gefällt hat. (66f.)

And just for a moment, let us follow Heine's train of associations before he has it come colliding with the present:

> He felled it calmly, that big oak that had once reached out its branches so proudly over England and Scotland, the royal oak in the shadow of which so many had flourished and in whose shade the elves of poetry once danced their sweetest roundelays;—he felled it calmly with his unhappy ax, and there it lies on the ground with all its lovely foliage and its crown;—unhappy ax! (151)
>
> Er hat sie ruhig gefällt, die große Eiche, die einst so stolz ihre Zweige verbreitete über England und Schottland, die Königseiche, in deren Schatten so viele schöne Menschengeschlechter geblüht, und worunter die Elfen der Poesie ihre süßesten Reigen getanzt;—er hat sie ruhig gefällt mit dem unglückseligen Beil, und da liegt sie zu Boden mit all ihrem holden Laubwerk und mit der unverletzten Krone;—unglückseliges Beil! (67)

It is at this point that these nostalgic ruminations about preindustrial craftsmanship come to a crashing halt:

> "Do you not think, Sir, that the guillotine is a great improvement?" Those were the squeaked words with which an Englishman standing behind me interrupted the sentiments I have just written down, sentiments that filled my soul with such sadness while I looked upon Charles's wounded neck in Delaroche's picture. It is painted a bit too bloodily. (151)

> "Do you not think, Sir, that the guillotine is a great improvement?" das waren die gequäkten Worte, womit ein Brite, der hinter mir stand, die Empfindungen unterbrach, die ich eben niedergeschrieben, und die so wehmütig meine Seele erfüllten, während ich Karls Halswunde auf dem Bilde von Delaroche betrachtete. Sie ist etwas allzugrell blutig gemalt. (67)

If the so-called progress of industrialized terror might hold a greater promise in terms of standardized efficiency, Heine's account reminds us that a quick and easy distinction between premodern and modernized modes of execution feeds into the fatal misapprehension of terror as mere function of brutality. The coloring and other aesthetic shortcomings that Heine finds in Delaroche's painting underline that any attempt to represent terror, and history in general, is subject to a failure produced by the fallacy of a presentism blind to the absence, delay, and deferral that define history and, and as a consequence, terror. Terror, in other words, relies on invisibility; the threat is the insidious absence and postponement of its consummation. Terror traumatizes by its delay, the suspense of deferral. It is ubiquitous and all-pervasive as long as it remains imminent, impending, anticipated, and therefore possible at any given moment. The perverse fact is that the consummation of its threat is its own undoing. It is that phantasmagoric moment of terror, its claim on the mind, that makes it so relentlessly powerful, reducing the mind to a mere body deprived of every meaning and claim to life. Dealing death is nothing more than cutting off a head of cabbage, the moment of death has become devoid of all meaning and significance—how could it ever be adequately represented?

Heine understands that capturing terror is possible only by exposing its strange dynamic, which hinges on the anxious and fraught play between the potential and the actual. Just like the metaphorical axe that felled Charles, terror is doomed to its own demise (*unglückselig*). Terror cannot be represented directly because it evades the present just like history and temporality in general. History and its extreme case, terror, can only be represented through figures of anticipation, delay, and deferral, by gesturing to what cannot be shown but only figured through the rearview mirror of deferred time and action, the staging of the belatedness of the afterward. The figure of belatedness allows at the same time, or so Heine suggests, an arresting of the vicious circle that exploits deferral and delay, thus preventing its decay into an instrument of terror and subjection. Heine's exposure and interruption of this mad and maddening structure unmasks the hidden grip of terror as the function of the dialectic of the absent. As a consequence, Heine's intervention turns this predicament from a situation of terror into a lever for liberation.

Heine leaves no doubt as to how pressingly contemporary, how timely, and how to the point the painting of Cromwell's return to the scene of his crime is:

> We feel [. . .] before the one painting how the great struggle of the age is not yet ended, how the ground still trembles beneath our feet; if we feel here the raging of the storm that threatens to tear down the world; if we still see here the gaping abyss that greedily devours the streams of blood, so that a ghastly fear of the apocalypse holds us in its grip. (152)
>
> Fühlen wir [. . .] wie der große Zeitkampf noch nicht zu Ende, wie der Boden noch zittert unter unsern Füßen; hören wir hier noch das Rasen des Sturmes, der die Welt niederzureißen droht; sehen wir hier noch den gähnenden Abgrund, der gierig die Blutströme einschlürft, so daß grauenhafte Untergangsfurcht uns ergreift. (68)

Heine does not end here, however, but drives the point home more pressingly, more directly, and more personally as he highlights the enduring legacy of terror unleashed:

> It grows difficult for me to remain calmly at my desk and finish writing my poor art report, my amicable judgment of paintings. And yet, if I descend to the street and someone recognizes me as a Prussian, some hero of the July Revolution will bash my brains in and all my art-full ideas will be squashed; a bayonet will stab my left side, where my heart is already bleeding, and maybe on top of that I'll be put in the local jail as a foreign mischief-spoiler. (153)
>
> Es wir mir schwer, ruhig am Schreibtische sitzenzubleiben und meinen armen Kunstbericht, meine friedliche Gemäldebeurteilung, zu Ende zu schreiben. Und dennoch, gehe ich hinab auf die Straße und man erkennt mich als Preußen, so wird mir von irgend einem Julihelden das Gehirn eingedrückt, so daß alle meine Kunstideen zerquetscht werden; oder ich bekomme einen Bajonettstich in die linke Seite, wo jetzt das Herz schon von selber blutet, und vielleicht obendrein werde ich in die Wache gesetzt als fremder Unruhestörer. (69)

Impersonating an art critic, Heine creates a discursive space where the grip of terror can no longer be sustained, not because it is exposed through representation but because he calls its bluff. The link Heine creates here between art criticism and political reality pointedly underlines the precarious nexus between the politics of historiography and representation. If art and its discourse seek to expose the murderous logic of terror, they can do so in critical self-reflection on the terms of representation they both rely on, as an instrument of domination and subjection in the case of terror, as a lever for critical exposure and liberation in the case of the aesthetic ambitions of art. This intertwining is what hampers but also enables the critical difference.

Heine reminds us that the only way to understand terror is by examining its mechanism of deflection: terror has no face, no direct, only an indirect presence through its absence, its screen. But its phantasmagoric production relies on the function of representation for it to work. As critical reflection on representation, art criticism thus assumes—in Heine's hands—importance as a form of critical examination that exposes, interrupts, and disarms the fatal collusion on which terror relies. Presenting representation by way of presentational refraction under the sign of delay, displacement, and substitution, that is, by reenacting, revisiting the scene of terror, terror's lethal threat is neutralized and turned against itself, or so Heine's visit to the Louvre suggests. When critical attention is given to the dynamic of the play of delay, deferral, and displacement in an aesthetically circumscribed manner, the repressive force of the absence that has been turned into terror loosens its lethal grip. The work of mourning that Heine's contemplative meditation initiates spells the promise of liberation from the grip of terror, a promise that defines the precarious distinction between terror as the extreme case of deferred action and its representation. It serves as a critical reminder of the difficulty of navigating the fine line of this distinction and the difficulty of theorizing temporality as itself always already a historically situated proposition.

If we can only reflect on history in hindsight and only through the prism of the particular perspectives we apply, it is precisely temporality's play of delay, deferral, and displacement that holds the promise of breaking the spell of terror. Caught in the bind of hindsight and afterwardness, this deferral also carries the promise of emancipation. The crack of time through which the messianic might enter the world at any given moment is no theological assurance. But it gives the nonconceptual its critical force to resist by reimagining temporality differently.

The Messiah in Golden Chains

Heine's extensive project of rethinking history and temporality reached a new stage with one of his most polemical writings, *Ludwig Börne: A Memorial*. There, at the end of Book 4, Heine narrates the story of the "Messiah in Golden Chains," which he claims he was told on a visit to Poland many years ago by a rabbi in Cracow:

"The Messiah," he told me, "was born on the day when Jerusalem was destroyed by the villain Titus Vespasian, and since then he dwells in the most beautiful palace of heaven, just like a king, but his hands are bound with golden chains!"

"What," I asked in surprise, "what do these golden chains mean?"

"They are necessary," replied the great rabbi, with a sly glance and a deep sigh; "without these fetters the Messiah, when he sometimes loses patience, would otherwise suddenly hurry down and undertake the work of salvation too soon, in the wrong hour. He is, after all, no calm sleepy-head. He is a handsome, very lean but immensely strong man: flourishing like youth. The life he leads, moreover, is very monotonous. The greatest part of the morning he passes with the customary prayers or laughs and jokes with his servants, who are distinguished angels, prettily singing and playing the flute. Then he has his long locks combed and he is rubbed with ointments and dressed in a regal purple robe. The whole afternoon he studies the Kabbalah. Towards evening he summons his old chancellor, who is a disguised angel, just as the four strong state councilors who accompany him are disguised angels. The chancellor must then read to his master out of a great book what has happened every day. All kinds of events occur about which the Messiah smiles with pleasure or shakes his head in annoyance. But when he hears how his people are treated down below, then he gets into the most terrible rage and howls so that the heavens tremble. The four strong state councilors must then hold the furious man back so that he will not hurry down to the earth, and they would surely not overcome him if his hands were not bound with the golden chains. They mollify him by saying gently that the time has not yet come, the right hour of salvation, and in the end he sinks onto his couch and covers his face and weeps." (S 103f.)

Der Messias, sagte er mit an, sei an dem Tage geboren, wo Jerusalem durch den Bösewicht, Titus Vespasian, zerstört worden, und seitdem wohne er im schönsten Palaste des Himmels, umgeben von Glanz und Freude, auch eine Krone auf dem Haupte tragend, ganz wie ein König . . . aber seine Hände seien gefesselt mit goldenen Ketten!

Was, frug ich verwundert, was bedeuten diese goldenen Ketten?

"Die sind notwendig"—erwiderte der große Rabbi, mit einem schlauen Blick und einem tiefen Seufzer—, "ohne diese Fessel würde der Messias, wenn er manchmal die Geduld verliert, plötzlich herabeilen und zu frühe, zur unrechten Stunde, das Erlösungswerk unternehmen. Er ist eben keine ruhige Schlafmütze. Er ist ein schöner, sehr schlanker, aber doch ungeheuer kräftiger Mann; blühend wie die Jugend. Das Leben, das er führt, ist übrigens sehr einförmig. Den größten Teil des Morgens verbringt er mit den üblichen Gebeten oder lacht und scherzt mit seinen Dienern, welche verkleidete Engel sind, und hübsch singen und die Flöte blasen. Dann läßt er sein langes Haupthaar kämmen und man salbt ihn

> mit Narden, und bekleidet ihn mit einem fürstlichen Purpurgewande. Den ganzen Nachmittag studiert er die Cabala. Gegen Abend läßt er seinen alten Kanzler kommen, der ein verkleideter Engel ist, ebenso so wie die vier starken Staatsräte, die ihn begleiten, verkleidete Engel sind. Aus einem großen Buche muß alsdann der Kanzler seinem Herrn vorlesen, was jeden Tag passierte . . . Da kommen allerlei Geschichten vor, worüber der Messias vergnügt lächelt, oder auch mißmütig den Kopf schüttelt . . . Wenn er aber hört, wie man unten sein Volk mißhandelt, dann gerät er in den furchtbarsten Zorn und heult, daß die Himmel erzittern . . . Die vier starken Staatsräte müssen dann den Ergrimmten zurückhalten, daß er nicht herabeile auf die Erde, und sie würden ihn wahrlich nicht bewältigen, wären seine Hände nicht gefesselt mit den goldenen Ketten . . . Man beschwichtigt ihn auch mit sanften Reden, daß jetzt die Zeit noch nicht gekommen sei, die rechte Rettungsstunde, und er sinkt am Ende aufs Lager und verhüllt sein Antlitz und weint . . ." (B 4, 120f.)

As Heine the narrator has the rabbi conclude, "certifying his reliability by reference to the Talmud," he notes that since the days of his visit to Poland, he has

> often had to think of his stories, especially in recent times, after the July Revolution. Indeed, in bad days I thought I heard with my own ears a rattling, as though of golden chains, and then despairing sobs. (S 104)

> oft an seine Erzählungen denken müssen, besonders in den jüngsten Zeiten, nach der Juliusrevolution. Ja, in schlimmen Tagen, glaubt ich manchmal mit eigenen Ohren ein Gerassel zu hören, wie von goldenen Ketten, und dann ein verzweifelndes Schluchzen. (B 4, 121)

Turning now to the present, Heine concludes this passage with an appeal to the Messiah and his guards that spells out the problem of *Nachträglichkeit* in harrowing terms:

> Oh, despair not, handsome Messiah, who wants not only to save Israel, as the superstitious Jews think, but all of suffering mankind! Oh, do not break your golden chains! Oh, keep him bound for a time so that he does not come too soon, the saving king of the world! (S 104)

> O verzage nicht, schöner Messias, der du nicht bloß Israel erlösen willst, wie die abergläubischen Juden sich einbilden, sondern die ganze leidende Menschheit! O, zerreißt nicht, Ihr goldenen Ketten! O, haltet ihn noch einige Zeit gefesselt, daß er nicht zu frühe komme, der rettende König der Welt! (B 4, 121)

As Heine, who never visited Cracow, seems to have made this wonderful story up, we can consider it a creative attempt to produce his own midrash[39] and remark, with Galileo Galilei: "se non è vero, è ben trovato." For this Midrash-style version of the messianic legend gives rise to some remarkable thoughts on the critical function of the messianic, and not just in the Jewish tradition.[40] While the notion does not appear in Jewish tradition until the Middle Ages, there is a medieval mystical Midrashic tradition that features a Messiah in chains.[41] Whether or not Heine knew about it, and whether or not he heard accounts reflecting this Midrashic tradition on his trip to Poland, is impossible to ascertain. But what is striking is that Heine's version resonates suggestively with such traditions and that his narrative stages them in a temporality of deferred action. In the wake of the seventeenth-century messianic movement inspired by the false Messiah Sabbatai Zvi, the imprisonment of the Messiah began to circulate as a common trope. After his arrest by the Turkish authorities, Sabbatai's life was spared and his sentence—against custom and expectations—commuted to imprisonment, a fact that his followers considered a miracle. Thanks to generous donations from the Jewish community, Sabbatai was moved to quite luxurious quarters where he received visitors like a dignitary. This may have inspired the idea of the Messiah in "golden" chains. In Poland, the epicenter of the Frankist movement in the eighteenth century, the Sabbatian tradition was alive and well in Heine's time. After all, Jacob Frank considered himself the reincarnation of Sabbatai Zvi.[42]

Now let us look at the way Heine frames this story. The legend is introduced as a citation of a past encounter with a Polish rabbi dating back to one of Heine's first publications, his series of articles *On Poland* published in 1823. A voice from the past in many ways, the fictional Polish rabbi's story resonates in Heine's memory as he sets out to frame how his relationship to history and the present distinguishes him from Börne, his one-time brother-in-arms and eventual unforgiving opponent whose stress on progress and advancement, Heine suggests, might in the larger scheme of history appear backward and retrograde: precisely because Börne mistook himself for the harbinger of a new world he failed to bring about. But again, it is tellingly only much later, in 1840, that the Cracow rabbi's story catches fire, years after the story was presumably told, or so Heine's narrator determines. Yet this "afterward," it is suggested, is never late because it is precisely its lateness—its working through, in a different scheme—that makes it so timely.

We will return to this image. It becomes a striking expression of Heine's claim to being in step with history despite apparently lagging behind; an image that draws a sharp contrast to Börne who, despite his brash pretense of being in step with the time, or even ahead of it, is blind to the past that holds the future and thus ultimately fails to recognize the transformative historical force of belatedness. With the story of the Messiah fettered with golden chains, Heine rehearses a literary form of *Nachträglichkeit*, that is, the afterward of belatedness, as his account surfaces over one-and-a-half decades after his fictional or fictionally reworked encounter with the rabbi of Cracow. This deferral of the narrative action frames the story of the Messiah in a context of continued belatedness, just as the Messiah's own reaction—when he hears at the end of the day about life on earth—must always be deferred: it is always late, if not too late. As "the chancellor must then read to his master out of a great book what has happened every day," the facts have already become the history that the Messiah himself seeks to correct. As a consequence, any meta-discourse on history is doomed to remain just another reiteration and repetition of the afterward, the belatedness, and therefore a deferral of action in the present. In other words, even in the heavens, there is no way to escape time and the temporality of history and textuality.

Deferred action can therefore never be translated into straightforward logic. It remains a self-recursive operation whose referent is never stable in itself, but works "itself" as a function of a delayed attempt at making sense in inevitable hindsight. This self-recursive mode, however, does not necessarily have to be simply limiting—permanent "chains"—since it also holds the promise of a transformative opening of, and into, history. The messianic does not denote only the moment of hope, but also that of activity, praxis, and action. Activating the image of deferral, this re-action performs itself through, as it were, a deferred action—a moment to be seized, after all—and one that Heine projects onto the scene as an emancipatory and transformative power.

Framed as a deferred narrative going back "many years" to his journey to Poland, the apocryphal mock or quasi-midrashic legend assumes a critical force that is pregnant with the hope of the future because it is so unabashedly grounded in the reference to a past that failed because "the moment to realize it was missed," as Adorno puts it in the opening sentence of *Negative Dialectics*. Opening the present to the past in this way, that is, a past that refers infinitely to the past in which it is situated, means opening the afterward to the force of the present as it embraces the future as the critical—analytical and emancipatory—moment of the present, or so Heine's rendering of the midrashic legend suggests.

A reminder of the dialectics of the afterward of deferred action, Heine's Messiah in golden chains illustrates the paradox of history and historical consciousness in modernity. The phenomenon of the false Messiah's impact and Heine's response to it demonstrates the degree to which modernity is defined by the crisis of tradition expressed in the image of the Messiah put in chains: the dynamic of the internal struggle of tradition's multiple aspects and motives expresses the predicament of a modernity defined by the counteracting pressures of a temporality that escapes teleologically straightforward alignment. In Heine, the Messiah in golden chains becomes the theological-political figuration of the conflicted situation of *Nachträglichkeit* that defines the condition of modernity.

Dream, Imagination, History: Going Forward Going Back

Hermann Levin Goldschmidt quotes Adrien Turel's grippingly suggestive question: "How far does one need to back up in order to jump further than where one stands?"[43] Turel's answer was of course that we need to go back as far as speculation allows us. For Heine, the answer seems to have been similar to the one that Freud would give. The poets, Heine argued, have a more genuine understanding of history than the historians with their fact-finding missions and purportedly naked facts. Heine formulates this view in his *Travel Pictures*' installment *Journey from Munich to Genoa*, a reflective meditation on the present as a journey back in time. Heine's programmatic statement of the poet's mission highlights the poet's often misunderstood political mandate, which for him was of course inseparable from the poetic aspect of his writing:

> Strange fancies these of the multitude! They seek their histories from the poet, and not from the historian. They ask not for bare facts, but those facts again dissolved in the original poetry from which they sprung. This the poets well know, and it is not without a certain mischievous pleasure that they mould at will popular memories, perhaps in mockery of pride-baked historians and parchment-minded keepers of State documents. [. . .] History is not distorted by the poets.[44] For they give the sense in all its truthfulness, though it be clothed in invented [Leland has: inverted] form and circumstance. [. . .] From the same point of view I would assert that Walter Scott's romances give, occasionally, the spirit of English history far more truthfully than Hume has done. (L 3, 27f.)

> Seltsame Grille des Volkes! Es verlangt seine Geschichte aus der Hand des Dichters und nicht aus der Hand des Historikers. Es verlangt nicht den treuen Bericht nackter Tatsachen, sondern jene Tatsachen wieder aufgelöst in die ursprüngliche Poesie, woraus sie hervorgegangen. Das wissen die Dichter, und nicht ohne geheime Schadenlust modeln sie willkührlich die Völkererinnerungen, vielleicht zur Verhöhnung stolztrockner Historiographen und pergamentener Staatsarchivare. [. . .] Die Geschichte wird nicht von den Dichtern verfälscht. Sie geben den Sinn derselben ganz treu, und sei es auch durch selbsterfundene Gestalten und Umstände. [. . .] In gleicher Hinsicht möchte ich behaupten, Walter Scotts Romane gäben zuweilen den Geist der englischen Geschichte weit treuer als Hume. (B 2, 330)

Heine goes on to point out that poets capture the essence of history just as dreamers capture through their inner feelings what their souls feel to be external causes,

> since they replace the latter [i.e. the real external causes] with totally different, dreamed-up causes, which, however, are fully adequate insofar as they bring forth the same feelings. (L 3, 28)[45]

> indem sie an die Stelle dieser letzteren [i.e. the real external causes] ganz andere äußere Ursachen erträumen, die aber insofern ganz adäquat sind, als sie dasselbe Gefühl hervorbringen. (B 2, 331)

Such a "dream-form" (*Traumgestalt*, L 3, 29; B 2, 331), as Heine calls it, captures the truth no less and, he suggests, potentially more precisely and more profoundly than an objective description by a sober chronicler (L 3, 27f.; B 2, 330). Let us keep in mind that at this point—as his *Rabbi of Bacherach* project demonstrates—Heine's bold and ambitious attempt, begun back in the days of the Verein für Cultur und Wissenschaft der Juden, to not only compose a historical novel à la Sir Walter Scott, but also to thereby produce historical source material for future historians, lies several years behind him. From that point onward—up to the conception of history he lays out in *On the History of Religion and Philosophy in Germany* of the 1830s and to his final literary legacy of *Romanzero* and particularly the *Romanzero*'s "Hebrew Melodies"—there is a continuous reflection on, and renegotiation of, history as a reality most adequately grasped by its creative poetic (re)imagination in poetical narrative and fiction. There are a couple of stops in the *Travel Pictures*' *Journey from Munich to Genoa*, however, that deserve our attention. Composed in 1828 and first published in 1828 and 1829, this text presents Heine's earliest extended reflection of history.

In visiting the battlegrounds of Marengo, this installment of the *Travel Pictures* enters a force field of historical memory, giving the narrator cause to wonder whether "world history were no longer a robber-legend (*eine Räubergeschichte*), but a ghost story (L 3, 103; B 2, 375). For a site that breathes as much history as the battlegrounds of Marengo—from which Napoleon emerged victorious as the great reformer of France and Europe's glorious harbinger of modernity—brings home the ghostly character that haunts history. Walking around the battlegrounds, Heine's narrator experiences the resurfacing of historical reflections in ghostly disguise, like stray dogs that have lost their masters (B 3, 378).[46] But the theme of the aftereffect of history writ large—the forgotten past that will make history proper, so to speak—is given further elaboration as Heine's narrator now asks some of the hard questions others so lightly dispatch:

> But alas! every inch which humanity advances costs streams of blood, and is not that paying rather dear? Is not the life of the individual worth as much as that of the entire race? For every single man is a world which is born and which dies with him; beneath every gravestone lies a world's

> history [—][47] "Be silent," Death would say "as to those who lie here"; but *we* still live, and will fight on in the holy battle for the freedom of humanity. (L 3, 108)
>
> Aber ach! Jeder Zoll, den die Menschheit weiter rückt, kostet Ströme Blutes; und ist das nicht etwas zu teuer? Ist das Leben des Individuums nicht vielleicht eben so viel wert wie das des ganzen Geschlechtes? Denn jeder Mensch ist schon eine Welt, die mit ihm geboren wird und mit ihm stirbt, unter jedem Grabstein liegt eine Weltgeschichte—Still davon, so würden die Toten sprechen, die hier gefallen sind, wir aber leben und wollen weiter kämpfen im heiligen Befreiungskriege der Menschheit. (B 2, 378)

If there is any poetically adequate expression of the moment of belatedness and the effect of the afterward that this passage so eloquently addresses, we can see it captured in this momentous but mute dash or break, which the German language so suggestively calls a *Gedankenstrich*: the punctuation mark that gives us pause for thought. Let us just focus on the operative moment that precedes this moment of silence and break:

> beneath every gravestone lies a world history.[48]
>
> unter jedem Grabstein liegt eine Weltgeschichte.

Rather than merely a burial ground for the bodies of the deceased victims of history, the battlefield is also the site of their dreams and aspirations: their hopes that live on and constitute a historical force precisely because their champions have died and the chance to realize their dreams was missed. Just as the dash separates from, but also links to, the statement that follows, the question of whether the dash fashions the pronouncement into a fragment awaiting completion or supplementation, or whether it should be considered a completely cutoff, stand-alone remark, becomes undecidable. Only the afterward will tell, that is, our lives and actions, as the text suggests: "But *we* still live, and will fight on in the holy battle for the freedom of humanity"; when, exactly, remains in question.

Similarly, the recurring figure of the "dead Maria" serves as a leitmotif that poses the question of temporality and the relation between past, present, and future in terms of repetition and the continuity of the discontinuous. History is not just what has passed but what informs the present and shapes the future. The enigmatic motif figures the return of the meaning of history as a repetitive reminder that history—never simply adding up—resists resolution into linear temporality. Like the Wittgensteinian musing at the end of Woody Allen's movie *Another Woman*, Heine's recursive motif poses the question: "Is memory something we have or something we have lost?"[49]

Nachträglichkeit's Aftereffects: Heine and Freud

Interestingly, Freud's theorizing on the afterward of deferred action is linked to Heine in such a way that we can see Freud working through remarkable aspects of Heine's aftereffect on Freud himself. The way this manifests itself in Freud not only highlights the profoundly systemic function of deferred action but also tracks a key connection between Heine, Freud, and Critical Theory.

If Heine plays a crucial role in Freud's theory formation, as we saw in Chapter 2, this holds true also for Freud's final publication *Moses and Monotheism*, his provocatively conflicted final word on the question of history and messianic hope. At the end of a rather long footnote early on in the book's second essay, Freud poses the question:

> And, incidentally, who suggested to the Jewish poet Heine in the nineteenth century a.d. that he should complain of his religion as "the plague dragged along from the Nile valley, the unhealthy beliefs of Ancient Egypt?"[50]
>
> Wer hat übrigens dem jüdischen Dichter H. Heine im 19. Jahrhundert n.Chr. eingegeben, seine Religion zu beklagen als "die aus dem Niltal mitgeschleppte Plage, den altägyptischen ungesunden Glauben?"[51]

It is very tempting to turn the question around and ask: Who gave Freud the idea to argue for the Egyptian origins of Judaism? If this seems like the kind of cheap shot Freud tries to get away with when he suggests that the Egyptian godhead "Aton" might be addressed in Judaism's core prayer of the "Sh'ma Israel," suggesting that the Hebrew "Adonai" might reference "Aton," a closer reading of Freud suggests that this footnote is hardly incidental, and communicates Freud's coy acknowledgment of Heine. Of course, this one occasional poem referred to in the footnote is not the only role Heine might have played in Freud's conception of his Moses book.[52]

Freud's *Moses and Monotheism* is a rather odd book: if we can, in fact, call this mix of three uneven texts a book at all. The textual quality of this series of essays poses a hermeneutic challenge of a severity that cannot be ignored. But bracketing the hermeneutic challenge of how to read this book or non-book, this trilogy of texts has the curious effect of encouraging a screening out of its self-critical dimension, of distracting from its compositional mode that twists its way through the text. Thus, we can easily forget our sense that this idiosyncratic and oddly conflicted piece of writing contains many doublings, reiterations, and duplications, as if built around a double bottom or false floor.

Unless we read Freud's *Moses and Monotheism* as a performative text that self-consciously announces a literary mode that is part and parcel of the critical function of the writing, a decisive aspect of Freud's argument will be lost. This approach warns us against focusing solely on Freud's rationalizations, and challenges us to attend to the tension-ridden struggle that underlies their articulation. This dual-level focus reveals Freud's strategic positioning of *Moses and Monotheism* as a critical intervention into the discourse of religion and modernity, secularization and revolution, and one in which Freud inserts himself self-consciously as an active player. The drama staged by this assemblage of texts shows us Freud following in the steps of Heine's writing while remaining careful and overly conscientious in giving his source full and due credit. Attention to the rich intertextual resonance with Heine—whose traces Freud refuses to mute—helps bring out the performative mode of Freud's *Moses and Monotheism*.

Freud's Moses book is, above all, a study concerned with the function of tradition, the role of doubling, repetition, and the phenomenon of *Nachträglichkeit*. If Freud is after the meaning and function of history, the study itself reflects its own embeddedness in the historical process. Freud suggests as much at the opening of the first essay "Moses, an Egyptian," where he emphasizes how science has grown increasingly cautious with regard to the transmission of traditions since "the early days of historical criticism."[53] This theme of belated discovery of a different origin continues to resurface throughout the speculative narrative that Freud presents.

While science or *Wissenschaft* as such is only a relatively reliable instrument, as Freud keeps cautioning us, his depth-psychological approach, he claims, will yield a better grasp of the way tradition, history, and religion function. Freud thus offers an alternative approach to history, one that bonafide historians can of course only consider anathema to their disciplinary convictions. Freud, to be sure, is primarily interested in a history of the psyche rather than in brute facts, although the facts he posits are no doubt rather brute in and of themselves.

Far less brutal is the way Freud's Moses book resonates with Heine. A brief survey of Heine's writing on the themes that Freud introduces provides us with the necessary background to situate Freud's effort in a more precise manner as an intervention in a critical discourse with a history of its own. For Freud's *Moses* is more than the brainchild of an aging psychoanalyst: we can read it as a pointed intervention in a larger discourse on the multiple origins of tradition, a discourse whose own historicity it critically reflects.

A review of some of the relevant passages in Heine's prose and poetry will help establish this intertext that underlies Freud's Moses book. In this context, Heine's enigmatic insertion of the story of the Messiah in golden chains, discussed above, represents a key passage around which Heine's other texts take on critical significance for Freud, for it is this text that poses the question of the relation between the messianic and history—revised in Freud's *Moses and Monotheism* as a theory of the differential origins of tradition, a position Freud uses Moses to explore—in explicit and challenging terms.

Eulogy of a Dying God and Moses's Creation of a People

While Freud's Moses book referenced a Heine poem from the early 1840s in which Judaism is cast as a disease the Jews carried with them when they departed from Egypt, the grand eulogy of "old Jehovah" that marks the finale of the second book of *On the History of Religion and Philosophy in Germany* deserves our attention, for it reads like a summary of Freud's theory of the genesis of monotheism:

> We have gotten to know him so well, from his cradle, in Egypt, where he was raised among the divine calves, crocodiles, holy onions, ibises, and cats—We saw him bid farewell to the playmates of his childhood, along with the obelisks and sphinxes of his homeland, the Nile valley, and become a small God-King in Palestine over a poor shepherd people, living in his own temple palace.—We saw later how he came into contact with Assyrian-Babylonian civilization and gave up his all-too-human passions, no longer spewed pure wrath and vengeance, or at least no longer went into rages about every little trifle.—We saw him emigrate to Rome, the capital city, where he gave up all national prejudice and proclaimed the heavenly equality of all peoples. With such splendid phrases, we saw him form a party in opposition to old Jupiter, intrigue long enough to come to power and rule from the Capitol over city and world, *urbem et orbem*.—We saw how he became even more ethereal, how he gently whined, how he became a loving father, a general friend of mankind, a benefactor of the world, a philanthropist—none of this could help him.
>
> Do you hear the bell ringing? Kneel down—Sacraments are being brought to a dying God. (OH 76)

> Wir haben ihn so gut gekannt, von seiner Wiege an, in Ägypten, als er unter göttlichen Kälbern, Krokodilen, heiligen Zwiebeln, Ibissen und Katzen erzogen wurde—Wir haben ihn gesehen, wie er diesen Gespielen seiner Kindheit und den Obelisken und Sphynxen seines heimatlichen Niltals Ade sagte und in Palästina, bei einem armen Hirtenvölkchen, ein kleiner Gott-König wurde, und in einem eigenen Tempelpalast wohnte—Wir sahen ihn späterhin, wie er mit der assyrisch-babylonischen Zivilisation in Berührung kam, und seine allzumenschliche Leidenschaften ablegte, nicht mehr lauter Zorn und Rache spie, wenigstens nicht mehr wegen jeder Lumperei gleich donnerte—Wir sahen ihn auswandern nach Rom, der Hauptstadt, wo er aller Nationalvorurteile entsagte, und die himmlische

> Gleichheit aller Völker proklamierte, und mit solchen schönen Phrasen gegen den alten Jupiter Opposition bildete, und so lange intrigierte bis er zur Herrschaft gelangte, und vom Kapitole herab die Stadt und die Welt, urbem et orbem, regierte—Wir sahen, wie er sich noch mehr vergeistigte, wie er sanftselig wimmerte, wie er ein liebevoller Vater wurde, ein allgemeiner Menschenfreund, ein Weltbeglücker, ein Philanthrop—es konnte ihm alles nichts helfen—
>
> Hört Ihr das Glöckchen klingeln? Kniet nieder—Man bringt die Sakramente einem sterbenden Gotte. (B 3, 591)

I am not claiming that Heine drafted the précis for Freud's cultural theory, but the resonances are so striking that we may wonder why Freud, who otherwise demonstrated such intimate familiarity with Heine, restricts himself to referencing a poem that only covers one aspect of his theory. This passage—in a now belated, but anticipatory construction—offers the principles of Freud's account of the God of the Hebrews, as first mouthed by an uncouth tribal chieftain, then received by the emperor, Pope ("Papa" as the Latin has it), and eventually ascending to the position of universal all-loving father of all humankind in Rome.

Let us consider another passage that presents an equally powerful vision, composed in Heine's last years when he was completely bedridden and arguing with God, tortured by the pain of his illness. In his "Confessions," as Heine entitled one of his very last publications in 1854, we find a striking portrayal of Moses who, despite his animosity against art, as Heine formulates it, was "nevertheless himself a great artist, and possessed true artist's spirit [*Genius*]."[54] And Heine continues:

> Only, this artistic spirit with him, as with his Egyptian countrymen, was applied to the colossal and the imperishable. But not, like the Egyptians, did he construct his works of art from bricks and granite, but he built human pyramids and carved human obelisks. He took a poor shepherd tribe and from it created a nation which should defy centuries; a great, an immortal, a consecrated race, a God-serving people, who to all other nations should be as a model and prototype: he created Israel. [With greater reason than the Roman poet is this artist, son of Amram and the midwife Yochevet, able to claim to have erected a monument that shall survive all creations made from ore].[55]

> Nur war dieser Künstlergeist bei ihm, wie bei seinen ägyptischen Landsleuten, nur auf das Kolossale und Unverwüstliche gerichtet. Aber nicht wie die Ägypter formierte er seine Kunstwerke aus Backstein und Granit, sondern er baute Menschenpyramiden, er meißelte Menschen-Obelisken, er nahm einen armen Hirtenstamm und schuf daraus ein Volk, das ebenfalls den Jahrhunderten trotzen sollte, ein großes, ewiges, heiliges Volk, ein Volk Gottes, das allen andern Völkern als Muster, ja der ganzen

> Menschheit als Prototyp dienen konnte: er schuf Israel! Mit größerm Rechte als der römische Dichter darf jener Künstler, der Sohn Amrams und der Hebamme Jochebet, sich rühmen, ein Monument errichtet zu haben, das alle Bildungen aus Erz überdauern wird! (B 6.1, 481)

But this is not where the significance of Heine's legacy for Freud ends. There is one additional crucial paragraph that highlights not only the concern of a dying "ex-God," as Heine calls himself just a few pages preceding the section on Moses,[56] a point that Freud's Moses book shares in a profound manner, as Miriam Leonard has recently demonstrated in such eloquent terms.[57] The Moses discourse also serves as a means for renegotiating the distinction between Hellenism and Hebraism, one Heine had already challenged earlier as a false distinction.[58] In this passage, he feels the need to reject this theory of mono-origin without reservation—not just with ironic ridicule, but as a matter of principle:

> I have never spoken with proper reverence either of the artist or of his work, the Jews; and for the same reason—namely, my Hellenic temperament, which was opposed to Jewish asceticism. My prejudice in favour of Hellas has declined since. I see now that the Greeks were only beautiful youths, but that the Jews were always men, strong, unyielding men, not only in the past, but to this very day, in spite of eighteen centuries of persecution and suffering. Since that time I have learned to appreciate them better, and, were not all pride of ancestry a silly inconsistency in a champion of the revolution and its democratic principles, the writer of these pages would be proud that his ancestors belonged to the noble house of Israel, that he is a descendant of those martyrs who gave the world a God and a morality, and who have fought and suffered on all the battle-fields of thought.[59]

> Wie über den Werkmeister, hab ich auch über das Werk, die Juden, nie mit hinlänglicher Ehrfurcht gesprochen, und zwar gewiß wieder meines hellenischen Naturells wegen, dem der judäische Ascetismus zuwider war. Meine Vorliebe für Hellas hat seitdem abgenommen. Ich sehe jetzt, die Griechen waren nur schöne Jünglinge, die Juden aber waren immer Männer, gewaltige, unbeugsame Männer, nicht bloß ehemals, sondern bis auf den heutigen Tag, trotz achtzehn Jahrhunderten der Verfolgung und des Elends. Ich habe sie seitdem besser würdigen gelernt, und wenn nicht jeder Geburtsstolz bei dem Kämpen der Revolution und ihrer demokratischen Prinzipien ein närrischer Widerspruch wäre, so könnte der Schreiber dieser Blätter stolz darauf sein, daß seine Ahnen dem edlen Hause Israel angehörten, daß er ein Abkömmling jener Märtyrer, die der Welt einen Gott und eine Moral gegeben, und auf allen Schlachtfeldern des Gedankens gekämpft und gelitten haben. (B 6.1, 481)

In other words: the Moses that Freud "inherited," as it were, came not from the "Egyptians," but from a notion of tradition that already viewed origins in a multiple, differential, and open form. A belated, as it were, but deeply original truth.

For Freud, not surprisingly, Moses represents the first Messiah.[60] And this sends us back to Heine's Messiah in golden chains. If we can say that Freud works out his relation to Heine in the Jewish sons' relation to Moses—a little bit pace Bloom—Freud needs to distort the predecessor figure to acquire his legacy in a different way. This is to say that Heine offers a view of tradition that Bloom never provides and towards which Freud only gestures, which is the following: that this process of encountering different origins is enjoyable, and that the guilt hides a pleasure that breaks traditional chains.[61] In Freud, Heine's Messiah might not be released from his golden—that his, historical—chains of *Nachträglichkeit*, but he is certainly reimagined as the Moses that Heine portrays.

Freud's final point might well have been this: the Jews are not, on the one hand, really to be seen as being responsible for the invention of Judaism, but rather only for their undying loyalty to it. The belated but contemporary meaning of his point, however, on the other Freudian hand, is that the Jews, or Jewish tradition—Freud is never too subtle about any such distinction—are certainly to be held responsible for the invention of Christianity and its differential tradition. Or, as Heine might retort with emancipatory openness, "Christianity is at present entirely in the hands of the Jews."[62]

To translate this point into less humorous parlance: Freud's most personal legacy, his conflicted but also liberating theory of Jewish tradition and history as a psychoanalytic case study, or rather speculation, or, more precisely, fantasy of how tradition and culture function, shows that working through an issue always means working it through one's predecessors. If Moses had been killed by the Jews, as Goethe had surmised,[63] Freud making him an Egyptian could perhaps save him from death at the hands of his own sons. Freud's footnoting of Heine might just have been another and more liberating way to acknowledge that a father—if only in spirit, and with rather extended family relations—might not always be just a form of repression but could also serve as a helpful guide to one's own freedom.

Temporality, the Paradox of Time, and Nonsimultaneity

In *Romanzero*, the penultimate volume of poetry he would complete, Heine explored in a poetic mode the question of temporality, the paradox of time, and the effect of the simultaneity of the nonsimultaneous. Revisiting the concepts of history, time, tradition, and identity, the figures of discontinuity, break, and innovation emerge as crucial aspects of modernity. History is no longer generalizable in the singular of a universal history but dissolves into a proliferating plurality of stories whose contingent and accidental character undermines all pretense of teleological closure, as Part 1, pointedly entitled *Historien* ("Histories"), signals. The stories these poems tell run counter to the desire for a grand-scheme approach to history, while the "Lamentations" of *Romanzero*'s Part 2 muster the incommensurability of the poet's sobering existential experience with any such scheme. Part 3, the "Hebrew Melodies" articulate a final critical move.

The order in which the poems "Prinzessin Sabbat," "Jehuda ben Halevy," and "Disputation" are arranged in the "Hebrew Melodies" amounts to an exploration of the dialectic of the simultaneity of the nonsimultaneous, as each poem addresses the intertwinement of present, past, and future through the guise of historical reflection. Caught between past and future, the noncontemporary emerges as the contemporary while the contemporary betrays features of the repression of its own noncontemporariness. If change seems to require a break in the flow of time, *Romanzero* also reminds its readers that change can occur only in and through time itself: continuity and discontinuity are interdependently constituting each other. History and the impression of the steady flow of time are possible only because rupture enables change, while change also requires continuity in order to be recognized as change. Benjamin's comment highlights the dialectical tension at the heart of the notions of time and history as an effect of constellations: "It may be that the continuity of tradition is mere semblance. But then precisely the persistence of this appearance of persistence provides it with continuity."[64] The "Hebrew Melodies" bring this point to its most mature expression as they address the paradox of time as the underlying condition of modernity.[65]

Rather than merely a critical reflection on the abortive attempts at emancipation, "Prinzessin Sabbat" reflects on the problem of time as an effect of the continual displacement of the messianic hope that reflects the paradox of time as the return of a repressed past that threatens to blind the present. Ignoring the paradoxical character of time, the poem suggests, would lock us into a conception of time that not only mistakes Jewish identity for a divided form of consciousness, but views such a split as the predicament of Jewish existence in modernity. Instead, "Prinzessin Sabbat" demonstrates that the unrelenting grip of the conventional notion of time and its tyrannical rule can only be critically addressed if the paradox of modernity—the paradox of time—is recognized as modernity's constitutive feature rather than the individual's fault. History emerges then as no longer the nemesis of time but as the process of renegotiating temporality in the here and now. Time, in turn, can then be grasped as the pacemaker of history, as that differential impulse that defines history ever anew, impregnating it with the past at every moment.

On the Jewish Sabbath, time comes to a standstill, or so it seems. Behind the traditional scene of a clear-cut dichotomy between the temporality of everyday life and messianic time, "Prinzessin Sabbat" comments on the subtle twist characteristic of the way modernity imposes normative expectations on the experience of time. The traditional scheme is worth recalling: the Sabbath celebrates the wonder of the creation of the world, a day set aside to meditate on creation, its completion and perfection, as a divine effort that spells eternal duration. Reflecting on creation and the creator's respite on the day of rest, the Sabbath recalls the moment when time is created through the parting of light from darkness. Time comes into being through this division and its repetition: as day follows night, time emerges through the distinction between before and after.

But while the distinction between continuity and interruption seems unproblematic, "Prinzessin Sabbat" challenges the dichotomous neatness of the division that informs it. In a resolute countermove to the romantic practice of stabilizing the anxiety over the loss of a clear boundary between reality and imagination by recourse to the uncanny, Heine exposes the problem of the recurrence of the fantastic by exposing modern reality and the conception of time that defines it as themselves fantastic constructions. Unlike the romantics, Heine no longer seeks to stabilize the conventional notion of time through simple reversal—the "infinity" of romantic irony—but instead exposes the repressive character of the modern construction of the concept of time directly.

"Prinzessin Sabbat" gives this problem subtle expression in the way it portrays the repetitive return of the weekly cycle. Citing the *Arabian Nights*, the poem opens with a fairy-tale cue that recalls a world inhabited by enchanted princes who at times regain their original appearance:

In Arabia's book of fables
We can see enchanted princes
Who at times regain their former
Human shape and comely figure:

Once again the hairy monster
Changes back into a princeling,
Dressed in brightly jeweled splendor,
Sweetly fluting amorous ditties.

But the magic respite ends,
And again all of a sudden
We behold his royal highness
Retransmuted to a monster. (D 651)

In Arabiens Märchenbuche
Sehen wir verwünschte Prinzen,
Die zuzeiten ihre schöne
Urgestalt zurückgewinnen:

Das behaarte Ungeheuer
Ist ein Königsohn geworden;

Schmuckreich glänzend angekleidet,
Auch verliebt die Flöte blasend.

Doch die Zauberfrist zerrinnt,
Und wir schauen plötzlich wieder
Seine königliche Hoheit
In ein Ungetüm verzottelt. (B 6.1, 125)

In the playful guise of Orientalizing fantasy, the poem repurposes Orientalism to turn the reader's expectation upside down as it replaces the fairy-tale fantasy with a miniature that tells the story of how Jewish tradition preserves human dignity under the conditions of repression and alienation in modernity. Israel, the poem informs us, is like a prince whose deformed features are the result of a witch's curse. While life in the diaspora seems like a curse that has reduced the Jewish people to a doglike existence, "Prinzessin Sabbat" refuses any simple reversal of time leading to a fantasy of triumphant Jewish restoration—a problematic form of messianism that would result in underwriting a circular movement of senseless repetition and, ultimately, historical stasis and paralysis. Instead, the poem critically enacts the tensions that define the existential predicament of temporal existence. Sheer repetition, it suggests, is no longer simply repetition but a sign of the repressed opportunities for contemporary Jewish emancipation. As a celebration of discontinuity and interruption of the regular flow of time, time's coming to a halt on the Sabbath no longer represents compliance with, and submission to, the grinding force of the eternal return of the same, but rather a creative break or "magic respite," as Draper (D 651) renders Heine's "Zauberfrist" (B 6.1, 125), the space in which repetition can be reimagined as the doorway to difference. The messianic promise of this opening offers a glimpse of a future that shows the present to be an opportunity for a break, change, and transformation.

The Sabbath is thus the promise of the perpetually recurring moment of the recovery of the messianic moment in time, the window to redemption in which the cursed prince "retransmutes" from doglike desolation to the dignity of human life, if only for the short respite of a day of holiday. The time of the Sabbath stands out as the moment when the dialectics of temporality gains its own emancipatory impetus, the chance for a break in which the imprisoning image of the past comes to the fore as the dictate of the alienated condition of modernity. As the celebration of the Sabbath holds out its transformative promise, it shatters the spell of the repressive grip of the grinding power of alienation, albeit only for the duration of a day. In turn, time no longer appears reduced to a fixed and linear order of repetitive moments of succession, but turns into a socially and historically mediated expression of creative life.

"Prinzessin Sabbat" both accentuates this emphatic standstill, punctuating the flow of time and, at the same time, underscores how such a break energizes time's course and direction. The magic cycle of transformation back into humanity and then, again, back into a doglike existence represents an experience of time that is both circular and linear, repetitive and progressive. Heine's description of repetition does not suggest the inescapability of the return of the same but, on the contrary, the possibility that what appears to be a return of the past is in fact the radically emancipatory prospect of, and opening to, a different present and future. Emancipation thus comes into view as something else than simply adjusting one's watch to standard time. Staging past and present in a reciprocal embrace, "Prinzessin Sabbat" spells out the messianic promise of a future that allows us to reimagine the present as more than merely the result of a rearview-mirror vision. Instead, the present appears as the moment that combines transition, rupture, and change, which—subject to reinvention—retrospectively transforms the past through a vision of the future that enables the present to become the moment of what at the same time interconnects and interrupts, thus creating a sense of time as what lasts and changes, each through the other.

While the doglike existence that submits to the dictate of an alienated vision of modernity is restored to its humanity for the elusive moment of the duration of the Sabbath, the return to the doggish world of an alienated modernity that thwarts the hopes for emancipation is inevitable as long as emancipation remains the privilege of those who submit to the dictate to surrender their particularity, a particularity that will always have to appear as the tail wagging the dog. For Heine, the promise of emancipation remains an empty promise as long as a creative Jewish appropriation of Schiller's "Ode to Joy" can only be figured comically as

> Schalet, shining gleam of Heaven,
> Daughter of Elysium! (D 653)

> Schalet, schöner Götterfunken,
> Tochter aus Elysium!" (B 6.1, 128)

And the worship of highbrow culture can only reject such a bold articulation of liberated culture as adulteration.

"Prinzessin Sabbat" exposes the view that casts the Jews as "divided selves" forever locked into their split relationship to time as a curious projection that superimposes modernity's paradox of time onto Jewish existence. Rehearsing this quid pro quo of mistaking modernity's split for a feature characteristic of Jewish identity, "Prinzessin Sabbat"'s phantasmagoric enactment of the drama of enchantment and transformation presents this split as modernity's own. Returning the criticism of Judaism's noncontemporaneity as divided consciousness to modernity itself rather than internalizing the rejection as the posing of "the Jewish question," Heine's poem invites a radically emancipatory understanding of Jewish tradition's enduring emancipatory impulse in modernity.

Echoing the critical line of the argument Marx developed a few years earlier in his essay "On the Jewish Question," Heine's critical plea for a more radical understanding of Jewish emancipation as a placeholder for the pressing need for universal emancipation resonates with the critical function that the unfinished project of Jewish emancipation carries in Benjamin, Adorno, and in Critical Theory more generally.

At the center of the trilogy of the three poems of the "Hebrew Melodies," "Jehuda ben Halevy" takes the reader to a past whose poetic imagination becomes the doorway to the future that is the reader's present. Heine's revisiting of the figure of the exemplary medieval poet Yehuda Halevi comprehends the link between tradition and innovation as constitutive for understanding the problem of history and Halevi's poetic creativity as the hallmark of the rejuvenating power of tradition. For Heine, the medieval poet-philosopher represents the creative power of the tradition (*Aggadah*) that gives the life and endurance that the normative elements (*Halacha*) require to live on. The poet's historical function consists in his or her poetic creation of a historical memory that transmits tradition's energy across generations even when the poets themselves are long gone. For Heine, the life-giving force of tradition rests less with its commentators and institutional custodians than with the creative art of the poet.[66]

"Prinzessin Sabbat" portrays the messianic futurity that the Sabbath offers as the sign that neither past nor present are to be understood without the perspective—however elusive—of messianic hope, a concern that for Benjamin and Adorno will assume a key role for anchoring their critique.[67] "Jehuda ben Halevy" expresses the concern that history and tradition are produced by the art of poetry that links past and present as the continuous effect of the transformative power of commemoration. Performing the process of the writing of history in the form of an ongoing retelling as counterhistory, "Jehuda ben Halevy" gives eloquent articulation to the insight that memory is a process that is always transformative. Transformation is the condition of tradition. Its recognition as emancipatory force is the promise of modernity.

Like a counterthrust, the third and concluding poem of the cycle, "Disputation," ends on a dark note that seems to return the reader back to the Middle Ages. But read together, the cycle of poems of the "Hebrew Melodies" gives voice to the project of reimagining past, present, and future as an inseparably interlinked context: if "Prinzessin Sabbat" is a reminder that the future is imagined through a past that remains present, and "Jehuda ben Halevy" reads the past through the present, the polemically edgy "Disputation" suggests that the present can only be grasped through a critique of the past: a past that reveals uncanny simultaneity with the present. It thus brings home the point reiterated throughout Heine's prose and poetry that, in the end, history is not defined by progress and triumph but characterized instead by standstill, repetition, and the simultaneity of the nonsimultaneous.

"And Only Time Remains"

In his notebooks, Heine comments that in modernity the secular Messiah will arrive by train (B 6.1, 648). As to the question of whether the mission of the Jews has come to an end, he writes:

> The Jews [. . .] Has their mission come to an end?—I believe so when the secular Messiah arrives: industry, work, joy—The secular Messiah arrives by train—Michael [i.e. Germany] paves the way—roses are strewn . . .
>
> Die Juden [. . .] Ist ihre Mission geendigt?—ich glaube, wenn der weltliche Heiland kommt: Industrie, Arbeit, Freude—Der weltliche Heiland kommt auf einer Eisenbahn—Michel bahnt ihm den Weg—Rosen werden gestreut auf . . . (B 6.1, 648)

We can appreciate the deeper meaning of this remark if we pay attention to the significance of the confluence of new technology and finance capitalism that literally brought about a new understanding of time and space, as Heine's visionary description of the effects of the new railways demonstrates. Heine addresses this nexus in an article he wrote in 1843 for the Augsburg *Allgemeine Zeitung*, for which he regularly reported about politics and current events from the "capital of the world," as he called Paris. Reporting on the opening of the new railway lines from Paris to Orleans and Rouen, Heine predicts that the new means of transportation will have profound and lasting consequences. They will not only provide unheard-of comfort, they will at the same time challenge our world in new and unheard-of ways:

> What marvelous changes must now enter into our methods of perception and action. Even the elementary ideas of space and time are tottering; for by the railway space is annihilated and only time remains. (L 8, 368)
>
> Welche Veränderungen müssen jetzt eintreten in unserer Anschauungsweise und in unseren Vorstellungen! Sogar die Elementarbegriffe von Zeit und Raum sind schwankend geworden. Durch die Eisenbahnen wird der Raum getötet, und es bleibt uns nur noch die Zeit übrig. (B 5, 449)

With the arrival of modernity, Heine argued, the old dearly held views of time and space as anchor points of our existence had become subject to changes brought about by the technological revolution. Nothing remained what it was in the face of such radical change, not even time and space, notions that Kant had held to be stable and secure intuitions on which we could rely with a priori certainty. For Heine, all that seemed to be conceptually solid had melted into air, as Marx and Engels would formulate it five years later in the *Communist Manifesto*[68] The challenge seemed so overwhelming that Heine felt the need to add a joke that anxiously underscored the significance of the profound changes ahead:

> Oh, that we had money enough to kill the latter [time] properly [as well]! (L 8, 368f.)
>
> Hätten wir nur Geld genug, um auch letztere anständig zu töten! (ibid.)

If once distant destinations have come into arm's reach and distances have shrunk to insignificance, time has at the same time expanded to such a degree that we might literally feel urged to kill it. With the acceleration of life in modernity, time has become a function of the modes of production and are subject to both expansion and contraction. As a result, time can no longer be taken as a reliable measure or fixing point, but has itself become liquefied and dynamic. In *The Harz Journey*, the dyed-in-the-wool Kantian Saul Ascher found himself pulling out worms when reaching into his pocket to retrieve his watch, an experience that defied his Kantian convictions: time, it turns out, is no longer a fixed notion, no longer steady a priori given reference on which knowledge can safely rely. But while the narrative of modernity is predominantly one of speeding up the tempo, Heine attends to the deeper underlying problem: the expansion rather than the contraction of time, that is, the phenomenon that there seems not only never to be enough time but also, at the same time, too much of it that we wish to kill. Modernity's problem with time might not be that we don't have enough, but always either too much or too little. But too much or too little: the ultimate challenge Heine poses is that of the ever-changing dynamic nature of time. For Heine, history, temporality, and the temporal relations of future, past, and present are no longer categories with a priori definable form or content, but the dynamic sites of critical renegotiation.

6

The Comedy of Body and Mind: Emancipation and the Power of the Affects

Heine's engagement in the struggle for liberation is informed by a vision of emancipation that resonates openly throughout his writing. His self-conscious presentation of himself first as a freedom fighter and only then as a poet reflects his poetics in a programmatic manner. This does not mean that Heine puts political commitments first but rather that his writing's critical purpose defines his poetics from the bottom up. For Heine, politics and poetics are interconnected at a deep level—but are also irreducible to each other, and he is adamant about their autonomy. Rather than identity, the connection between literature and politics is for Heine one of a productive challenge and tension; a challenge that in each and every case needs to be worked out by way of creative negotiation and with an eye to the particular historical context in which the poet gives articulation to form that formulates content dialectically. Giving voice to the project of emancipation can only gain universal traction as long as this call reflects its own specific situation critically. Emancipation understood this way, Heine reminds us, does not recognize any form of universalization that includes the privileging of any one particularism over another. For that would only lead to a sort of indentured servitude for strategic or "practical" reasons:

> But what is the great question of the age?
>
> It is that of emancipation. Not simply the emancipation of the Irish, Greeks, Frankfort Jews, West Indian Negroes, and other oppressed races, but the emancipation of the whole world, and especially that of Europe, which has attained its majority, and now tears itself loose from the iron leading-strings of a privileged aristocracy. (L 3, 104f.)
>
> Was ist aber diese große Aufgabe unserer Zeit?

> Es ist die Emanzipation. Nicht bloß die der Irländer, Griechen, Frankfurter Juden, westindischen Schwarzen und dergleichen gedrückten Volkes, sondern es ist die Emanzipation der ganzen Welt, absonderlich Europas, das mündig geworden ist, und sich jetzt losreißt von dem eisernen Gängelbande der Bevorrechteten, der Aristokratie. (B 2, 376)

For Heine, emancipation is the great task of our time that unites the whole world in all its irreducible differences. The proportions of this project cannot be contained within any sort of political frame. Rather, this task requires a vision based on a rigorous critique whose fuller implications Marx will begin to develop a decade later, but which Heine already grounds in a resolute rethinking of the basic terms of a post-idealist, non-dualist notion of human nature and human needs. Because body and mind are two inseparable but different aspects of human nature, emancipation cannot be abstracted from the way it approaches its task, that is, through a form of language that must reflect on its own materiality—genre, style, tone, diction, and so on. In this context, Heine's following statement receives its full critical significance:

> I really do not know whether I deserve that a laurel wreath be laid on my coffin. Poetry, dearly as I have loved it, has always been to me only a holy plaything or a consecrated means whereby to attain a heavenly end. I have never attached much value to a poetic reputation, and I care little whether my songs are praised or found fault with. But ye may lay a sword on my coffin, for I was a brave soldier in the war of freedom for mankind. (L 3, 114)

> Ich weiß nicht, ob ich es verdiene, daß man mir einst mit dem Lorbeerkranze den Sarg verziere. Die Poesie, wie sehr ich sie auch liebte, war mir immer nur heiliges Spielzeug, oder geweihtes Mittel für himmlische Zwecke. Ich habe nie großen Wert gelegt auf Dichter-Ruhm, und ob man meine Lieder preiset oder tadelt, es kümmert mich wenig. Aber ein Schwert sollt Ihr mir auf den Sarg legen; denn ich war eine braver Soldat im Befreiungskriege der Menschheit. (B 2, 382)

For Heine, emancipation is connected to the rehabilitation of the flesh, the acknowledgment of the needs of the body, the dynamics of pleasure, joy, and suffering, and the fundamental role of the affects. Heine adopts one of the Saint-Simonists' catchiest phrases—that of the "the rehabilitation of matter" or "the rehabilitation of the flesh"—but not without giving it a saucier twist than the sect's sanctimonious vision could accommodate.[1] With Heine, the call for the rehabilitation of the flesh assumes a liberatingly irreverent stance that goes beyond the Saint-Simonist project of social engineering with its modernized form of convent mentality under the strict authority of its self-appointed elders. Heine's call for the rehabilitation of the flesh is a revolutionary call for the liberation of the senses; a sensibility that gives sensualism new meaning as it envisions beauty as a function of joy and pleasure. In revolt against the aesthetics of perfection—which for Heine could only mean an aesthetics of containment—the rehabilitation of matter, the senses, and the flesh promises a liberation from all obsequious submission to conventional forms of authority, rule, and domination.[2]

If Heine had initially hoped to find brothers-in-arms in the Saint-Simonists, he was soon disappointed by the sect's authoritarian organization, which betrayed the very idea of emancipation and instead submitted people to yet another regime that denied them their right to individuality. But while the experience with Saint-Simonism had been disappointing, it provided Heine with an opportunity to advance his own vision of the rehabilitation of the flesh with renewed resolve and in a more sophisticated fashion. If Heine's struggle for emancipation from all forms of repression points far beyond the rehabilitation of the flesh alone, it is because his project is grounded in a theoretically more solid framework than that of the Saint-Simonists, albeit one that bears a significant family resemblance to their vision. The theoretical foundation underlying Heine's stance is one that serves as a critical counterpoint to the powerful discourses of Kant, Hegel, and German Idealism, which determined not only the general philosophical atmosphere of the time but also informed its canonical literary production.

Spinoza's Return

This counterpoint is found in Spinoza, who served Heine as an alternative approach to philosophy, an approach that in Heine's reading offers decisive theoretical leverage for a post-idealist stance. Heine's writing is grounded in an engagement with Spinoza's thought that brings out the emancipatory impulse at the heart of Spinoza's philosophy as a critical project that lays the groundwork for rethinking the relationship between mind and body, the psychosomatic foundation of the affects, and the nature of reason from a consistently post-Cartesian view. It is a project that addresses the problem of the theological-political complex and the desire for teleological closure as fundamental stumbling blocks for a progressive and universal emancipation. Heine's resolute embrace of Spinoza offers a literary enactment of some of the signal ideas of Spinoza's thought that—in line with Spinoza's immanent thinking—does not reproduce or imitate Spinoza's propositions but sets the critical force of his thought free through the performative enactment of their implications in his literary production.

Heine had taken a keen interest in Spinoza long before he encountered Saint-Simonism. He was introduced to Spinoza by one of his closest school friends, an avid and apparently radicalized Spinozist, with whom he spent hours on end reading and discussing the philosopher. We only know Heine's young companion by the names "herring philosopher" and "the atheist." Nearly outcast by his father because of his Spinozism, Heine's brother Max tells us, this son of a wealthy grain merchant was rarely found at his family's dinner table, but instead carried a piece of bread and a herring in one pocket and philosophical writings in another. The odd fellow—as Heine's brother characterizes him—died young due to an illness. But he also notes:

> For one, it is certain that the two young men read Spinoza's works together, got acquainted early on with rationalist writings, and generally entertained very serious discussions that were not in keeping with their age.
>
> Gewiss ist, dass die beiden jungen Leute gemeinschaftlich Spinoza's Werke gelesen, sich mit rationalistischen Schriften früh vertraut, und überhaupt sehr ernste, gar nicht ihrem Alter gemäße Discussionen geführt haben.[3]

And, Max adds,

> My brother never liked to talk about the young yellowish pale fellow with the uncanny regard.
>
> Mein Bruder sprach nie gern über den jungen gelbbleichen Menschen mit dem unheimlichen Blicke.[4]

While Heine's brother Max may have enriched his account with a good deal of his own opinion, the anecdote is illuminating not only for showing that Heine encountered Spinoza at an early age but also for the light it sheds on the particular tradition of Spinoza reception to which he first was exposed. For at this early stage, the Spinoza to which Heine was introduced was not the "Jewish," God-intoxicated thinker that Herder, Goethe, and Novalis would extol, but the champion of subversive, anti-religious, and materialist thought embraced by the radical French philosophers of the late eighteenth century. If Spinoza became a reliable anchor for Heine's critical thinking early on, this grounding from the beginning accentuated the radical, critical, and subversive thrust of Spinoza's thought rather than the sublime, spiritual, and religious impulse Heine would later mobilize as well for strategic reasons.

Understanding the roots of Heine's politics of emancipation in Spinoza requires accounting for Spinoza's subversive and materialist impulse together with his prophetic and messianic impulse in a manner that is unafraid of acknowledging Jewish sources as an equally important aspect of Spinoza's critical thrust. Reducing Spinoza to one or the other only defuses the emancipatory force of his thought. Heine was drawn precisely to the way Spinoza grasped the constitutive, inseparable link between the social/political, the material, and the personal/subjective. Heine's early and intense discussions with his friend opened up the possibility of embracing Spinoza as the revolutionary thinker who understood emancipation as the moment in which the universal and the particular are brought together.

For Heine, Spinoza serves as a resource that allows him to give voice to his own thinking without submitting to the oppressive pressures of the dominant forms of philosophical discourse, be it in the consummate shape of Hegel's philosophy or in the derivative and philosophically less impressive, but no less domineering, form of Saint-Simonism. We find traces of Spinoza throughout Heine's poetry and prose, in his fiction and critical writings alike, from his earliest writings in the 1820s to the last lines written in his "mattress grave," in the unrelenting face of death.[5] Spinoza kept Heine theoretically grounded, and rather than following him as an alternative to philosophers such as Kant, Hegel, or Schelling, Heine made use of Spinoza to formulate his own stance freely and self-confidently. This comes as no surprise. From his earliest reception, Spinoza fostered readers' reliance on their own thinking. Beginning with the circle of his friends, his readers would form free discussion groups. Initially enjoying the privilege of being able to passing on queries to the author whose answers were in turn read and discussed by the group, this tradition of Spinoza reception turned after his death into one of studying Spinoza together on their own. Heine and his friend's intense conversations are an important link of this transmission mode of Spinoza reception that some of his most dedicated readers cultivated as they engaged with the philosopher in intimate discussion groups such as the ones Lessing and Mendelssohn or Goethe and his circle formed at decisive moments of their intellectual careers.[6] The form and structure of Spinoza's *Ethics* as a kind of manual for the self-empowerment of the mind through recognition of the psychodynamic power of the affects led his friend Ehrenfried Walther von Tschirnhaus, for example, an early reader and interlocutor, to fashion his own *Medicina mentis*, a therapeutic manual for the mind.[7] This "dialogical" moment is a constitutive part of the therapeutic design of Spinoza's *Ethics* and *Treatise on the Emendation of the Intellect*. It is this open structure of Spinoza's thought that allows Heine to anchor his writing in Spinoza in a creative fashion.

To Heine, Spinoza offers recourse to an alternative approach to reimagining the individual, society, culture, politics, and ethics in contrast to the way philosophy was practiced at the modern German university spearheaded by the University of Berlin during Hegel's tenure and in the circle of young Hegelians like Eduard Gans, Ludwig Markus, and Moses Moser, who were instrumental in shaping the agenda of the Verein für Cultur und Wissenschaft der Juden. Like Hegel, whom Heine on occasion encountered in person, these friends played an important role in Heine's intellectual life as interlocutors with whom he shared common interests but with whose philosophical commitments he did not always agree.

In the lead article of the inaugural issue of the Verein's journal *Zeitschrift für die Wissenschaft des Judenthums*, Immanuel Wolf (i.e., Wohlwill) singled out Spinoza as the key intellectual force expressing the association's aspirations of advancing cultural renewal in the context of the Jewish emancipation, a view that would resonate with Heine's later experience that reading Spinoza felt like the morning breeze he so suggestively described as whiffling through Spinoza's works.[8] For Heine and his friends, Spinoza had become the Jewish entry point to philosophy that Hegel and others seemed to deny their Jewish fellow beings, as they were only prepared to grant such entry to Jews if they were willing to check their Jewish identity at the door of German culture.[9] In contrast, Spinoza stood for a vision that held the promise of a universal and holistic liberation that would no longer distinguish between religious and other forms of social association, but declare every human's potential ability to emancipate themselves regardless of their background, provenance, or social class.

Spinoza's *Ethics* offers a sustained vision of self-emancipation that leads from bondage and servitude to freedom. The process of liberation is powered by the affects, whose liberating force is released through Spinoza's critical move to end the deadlock enforced by the Cartesian separation of body and mind. Spinoza's recourse to the affects as the driving force at the interface of body and mind—which refuses reduction to one or the other—recovers a new paradigm for understanding action and praxis, one that leads to a new appreciation of the complex ways in which body and mind interrelate. As a result, Spinoza emerges as the philosopher whose recovery of the dynamic power of the affects sets the stage for rethinking the dynamic function of joy, pleasure, and sadness with a new focus on their materiality.

Spinoza plays a critical role in Heine, a role his writing reflects in occasionally striking fashion. Heine's fictionalization of Spinoza recovers a critical aspect of Spinoza's liberation philosophy, which the academic discipline of philosophy had eclipsed and which Heine took great pains to recover. But Heine's renegotiation of Spinoza's place in the history of philosophy does not just affect the historiography of philosophy, it also carries deeper implications. It is directly linked to Heine's agenda of the rehabilitation of the flesh, the fight for universal emancipation and freedom of speech, art, and the recognition of the emancipatory role of fiction. Heine's embrace of Spinoza also has important implications for a critical reexamination of the conditions of the production of knowledge more generally, as well as for rethinking politics and social questions of justice and equality. In Heine, these issues form an irreducible nexus just as they do in Spinoza. This agenda animates every line and verse of Heine's writings. The liberating force of Heine's prose and poetry derives its thrust from this vigorous appropriation and adoption of Spinoza or, more precisely, from the fresh and original rereading of Spinoza that Heine's writing instantiates.

Heine first introduces Spinoza in his writing, if apparently only in passing, in *The North Sea, Part 3*, an early part of the *Travel Pictures*. This is the passage from which Freud lifts Heine's reference to Spinoza as his "fellow unbeliever" (*Unglaubensgenosse*), as detailed in Chapter 2.[10] The passage deserves attention because the reference to Spinoza is, at this early point in Heine's writing career, neither to his *Ethics* nor the *Theological-Political*

Treatise, but to the less known *Political Treatise*, a reference that indicates more than a superficial familiarity with Spinoza.[11] More significantly, it suggests Heine's appreciation of Spinoza's view of power as a complex interlinking of the sphere of law with the theological-political and the dynamic play of the affects, whose dual aspect of body and mind makes up the life force of existence Spinoza calls *conatus*. Apparently an illustration of Spinoza's critical tenet that "might is right,"[12] Heine's comment demonstrates a sophisticated view of Spinoza's understanding of power, which he musters here to buttress the fight for emancipation announced in the passage quoted at the opening of this chapter.

The passage in question in *The North Sea* comments on the recent mediatization of the German states as a result of the dissolution of the Holy Roman Empire of the German nation in the wake of the French Revolution and the Napoleonic reforms in Prussian-ruled territories and their reversal after the French army's departure. As the collapsing empire dissolved into various power struggles, the retired aristocracy returned with their ancient claims to equal the royalty in rank and birth, demonstrating an appreciation for genealogy equal to that which Arabs show for the pedigree of their horses,

> and indeed with the same object, as they well know that Germany has been in all ages the great princely stud from which all the reigning neighbouring families have been supplied with mares and stallions. (L 2, 249f.)

> und zwar aus derselben Absicht, indem sie wohl wissen, daß Deutschland von jeher das große Fürstengestüte war, das alle regierenden Nachbarshäuser mit den nötigen Mutterpferden und Beschälern versehen muß. (B 2, 232)

Lamenting the loss of their sovereign rights in the wake of the revolution, the aristocrats seem to have forgotten that the historical conditions on which their rule depended have long since changed. In a move that challenges any legitimation of power based on historical rights, and subjects all such claims to radical revolutionary scrutiny, Heine notes:

> These persons have of late suffered great injustice, inasmuch as they have been robbed of a sovereignty to which they had as good right as the greater princes, unless, indeed, any one will assume, with my fellow-unbeliever Spinoza, that that which cannot maintain itself by its own power has no right to exist. (L 2, 248f.)

> Diesen Leuten ist in der letzten Zeit ein großes Unrecht geschehen, indem man sie einer Souveränität beraubte, wozu sie ein eben so gutes Recht habe, wie die größeren Fürsten, wenn man nicht etwa [*etwa nicht, wie mein Unglaubensgenosse Spinoza,*] annehmen will, daß dasjenige, was

> sich nicht durch eigene Kraft erhalten kann, auch kein Recht hat, zu existieren. (B 2, 232)

Putting this demonstration of sympathetic understanding into perspective, however, Heine continues:

> But for the greatly divided Germany, it was a benefit that this array of 16mo [sextodecimo, i.e. pocket book] despots were obliged to resign their power. It is terrible when we reflect on the number which we poor Germans are obliged to feed, for although these mediatised princes no longer wield the sceptre, they still wield knives, forks, and spoons, and do not eat hay, and if they did, hay would still be expensive enough. (L 2, 249)
>
> Für das vielzersplitterte Deutschland war es aber eine Wohltat, daß diese Anzahl von Sedezdespötchen ihr Regieren einstellen mußten. Es ist schrecklich, wenn man bedenkt wie viele derselben wir armen Deutschen zu ernähren haben. Wenn diese Mediatisierten auch nicht mehr das Zepter führen, so führen sie doch noch immer Löffel, Messer und Gabel, und sie essen keinen Hafer, und auch der Hafer wäre teuer genug. (B 2, 232)

By exposing the retired aristocracy's attempts to return to the queue for power—by claiming an equality of birth they deny to their former subjects—Heine exposes the hypocrisy of their obliviousness to their own robbery of others. If Spinoza's point was that rights arise only from actual and sustainable power, that is, an ability to act, rather than from underhanded theft, robbery, and crime, Heine's recourse to Spinoza brings home the faulty logic of the nobility's claim of ancient rights, and highlights the subversively critical character of Spinoza's approach:

> Each natural thing has as much right by nature as it has power to exist and have effects.[13]
>
> Unamquanque rem naturalem tantum juris ex natura habere, quantum potentiae habet ad existendum et operandum.[14]

Heine's showcasing of Spinoza—initially explicitly, and in later editions implicitly—as a critical political theorist with far-reaching philosophically critical implications, carries a strong signal that runs against the grain of the Spinoza reception of his day. This exposure of the underlying nexus of Spinoza's dual-aspect monism—in which body and mind are two different aspects of the same being—against the Cartesian view that two different substances are miraculously coordinated with each other, is a crucially critical moment in Heine's approach to the complex of power and politics.[15] This approach is in pointed opposition to the popular reception of Spinoza that began with Jacobi's ignition of the pantheism controversy in the eighteenth century, which fixated on the metaphysical aspects of Spinoza's philosophy and went on to define (with the exception of the same Jacobi, who had just a few years earlier publicly embraced Spinoza's progressive political outlook)[16] the philosophical debates surrounding Spinoza, from Leibniz to Hegel and the German idealists.[17]

A few years later, in *On the History of Religion and Philosophy in Germany*, Heine has Spinoza take center stage as the hidden but central philosophical force of modern German thought. Heine's dramatic introduction of Spinoza deserves attention for the way it foregrounds the palpably materialist aspect of Spinoza's thought. In the guise of a description of Spinoza's powerful affective resonance with his readers, Heine highlights the immanentist stance of his philosophy. His presentation enacts a literary description of Spinoza's effects on readers that reproduces this same readerly experience in striking fashion, bringing home his philosophy's immanent thrust. This way, Heine's evocatively embodied language rehearses the critical principle of immanence with stunning eloquence.

For Heine, then, Spinoza serves as critical reminder that philosophy, as well as literary production and critique in general, can no longer ignore the material conditions on which they rest:

> When we read Spinoza, we are seized with a feeling like that of seeing nature at its grandest in most vigorous repose: a forest of thoughts, tall as the sky, whose blooming tree-tops sway back and forth, while imperturbable trunks stand rooted in the eternal soil. There is a certain soft breeze in the writings of Spinoza which is inexplicable. It stirs the reader with the winds of the future. The spirit of the Hebrew prophets still rested perhaps on their late descendant. (OH 50f.)
>
> Bei der Lektüre des Spinoza ergreift uns ein Gefühl wie beim Anblick der großen Natur in ihrer lebendigsten Ruhe. Ein Wald von himmelhohen Gedanken, deren blühende Wipfel in wogender Bewegung sind, während die unerschütterlichen Baumstämme in der ewigen Erde wurzeln. Es ist ein gewißer Hauch in den Schriften des Spinoza, der unerklärlich. Man wird angeweht wie von den Lüften der Zukunft. Der Geist der hebräischen Poeten ruhte vielleicht noch auf ihrem späten Enkel. (B 3, 561f.)

The rich imagery, interwoven with references from the Bible and Goethe's poetry (which Heine will call an illustration of Spinoza's thought),[18] emphasizes how Spinoza affects his readers, touching them as if by the breath that emanates from his thought. Heine's palpably physical poetic imagery plays here with the biblical notion of the divine breath that animates creation but which, rather than being disembodied, has powerfully physical as well as ethereal connotations. A metaphor for immanence, the description enacts the experience of immanence in a speech act that performatively invokes the reaction it describes, illustrating the bodily undercurrent of Heine's poetics as the powerful imagery seizes the reader's imagination.

Remarkably, Heine concludes his excursus on Spinoza in *On the History of Religion and Philosophy in Germany* by pointing to the *Political Treatise* as evidence of Spinoza's sovereign grasp of politics (OH 52; B 3, 563). The French translation, with its recommendation to read the *Political Treatise*, is even more direct in encouraging engagement with Spinoza.[19] As Heine goes on to elaborate how pantheism's materialist grasp of reality constitutes the best of modern German philosophy's critical substance, he notes that pantheism is less a term he uses to describe Spinoza's "system" than his way of referring more generally to a certain "way of thinking" (*Anschauungsweise*, OH 54; B 3, 565).

Heine's agenda—to "rehabilitate matter, to reinstate it in its dignity, to recognize its moral worth and give it religious consecration, to reconcile it with spirit" (OH 56; B 3, 568)—formulates the program of emancipation that pantheism in the raw form of pagan Germanic folklore had anticipated in premodern times and to which Spinoza had given philosophically refined expression. The narrative Heine unfolds is the story of the development of modern German thought and culture out of the struggle between sensualism and spiritualism. *On the History of Religion and Philosophy* tracks the course of intellectual history as the double movement of the emancipation of matter from the tutelage of the spirit and the mind's emancipation from domination by the body. We will see in the next chapter how Heine's narrative addresses the problem of history writing as a form of secularization. For the purpose of this chapter, the relevant point is that Spinoza serves as the philosophical guarantor for the theoretical soundness of the program of the rehabilitation of matter.

Spinoza serves also as connection that bridges Heine's discussion of the battle between Christianity and local forms of pagan pantheism in German lands in Part 1 of the essay and Heine's presentation of Goethe's most accomplished poetry as sublime pantheism in Part 3. Heine deepens the significance of Spinoza's philosophy, but not without reiterating the profoundly materialist implication his thought had, especially for Goethe, the most refined exemplar of German poetry before Heine.

In Part 3, Heine returns to Spinoza through a unique appreciation of Goethe:

> Goethe's pantheism is thus very different from that of the heathen. To express myself concisely: Goethe was the Spinoza of poetry. All of Goethe's poems are suffused by the same spirit which stirs us in Spinoza's writings. (OH 98f.)
>
> Der Pantheismus des Goethe ist also von dem heidnischen sehr unterschieden. Um mich kurz auszudrücken: Goethe war der Spinoza der

> Poesie. Alle Gedichte Goethes sind durchdrungen von demselben Geiste, der uns auch in den Schriften des Spinoza anweht. (B 3, 618)

The image of the spirit/breeze that blows through the pages of Spinoza's writings becomes the metonymic reminder that connects Spinoza with Goethe, underscoring their shared acknowledgement of matter and the body. As Heine adds assertively,

> There is no doubt that Goethe paid tribute without reservation to the doctrine of Spinoza. (OH 99)
>
> Daß Goethe gänzlich der Lehre des Spinoza huldigte, ist keinem Zweifel unterworfen. (B 3, 618)

Two pages later, the characterization of Goethe's literary works climaxes, as if accentuated by a drumbeat, in this conclusion:

> But it is in the small songs that Goethe's pantheism is documented most purely and charmingly. Spinoza's doctrine has emerged from its mathematical chrysalis and flutters around us in Goethean song. Thus the rage of our Orthodox and Pietists against Goethe's songs. They grope with their pious bear claws at this butterfly, which constantly eludes them. For it is so delicately ethereal, so softly winged. You French cannot understand it if you do not know the language. These Goethe songs have a mischievous magic which is indescribable. The harmonic verses wrap themselves around your heart like an affectionate lover. The word embraces you, while the thought kisses you. (OH 100)
>
> Aber am reinsten und lieblichsten beurkundet sich dieser Goethesche Pantheismus in seinen kleinen Liedern. Die Lehre des Spinoza hat sich aus der mathematischen Hülle entpuppt und umflattert uns als Goethesches Lied. Daher die Wut unserer Orthodoxen und Pietisten gegen das Goethesche Lied. Mit ihren frommen Bärentatzen tappen sie nach diesem Schmetterling, der ihnen beständig entflattert. Das ist so zart ätherisch, so duftig beflügelt. Ihr Franzosen könnt Euch keinen Begriff machen, wenn Ihr die Sprache nicht kennt. Diese Goetheschen Lieder haben einen neckischen Zauber, der unbeschreibbar. Die harmonischen Verse umschlingen dein Herz wie eine zärtliche Geliebte; das Wort umarmt dich, während der Gedanke dich küsst. (B 3, 620)

One the one hand an illuminating commentary on the plasticity of Goethe's poetry, the passage articulates at the same time the critical impetus of Heine's own Spinozist poetics. In contrast to Heine's criticism of Goethe's occasionally indifferentist stance and its politically conservative tendencies, Heine's emphasis on Goethe's Spinozist inclinations reclaims the liberating impulse of Goethe's legacy. In associating Goethe with

Spinoza and, through Spinoza, with the powerful undercurrents of ancient pantheism, Heine recovers the hidden force of Goethe's writing and its profoundly liberating thrust, which he pits against the repressive attempts at canonization by the nationalistic tendencies of the emerging literary historiography.

Heine describes the difference between Spinoza and Goethe in terms of the difference between a "mathematical shell" and a poetic core. The image of the chrysalis transforming into a butterfly links Goethe—and, by extension, Heine—to a genetic model that casts literature and philosophy as different stages of life animated by one and the same life force, or what Spinoza calls *conatus*.

This return of body and matter, of the material conditions underlying every form of life, runs through Heine's writing as a recurrent theme. It assumes at times a less refined artistic form than Goethe had been able to impart. But even in Goethe, the carefully wrapped return of the senses runs on the energy of the liberating power of comedy. A more explicitly comedic and pleasure-affirming, hands-on version of this return can be found in Heine's treatment of the odd couple Don Quixote and Sancho Panza.

Brain and Belly: Don Quixote and Sancho Panza

The Romantic School (*Die Romantische Schule*), which Heine finished shortly before he began to write *On the History of Religion and Philosophy in Germany*, introduces Cervantes's *Don Quixote* as an exploration of the dialectic that informs the struggle between body and mind under spiritualist rule. Like Kafka's motley cast of subaltern characters, Sancho Panza and the various aspects of the materiality of life that creep into the novel to subvert and expose the repressive character of life lived under the domination of the mind bring out the counterforce without which life would not only be not worth living, it would be impossible.[20] For Heine, Cervantes's odd protagonist couple assumes paradigmatic significance for understanding life's bare necessities, including the profound role played by joy and pleasure in the life of the mind. Discussing Cervantes's intentions, Heine remarks:

> Did he allegorise the soul in the form of Don Quixote and the body in that of Sancho Panza? And is the whole poem a great mystery, in which the question of spirit and matter is discussed with terrible truthfulness? This much I see in the book, that the poor material Sancho must suffer much for the spiritual Don Quixote, that he gets for the noble views of his master the most ignoble stripes, and that he is always more sensible than his high-trotting master, for he knows that lashes and cuffs have an evil taste, but the little sausages in an *olla podrida* a very good one.

> Indeed, the body often seems to have more insight than the soul, and man thinks frequently far better with his back and belly than with his head. (L 5, 358)

> Hat er vielleicht in der Gestalt des Don Quixote unseren Geist, und in der Gestalt des Sancho Pansa unseren Leib allegorisiert, und das ganze Gedicht wäre alsdann nichts anders als ein großes Mysterium, wo die Frage über den Geist und die Materie in ihrer gräßlichsten Wahrheit diskutiert wird? So viel sehe ich in dem Buche, daß der arme materielle Sancho für die spirituellen Don Quixoterien sehr viel leiden muß, daß er für die nobelsten Absichten seines Herren sehr oft die ignobelsten Prügel empfängt, und daß er immer verständiger ist, als sein hochtrabender Herr; denn er weiß, daß Prügel sehr schlecht, die Würstchen einer Olla-Potrida aber sehr gut schmecken. Wirklich, der Leib scheint oft mehr Einsicht zu haben als der Geist, und der Mensch denkt oft viel richtiger mit Rücken und Magen als mit dem Kopf. (B 3, 431)

Referring to Tieck's translation of *Don Quixote*, Heine points out the irony:

> It is droll enough that the Romantic school has given us the best translation of a work in which its own folly is most amusingly ridiculed. (L 5, 357 note 2)

> Spaßhaft genug ist es, daß gerade die romantische Schule uns die beste Übersetzung eines Buches geliefert hat, worin ihre eigne Narrheit am ergötzlichsten durchgehechelt wird. (430)

As early as 1820, Heine had singled out romanticism's conflicted relationship to spirituality and the senses as the key problem compromising modern thought and literature. He saw the continuation of medieval forms of Christianity and feudalism as obscuring the challenge that modernity poses to the dualist worldview behind Christian spiritualism. With the arrival of modernity, Heine suggested, the narrative of the struggle between spiritualism and sensualism could no longer be viewed as an embodiment of the battle between good and evil. Against such a metaphysically repressive form of romanticism, Heine offered an alternative vision devoid of the theological-political implications of German romanticism, which even in its ostensibly irreligious variations remained steeped in Christian-inflected notions of privileging mind over body. As Heine puts it in his short but programmatic essay "Die Romantik,"

> But many who noted the immense influence of Christianity—and of knighthood in its wake—on Romantic poetry believe they must now mix both into their poetry in order to imprint it with the character of Romanticism. However, I believe that Christianity and knighthood were only means of getting Romanticism through the door; its flames have long

> been burning on the altar of our poetry; no priest has to add any more sacred oil, and no knight has to stand guard. Germany is now free: no cleric [Pfaffe] any longer has the power to whip German bodies to work, and because of this the German muse shall again be a free, blossoming, unaffected, true German maiden, no languishing nun, and no haughtily aristocratic knight's lady.
>
> Viele aber, die bemerkt haben, welchen ungeheuren Einfluß das Christentum, und in dessen Folge, das Rittertum, auf die romantische Poesie ausgeübt haben, vermeinen nun beides in ihren Dichtungen einmischen zu müssen, um denselben den Charakter der Romantik aufzudrücken. Doch glaube ich, Christentum und Rittertum waren nur Mittel, um der Romantik Eingang zu schaffen; die Flamme derselben leuchtet schon längst auf dem Altar unserer Poesie; kein Priester braucht noch geweihtes Öl hinzugießen, und kein Ritter braucht mehr bei ihr die Waffenwacht zu halten. Deutschland ist jetzt frei; kein Pfaffe vermag mehr die deutschen Leiber zur Fron zu peitschen, und deshalb soll auch die deutsche Muse wieder ein freies, blühendes, unaffektiertes, ehrlich deutsches Mädchen sein, und kein schmachtendes Nönnchen, und kein ahnenstolzes Ritterfräulein. (B 1, 401)

At the heart of German romanticism, the dualist split between mind and body carried the metaphysically infused dichotomy between spiritualism and sensualism into modernity, where it continued to propagate an anachronistic "medieval" mindset. Heine's later work on the romantic school and on the historical development of religion and modern thought in Germany would further expose this view of the absolute sovereignty of the spirit over the body as blind to the reality behind the immense battle between the spiritual and the sensual impulses, respectively embodied by Christianity on the one hand and by raw pagan undercurrents on the other, which Heine addressed as primitive forms of pantheism.

In 1820, at the time of the conception of Heine's essay, such a view was still provocatively subversive. In Heine's mind, however, it is clear that modernity means a departure from metaphysically entrenched dualism and a move to reclaiming the sovereign rights of the senses—and not just in aesthetic terms. As the young poet and critic who wrote the short essay on romanticism, Heine concluded his first manifesto on literature thus:

> If only this view were shared by many! Then there would soon be no more dispute between Romantics and sculptors. Yet many a laurel must wilt before the olive leaf grows again on our Mount Parnassus.
>
> Möchten doch viele diese Ansicht teilen! Dann gäbe es bald keinen Streit mehr zwischen Romantikern und Plastikern. Doch mancher Lorbeer muß welken, ehe wieder das Ölblatt auf unserem Parnassus hervorgrünt. (B 1, 401)

It is no coincidence that as paradigmatic "Plastiker," or literary sculptors, Heine singled out both Goethe and August Wilhelm von Schlegel (B 1, 400), his seminal academic teacher who at the time encouraged him to pursue his poetic calling. While Heine became increasingly critical towards Schlegel, Goethe remained a supreme yet sovereignly freestanding figure toward whom he continued to feel a deep underlying affinity despite all differences.

The drama of this struggle to break free from the hold of Christian repression and reinstate the dignity of the senses is acted out in the story of Don Quixote and Sancho Panza, the boisterous relationship between the ascetic spiritualist and the hedonistic sensualist. For Heine, they represent two sides of the same coin of human existence. Neither of them is able to live without the other, and their intertwined relationship defines the condition of human life. Taken together as one figure, they represent, Heine suggests, the novel's true protagonist. Contrasting opposites, they exemplify the feisty antagonism that drives human existence: the enduring reciprocal relationship between body and mind. If separated, their lives would end. Yoked together, they serve as an allegory for the predicament of human existence and as an object lesson on the consequences of the repression of either and the elevation of one over the other. Heine developed these ideas in his introduction to an illustrated edition of a German translation of Cervantes's novel in 1837, which he was commissioned to write. In this introduction, he notes:

> Now, with regard to the two characters called Don Quixote and Sancho Panza, who constantly parody and yet so wonderfully complement each other that they constitute the novel's actual protagonist, they both testify equally to the author's grasp of art and intellectual profundity.[21]
>
> Was nun jene zwei Gestalten betrifft, die sich Don Quichote und Sancho Pansa nennen, sich beständig parodieren und doch so wunderbar ergänzen, daß sie den eigentlichen Helden des Romans bilden, so zeugen sie im gleichen Maße von dem Kunstsinn, wie von der Geistestiefe des Dichters. (B 4, 165)

In a remarkable instance of self-quotation from the *Travel Pictures*, Heine opens the introduction with a flashback to his first encounter with the novel. He conjures the setting of this reading experience in a way that spells out this hermeneutic situation's complex material conditions, which will inform the young reader's future poetics:

> *Strange*! "The Life and Deeds of the Sagacious Knight, Don Quixote de la Mancha," written by Don Miguel de Cervantes Saavedra, was the first book which I read after I had attained a tolerably boy-age of discretion and had become to a certain degree familiar with the nature of letters. (L 3, 320)

> Seltsam! *Leben und Taten des scharfsinnigen Junkers Don Quixote von La Mancha, beschrieben von Miguel de Cervantes Saavedra* war das erste Buch, das ich gelesen habe, nachdem ich schon in ein verständiges Knabenalter getreten, und des Buchstabenwesens einigermaßen kundig war. (B 4, 151; B 2, 522)

Heine continues the extended self-quotation, invoking the romantic composition of this literary encounter that now, in its reiteration, serves to evoke the enchanted world of the novel:

> I can well remember the bit of leisure time when I early one morning stole away from home and hastened to the Court Garden, that I might read "Don Quixote" without being disturbed. It was a beautiful May-day; the blooming spring lay lurking in the silent morning light, listening to the sweet praises of her flatterer the nightingale; and the bird sang so softly and caressingly, with such melting enthusiasm, that the most shame-faced buds sprang into life, and the love-longing grass and the sun-rays quivering in perfume kissed more hurriedly, and trees and flowers trembled for sheer rapture. (L 3, 320f.)
>
> Ich erinnere mich noch ganz genau jener kleinen Zeit, wo ich mich eines frühen Morgens von Haus wegstahl, und nach dem Hofgarten eilte, um dort ungestört den *Don Quixote* zu lesen. Es war ein schöner Maitag, lauschend im stillen Morgenlichte lag der blühende Frühling, und ließ sich loben von der Nachtigall, seiner süßen Schmeichlerin, und diese sang ihr Loblied so karessierend weich, so schmelzend enthusiastisch, daß die verschämtesten Knospen aufsprangen, und die lüsternen Gräser und die duftigen Sonnenstrahlen sich hastiger küßten, und Bäume und Blumen schauerten, vor eitlem Entzücken. (B 2, 522; B 4, 151)

In fact, as the self-citation continues, the reader finds him or herself, along with the narrator, already immersed in the enchanted world of the novel. The mimetic gesture of reproducing the novel's interior highlights its proto-romantic features as cues for the significant role material conditions play in literary imagination. Heine stages this moment of poetic revelation as a replay of romantic irony's double reflection:

> But I sat myself down on an old mossy stone-bench in the so-called "Walk of Sighs," near the waterfall, and solaced my little heart with the great adventures of the daring knight. In my childish uprightness of heart, I took it all in sober earnest, and ridiculously as the poor hero was treated by luck, I still thought that it was a matter of course, and must be so, the being laughed at as well as being wounded, and that troubled me sadly as I sympathised with it all in my soul. (L 3, 321)

> Ich aber setzte mich auf eine alte moosige Steinbank in der sogenannten Seufzerallee unfern des Wasserfalls, und ergötzte mein kleines Herz an den großen Abenteuern des kühnen Ritters. In meiner kindischen Ehrlichkeit nahm ich alles für baren Ernst; so lächerlich auch dem armen Helden von dem Geschick mitgespielt wurde, so meinte ich doch, das müsse so sein, das gehöre nun mal zum Heldentum, das Ausgelachtwerden eben so gut wie die Wunden des Leibes, und jenes verdroß mich eben so sehr, wie ich diese in meiner Seele mitfühlte. (B 2, 522; B 4, 151)

The reader's naivety—as that of an unsuspecting child—cancels the reflective distance on which the novelist's contract with the reader depends. But by misunderstanding and misconstruing the fictional "contract," the narrator repeats the critical move by which the novel sustains its continuous ironic exposure of the snares of fiction, all the while highlighting the vividly brimming animation that is the result of the text's self-reflective attention to the material aspects of its fiction. In a pointedly post-romantic manner, the materiality of this experience is no longer shut out, but is embraced as the engine of a form of irony that, Heine claims, is Cervantes's legacy: an irony grounded squarely in the material conditions of life, an irony whose liberating force works against the paralyzing lure of the domesticated forms of romantic irony that defined the romanticism of the Schlegel brothers—Tieck, Novalis, Hoffmann, and Eichendorff, among others. In mimetic but at the same time parodic fashion, Heine exposes the poverty of such forms of appropriating romantic irony by mustering *Don Quixote* both as its original paradigm and as a safeguard against the allure of such a romanticism, which Cervantes had already lampooned:

> I was a child, and knew nothing of the irony which God had twined into his world as he created it, and I could have found it in my heart to weep the bitterest tears when the noble knight, for all his heroic courage, received only ingratitude and blows. (L 3, 321)
>
> Ich war ein Kind und kannte nicht die Ironie, die Gott in die Welt hineingeschaffen, und die der große Dichter, in seiner gedruckten Kleinwelt nachgeahmt hatte—und ich konnte die bittersten Tränen vergießen, wenn der edle Ritter, für all seinen Edelmut, nur Undank und Prügel genoß. (B 2, 522; B 4, 151)

And so it is precisely a naïve readerly disposition that is able to pick up on the literary cues to which more experienced readers have become oblivious in learning to disregard their affects, that is, their bodily responses. As an unrefined and unschooled child reader, the narrator is less subject to censorship and more openly responsive to the bodily pleasures that come with the joy of reading. The passage continues:

> And as I, who was as yet unpractised in reading, pronounced every word aloud, it was possible for birds and trees, brook and flowers, to hear everything with me, and as such innocent beings of nature knew as little as children of the irony of the great world, they took it all for sober earnest, and wept with me over the sorrows of the poor knight; even a worn-out old oak sighed deeply, and the waterfall shook more rapidly his white beard and seemed to scold at the wickedness of the world. (L 3, 321f.)

> Und da ich, noch ungeübt im Lesen, jedes Wort laut aussprach, so konnten die Vögel und Bäume, Bach und Blumen alles mit anhören, und da solche unschuldige Naturwesen, eben so wie die Kinder, von der Weltironie nichts wissen, so hielten sie gleichfalls alles für baren Ernst, und weinten mit über die Leiden des armen Ritters, sogar eine alte ausgediente Eiche schluchzte, und der Wasserfall schüttelte heftiger seinen weißen Bart, und schien zu schelten auf die Schlechtigkeit der Welt. (B 2, 522f.; B 4, 151f.)[22]

Unaware of the "irony of the great world" (*Weltironie*), the young and inexperienced reader might take fiction for reality but, ironically, by ignoring the fictional contract, he brings out the deeper ironies that are lost on the more sophisticated literary consumers who, reading for Romantic irony, miss the challenging aspects of the more material side of ironies that are devoid of any poetic sheen. While the more sophisticated readers' temptation is to instrumentalize literary imagination for the purpose of consumption, such reading comes at the cost of rarefying the materiality of readerly experience into a hermeneutic exercise that substitutes aesthetic experience for pleasure. In Heine's reading, Cervantes exposes the dialectics of sublimation, a subversive act of recognition that liberates the oppressive force of sublimation and sets free the explosive power of pleasure that drives the act of unrestrained reading that conventional hermeneutics seeks to exorcise.

While the young Heine may have misconstrued the point of the novel and the melancholy lesson of real life, he retains a crucial aspect of literary fiction that more mature readers might easily discard: the process of reading operates on a level of the dynamic play of affects that defies a neat and tidy reduction to any particular effect. Instead, fiction extends the conflicts it narrates to the reader, a shift that complicates the escape route that romantic irony had meant to offer. The false heroism of the failed knight is a story about the high costs of the separation of body and mind in which the reification of this dichotomy results in the atrophy of life. Heine's identification of the romantic scene of his experience of reading highlights the material conditions of literary consumption, bringing home the point that the poetics of fiction cannot be separated from its material context. The naïve resistance of a child's reading is powerful enough to call the bluff of the high canonical construct of literature as escape, reclaiming literature's critical power of disenchantment by way of charming the reader, a dialectic of which romantic irony is a symptom rather than the cure.

In returning to the *Don Quixote* of his childhood days, Heine constructs a genealogy of his own literary *Bildungsroman* that grounds his critique squarely in an experience that precedes the spiritualist regime of the separation of body and mind. Restaging the primal scene of Heine's socialization as a reader, this flashback reclaims the subversively emancipatory power of fiction as it frames the rehabilitation of matter and of flesh as the primary experience of literary imagination.

If Heine's self-citation brought out the deep connection his immersion in Cervantes's world established for him as a child, *The City of Lucca* took the comparison a step further. In a suggestive move, Heine had preluded the description of his formative encounter with Cervantes's novel with the comment that the relationship between reader and author is analogous to that between Sancho Panza and Don Quixote. Like Sancho Panza, Heine notes, the reader is forced to follow the "crazy poet" on his wanderings (L 3, 320; B 2, 521). This seemingly innocuous aside signals that the story of Heine's experience as an impressionable young reader has more than just anecdotal significance. It underlines the fundamental role of materiality in the relationship between author and critic as one that informs the process of reading. The description of the material existence of the reader as Sancho Panza highlights both readers' need and desire to follow their hero while reminding us that without readers, authors, books, and literary fiction in general do not go anywhere at all.

The tug-of-war between author and reader figured in the back-and-forth of the odd coupling of Don Quixote and Sancho Panza does not only reflect the quandary of the hermeneutic situation but shows it to be very much defined by the material conditions that inform the institution of literature or, more precisely, the conditions for the production and consumption of literature more generally. Ironically, this leads Heine, who used to see himself as siding more with Sancho Panza when it came to the recognition of the imponderables of the materiality of human existence, to cast himself in literary fiction as Don Quixote.[23] This self-ironic reversal plays itself out with the same semblance of rigor Heine tries to impart to his reader:

> Perhaps you are in the right, and I am only a Don Quixote; and the reading of all manner of strange books has turned my head, as the knight of La Mancha's was turned; and Jean Jacques Rousseau was my Amadis de Gaul, Mirabeau was my Roland or Agramanto, and I have studied too deeply in the heroic deeds of the French Paladins, and of the Round Table of the National Convention. It is true that my madness and the fixed ideas which I have gathered from those books are of a diametrically different description from the monomania and madness of the Manchan. He was desirous of restoring decaying chivalry to its pristine splendour, while I, on the contrary, would utterly destroy all that there is as yet

> remaining from those days; and we, consequently, work with views at utter variance. (L 3, 326f.)
>
> Vielleicht habt Ihr doch Recht, und ich bin nur ein Don Quixote und das Lesen von allerlei wunderbaren Büchern hat mir den Kopf verwirrt, ebenso wie den Junker von La Mancha, und Jean-Jacques Rousseau war mein Amadis von Gallien, Mirabeau war mein Roland oder Agramanth, und ich habe mich zu sehr hineinstudiert in die Heldentaten der französischen Paladine und der Tafelrunde des Nationalkonvents. Freilich, mein Wahnsinn und die fixen Ideen, die ich aus jenen Büchern geschöpft, sind von entgegengesetzter Art, als der Wahnsinn und die fixen Ideen des Manchaners: dieser wollte die untergehende Ritterzeit wieder herstellen, ich hingegen will alles, was aus jener Zeit noch übrig geblieben ist, jetzt vollends vernichten, und da handeln wir also mit ganz verschiedenen Ansichten. (B 2, 525f.)

This intimate proximity to Cervantes prepares Heine to contrast the otherwise opposite nature of the commitment that separates him from Don Quixote. But Heine is willing to sustain this affinity only in order to bring out the contrastive difference that puts him ultimately on the opposite side, and more closely at the side of the figure on which Don Quixote is bound to rely, Sancho Panza:

> My colleague regarded windmills as giants; I, however, in the braggart giants of the day see only noisy windmills. (L 3, 327)
>
> Mein Kollege sah Windmühlen für Riesen an, ich hingegen kann in unseren heutigen Riesen nur prahlende Windmühlen sehen. (B 2, 525)

Heine's deflationary humor will always side with Sancho Panza, but it never does so without acknowledgment of Don Quixote as Panza's other. A unit, they exemplify the mutual irreducibility of body and mind.

But if Sancho Panza is the unfortunate body that attracts the beatings that the mind—Don Quixote—provokes, visualizing the bodily harm the spirit causes, Heine does not lose track of the "imagined pain" that Don Quixote so poignantly feels and that does not hurt any less just because it is imagined (L 3, 328; B 2, 527). Heine's odd couple illustrates a knowing grasp of suffering and pain that resists reduction of one form of pain to the other, but recognizes the fact of pain as an irreducible reality of the dual aspect of human nature. Pain, however, regardless of any wish we may have to reduce it to a solely physical or solely mental reality, remains unacceptable and calls for change.

In a remarkable reversal that precedes the comment concerning Sancho Panza as the reader of the crazy poet, Heine not only declares the "great mass of people"—*die große Volksmasse*—a colossal Sancho Panza, he does so by including philosophers in that mass. But this Sancho Panza on the other hand represents the very mass of human nature that made the Don-Quixotic phenomenon of human existence possible in the first place:

> The cool, calm, cunning philosophers! How compassionately they smile on the self-torture and mad freaks of a poor Don Quixote, yet with all their school-wisdom do not perceive that that Don Quixotery is the most laudable thing in life, yes, life itself, and that it inspires to bolder effort the whole world, and all in it which philosophises, plays, plants, and gapes! For the great mass of the people with the philosophers is, without knowing it, nothing but a colossal Sancho Panza who, despite all his sober dread of whippings [. . .] (L 3, 319f.)
>
> Die kühlen und klugen Philosophen! Wie mitleidig lächeln sie herab auf die Selbstquälereien und Wahnsinnigkeiten eines armen Don Quixote, und in all ihrer Schulweisheit merken sie nicht, daß jene Donquixoterie dennoch das Preisenswerteste des Lebens, ja das Leben selbst ist, und daß diese Donquixoterie die ganze Welt, mit allen was darauf philosophiert, musiziert, ackert und gähnt, zu kühnerem Schwunge beflügelt! Denn die große Volksmasse, mitsamt den Philosophen, ist, ohne es zu wissen, nichts anders als ein kolossaler Sancho Pansa, der, trotz all seiner nüchternen Prügelscheu [. . .]. (B 2, 521)

Freud will need to take only one step to shift this conceptual content to the nomenclature of a struggle between the Id and the Superego, the pleasure-seeking drive pitched against the principle of sublimation and resignation. In this relationship, the seat of reason has become strangely insecure as it hovers between Don Quixote and Sancho Panza, never to be claimed exclusively by either, as Kafka has suggested as well. The reversal from reason to madness and back again to reason remains ever precarious, exemplifying the volatile dynamic of body and mind. The almost Dionysian outlook of this relationship highlights the explosive force of this dynamic. As Heine concludes this long sentence,

> For the great mass of the people with the philosophers is, without knowing it, nothing but a colossal Sancho Panza who, despite all his sober dread of whippings and homely wisdom, still follows the knight in all his dangerous adventures, lured by the promised reward in which he believes because he longs for it, but still more attracted by the mystic power which enthusiasm always exerts on the masses as we see in all political and religious revolutions, and it may be, also, daily in the smallest events. [L 3, 319f.)
>
> Denn die große Volksmasse, mitsamt den Philosophen, ist, ohne es zu wissen, nichts anders als ein kolossaler Sancho Pansa, der, trotz all seiner nüchternen Prügelscheu und hausbackner Verständigkeit, dem wahnsinnigen Ritter in allen seinen gefährlichen Abenteuern folgt,

> gelockt von der versprochenen Belohnung, an die er glaubt, weil er sie wünscht, mehr aber noch getrieben von der mystischen Gewalt, die der Enthusiasmus immer ausübt auf den großen Haufen—wie wir es in allen politischen und religiösen Revolutionen, und vielleicht täglich im kleinsten Ereignisse sehen können. (B 2, 521)

This volatile mass phenomenon illustrates the precariously fragile and potentially explosive relationship between body and mind whenever they are imagined as separate entities simply opposed over and against each other in freestanding isolation. Pain and suffering arise where this dynamic comes under pressure. While Sancho Panza appears as the manifest physical bearer of the mind, Don Quixote's pain and suffering is no less a result of the separation of body and mind than Sancho Panza's. Whereas Don Quixote gives voice to the pain he experiences for the sake of the life of ideas, his seemingly clueless companion rides his donkey through life closer to the ground, attentive to physical needs. But he relies just as well on his master. For without his master's vision—if mostly deluded—the servant's materialism would be left blind and cluelessly lost along the road. As in in Hegel's dialectics of master and servant, their lives remain inseparably intertwined and mutually interdependent.

The imperative to give voice to suffering and to the primary significance of bodily needs—what Heine at some point calls "the great soup question" (*die große Suppenfrage*, B 1, 340)—informs his writing as a central aspect of the project of universal emancipation. For Heine, the two concerns represent one and the same cause. As an allegorical figuration of literary imagination, Don Quixote serves as a reminder that this quest is possible only as long as it attends to the material base and its base, trivial, and lowly aspects that make life possible and sustain it in the first place. But the boisterous relationship between Sanso Panza and Don Quixote furthermore realizes the relationship between the author and his audience, between the process of literary production and the marketplace. Comedically enacted, pain and suffering figure in this context as transferentially negotiated moments of the transaction between the act of writing and the act of reading. The latter, also, are only understandable as moments that encompass the mind and the body and the life of the affects.

Heine's staging of the mind-body comedy presents the relationship between Sancho Panza and Don Quixote in a way that anticipates central aspects of Freud's theorizing of the Ego as the enduring scene of the tug-of-war between Id and Superego. It is the same interface that will gain critical importance in the way Adorno frames the recognition of the bodily dimension of the life of the mind and its fundamental importance for truth. This critical attempt to rethink the interrelation of body and mind underlies the central move of Adorno's approach to Critical Theory. In a carefully refined rethinking of Marx's view that material conditions inform consciousness down to its most minute manifestations, Adorno's *Minima*

Moralia follows Benjamin's cues in *Berlin Chronicle* and elsewhere in tracking the formative role that material conditions play in producing the philosopher's subjectivity. But it is in *Negative Dialectics* that Adorno sums up this critical concern in his most succinct formulation:

> The need to lend a voice to suffering is a condition of all truth. For suffering is objectivity that weighs upon the subject: its most subjective experience, its expression, is objectively conveyed.
>
> Das Bedürfnis, Leiden beredt werden zu lassen, ist Bedingung aller Wahrheit. Denn Leiden ist Objektivität, die auf dem Subjekt lastet; was es als sein Subjektivstes erfährt, sein Ausdruck, ist objektiv vermittelt.[24]

Adorno's insistence that the material satisfaction of bodily needs remains a necessary condition of all intellectual and mental fulfillment sheds light on the deeper critical meaning of Heine's slapstick comedy of Sancho Panza and Don Quixote. Adorno signals the fundamental importance of this point by positioning it at the conclusion of the centerpiece of *Negative Dialectics*, the section entitled "Negative Dialectics: Concept and Categories." Expressing a concern at the heart of Adorno's project of Critical Theory, the passage echoes Heine's project in theoretically stringent fashion:

> [Materialism's] great desire would be the resurrection of the flesh, a desire utterly foreign to idealism, the realm of the absolute spirit. The perspective vanishing point of historical materialism would be its self-sublimation, the spirit's liberation from the primacy of material needs in their state of fulfillment. Only if the physical urge were quenched would the spirit be reconciled and would become that which it only promises while the spell of material conditions will not let it satisfy material needs. (ND 207)
>
> Seine [Materialismus] Sehnsucht wäre die Auferstehung des Fleisches; dem Idealismus, dem Reich des absoluten Geistes, ist sie ganz fremd. Fluchtpunkt des historischen Materialismus wäre seine eigene Aufhebung, die Befreiung des Geistes vom Primat der materiellen Bedürfnisse im Stand ihrer Erfüllung. Erst dem gestillten leibhaften Drang versöhnte sich der Geist und würde, was er so lange nur verheißt, wie er im Bann der materiellen Bedingungen die Befriedigung der materiellen Bedürfnisse verweigert. (GS 6, 207)

If the theological, more precisely "Catholically" inflected overtones signaled by the formulation "resurrection of the flesh" sound somewhat disappointing in the context of a phrasing that subliminally broadcasts a powerful political vision of emancipatory thinking, closer examination shows that Adorno is closer to Heine's notion of the emancipation of the body than the wording suggests. Just as for Heine, for Adorno the body's satisfaction is not merely an end in itself; it is also a condition of the mind's eventual release from its oppression by the body and itself. As mentioned in Chapter 3, the exact wording of this passage of *Negative Dialectics* gives conceptual precision to the idea that the reconciliation of body and mind can come only after the satisfaction of bodily needs. At that point, the mind or spirit is able to reconcile itself with the body whose material needs it no longer denies.

For Adorno, the master-servant dialectic of body and mind leads to the fatal mutilation of the relation to the body. The "mortification of the flesh by power was nothing other than the ideological reflection of the oppression practiced on them"[25] (*daß die Erniedrigung des Fleisches durch die Macht nichts anderes war als das ideologische Spiegelbild der an ihnen selbst verübten Unterdrückung*).[26] Adorno's description of the "love-hate toward the body" casts the body as what is ridiculed and jibed and at the same time desired as the forbidden, reified, and alienated (ND 193; GS 6, 247). This discussion in the section "Interest in the Body" in the notes to the *Dialectic of Enlightenment* seems like a distant but concise echo of the darker side of Heine's comedic figuration of Sancho Panza and Don Quixote. What Heine figured in the raucous comedy of Don Quixote and Sancho Panza, Adorno articulates theoretically in a way that illuminates the firepower of Heine's slapstick comedy, that is, Adorno translates the analysis of the dialectics of a dysfunctional relationship from Heine's exuberant prose into the stringent language of the concept:

> In humanity's self-abasement to the *corpus* nature takes its revenge for the debasement of the human being to an object of power, to raw material. (ND 193)
>
> In der Selbsterniedrigung des Menschen zum corpus rächt sich die Natur dafür, daß der Mensch sie zum Gegenstand der Herrschaft, zum Rohmaterial erniedrigt hat. (GS 6, 247)

Adorno shares with Heine the recognition of the importance of the historical undercurrent of repression and distortion of human instincts and passions (ND 192f.; GS 6, 246). The insistence on the primary importance of the liberation of the life of the affects reclaims a vision of freedom that recognizes the rehabilitation of the flesh as the linchpin of the emancipation from exploitation and domination by the status quo. In Adorno's formulation, Heine's critical exposure of the insidious mechanism of the repressive split between body and mind returns with the same critical force:

> In the relationship of individuals to the body, their own and that of others, is reenacted the irrationality and injustice of power as cruelty; and that irrationality is as far removed form judicious insight and serene reflection as power is from freedom. (ND 193)

> Im Verhältnis des Einzelnen zum Körper, seinem eigenen wie dem fremden, kehrt die Irrationalität und Ungerechtigkeit der Herrschaft als Grausamkeit wieder, die vom einsichtigen Verhältnis, von glücklicher Reflexion so weit entfernt ist, wie jene von der Freiheit. (GS 6, 247)

For Adorno as for Heine, then, the affects assume a critical role as the site of liberation. As the scene of the mediating dynamics of the interface between body and mind, they come into play not just as a theme but more importantly as a constitutive momentum in the process of writing itself: writing engages the affects as an emancipatory force. We can now see how Heine's writing is, that is, enacts—by engaging in a release of the dynamics of the play of the affects and thereby reconfiguring their economy in a transformative manner—the very act of liberation Adorno theorizes. This release of the dynamics of the affects sets free the emancipatory power of critical thinking as it enables a creative reimagination that transcends the normatively crippling limitations of the fixation on the status quo. Heine's freewheeling writing is so liberating because it provocatively reclaims the possibility of thinking otherwise. Creatively reimagining the relationship between the material and the spiritual, the body and the mind, Heine advances the central emancipatory move of Adorno's Critical Theory.

Undermining the regime that imposes the dichotomy between body and mind, the recognition of the material base of human existence is no longer a liability but comes to the fore as emancipation's empowering condition. The critical thrust of this materialist stance shields against the false ideological forms of idealism, which it exposes as the ultimate instrument of domination and oppression. In Heine's hands, *Don Quixote* stands out as a unique reminder that highflying but disembodied ideals, norms informed by obsolete claims, and a morality that submits to the powers that be remain complicit with oppression and exploitation. It is not the material conditions, Heine's raucous comedy reminds us, that keep the oppressive forces in power. On the contrary, the material conditions stand as an uncompromising reality that not only pose a challenge and a provocation to lazy thinking, they also hold out the promise of change and freedom. Heine's transformative reversal and redemption of the materiality of human nature into the chance and promise of emancipation gives eloquent expression to a social vision whose critical edge pushes for a messianic recognition of materiality as life's most redemptive aspect. This irreverent materialism resists submission to ideological closure and takes its strength from a critical commitment to the singularity of each individual's specific form of human life. In a move similar to Adorno's critical recourse to the biblical layers of Jewish and Christian traditions, Heine embraces these traditions' recognition of the role of the material aspect of life but, unlike Adorno, he does so in self-confident association with Spinoza.[27]

Seraphine

A striking formulation of the revolutionary power of the call for liberation of the senses stands at the center of the collection of poems grouped under the title "Seraphine," a call that steers clear of bleak reductionism and the celebration of sensualism for its own sake. Number VII of this group published in 1844 in *Neue Gedichte*, the poem is part of a cycle that presents variations on the theme of sensual love (D 332; B 4, 325). But closer examination makes it clear that sensual love does not represent for Heine a goal for its own sake but stands rather as an expression of a deeper concern. The opening line "Auf diesem Felsen bauen wir" ("Upon this rock we'll build a church") plays with Luther's lyrics and Saint-Simonist aspirations, but turns all ecclesiastical pretensions upside down. Instead, the poem communicates a genuine notion of revolutionary insurgence committed to the dignity of every individual. To fully appreciate its critical movement, it is important to consider the note on which the preceding poem ends, that is, a reference to the lyrical I's heart where the sun has taken refuge:

> Oh, do not weep—it is not dead,
> Not dead beyond reclaiming:
> The sun lies hid within my heart
> And there it still is flaming. (D 332)
>
> O weine nicht, die Sonne liegt
> Nicht tot in jenen Fluten;
> Sie hat sich in mein Herz versteckt
> Mit allen ihren Gluten. (B 4, 325)

In a dramatic reversal, the lyrical I serves as the rock to which the following poem number VII refers. In this poem, the heart is identified as the poetic site dually occupied by mind and body, or more precisely, the conventional seat of the affects, that is, the embodied place where body and mind, matter and spirit meet or unite:

> Upon this rock we'll build a church
> All suffering transcended—
> The church of the third New Testament;
> The days of pain are ended.
>
> Annulled the great Antithesis
> That held us long deluded;
> The stupid torments of the flesh
> Are over now, concluded.
>
> Do you hear God on his dark sea?
> He speaks with a thousand voices.

And do you see how his sky overhead
With a thousand candles rejoices?

God dwells both in the heaven's light
And ocean's dark abysses;
God's spirit dwells in all that is—
He dwells in our kisses. (D 332)

Auf diesem Felsen bauen wir
Die Kirche von dem dritten,
Dem dritten neuen Testament;
Das Leid ist ausgelitten.

Vernichtet ist das Zweierlei,
Das uns so lang betöret;
Die dumme Leiberquälerei
Hat endlich aufgehöret.

Hörst Du den Gott im finstern Meer?
Mit tausend Stimmen spricht er.
Und siehst du über unserm Haupt
Die tausend Gotteslichter?

Der heilge Gott der ist im Licht
Wie in den Finsternissen;
Und Gott ist alles was da ist;
Er ist in unsern Küssen. (B 4, 325)

Playing with the aspirations of Saint-Simonist social reform and religious and cultural renewal, the poem gives voice to a devastating critique of any form of organized religion and institutionalization. A resolute rejection of the dichotomy of body and mind and the ideological blinding it entails, the poem welcomes the final demise of the exploitation of the body by way of spiritual oppression. Only after the split between body and mind is overcome does it become possible to recognize God as "all that exists," that is, beyond any form of dichotomy. The irreverent impulse of the first two stanzas suggests that Saint-Simonism remains in the final analysis complicit with the exploitation of the body by the mind—for, despite proclaiming the end of the dichotomy of body and mind, the authoritarian structure of the sect's beliefs and organization reinforces what it claims to abolish. By contrast, the poem no longer accepts any external authority but sees guidance as originating in the individual "heart," that is, as the connection between mind and body, which is to say the site of the psychosomatic dynamics of the individual's affects. At this moment, the individual is open to perceiving the divine character of nature residing in everything that exists. God is no longer a function of a transcendent regime of control but represents the empowering omnipresence of the promise of the redemptive power of joy and love. They are not figured as a final state of bliss but in the image of an allegory of creative interaction. For a kiss signals that symbolic transaction whose sensual pleasure exists only in the face of the presence of the mental consensus whose minimal threshold the law calls consent.

In contrast to the Saint-Simonist claim to represent the third testament, Heine envisions the messianic state of the third era as one where there is no more suffering (*Das Leid ist ausgelitten*). The poem trumps not only Saint-Simonism but any institutionalized desire to impose any law that is not grounded in the heart and in a human nature figured as the dual-aspect monism where body and mind meet to "kiss." God is no longer to be imagined as residing in one or the other human being; rather, God manifests divine presence in between human beings, in the process of activity: "He dwells in our kisses."

This is when redemption and emancipation reach their realization. Poem number VII articulates a theological-political intervention that highlights the terms of the relationship between body and mind as the critical site of the project of universal emancipation.

The poem resonates with the central argument advanced in *On the History of Religion and Philosophy in Germany*, which was written around the same time. There, Heine introduced pantheism and its powerfully critical thrust in the theoretically refined form of Spinoza's philosophy. In his prose, Heine formulates the poem's point in the following way:

> To rehabilitate matter, to reinstate it in its dignity, to recognize its moral worth and give it religious consecration, to reconcile it with spirit. (OH 56)
>
> Die Rehabilitation der Materie, die Wiedereinsetzung derselben in ihre Würde, ihre moralische Anerkennung, ihre religiöse Heiligung, ihre Versöhnung mit dem Geiste. (B 3, 568)

This is a program that expresses the same promise to which Heine's poem gives poetic expression. But the kind of beauty and pleasure it evokes derives its power from a Spinozist vision of aesthetics that moves beyond the historical divisions of form and matter to reimagine new ways in which the dialectics of form and content can be liberated to free play.

This pantheism, Heine stressed in theological shorthand, no longer claimed that God had been incarnated in man. Heine boldly turned the story upside down. No longer would he force the heavens down to earth; it would rather elevate earthly existence into the heavens:

> God is identical with the world. He manifests himself in plants [. . .] He manifests himself in animals [. . .] But most magnificently, he manifests himself in the human being, who feels and thinks at the same time [. . .] In the human being, divinity comes to self-consciousness, and such self-consciousness again itself reveals the divine by means of the human being.

> But this revelation does not occur in and through the individual human being, but rather in and through the entirety of humanity, so that each person only grasps and represents a part of the God-World-Universe, but all of humanity together will grasp and represent the entire God-World-Universe in idea and in reality. (OH 57)
>
> Gott ist identisch mit der Welt. Er manifestiert sich in den Pflanzen [. . .]. Er manifestiert sich in den Tieren [. . .]. Aber am herrlichsten manifestiert er sich in dem, Menschen, der zugleich fühlt und denkt [. . .]. Im Menschen kommt die Gottheit zum Selbstbewußtsein, und solches Selbstbewußtsein offenbart sie wieder durch den Menschen. Aber dieses geschieht nicht in dem einzelnen und durch den einzelnen Menschen, sondern in und durch die Gesamtheit der Menschen: so daß jeder Mensch nur einen Teil des Gott-Welt-Alls auffaßt und darstellt, alle Menschen zusammen aber das ganze Gott-Welt-All in der Idee und in der Realität auffassen und darstellen werden. (B 3, 569)

While this translates into the formula "one can justly say of humanity in its entirety, it is an incarnation of God!" (OH 57; B 3, 569), God is not a transcendent being but immanent to what exists:

> "God"—which Spinoza calls the one Substance and the German philosophers call the Absolute—"is everything that is," matter as well as spirit. Both are equally divine, and whoever insults holy matter is just as sinful as one who sins against the Holy Spirit. (OH 54)
>
> "Gott," welcher von Spinoza die eine Substanz und von den deutschen Philosophen das Absolute genannt wird, "ist alles was da ist," er ist sowohl Materie wie Geist, beides ist zugleich göttlich, und wer die heilige Materie beleidigt, ist eben so sündhaft, wie der, welcher sündigt gegen den heiligen Geist. (B 3, 565f.)

Neither a profanation of the divine nor a leveling down of all that is sacred, Heine's emancipatory push points in the opposite direction. Reclaiming the divinity of nature and man, this countermove seeks to recover the divine dignity of all that exists, whether it manifests itself under the aspect of matter or of spirit. The Saint-Simonists "have understood, and desired, something like this." But "the materialism around them beat them down" and neutralized their progressive potential—at least for a time, as Heine notes (OH 58; B 3, 570). The political revolution that was launched on the back of French materialism will be welcomed by the pantheists but, as Heine suggests, it will encounter in the pantheist a deeper, more profound source of conviction than materialism has to offer:

> We support the wellbeing of matter, the material happiness of people, not because we are contemptuous of the spirit, like the materialists, but

> because we know that the divinity of the human being is also revealed in his bodily appearance, that misery destroys or demeans the body, the image of God, and that the spirit is destroyed thereby as well. (OH 58)
>
> Wir befördern das Wohlsein der Materie, das materielle Glück der Völker, nicht weil wir gleich den Materialisten den Geist mißachten, sondern weil wir wissen, daß die Göttlichkeit des Menschen sich auch in seiner leiblichen Erscheinung kund gibt, und das Elend den Leib, das Bild Gottes, zerstört oder aviliert, und der Geist dadurch ebenfalls zu Grunde geht. (B 3, 570)

Heine's critical distance from materialism is philosophically motivated, but it also rests on a critical awareness of the theological-political pitfalls of a radically materialist position, a position that would only succumb to the temptation to replace one deadly despotism for another. Against this, Heine's Spinozism offers a safeguard:

> The great motto of the revolution expressed by Saint-Just: "Bread is the right of the people" reads for us "Bread is the divine right of the human being." We do not fight for the human rights of the people but for the divine rights of the human. (OH 58)
>
> Das große Wort der Revolution, das Saint-Just ausgesprochen: le pain est le droit du peuple, lautet bei uns: le pain est le droit divin de l'homme. Wir kämpfen nicht für die Menschenrechte des Volks, sondern für die Gottesrechte des Menschen. (B 3, 570)

This seemingly simple theological point carries theological-political implications as the continuation demonstrates:

> In this and several other things, we differ from the men of the revolution. We want to be neither *sans-culottes*, nor frugal citizens, nor parsimonious presidents; we will found a democracy of gods, equally glorious, equally joyous. (58)
>
> Hierin, und in noch manchen anderen Dingen, unterscheiden wir uns von den Männern der Revolution. Wir wollen keine Sansculotten sein, keine frugale Bürger, keine wohlfeile Präsidenten: wir stiften eine Demokratie gleichherrlicher, gleichheiliger, gleichbeseligter Götter. (570)

Rather than singling out any particular subset of human beings, this deification of human life is pointedly collective. It comprehends all human beings without exception, with all their diverse and enriching national and cultural differences. Instead of being assimilated to a universal mold of human nature, Heine's vision celebrates the singularity of each individual human existence and the differences it represents as one of the infinite instantiations of the divine making itself manifest in matter and mind:

> You demand simple clothes, abstemious morals, and spiceless enjoyments; we, on the other hand, demand nectar and ambrosia, kingly robes, costly fragrances, sensuality and splendor, the dances of laughing nymphs, music, and comedies. (OH 58)
>
> Ihr verlangt einfache Trachten, enthaltsame Sitten und ungewürzte Genüsse; wir hingegen verlangen Nektar und Ambrosia, Purpurmäntel, kostbare Wohlgerüche, Wollust und Pracht, lachenden Nymphentanz, Musik, Komödien. (B 3, 570)

A decade later, the opening stanzas of *Germany: A Winter's Tale* (*Deutschland. Ein Wintermärchen*) will reinforce the critical link between the Spinozist dual-aspect monism Heine champions and his particular understanding of pleasure as the key empowering moment in the economy of the affects, such that satisfying one's material and intellectual needs receives a fundamental emancipatory function. The dynamics of the affects are the central lever that determines how material conditions inform the theological-political parameters of human existence. The provocative irreverence of pleasure is so subversive not just because it exposes the conventional forms of organized piety in their sanctimonious pretense. More critically, the subversive power derives its thrust from the undeniable legitimacy of its call for a more just distribution of the resources that determine material conditions, for genuine and universal equality of access to the fruits of our labor—and not just in name:

> A newer song, a better song,
> My friends, let's bring to birth now!
> We shall proceed right here to build
> The Kingdom of Heaven on earth now. (D 484)
>
> Ein neues Lied, ein besseres Lied,
> O Freunde, will ich Euch dichten!
> Wir wollen hier auf Erden schon
> Das Himmelreich errichten. (B 4, 578)

Again, the movement is one of sanctification rather than profanation: the earth shall be heaven, a new earth and a new heaven. The biblical resonance with Isaiah 65:17 and 66:22 combines with a modern clarion call for emancipation that unites ancient sources of Jewish traditions and their prophetic and messianic expectations with a post-idealist dual-aspect monism. As biblical, prophetic, and messianic traditions converge with the post-idealist form of a modern Spinozist notion of the body-mind relation, the function of the affects, and the emancipatory power of joy and pleasure, Heine articulates a vision of modernity that is unafraid of its multiple ancient and modern sources. Instead, it joyfully embraces them as empowering visions of the promise of diversity and its liberating power in modernity. This is not a simple hedonist or Dionysian endorsement of pleasure but one informed by an emancipatory vision of self-determination that embraces pleasure as a condition of its existence under the sign of a liberated notion of work devoid of exploitation and expropriation.

We wish to be happy here on earth,
All want eradicated,
The idler's belly shall not consume
What toiler's hands have created.

The soil produces bread enough
For all mankind's nutrition,
Plus rose and myrtle, beauty and joy,
And sugar peas in addition. (D 484)

Wir wollen auf Erden glücklich sein,
Und wollen nicht mehr darben;
Verschlemmen soll nicht der faule Bauch
Was fleißige Hände erwarben.

Es wächst hienieden Brot genug
Für alle Menschenkinder,
Auch Rosen und Myrten, Schönheit und Lust,
Und Zuckererbsen nicht minder. (B 4, 578)

The poem's firepower and subversive thrust—what made Heine's poetry so fierce and so feared by the reactionary regimes in Metternich's Austria and in Prussia—consists in its intense interweaving of the social, political, and theological-political motifs with a critical recognition of the primacy of material conditions. In a subversive and liberating move of profanation—or consecration—Heine hammers home the profound nexus of the theological-political complex:

Yes, sugar peas for everyone
Piled high upon the barrows!
The heavens we can safely leave
To the angels and the sparrows. (D 484)

Ja, Zuckererbsen für jedermann,
Sobald die Schoten platzen!
Den Himmel überlassen wir
Den Engeln und den Spatzen. (B 4, 578)

Heine's call for a critical approach to secularization resonates powerfully not only with Marx, Freud, and Nietzsche, but also with their heirs and especially with the Critical Theory of the Frankfurt School, who would find their own calls for the emancipation of body and mind pleasurably prefigured in Heine's joyous play with comedy. If tragedy is followed by farce, as Heine suggested, his comedy ushers in theory's most critical concerns.

7

Myths of Enlightenment: Heine's Secularization Narratives

If Heine was among the first to respond critically to secularization narratives, he did so with a difference, upping the ante. It is no coincidence that the only other author with a similarly critical stance with regard to secularization was Goethe. Goethe's Spinozist sensibilities certainly aligned him closely with Heine when it came to the way he viewed the function of religion. In his *Wilhelm Meister's Journeymen Years*, which Heine called "the best model for a novel" (*das beste Muster eines Romans*),[1] Goethe had offered, in the ironic mode that defined his mature style, a striking object lesson on how to address the issue. It occurs in a passage of the novel that comically exposes the inadequacy of the aesthetic program of the Nazarenes—a group of epigonal painters whose neo-devout attitude was, in Goethe's eyes, in poor taste—while also speaking to a deeper point about the project of *Bildung* as a social, political, and theological-political critique of modernity. In the first novel's pages, the protagonist Wilhelm Meister encounters a character called Joseph II, accompanied by his pregnant wife, Mary, riding a donkey. Goethe spares us the name of the unborn child, but the play with genealogical pretension is obvious. The parody of the Holy Family exposes the irony that follows from a willfully naive implementation of the call for *imitatio Dei*, that is, to follow in the footsteps of Jesus Christ. The first lesson in the quest for what *Bildung*—that is, formation, education, and self-making—means to a modern subject is a satirical demonstration of what happens when "life imitates art." The more this exceedingly pious family tries to emulate its divine and sacred model, the more obvious the sheer impossibility of their goal becomes. When Joseph II attempts to copy the biblical Joseph by painting the throne his namesake was commissioned to make for Herod, the reader begins to pick up on some of the intricacies of the dialectics of secularization that flow from even seemingly simple acts of devotion. Joseph II's blind devotion to a religious lifestyle causes him to take possession of and rebuild a small chapel that had fallen into ruins and move into it with his family. His appropriation of the house of God leads to unexpected consequences. Ironically, the desire for the sacred for its own sake leads to a domestication of the sacred, because religious objects of desire are reinvented in the image of the person who desires them. Consequently, such desire is, in the final analysis, an act of profanation. By taking piety to its extreme, Goethe illustrates that the search for religion is—and necessarily so—a form of secularization. Wilhelm and his lucky son Felix learn from Joseph II that imitation and repetition, that is, appropriation and production by mimesis, cannot be the answer to the search for authentic life in modernity.

For Goethe, religion is not a pristine and privileged access to transcendence but an invention and practice of tradition. When bidding farewell to the Pedagogical Province, Wilhelm encounters a visual representation of the way the ideologues of the Pedagogical Province construct modern religion for their pupils. The statically didactic images are faded representations of what were once lively, dynamic traditions. The images turn Judaism and Christianity into relics whose narratives have been appropriated to legitimize traditional culture and education as a curious halfway house of secularization. Exposing the conditions of secularization as the defining feature of the way modern man experiences religion serves as a critical reminder that the very desire for a return of religion is the ultimate consequence of the formative power of secularization. In this vein, the novel offers a series of alternatives that are all exposed to the skepticism of the protagonist, who comes to realize that *Bildung* is an open-ended, lifelong project. The first stage of *Bildung*, or rather its misconception, is that of naïve emulation. But imitation, the novel suggests, is not a viable option. Goethe responds to the claim that religion is on the wane in modernity with the insight that religion is a product of secularization. Recognizing secularization as a religious concept demands that we examine the concept of religion as itself a result of secularization.

Guided by the same critical insight, Heine takes up and rehearses various secularization narratives. His poetry, fiction, and critical prose challenge the terms for theorizing religion and the consequences of secularization in modernity from the bottom up. Responding to Hegel's cues with a critical twist, Heine's interventions are punctuated with remarks addressing secularization as a process that informs modernity's discontents if not its inability to face its religious traditions as its own underlying condition. Heine recognized as a defining aspect of modernity what Horkheimer and Adorno's *Dialectic of Enlightenment* would later diagnose as modernity's danger, that is, the danger of submitting to the very myths it seeks to subdue, contain, and ignore. Similarly, Benjamin's recognition of the theological-political nexus that modernity cannot escape; Kracauer's analysis of the enduring sway of religion; and what Bloch, Marcuse, Fromm and others saw as the ability of religious tradition to be both repressive and liberating, oppressive and empowering—all resonate with Heine's strategy of reimagining secularization narratives differently.

Over a century later, Hans Blumenberg will note in *The Legitimacy of the Modern Age*—Blumenberg's answer to *Dialectic of Enlightenment*, as Tracie Matysik suggests—that secularization is "a last theologoumenon that the consciousness of guilt imposes on the heir of theology for their inheritance."[2] As Blumenberg quotes Nietzsche's close friend Franz Overbeck, theology is itself "nothing else but a piece of the secularization of Christianity."[3]

While the exponents of the Frankfurt School shared a profound discontent with the dominant secularization narratives—whose Weberian-style cogency betrays signs of subliminal commitments to Christianity they were loath to share—Heine's counternarratives act out this resistance more directly, playfully, and with a sanguine enjoyment of pleasure that Critical Theory often seems to browbeat. Openly and provocatively marking Jewish opposition, Heine exposes the blind spots of the dominant secularization narratives' theological rationalizations. As a result, Heine's approach brings out the problems that Critical Theory's tentative stance on secularization theory left unaddressed. Heine's subversive comedy of secularization narratives reflects in a pleasurably liberating fashion the concerns that Critical Theory faced as it critically addressed the theological-political implications that haunt secularization theory.

The theme of contention between religions, or more precisely the religious and theological contentions between the Jewish traditions and Christianity, can be found throughout Heine's prose and poetry. It acts out what Siegbert Prawer calls Heine's "Jewish Comedy."[4] By acting out this comedy—initially covertly but, with time, increasingly out in the open—Heine addresses point blank the predicament of Jewish experience in the face of a secularization discourse that excludes Jewish existence a priori by casting it as a failure and aberration Christianity has come to expunge. While every universalist stance, from Voltaire to Marx, was informed by notions of the secular that were the product of the theological tradition of European Christianity, Heine's fresh and irreverent approach breaks the theological-political spell that would otherwise force those acting according to the rules of engagement into compliance with the theological commitments required by the dominant discourse. Interrupting, undermining, and breaking this discourse apart and exposing its "*partie honteuse*"[5]—as Marx defined the liberating force of critique—Heine drags the dark family secrets of the dysfunctional Jewish-Christian relationship into open daylight. With dauntless resolve—the refreshingly openhearted chutzpah he wears on his sleeve—Heine expresses his critique with a frankness the Frankfurt School can match only with the restrained guise in which it exposes the process as the dialectic of the concept that leaves the decisive moments of exclusion unaccounted for. The manner in which Critical Theory negotiates secularization theory becomes more legible in its critical force when read with Heine's comedic dramatization in mind, which confronts the secularization narratives as (re)iterations of a theological culture they claim to have overcome. Heine's interventions bring out in a pointed fashion the "Jewish" difference that drives the resolve of the Frankfurt School's critical project: a Jewish difference that in Critical Theory itself is curiously muted.

Heine's tracking of the continuous, irreducible nexus of religion and secularization as a mutually interlocking function provides a framework for contextualizing the underlying discourse on secularization and its critique that informs the project of Critical Theory. The wider context of this discourse is defined by the theological-political renegotiations that begin with Spinoza, if not Montaigne, and continue to Derrida and the present debates on secularization. These renegotiations have produced their own forms of rethinking the relationship between religion and the secular, including its most recent iteration in the debate on the return of religion and the post-secular.

Protestant Secularization: *The City of Lucca*

From his earliest writings, Heine critically reflects the conundrum of the theological-political conditions of secularization and its discourse. But it is in the seminal form of the blend of prose and poetry that defines the genre he goes on to invent, the *Travel Pictures*, that Heine explores the problem of secularization from up close. In Part 4 of the *Travel Pictures*, *The City of Lucca*, the issues that attend the conception of the secular and the dialectics that define secularization come to a head. Presented as a human—or divine—comedy, the Lucca episodes are preluded and framed by *The Baths of Lucca*, a persiflage on two Jewish converts desperately looking for acceptance in society; a society whose Italian-style sensualist *dolce vita* remains enough under the sway of doctrinaire Catholicism to make Christianity a formidable proposition even for those new Christians most eager to demonstrate the zealousness only converts can muster.

We've already encountered Hirsch-Hyazinth—in Freud's appreciation, Heine's arguably most amusing character who serves at the same time as his comedic self-characterization. The Jewishly inflected episodes in *The Baths of Lucca* set the stage for *The City of Lucca*. Against the backdrop of Italian Catholicism and English Protestantism, the protagonists Hirsch-Hyazinth and Gumpelino—Jewish converts to Protestantism and Catholicism, respectively—frame and act out the difference between the two confessions in comically Jewish terms. In other words, Christian religious difference is performed as a matter and concern completely internal to Jewish experience. Modeled on the master-servant relationship of Cervantes's Don Quixote and Sancho Panza, the Christian stance thus is reversed as Christianity performed, that is, translated and converted into a Jewish comedy of supersession. Staged as the comedy of Jewish assimilation, Christianity's supersession is turned comically upside down. With its reversal of the frame of reference of the discourse on religion and secularization, Heine's dramatic farce of supersession brings the point home that religion itself is already a secular product of secularization. As a consequence, secularization becomes legible as a religious phenomenon that can never be fully extricated from the sphere of religion. Moving between religions, Heine's incorrigibly Jewish characters suggest, never means moving out of or outside religion but rather substituting or superseding one frame of reference for another.

As the narrator enters the city of Lucca, the stage is set for him to present everything from a displaced frame of reference that reconfigures his experiences in flagrantly non-Christian terms. Rather than simply anti-Christian—as the Voltairean mode would have it—Heine's narrator embraces a position with regard to Christianity that addresses its content in a parodistically literal fashion that brings out the comedic aspects of religious pretentions as they present themselves to the eyes of a Jewish observer. Performed as the persiflage of a convert whose enthusiastic embrace of his new religion only undermines what it enshrines the more fervently he seeks to subject himself to its order, Heine highlights the comic aspects of the dialectic that turns religion into a form of secularization and secularization into a form of religion.

Entering the city of Lucca at night, the narrator witnesses a solemn and somber Catholic procession. From the narrator's humorously defamiliarized perspective, the religious procession suggests the appearance of a nocturnal spook:

> Has an entire race risen spectre-like from the grave to mock life with the maddest mummery? (L 3, 263)
>
> Ist ein ganzes Volk als nächtliches Gespenst aus dem Grabe gestiegen, um im tollsten Mummenschanz das Leben nachzuäffen? (B 2, 488)

With comments whose anthropological acuity exposes Christianity's violent forms of supersession, Heine brings out the implications of shifting the frame of reference from a Christian to a Jewish perspective. In a stunning turn that gives new meaning to the radical thrust of Heine's play with secularization, the narrator dryly notes:

> If the Jews had formed the great mass of the people, and if their religion had been the established religion, the aforesaid psalmodising would have been characterized with the name of "mauscheln." (L 3, 265)
>
> Wären die Juden die größere Volksmenge, und ihre Religion wäre die Staatreligion, so würde man obiges Gesinge [the chanting of the procession] mit dem Namen "Mauscheln" bezeichnen. (B 2, 489)

Continuing the discussion, the narrator turns to those secular aspects that, as Heine's comments subtly suggest, provide the foundation that makes religion possible in modern times, even in a country as deeply steeped in Catholicism as Italy appears to be:

> Fortunately one could only half hear it, since there marched behind the procession, with a full accompaniment of drums and fifes, several companies of troops, besides which there was on each side, near the priests in their flowing robes, grenadiers going by two and two. There were almost as many soldiers as clergy, but it requires many bayonets now-a-days to keep up religion, and even when the blessing is given, cannon must roar significantly in the distance. (L 3, 265f.)
>
> Glücklicherweise konnte man es nur zur Hälfte vernehmen, indem hinter der Prozession, mit lauten Trommeln und Pfeifen, mehreren Kompanien Militär einherzogen, so wie überhaupt an beiden Seiten neben den wallenden Geistlichen, auch immer je zwei und zwei Grenadiere marschierten. Es waren fast mehr Soldaten als Geistliche; aber zur Unterstützung der Religion gehören heut zu Tage viel Bajonette, und wenn gar der Segen gegeben wird, dann müssen in der Ferne auch die Kanonen bedeutungsvoll donnern. (B 2, 489)

The choreography of this balancing act between state power and religion subtly transforms under the reader's eyes into a precariously questionable act of secularization:

> When I see such a procession, in which clergymen amid military escort walk along so miserably and sorrowfully, it strikes painfully to my soul, and it seems to me as though I saw our Saviour himself surrounded by lance-bearers and led to judgment. (L 3, 266)
>
> Wenn ich eine solche Prozession sehe, wo unter stolzer Militär-Eskorte, die Geistlichen so gar trübselig und jammervoll einherwandeln, so ergreift es mich immer schmerzhaft, und es ist mir als sähe ich unseren Heiland selbst, umringt von Lanzenträgern, zur Richtstätte abführen. (B 2, 489)

The procession's recreation of the imagined original scene of Christ's walk to crucifixion reveals the secular underpinnings of religious ritual and symbolism as the narrator attends to the double meaning of every manifestation of religion in *this* world, which defines the civic dimension necessarily assumed by every display of religious meaning.

The next chapter opens with a curious *quid pro quo* that serves, as it were, as a sort of secularization in reverse; the opening cites eight verses from Homer's *Iliad* (1: 596–604) portraying a feast of the Greek gods where food is abundant and wine, music, and song flow all day long as

Hephaistos waits on the gods and Apollo entertains his colleagues with the lyre accompanied by the muses:

> He then also poured forth to the other immortals assembled
> Sweetest, pleasantest nectar, the goblet quickly exhausting,
> And still an infinite laughter rang from the happy immortals
> As they saw how Hephaestos around was so cleverly passing.
> Thus through the live-long day, until the sun was declining,
> The feast went on, nor was wanting through all the genial banquet
> Either the sound of the strings of the exquisite lyre of Apollo,
> Nor the soft song of the Muse with voices sweetly replying.
> (L 3, 270)[6]

> Jener schenkte nunmehr auch der übrigen Götterversammlung,
> Rechtshin, lieblichen Nektar dem Mischkrug emsig entschöpfend.
> Doch unermeßliches Lachen erscholl den seligen Göttern,
> Als sie sahn, wie Hephästos im Saal so gewandt umhering.
> Also den ganzen Tag bis spät zur sinkenden Sonne
> Schmausten sie; und nicht mangelt' ihr Herz des gemeinsamen Mahles,
> Nicht des Saitengetöns von der lieblichen Leier Apollons,
> Noch des Gesangs der Musen mit holdantwortender Stimme.
> (Vulgata) (B 2, 492)

As the source of the quote, Heine references the *Vulgata*, the Church-authorized Latin Bible translation. The farcical substitution of the source text comically undermines the distinction between Greek and Hebrew tradition. In addition it performs, in a simultaneous double move, secularization and its reversal, underlining the ambivalent double nature of secularization as both a secular and religious process. Homer, whose name had, since Winckelmann, come to assume the authority for the heretic confession of sensualist indulgence, is pitted—in direct provocation—over and against Christian sensitivities as Christ arrives to crash the party, plonking his big wooden crucifix onto the dinner table where the gods are gathered:

> Suddenly there came gasping towards them a pale Jew, dripping with blood, a crown of thorns on his head, bearing a great cross of wood on his shoulder, and he cast the cross on the high table of the gods, so that the golden goblets trembled and fell, and the gods grew dumb and pale, and ever paler, till they melted in utter mist. (L 3, 270)

> Da plötzlich keuchte heran ein bleicher, bluttriefender Jude, mit einer Dornenkrone auf dem Haupte, und mit einem großen Holzkreuz auf der Schulter; und er warf das Kreuz auf den hohen Göttertisch, daß die goldnen Pokale zitterten, und die Götter verstummten und erblichen,

> und immer bleicher wurden, bis sie endlich ganz in Nebel zerrannen. (B 2, 492)

Note the way this imagined description of Christianity's ascendance presents itself as a version of secularization *avant la lettre*:

> Then there were dreary days, and the world became grey and gloomy. There were no more happy immortals, and Olympus became an hospital, where flayed, roasted, and spitted gods went wearily, wandering round, binding their wounds and singing sorrowful songs. Religion no longer offered joy, but consolation; it was a woeful, bleeding religion of transgressors [*Delinquentenreligion*]. (L 3, 271)
>
> Nun gabs eine traurige Zeit, und die Welt wurde grau und dunkel. Es gab keine glücklichen Götter mehr, der Olymp wurde ein Lazarett wo geschundene, gebratene und gespießte Götter langweilig umherschlichen, und ihre Wunden verbanden und triste Lieder sangen. Die Religion gewährte keine Freude mehr, sondern Trost; es war eine trübselige, blutrünstige Delinquentenreligion. (B 2, 492f.)

With the "holiday gods" (*Festtagsgötter*, L 3, 271; B 2, 493) gone and their sensual feasting ended, suffering has replaced the joy of life as the highest value, Hellenism is substituted by Hebraism:

> Pity is the last consecration of love, it may be love itself. (L 3, 271)
>
> Das Mitleid ist die letzte Weihe der Liebe, vielleicht die Liebe selbst. (B 2, 493)

With these thoughts, the narrator takes refuge from the dark atmosphere of Lucca's streets, ducking into a church of all places. While, outside, the procession unfolds with the somber display of mummery, the peaceful haven of the church has a reassuring effect on the fugitive. But not for long. In a corner the narrator spots the young and passionate Francesca, who takes him in her arms and showers him with kisses. But alas, the kisses of this sensual southern sultry beauty are meant for somebody else! He hears Francesca whisper with yearning: "Cecco, Cecco, caro Cecco!" (L 3, 274; B 2, 495)—the name of a young Bolognese abbé and devout servant of the Roman Catholic Church. Yet Heine's narrator has no scruples when it comes to appropriating these favors of love, especially since redirecting them comes with the bonus of a good conscience:

> As a Protestant, I did not scruple to appropriate to my use the goods of the Catholic Church, and I consequently secularised the pious kiss of Francesca on the spot. (L 3, 275)

> Als Protestant machte ich mir kein Gewissen daraus, mir die Güter der katholischen Geistlichkeit zuzueignen, und auf der Stelle säkularisierte ich die frommen Küsse Franscheskas. (B 2, 495)

While Heine certainly was justified in calling himself a protestant, that is, he was at least correct in name, it was precisely his baptism that marked him all the more indelibly as a Jew whose Judaism, he had to learn, could not be washed off by holy water.[7] The qualification "as a protestant" suggests the shift to functionality that, in modernity, we relate to the sacred and divine as a function of our subject position. This function defines a particular experience as sacred or profane according to how we relate to it, a relation that is always informed by the religious affiliation that we are assigned. Even morality, it turns out here, is defined by its function and linked to the religious form of practice in which it arises. Secularization is then a distinctly religious operation or, more precisely, a process that operates in the name of religion, that is, on the basis of religious legitimation; more precisely, its delegitimating function is based on religious difference rather than the opposition between religion and plain nonbelief. Declaring himself "a protestant," the narrator posits his position as irreducible to one or the other religion, suggesting instead that in modernity there is no position simply outside of religion. Instead, in Heine, Judaism and Christianity represent multiple and conflicting strands of religious affiliations that remain mutually invested in each other.

But if secularization comes as easily as offering yourself as beneficiary for the redirection of goods owned by religious institutions, a closer look suggests that secularization is always already "naturally" under way. For Francesca's act of piety harbors a this-worldly and rather sensual impulse that the church, represented by the beloved abbé, seems only too eager to welcome. Continuing the idea of protestant secularization of the property of the Catholic Church, the story takes an illuminating turn as the Catholic double entendre of body and spirit is taken to the next level: transubstantiation. In a tight *pas-de-deux* of letter and "spirit," Heine brings out the inherently secular impulse that informs the precise moment of the distinction between the sacred and profane. In the same movement, the text highlights the intricate entwinement of spiritualism and sensualism as mutually constitutive of each other.

Provocatively coupling the description of the moment of transubstantiation in the Eucharist, at which the wafer assumes the divine properties of Christ as determined by the Fourth Council of the Lateran in 1215, with the extolment of the sultry beauty of the object of the narrator's desire, Francesca, Heine stages the convergence of the two—the *coincidentia oppositorum*, as it were, of the Catholic mass and the profane declaration of sexual desire—as identical in terms of the linguistic performance that subversively exposes in one and the same speech act the indistinguishable nature of their worship. This literal and scandalously irreverent reversal in the form of the secularization of the most sacred moment of the Catholic mass turns into a stunning sanctification of the flesh. The moment highlights the uncanny return of the repressed sensualism of a religion that relies on the suppression of its most humane features. Humorously, Heine the Jew posing as a Protestant brings out the irony that the most extreme expression of the secular is the most extreme expression of the religious:

> "Francesca!" I cried, "Star of my thoughts! Thought of my soul! *vita della mia vita!* My beautiful, oft-kissed, slender, Catholic Francesca! for this one night, if thou wilt grant it to me, I will become a Catholic—but only for this night! Oh the beautiful, blessed, Catholic night! I will lie in thy arms, with deepest Catholicism, I will believe in the heaven of thy love, we will kiss the sweet confession from our lips, the Word will be made flesh, Faith will become corporeal in body and in form! oh what religion! Ye priests, ring forth meanwhile in joy your Kyrie Eleison, ring, burn incense, sound the bells! let the organ be heard, peal out the mass of Palestrina—that is the Body!—I believe, I am blest, I sleep—but so soon as I awake on the next morning, I will rub away sleep and Catholicism from my eyes, and see again clearly the sunlight and the Bible, and be as before, Protestant, reasonable, and sober. (L 3, 275f.)

> "Franscheska!" rief ich, "Stern meiner Gedanken! Gedanke meiner Seele! Vita della mia vita! Meine schöne, oftgeküßte, schlanke, katholische Franscheska! für diese einzige Nacht, die du mir noch gewährst, will ich selbst katholisch werden—aber auch nur für diese einzige Nacht! O, die schöne, selige, katholische Nacht! Ich liege in deinen Armen, strengkatholisch glaube ich an den Himmel deiner Liebe, von den Lippen küssen wir uns das holde Bekenntnis, das Wort wird Fleisch, der Glaube wird versinnlicht, in Form und Gestalt, welche Religion! Ihr Pfaffen! jubelt unterdessen Eur Kyrie Eleison, klingelt, räuchert, läutet die Glocken, laßt die Orgel brausen, laßt die Messe von Palestrina erklingen—das ist der Leib!—ich glaube, ich bin selig, ich schlafe ein—aber sobald ich des anderen Morgens erwache, reibe ich mir den Schlaf und den Katholizismus aus den Augen, und sehe wieder klar in die Sonne und in die Bibel, und bin wieder protestantisch vernünftig und nüchtern, nach wie vor." (B 2, 495f.)

If profanation can be perfected as a form of high art, Heine certainly offers a formidable example. But at the same time, this act of profanation performs a sanctification.

We have seen in Chapter 6 how the coincidence of the two movements, the simultaneity of the human and the divine, the sensual and the spiritual, represents a central concern in Heine, a concern whose fundamental significance cannot be stressed enough. Addressed in terms of secularization,

Heine's Italian travel picture underlines the fact that secularization does not operate in a neutral sphere, as it were, outside of religion in a context devoid of religious meaning. Rather, secularization's theological-political implications rear their head with indefatigable resilience. Heine's extravagant mix of sex and religion drives the point home that religion is not a pure product of divine spirituality but always already contingent on the process of secularization in which it is steeped, but which it seeks at the same time to deny, repress, and transcend. For Heine, secularization represents a process that is continuous with religion.

Just like the opposition between day and night, the secular and sacred, so do Catholicism and Protestantism stand in a complementary relationship that conceals their common but hidden origins. The claim of each to the monopoly they in fact share eclipses the rights of that other, third religious tradition that disagrees with the Pauline distinction between letter and spirit that both confessions presuppose—and necessarily so—as the very condition of their right to existence. While they might fancy sharing their power the way day and night together rule all of life on earth—an aspiration and fantasy prefigured in the pope's 1494 decision to divide the world into two equal hemispheres between Portugal and Spain—the Protestant wake-up call brings with its forced sobriety the silent memory of what goes unmentioned but is recalled by the text as Christianity's repressed: the Jewish body that Christianity spiritualizes and thus instrumentalizes in an act of secularization of its own, albeit to a dubious theological-political end.

Heine's double entendre confuses and mixes up flesh and spirit, body and mind and so undoes the key distinction on which the theological underpinning of Christianity hinges. The reinstatement of the senses and the resurrection of the body is thus bound up with the act of secularization and is at the same time more than just the profanation of the sacred. For it functions simultaneously as a sanctification of what religion itself had secularized, that is, expelled beyond the proper sphere of religion as defined by Christianity in either its Catholic or Protestant iteration—and in sharp distinction to the Jewish tradition the two confessions claim to have superseded.

This critical concern announces itself in the seemingly innocuous presentation of the narrator "as a Protestant." Heine's program of reclaiming the rights of the senses and the rehabilitation of the flesh, the emancipation of the body, and the recalibration of the function of the mind as a function of the dynamics of the affects emerge in the context of a renegotiation of the theory of secularization that insistently brings home the point that the Christian paradigm of theorizing secularization is problematic and requires critical correction. More than just a frivolous or iconoclastic move, Heine's intervention signals the recovery of the Jewish voice as a necessary condition of any genuine praxis of universal emancipation true to its name.

For Heine, then, secularization is anything but a straightforward process that signals the demise of religion. Rather, secularization comes into view as dialectically interrelated with religion. As a consequence, civil society and the state do not represent a base-level rationality where religion has been contained as a private affair of personal faith and belief. On the contrary, the state and civil society are the result of a process in which religion is the driving force of a process of secularization that brings out religion's emancipatory potential:

> Only so long as religions are rivals, and more persecuted than persecutors, are they noble and worthy of honour [. . .] The monopoly of system is as injurious to religions as to trades; they are only strong and energetic by free competition, and they will again bloom up in their primitive purity and beauty so soon as the political equality of the Lord's service, or, so to speak, so soon as the trades-freedom of the divinities, is introduced. (L 3, 314f.)

> Nur so lange die Religionen mit anderen zu rivalisieren haben, und weit mehr verfolgt werden als selbst verfolgen, sind sie herrlich und ehrenswert. [. . .] Wie den Gewerben ist auch den Religionen das Monopolsystem schädlich, durch freie Konkurrenz bleiben sie kräftig, und sie werden erst dann zu ihrer ursprünglichen Herrlichkeit erblühen, sobald die politische Gleichheit der Gottesdienst, so zu sagen die Gewerbefreiheit der Götter eingeführt wird. (B 2, 518)

For Heine, the notion of "state religion" is just another name for the problematic entanglement of state and religion, a "freak" or "monster" (Missgeburt) produced by the unfortunate affair between secular and religious power (B 2, 517). In contrast, where there is no special state-sponsored monopoly of one religion over others and religions are left to themselves, their lack of privileged state support guarantees an equality that will only benefit and bring out the best, that is, the emancipatory impulse that underlies the mission of religions at their best. As Heine had playfully suggested in an earlier chapter of *The City of Lucca*: while the shared profession of religious leaders might result in their sharing similar features, posture, and facial expressions, their differences are defined by the material conditions that dictate their property regimes:

> It is a well-known observation that priests, all the world over, whether Rabbis, Muftis, Dominicans, Councillors of the Consistory, Popes, Bonzes, in short, the whole diplomatic corps of the Lord, have a certain family likeness in their faces, such as we are accustomed to find in those who follow the same trade. Tailors in every quarter of the globe have weak legs, butchers and soldiers all have a fierce colour and style, and the Jews have their own peculiar honourable expression, not because they spring from Abraham, Isaac, and Jacob, but because they are business men, and

> the Frankfort Christian shopman looks as much like a Frankfort Jewish shopman as one rotten egg looks like another. And the spiritual shop-people, such as get their living by the religion business, also acquire by it a resemblance in countenance. (L 3, 259f.)
>
> Ist es doch eine bekannte Bemerkung, daß die Pfaffen in der ganzen Welt, Rabbinen, Muftis, Dominikaner, Konsistorialräte, Popen, Bonzen, kurz das ganze diplomatische Corps Gottes, im Gesichte eine gewisse Familienähnlichkeit haben, wie man sie immer findet bei Leuten, die ein und dasselbe Gewerbe treiben. Schneider, in der ganzen Welt, zeichnen sich aus durch Zartheit der Glieder, Metzger und Soldaten tragen wieder überall denselben farouschen Anstrich, Juden haben ihre eigentümlich ehrliche Miene, nicht weil sie von Abraham, Isaak und Jakob abstammen, sondern weil sie Kaufleute sind, und der Frankfurter christliche Kaufmann sieht dem Frankfurter jüdischen Kaufmanne eben so ähnlich, wie ein faules Ei dem andern. Die geistlichen Kaufleute, solche die von Religionsgeschäften ihren Unterhalt gewinnen, erlangen daher auch im Gesichte eine Ähnlichkeit. (B 2, 486)

Whereas the servants of God of all the various religious traditions show a "certain family resemblance" (*Familienähnlichkeit*), the differences between the material conditions that define their occupation, status, and the way they relate to the means of production—property or lease—inform the life of organized religion right down to the subtleties of their theological distinctions:

> Of course certain shades of difference result from the manner and fashion in which they do business. The Catholic priest manages it like a clerk who has a place in an extensive establishment. The firm of the Church, at whose head is the Pope, gives him a regular occupation and a regular salary; he works leisurely or lazily, like every man who is not in business on his own account, and has many fellow-labourers, and who escapes observation among the multitude; only he has the credit of the house at heart, and still more its permanence, since by a bankruptcy he would lose his means of support. (L 3, 260)
>
> Freilich, einige Nuancen entstehen durch die Art und Weise wie sie ihr Geschäft treiben. Der katholische Pfaffe treibt es mehr wie ein Commis, der in einer großen Handlung angestellt ist; die Kirche, das große Haus, dessen Chef der Papst ist, gibt ihm bestimmte Beschäftigung und dafür ein bestimmtes Salär; er arbeitet lässig, wie jeder, der nicht für eigne Rechnung arbeitet und viele Kollegen hat, und im großen Geschäftstreiben leicht unbemerkt bleibt—nur der Kredit des Hauses liegt ihm am Herzen, und noch mehr dessen Erhaltung, da er bei einem etwaigen Bankerotte seinen Lebensunterhalt verlöre. (B 2, 486)

While the priest of the Catholic denomination acts like the clerk of a big corporation and is less concerned about short-term sales and profit than about the solidity and longevity of the firm, the Protestant reverend foreshadows the features of the self-reliant entrepreneur that Max Weber will identify as the driving agent of capitalism in his *Protestant Ethics and the Spirit of Capitalism*:

> The Protestant clergyman is, on the contrary, everywhere himself principal, and he carries on the religion business on his own account. He does not drive a wholesale business like his Catholic colleague, but only a small retail trade, and as he represents his own interests, it would never do for him to be negligent. He must cry up his articles of faith to the people, depreciate those of his rivals, and, like a real retailer, he stands in his small shop, full of professional envy of all the large houses, particularly of the great firm in Rome, which salaries so many thousand bookkeepers and salesmen, and has its factories in every quarter of the globe. (L 3, 260f.)
>
> Der protestantische Pfaffe hingegen ist überall selbst Prinzipal, und er treibt die Religionsgeschäfte für eigene Rechnung. Er treibt keinen Großhandel wie sein katholischer Gewerbsgenosse, sondern nur einen Kleinhandel; und da er demselben allein vorstehen muß, darf er nicht lässig sein, er muß seine Glaubensartikel den Leuten anrühmen, die Artikel seiner Konkurrenten herabsetzen, und als echter Kleinhändler steht er in seiner Ausschnittbude, voll von Gewerbeneid gegen alle großen Häuser, absonderlich gegen das große Haus in Rom, das viele tausend Buchhalter und Packknechte besoldet und seine Faktoreien hat in allen vier Weltteilen. (B 2, 486f.)

But again, while theological distinctions point to differences in material conditions, what unites the two entrepreneurial modi operandi is their subliminal resemblance to the business to which they sought to reduce the Jews, and not only in the Frankfurt ghetto. This discussion of the business practices of administered religion serves as a transition to prepare for the narrator's entering the city of Lucca. In the lead-up to the following punch line, the reader's attention is drawn to flaws in the two confessions' claim to legitimacy and to the fact that such business methods do not bode well for truth in advertising:

> A Catholic priest walks as if heaven belonged to him; a Protestant clergyman, on the contrary, goes about as if he had taken a lease of it. (L 3, 261)
>
> Ein katholischer Pfaffe wandelt einher als wenn ihm der Himmel gehöre; ein protestantischer Pfaffe hingegen geht herum als wenn er den Himmel gepachtet habe. (B 2, 487)

Rather, the framing of the narrative in *The City of Lucca*, with the narrator availing himself of the kisses of sultry Francesca and provocatively substituting her body for the body of Christ, suggests that secularization is the moment in which religion comes to exist in the world.

Secularization Theory as Counternarrative Heine's Intellectual History

If Heine's fiction and poetry do not address secularization as a process that renders religion obsolete, but cast it instead as the central operation of religion, his *On the History of Religion and Philosophy in Germany* offers a counternarrative of history that advances a theory of secularization with a critical difference. In contrast to Hegel's narrative—to which it responds, among others—which builds on Christianity as its sole point of reference, Heine's framework produces a history that sees Christianity in a larger context in which Judaism and paganism are more than just preliminary stages in a teleological scheme that posits Christianity as the sole candidate for the role of ushering in redemption. Rather, Heine's counternarrative challenges the Christian perspective and its supersessionist implications, which endured even in one of Christianity's most formidable critics, Voltaire. Voltaire, Heine explains, was only able to hurt the body, that is, the form, of Christianity, while its idea lived on unharmed (OH 10; B 3, 515):

> For Christianity is an idea and, as such, is indestructible and immortal like any idea. (OH 11)
>
> Denn das Christentum ist eine Idee, und also solche unzerstörbar und unsterblich, wie jede Idee. (B 3, 516)

Ideas call for a particular form of history.[8] Having no life of their own, they are contingent on the material conditions from which they arise. As their products, however, they have diagnostic significance and their study is anything but trivial as long as it is not taken hostage by speculative pretension but remains grounded in a critical consideration of the dynamics of the social and political forces that produce them.

In decentering the narratives and reframing religious history less in terms of a history of salvation than as a salvation of history, that is, the recognition of history as a category no longer subject to one or another privileged view on religion, Heine advances an approach to theorizing secularization that would replace the scheme of the distinction between the religious and the secular with a dialectical conception that takes account of the recognition that this distinction is itself already a product of secularization.

But, as Heine notes, "a true history of Christianity does not yet exist" (OH 10; B 3, 516) precisely because it is "an idea" rather than a phenomenon defined by its manifestations. Heine's point is to offer a history that accounts for the curious metaphysical nature of its subject, which in this case means that historiography is contingent on a speculative moment that requires that an idea prescribe the historian's grasp of the empirical forms in which the idea of Christianity manifests itself here on earth. However, this idea does not reveal itself through the study of all the tomes of church history or by attempting to make sense of the various doctrinal theological distinctions. Rather, Heine suggests, the idea of Christianity emerges through the study of the social forces that define individual biographies and the thoughts they produce. Examined this way, material history sheds light on Christianity as a particular idea or vision that has emerged historically over time. As Heine notes, this history is not straightforward and detached from the course of the rest of history, but as a history of ideas it is contingent on the material conditions that drive the processes of institutionalization, though not necessarily in a causally direct fashion. Rather, the idea of Christianity emerges as a sort of compromise formation in friction with the forces it opposes.[9] While Manichaeans and Gnostics, for instance, were outlawed and persecuted by the church, their impact on the formation of its theological doctrines was decisive. Not only did their symbolism shape Catholic art, "their way of thought (*Denkweise*) pervaded the entire life of the Christian peoples" (OH 12; B 3, 517). Notice the genealogy that Heine offers for the genesis of the idea he calls Christianity:

> At base, the Manicheans are not very different from the Gnostics. A characteristic of both is the doctrine of the two principles, good and evil, which battle each other. The former group, the Manicheans, took this doctrine from the ancient Persian religion, where Ormuz, light, is the enemy of Ahriman, darkness. The latter group, the true Gnostics, believed also in the pre-existence of the good principle, and they explained the origin of the evil principle by means of emanation, through the generation of eons [. . .] This Gnostic worldview was authentically Indian. It included the doctrines of divine incarnation, of the mortification of the flesh, of spiritual introversion, and it gave rise to the ascetic contemplative monastic life, which is the purest outgrowth of the Christian idea. This idea was expressed only in a very confused way in dogma and only very dimly in the cult. But everywhere we see the doctrine of the two principles in evidence: opposed to the good Christ stands the evil Satan; the world of spirit is represented by Christ, the world of matter by Satan; our soul belongs to the former, our body to the latter; and the whole world of appearance, nature, is thus originally evil; Satan, the Prince of Darkness, will thereby lure us to perdition; and it is essential to renounce all the sensual joys of life, to torment our body, Satan's fief, so that the soul can rise aloft, all the more nobly, into the lucid sky, into the bright kingdom of Christ. (OH 12f.)

> Die Manichäer sind ihrer letzten Gründe nach nicht sehr verschieden von den Gnostikern. Die Lehre von den beiden Prinzipien, dem guten und dem bösen, die sich bekämpfen, ist beiden eigen. Die einen, die Manichäer, erhielten diese Lehre aus der altpersischen Religion, wo Ormuz, das Licht, dem Ariman, der Finsternis, feindlich entgegengesetzt ist. Die anderen, die eigentlichen Gnostiker, glaubten vielmehr an die Präexistenz des guten Prinzips, und erklärten die Entstehung des bösen Prinzips durch Emanation, durch Generationen von Äonen [. . .] Diese gnostische Weltansicht ist urindisch und sie führte mit sich die Lehre von der Inkarnation Gottes, von der Abtötung des Fleisches, vom geistigen Insichselbstversenken, sie gebar das asketisch beschauliche Mönchsleben, welches die reinste Blüte der christlichen Idee. Diese Idee hat sich in der Dogmatik nur sehr verworren und im Kultus nur sehr trübe aussprechen können. Doch sehen wir überall die Lehre von den beiden Prinzipien hervortreten: dem guten Christus steht der böse Satan entgegen; die Welt des Geistes wird durch Christus, die Welt der Materie durch Satan repräsentiert; jenem gehört unsere Seele, diesem unser Leib; und die ganze Erscheinungswelt, die Natur, ist demnach ursprünglich böse, und Satan, der Fürst der Finsternis, will uns damit ins Verderben locken, und es gilt allen sinnlichen Freuden des Lebens zu entsagen, unsern Leib, das Lehn Satans, zu peinigen, damit die Seele sich desto herrlicher emporschwinge in den lichten Himmel, in das strahlende Reich Christi. (B 3, 517f.)

This storyline of the seamless transfer, assimilation, and incorporation of ancient Persian and Indian heritage brings home the point that the idea of Christianity is not the result of a unique vision grounded in a pristine epiphany of divine revelation but the product of a complicated, multifaceted negotiation of a diverse range of multiple and seemingly incompatible traditions. Given the richness of its genealogical filiations, the "Christian idea" arises as the result of a complicated and long-winded historical development whose constitutive features are shaped by a particular history of secularization. Casting Christianity as an idea predestines its historical manifestations to appear as instantiations of secularization as they manifest otherworldly aspects of a divinity whose transcendence can only be maintained as present in this world through secularization. Consequently, as a product of secularization, religion's claim to authenticity becomes problematic as its manifestation comes into view as a continuous reiteration of displaced origins.

Heine's discussion thus makes clear that writing the history of an idea is a contentious proposition that calls for a framework that must reflect the process of secularization on which any form of an idea of the divine necessarily hinges. This is the implicit assumption if this idea is to be grasped by the historian of ideas or to be claimed as property by the institutions that claim to represent this idea in the world. The historian of ideas thus faces the challenge that, in methodologically strict terms, his or her work represents itself a form of secularization that calls for critical reflection of the social and material conditions that define it.

The project of Christianization entails a further layer of secularization as Christianity repurposes ancient Gods and Goddesses as demons, ghosts, spooks, goblins, imps, elves, and so on. As a consequence, Christianity emerges as a religion that depends on secularization as its very means of existence. From Heine's account, it becomes clear that secularization is anything but a neutral operation; rather it is one saturated with religious implications and struggles for power.

Appropriating Judaism and transforming ancient mythologies, Christianity turns the world upside down, transforming a world breathing with divine presence into a rarefied and lifeless spirituality that stands in stark contrast to the pantheism of old, a pantheism that was brimming boisterously with life and replaced with a bleak vision of suffering and martyrdom. The loss of the diverse and rich forms of animist superstition attests, according to Heine, less to the triumph of Christianity than to an atrophy of life due to the insidious consequences of a desiccated spiritualism. Leaving behind the wreckage of bodies reduced to dead and meaningless matter, the vision of spiritual perfection comes at the cost of the final depletion of life. The result is a split world where Christian piety rules by day and the spirits, ghosts, and elves return to rule by night. This nocturnal realm of the repressed proliferates under the sign of a divided consciousness whose spiritualism relies on the repressed it denies. Christianity is built on the premise of the repression of the realm of evil it creates in order to suppress:

> This came about because the Christian clergy did not simply dismiss the pre-existent national gods as empty products of the imagination, but rather conceded them an actual existence. They maintained, though, that all of these gods were nothing but male and female devils, who had lost their power over people with the victory of Christ [. . .] The Olympic pantheon thus became an airy hell. (OH 16)

> Dieses entstand dadurch, daß die christliche Priesterschaft die vorgefundenen alten Nationalgötter nicht als leere Hirngespinste verwarf, sondern ihnen eine wirkliche Existenz einräumte, aber dabei behauptete, alle diese Götter seien lauter Teufel und Teufelinnen gewesen, die durch den Sieg Christi ihre Macht über die Menschen verloren [. . .] Der ganze Olymp wurde nun eine luftige Hölle. (B 3, 522)

The topographic reversal of the top of the world into abject repression could not be more graphic. It illustrates how profoundly repression and what it represses defines the "idea" of Christianity. This reversal or revolution—what Nietzsche will later describe as the revolt of the slaves—is characterized in terms of a process of secularization that occurs in the name of religion. Christianization thus "perverted" the religion it found among the ancient Germanic nations, turning their pantheist worldview into a vision of the world as pandemonium (OH 22; B 3, 529). While Christianity is defined by a categorical denial of sensualism, curiously, it depends on it at the same time as the very presupposition it would repress. As Heine puts it,

> Catholicism was a sort of Concordat between God and the Devil, that is, between spirit and matter, in which the full sovereignty of the spirit was proclaimed in theory, but that in practice, matter was put in the position of being able to exercise all of its annulled rights. (OH 24)
>
> daß der Katholizismus gleichsam ein Konkordat war zwischen Gott und dem Teufel, d.h. zwischen dem Geist und der Materie, wodurch die Alleinherrschaft des Geistes in der Theorie ausgesprochen wird, aber die Materie in den Stand gesetzt wird alle ihre annullierten Rechte in der Praxis auszuüben. (B 3, 531)

Ironically, this religious scheme creates an alliance that betrays religion to be profoundly dependent on the secular it so vehemently denounces and rejects:

> Thus, there arose a shrewd system of concessions to sensuality made by the Church, but granted always in such a way that each act of sensuality was denounced, and the spirit was secured against any scornful usurpations. (OH 24)
>
> Daher ein kluges System von Zugeständnissen, welche die Kirche zum Besten der Sinnlichkeit gemacht hat, obgleich immer unter Formen, welche jeden Akt der Sinnlichkeit fletrieren und dem Geiste seine höhnischen Usurpationen verwahren. (B 3, 531)

Turning to the fund-raising scheme of the letters of indulgence with which the Catholic Church made a fortune, Heine insists that this was not an aberration but a logical consequence of the whole system of the Catholic Church. Yet this pact with the devil, as it were, has its very secular and very mundane implications. For with the proceeds from the sale of the letters of indulgence, the church financed the lavish construction of Saint Peter's Cathedral,

> so that it was actually sin which gave the money to build this church, which was as it were a monument to the pleasure of the senses. (OH 25)
>
> so daß die Sünde ganz eigentlich das Geld hergab zum Bau dieser Kirche, die dadurch gleichsam ein Monument sinnlicher Lust wurde. (B 3, 532)

And Heine adds mockingly:

> It is thus perhaps more accurate to say that this house of God was built by the devil than the Cologne Cathedral. This triumph of spiritualism, that sensualism itself had to build it its most beautiful temple. (OH 25)
>
> Von diesem Gotteshause könnte man vielleicht eher als von dem Kölner Dome behaupten, daß es durch den Teufel erbaut worden. Diesen Triumph des Spiritualismus, daß der Sensualismus selber ihm seinen schönsten Tempel bauen mußte. (B 3, 532)

But this triumph, Heine suggests at the same time, is precarious. If sin, sensualism, and even demonization are decisive features of the Catholic Church, secularization emerges not just historically but also theologically as its constitutive moment, which in turn prepares the ground for Luther's reformation, which will initiate a second-order secularization by reappropriating the goods of the Catholic Church in the name of a new spirituality meant to supersede Catholicism in the name of Protestantism—from which, eventually, modern German philosophy will emerge.

In pointed distinction to Hegel's secularization narrative, which grounds philosophy in the Protestant spirit, Heine's version presents the history of religion and philosophy with a bill of the costs of the repression and containment of what it excludes, domesticates, and silences. Heine's account of secularization is inextricably bound up with the moment of secularization that informs Christianity from the start as a movement whose supersessionism defines it as intrinsically expropriatory. As Christianity recasts the sacred in relation to the Jewish tradition it expropriated, it produces the secular as a theologically necessary category. This move is driven by the dichotomy that pitches spiritualism over and against sensualism as mutually exclusive modes of existence, as Heine never ceases to remind us. Heine's implied critique of Hegel is that he turns a blind eye to the emancipatory moment of the sensual and rarefies his secularization narrative into an exclusive affair of faith as a form of consciousness that has long become spirit, thus shedding its bodily function and reducing "nature" to mere matter.

Heine's theory of secularization contradicts the narratives of the functional transformation of religious to secular forms, suggesting to the contrary that the distinction between the divine or sacred and the secular remains—fraught with theological assumptions—problematic and contingent on the theological-political regime that defines the distinction. Exposing this distinction as itself theological, Heine's version of the secularization narrative counters both its complementary one-sided Enlightenment and romantic versions while advancing a distinctly post-secular approach that—far from, and critical of, any supposition of a return of religion—attends to the profoundly historical nature of both religion and reason as both its weakness and its potential strength. For Heine as for Spinoza, religious traditions may lend themselves to use as a means of domination, but historically they have also served—and thus carry the promise of continuing to do so in the future—as empowering levers for liberation. Similarly, for Heine, it is not the theological-political aspects of religion that are the problem but the complicity of organized religion in submitting to the lure of political power and the temptation of oppression for ulterior political motives.

To put it differently, for Heine, religions are fluid social practices that are to be understood differentially in relation to the specific social and political circumstances in which they arise. If they might be used as powerful instruments of domination and oppression, the reason for this is that they seize on the hopes and dreams of redemption. If Heine opposed Christianity, he did so from a renegade Jewish point of view that brought the most liberating force of prophetic critique and messianic hope to the fore. Where he opposed Catholicism he did so from a "Protestant" point of view, all the while suggesting this Protestantism's Jewish sources. And where he exposed the problematic aspects of this Protestantism, he did so by accentuating the redemptive force of Catholicism. Equally critical of the doctrinaire aspects of certain accentuations of Jewish tradition, he did not shy away from exposing its problematic nature from a "Christian" point of view. Heine's negotiation of a differential position between religions not only highlights the differential character that defines religious traditions as mutually contingent on each other, but articulates an original way of addressing the notion that there is no theological–politically neutral position "outside" or beyond religion. Rather, the post-secular stance that Heine's negotiation of secularization narratives articulates is one that, in the wake of Spinoza, Lessing, and Kant, attends to the practical meaning of religion as a sociological function irreducible to, and incommensurate with, truth claims. As expressions of visions of the hope for universal emancipation, religion's multiple traditions offer themselves as unique resources for enabling a rethinking of the terms of modernity.

Heine brings the dissonant Jewish perspective into play as a critical corrective or counterthrust that challenges all unexamined recourse to the secular as unaffected by the theological-political nexus that informs the distinction between the secular and the religious. As a consequence, Heine switches the frame of reference by suggesting different perspectives that challenge the entrenched hermeneutic horizons. Introducing a notion of constellation that suggestively preludes the later concept operative in Benjamin and Adorno, Heine's provocatively pleasurable play with the differential aspects of the multiple strands of religious traditions articulates a critical resistance against the presumption of a meta-level where secularization could be theorized without consideration of the theological-political conditions that define it.

This critical resistance drives the silent recourse to Jewish tradition in Benjamin, Kracauer, Adorno, Bloch, and—in more subdued fashion—in

Horkheimer and Marcuse. It is the critical lever that emphatically reclaims the moment of redemption as its own, because religion already is the secularization it seeks to deny it is. Heine's secularization narratives advance a dialectical rethinking of the interplay between secularization and religion, one that sets free the emancipatory force of thinking in constellations.

8

Another Abraham, Another Sarah: Heine's Frankfurt Shul in *The Rabbi of Bacherach*

This concluding chapter explores Heinrich Heine's story *The Rabbi of Bacherach* as a critical renegotiation or, if you wish, a modern midrash on Abraham, Sarah, and Isaac. The fragmentary story takes us to the Frankfurt ghetto's synagogue on the first day of Passover; for Abraham and Sarah, who have just escaped the pogrom in Bacherach, this will prove to be only the penultimate stop. Leaving the Frankfurt synagogue, they meet Don Isaac, with whom they end up at a restaurant where they can finally enjoy the meal that had been so violently interrupted the day before on the first night of Passover. The story's conclusion at Schnapper-Elle's restaurant becomes a celebration of the reconciliation of the multiple strands of tradition in which diversity becomes the life-affirming act of restoring the pleasure of the difference that sustains the life of tradition. We can then read Heine's *Rabbi of Bacherach* as a story that captures the Frankfurt School's vision of difference as the openness that powers the emancipatory impulse. If Heine's story is a fragment that is open to the future and looks toward the "restaurative" moment of redemptive experience, it also attends to the central categories of the dissonant aesthetics and critical commitments that Critical Theory will articulate in striking affinity with him. Just as for Heine the pleasures of Schnapper-Elle's kitchen hold the "restaurative" promise of the multiple origins of tradition, so the messianic impulse returns in Benjamin, Adorno, Marcuse, Fromm, and their associates as the "tiger's leap": the empowering recovery of the emancipatory force of the past that was missed but lives on through the redemptive move of critical retrieval. Like Heine's Don Isaac, who proudly bears the lion in his coat of arms, that other feline's move, the tiger's leap, sets free the repressed multiple origins of tradition. If the Frankfurt School has long been reduced to secularized modes, Heine's Frankfurt shul reminds us that the trajectory of its Critical Theory comes into full view only if we grasp the critical importance of the singularity of its own positionality, that is, the particular stance from which it addresses Jewish tradition as a critical resource. Reading Heine's Jewish historical novel with Critical Theory in mind not only opens possibilities for understanding Heine's story, it also illuminates the inner tensions and promise of Critical Theory's emancipatory project.

Heine began work on what he envisioned would be his signal contribution to the Jewish historic novel—in the style of, but also in critical distance to, Walter Scott, whose *Ivanhoe* was certainly a source of inspiration—in the 1820s in Berlin in the context of his collaboration with the Verein für die Cultur und Wissenschaft der Juden, the circle of young and aspiring students of Hegel, foremost among them Eduard Gans and Leopold Zunz, the pioneering figures of the Wissenschaft des Judentums. But it was not until 1840—when Heine, working as foreign correspondent for the German press in Paris, witnessed the rage around the Damascus affair, during which the Jews of Damascus were accused of blood libel—that he decided to publish *The Rabbi of Bacherach*. In the capital of the nineteenth century, the return of the age-old accusation had a particular sting, recalling that even his city of exile and hope, the city of modernity, the Paris that always had been worth a mass, had, after all, not shed all its medieval trappings, but could still succumb at a moment's notice to dangerous religious anachronisms.

This is the context in which Heine decided to return to publish his story, and Heine scholarship has been quick to point out the specific contemporary dimension of the historical novel. While this work—one of Heine's most enigmatic—has recently been the subject of some renewed attention, surprisingly the figures at the center of the plot, Abraham and Sarah, remain underexposed. To be sure, they have been read as characters in terms of the plot, but the question that calls for examination—the question of how to read them in relation to the biblical subtext and Jewish tradition in general—has received little if any critical attention. It has of course not escaped the attention of most critics that Abraham and Sarah appear to function as allegorical figures. But this only raises the question of who is really who in this allegory, and of how this allegory, if it is one, is to be read. Heine's somewhat anemic depiction of Abraham and Sarah as typologically sketched figures rather than fully embodied life-breathing characters may have led to such reductive responses that focus on the plot while ignoring the intertextual allusions. But I would argue that while Heine interacts playfully with such readings, the text points at the same in a different direction, inviting us to rethink the way Abraham, Sarah, as well as Isaac have been seen and figured through the ages.[1]

Heine invites his readers to think about Jewish tradition in terms of a continual reinvention and renegotiation. His text, I argue, is informed by a creative, midrashic impulse that contributes in a critical manner to the life of Jewish tradition. His bold intervention consists of rethinking and reimagining Jewish modernity as a vital player in a modernity that has yet to emerge and to which Jewish tradition has much to contribute. This at least is what a close reading of *The Rabbi of Bacherach* suggests.

The story plays around the year 1487 in Bacherach, a small town on the Rhine River.[2] It is the evening of the first Seder of Passover and a large group of family and friends has gathered in the house of Abraham, the rabbi of Bacherach, and his wife Sarah. While the house resounds during the festivities with the life of children, the young couple has none of their own. Abraham and Sarah can be read here either as suggestively opposite, contrasting characters to those of the biblical story, or else as representing the couple at an early stage prior to the two divine messengers' visit and announcement of Sarah's conception of Isaac.

At the moment when the Seder requires that the host open the door and welcome everybody who is hungry to join and share in the dinner, two strangers enter the dining room. They are welcomed to join and sit down at the table. Unlike the two biblical messengers sent to announce the conception of Isaac, which sets Abraham and Sarah at ease, the story's scene stages the familiar past as the uncanny present:

> Then the hall-door opened, and there entered two tall, pale men, wrapped in very broad cloaks, who said: "Peace be with you. We are men of your faith on a journey, and wish to share the Passover-feast with you!" (L 1, 186)[3]
>
> Da öffnete sich die Saaltüre, und hereintraten zwei große blasse Männer, in sehr weiten Mänteln gehüllt, und der eine sprach: "Friede sei mit Euch, wir sind reisende Glaubensgenossen und wünschen das Paschafest mit Euch zu feiern." (B 1, 467)

Abraham invites them to join and resumes the chanting of the Haggadah. At some point Abraham realizes with fright that the two guests have planted the body of a dead child under the table. Carrying on as if nothing has happened, Abraham ushers Sarah out of the dining room and escapes with her at once. They escape in a rowboat on the Rhine River with the help of "Dumb Wilhelm" (L 1, 191; B 1, 470), a German neighbor's loyal and mute son, who seems to have expected them. The next morning, they arrive safely in Frankfurt on the Main River and are let into the ghetto just in time for the morning service. As Abraham chants the Kaddish for the entire Bacherach community, Sarah realizes that all the friends and relations they left behind have fallen victims to the Easter pogrom. After the service they are invited to supper at Schnapper-Elle's restaurant with some of Frankfurt's more colorful characters.

While the choice of the protagonists' names may at first seem simply fortuitous and suggestive, the description of the service at the synagogue takes a telling turn:

> When on the platform, the velvet cover as well as the wrappings covered with illuminated letters were removed, and the chief singer, in the peculiar intonation which in the Passover service is still more peculiarly sounded, read the edifying narrative of the temptation of Abraham. (L 1, 221)

> Auf der erwähnten Bühne zog man von dem heiligen Buche das samtne Mäntelchen, so wie auch die mit bunten Buchstaben beschriebenen Windeln, womit es umwickelt war, und aus der geöffneten Pergamentrolle, in jenem singenden Tone, der am Paschafest noch gar besonders moduliert wird, las der Vorsänger die erbauliche Geschichte von der Versuchung Abrahams. (B 1, 489)

Describing the narrative as "edifying" signals more than just irony. For the events in Bacherach that enabled the escape of the two survivors are a stirring reminder of the larger meaning of this "edifying narrative." Beneath the apparently detached description, the startling use of the word "edifying" in the context of the Akedah, the Binding of Isaac, expresses profound pain. Grimm's dictionary offers the following words as synonyms for "edifying" (*erbaulich*): "salutary, wholesome, beneficial" (salutaris, heilsam, nützlich), but notes: "often used ironically for repugnant, unpleasant, unedifying" (oft ironisch für widrig, unangenehm, unerbaulich). The jarring note in Heine's use of the word creates a dissonance that causes the reader to pause and wonder. Abraham's temptation is a theme the text underlines with explicit emphasis. This hint assumes pointed significance if we recall that the Akedah is not what the Passover reading of the Torah addresses. Rather, the portion read out from the Pentateuch on the first day of Passover addresses a different, yet no less central episode to Heine's plot: the exodus from Egypt. In an intricately spun dialectics, the escape from Bacherach to Frankfurt represents both an escape to freedom and, at the same time, a modern-day version of the temptation to return to the very fleshpots of Egypt from which the Hebrews once took leave.

But this dialectics is only intimated as Heine directs the reader's attention to the figures of Abraham and Sarah. While their story may not be part of Passover, it is part of the Rosh Hashanah or New Year service. Whether or not Heine was aware of this fact, whether this was an error on his part or intended, is of little consequence. The point is that this passage links Heine's text with more than just the names of Abraham and Sarah. It invites the reader to attend to the deeper resonances and affinities with a tradition that this text not only stages anew but also creatively renegotiates.

But what kinds of readings does Heine solicit? A telling instantiation of what it means to read is exemplified by Sarah's dreamful blending of biblical figures while Father Rhine gently rocks her to sleep when she escapes on the river. The reading indicated by her dreamt staging is suggestively different from Abraham's rabbinic approach to tradition. But even he has to learn that reading the words of the Passover Haggadah ultimately means more than simply following and repeating them. As the appearance of the guests and their smuggling of the body of the dead boy suggests, every repetition is at the same time also different: there is no repetition without difference, change, and transformation; and no life of tradition without break and rupture.[4] In other words, the prayers are indeed performative speech acts that change every time they are spoken in different contexts, representing in these changing contexts ever new and unique reiterations of always singular and unique pronunciations. Tradition cannot be imagined as unchangeable; it changes with each and every appeal to itself.

Transmission literally rests on the uncanny function of substitution. The dramatic case of planting the corpse of a boy as the "corpus delicti" does not only represent the continual threat of the end of tradition. It also functions as the uncanny hinge on which repetition in difference, which gives life to tradition, depends. The plot, however, stages the instrumentalization of death as a misguided attempt to renew one tradition by killing another, using the death of one's own tradition in order to cause the death of another. It will only be through the embrace of life—of a life that returns, if unexpectedly, as the story will suggest at a later point—that the substitution of death, rather than the instrumentalization of its substitution, will bring back life and the life of tradition. The substitution of martyrdom replaces the martyrdom of substitution whose transferential economy the story exposes as the insidious threat of a manipulative quid pro quo that not only suggests a dark commentary on the children's traditional search for the afikomen[5] but also ultimately deprives the dead of their dignity as it subjects them to the ultimate violation of turning them into the cause for the compulsive repetition of their fate: murder and death.

But let us return to Sarah, who in this story experiences what Abraham has yet to learn. Allegorically overdetermined, Sarah and Abraham figure also as representatives for opposed yet complementary approaches to reading and tradition. With this story, Heine adds to the tradition a midrash that does not simply oppose or reject dominant views of the tradition but opens tradition up to a richer approach to interpretation. Abraham and Sarah are characters that vary as they repeat, change, and transform, even while they remain bearers of a continuity that hinges on the discontinuity of break, rupture, and substitution that makes tradition and its continuity possible in the first place. This may relate to why Heine calls the story "a fragment." As it breaks off open-ended, the story highlights the fact that in modernity, tradition remains always just that: a fragment. Yet Heine's post-romantic take casts the fragment as the placeholder of a totality that exists only thanks to rupture and discontinuity, the interpretative play that reconstitutes its continuity through the emancipatory move of imaginative reappropriation. The incomplete, unfinished, open-ended quality makes tradition a "fragment," that is, a work in progress that hinges on the future as the ever-changing perspective from which the past opens in ever newly reconfigured constellations.[6]

As the story unwinds in the relaxed atmosphere of conversations over dinner at Schnapper-Elle's restaurant, Heine's creative way of reimagining tradition in general, and Jewish tradition in particular, takes center stage as a tradition provided by knowing women and their art of cooking, a tradition that goes through the stomach. This is a theme that runs through Heine's work, and the proponent of this alternative approach to tradition in *The Rabbi of Bacherach* is the glamorous Don Quixote-like figure Don Isaac Abarbanel, Heine's playful and conflicted alter ego.

We have now approached the question of how to read this story in terms of the hermeneutic guidance the text provides. There is more to say in that respect, and the entire manner in which Heine describes the education of Abraham at home in Ashkenaz and abroad in Spain gives additional clues. Abraham's and Sarah's different ways of addressing tradition and scripture not only highlight different but complementary forms of hermeneutic practice, they also make clear, more importantly, that neither of them alone represents the whole of Jewish tradition. Rather, it is in marriage and creative exchange that the individual approaches are brought to fertile realization. The absence of children in their marriage may indicate that taken for themselves, neither of their hermeneutic practices will do and that only once they both accept and embrace each other with love will they create the grounds for living transmission. Young as Abraham and Sarah are in the story, they remind the reader that the stage of creative continuity may well still lie in the future, at a time when their marriage will be truly consummated in the biblical sense of mutual recognition—a possibility suggested by the story's description of the couple's rather sterile living arrangements in Ashkenaz.

The text thus articulates a protocol for reading and interpretation that calls for a more attentive approach to the way its characters are configured. Sarah seems the more passive figure in this story, but it is also she who represents the emancipatory force of poetic imagination. No wonder that, while Abraham is Isaac Abarbanel's intimate friend, Isaac—Heine's charming double—seems to be drawn to Sarah as the lady of his desires. Sarah represents more the haggadic and imaginary side of Jewish tradition, whereas Abraham represents the cool of halachic reasoning. But in her suffering, Sarah is also pointedly different from her biblical model. It is as if with the absence of Isaac the power and liberating force of laughter has been suspended. Delegated to Isaac Abarbanel, mockery, irony, poetic imagination, and humor are correlated with Sarah. At first, however, she seems no longer capable of recognizing Isaac as her own. His pledge to serve as her knight is gently but firmly refused when offered during his entrance, his extravagant street performance. The decisive link between laughter, creativity, and Jewish tradition has been severed and awaits future reconstitution. Interestingly, it is Abraham who will instantly put both Sarah and Isaac at ease; but he will also be what initially prevents their quick and easy meeting. With Abraham's recognition of his old friend from his student days, the relationship between Isaac and Sarah is at once transformed from one of erotic desire—solicited by Isaac and refused by Sarah—to a more solid, lasting, but also creative form of family relation. The play of sublimation and redirection of desire reconstitutes the interfamilial relationships as it brings the Sephardi and Ashkenazi sides together in an economy of the affects and emotions that transcends individual desire and sets free an alternative vision of the patronage of art.

As Isaac is forced to abandon his initial attempt to imitate the Christian-coded eroticism of the ascetic troubadour poet dependent on patronage—a relationship that came to define the role and function of art at large—his art is given the chance to figure as an independent and autonomous form of creativity no longer subject to the whims of the powers that be. The *Romanzero*'s "Hebrew Melodies" will make the point of this scene more explicit in its densely overdetermined meaning. There, the description of Yehuda Halevi, the lyric I's alter ego, is couched precisely in the terms of independence, autonomy, and poetic sovereignty that the figure of the medieval troubadour could only dream of in moments of exalted aspiration. Famously, the "Hebrew Melodies" will conclude with the anticlimactic note of Queen Blanche's verdict on the rabbi and monk as both despicable characters who "stink." In critical contrast, Sarah will not accept Isaac as a servant who seeks her patronage, but does eventually welcome him as the friend of her husband and as an equal: the lost son who reconstitutes the family, although on new terms.[7]

In Heine's story, Abraham is characterized by his youth; and with his parents deceased, he is more the exponent of an epigonal existence than his biblical equivalent who leaves home to create a new people. Heine's Abraham appears more like the end point rather than the beginning of the Jewish people. His personality is complicated, erratic, and opaque, whereas the biblical patriarch is known for his pure simplicity and unwavering character. Like his biblical counterpart, the rabbi leaves his home to move to a foreign country. But unlike his biblical predecessor, he returns after seven years; as if to guarantee his future return, the rabbi of Bacherach performs the marital vows declaring Sarah his wife as he rushes to take leave. The seven-year hiatus is of course a playful reference to Jacob's—Isaac's second son's—courting of Rachel but getting Leah first instead, and Rachel only after seven additional years of serving her father. The young rabbi Abraham seems to spend his life locked inside a circle of the self-fulfilling prophecies of a spurious commentator. In an underhanded way, Heine's story seems to suggest that it might be the hermeneutically vicious circle of epigonal supplication that leads to the rabbi's failure as far as his desire for biblical succession—reduced to mere imitation and repetition—is concerned. Only thanks to the grace of Sarah, whom he seems to guide and lead, is Abraham shown his own way. Without Sarah's haggadic imagination, Abraham's halachic reasoning would remain blind.

Despite all his righteousness, Abraham displays one major flaw. It is so preposterous that it qualifies to be seen as profoundly tragic: Abraham's escape with Sarah on the Seder night comes with the heavy burden of leaving behind a bloodbath in which all his friends and relatives will find certain death. This is an unbearable dilemma. The story challenges the reader with an ethical question it poses only tacitly, but therefore all the more eloquently, as the silent question that looms over the story. Its uncanny, unspoken presence throws a dark shadow over the story, endowing it with a bleakness from which commentators and critics recoil in horror. As a moment that seems beyond the conventional parameters of ethics, it appears as an uncanny repetition of Abraham's challenge on Mount Moriah. It is the dilemma and paradox of the obligation of Kiddush Hashem, the sanctification of God by self-sacrifice: if young rabbi Abraham refuses to escape certain death with his community, there will be no witness and no continuation of life. If, on the other hand, he is lucky enough to escape with Sarah, the question poses itself irresistibly: What kind of life will this be? If the ethical dilemma transports the situation beyond the question of guilt and innocence, Heine's story frames its radical challenge in stark difference to Kierkegaard's logic of foregone conclusion. Interestingly, in Heine's account the outcome is not faith but a practice that undergoes transformation as it is enriched by the marriage with Sarah and consequently the marriage of Halacha and Aggadah. The terms of the logic of the ethical dilemma are thus staged in a context that is profoundly different from the morally determined framework that defines Kierkegaard's captive logic.[8]

In Heine, the repetition of the Akedah is without divine intervention. But the question remains: Has Abraham lost his faith, as he does not await the course of events but prudently makes for a safe exit for himself and Sarah? The biblical Abraham's situation cannot be repeated *tel quel*, the story seems to suggest. The rabbinic variant of Abraham, the rabbi of Bacherach, has all the scholarship, wisdom, and authority of a long tradition. But the heart of the lion poised to protect Israel with the sword of sharp wit and humor resides in Isaac Abarbanel—that is, the historic figure of Yehuda Abarbanel, also known as Leone Ebreo. Claiming Davidian lineage, the Abarbanel family featured Judah's coat of arms with a lion. Don Isaac, however, flaunts his feline nature with an ironic pride that braves the world but shies away from water—the water of baptism, as he emphatically notes. Rabbi Abraham finds himself in the dilemma that defines the Akedah and which Emil Fackenheim identifies in the face of the Holocaust: What is more important, saving Judaism or the life of Jews—and how could the two possibly be distinguished?[9] The predicament of choosing between life and death, the deadlocked dilemma between choosing Jewish life or Jewish faith, remains irresolvably caught up in paradox. Heine's story seems to suggest that Kiddush Hashem, the final resort of Jewish martyrdom often practiced in medieval Ashkenaz, rubs problematically against a reading of the Akedah that brings home its liberating, revolutionary, and very secular implications. Ultimately, the biblical figure of Abraham trumps his rabbinical counterpart and Halacha is kept in check by Aggadah. While the biblical Abraham receives his blessings and divine intervention turns the course of events around, making his attempt at sacrifice an instant of divine transformation, rabbi Abraham's halachic literalism realizes the law, but only with regard to the letter and at the expense of the spirit. Because he follows the law, he eventually becomes a "renegade," whereas Isaac Abarbanel, the openly confessed renegade, is the true bearer of his name. He is the Isaac this late medieval or early modern Abraham will never have, or at least not until he has freed himself from reducing the law to the letter and released the internal openness of Jewish tradition he has so far contained in keeping the past of his Sephardic experience from his Ashkenazi present.

If Isaac Abarbanel is the son Abraham has not—yet—had, Abraham is the father Isaac Abarbanel has been missing. Isaac's bid to protect Sarah shifts from romantic to existential as Sarah pronounces the protocol of the protection she would require from her knight: a Jewish mother's catalogue whose irony at the same time bears a deeper meaning (L 1, 231f.; B 1, 495f.). Rabbi Abraham, Sarah, and their "lost" son Isaac: Heine's family romance suggests a playful approach to reimagining Jewish modernity, one whose modernity consists in its reinterpretation of the rich texture of Jewish tradition in critical response to its own internal differences, thereby disclosing new ways of grasping its ancient sources.[10]

Just like Don Isaac, the lost son whose return is welcomed with the fraternal embrace of the rabbi and the gracious gesture of Sarah—who now recognizes behind the guise of the evasive, outlandish dandy the creative power of poetic imagination and humor that embraces difference as the driving force of the life of tradition—Heine stages the creative act of interpretation as the moment that strikes closest to the heart of the text.

Let us consider the startling midrash Fackenheim cites in his discussion of the question of Abraham's significance for philosophy:

> The Midrash tells how once Nebuchadnezzar erected an idol and assembled three men from every nation to bow down to it. Hananiah, Mishael, and Azariah, the three Jews selected, consulted the prophet Ezechiel as to their duty, and the prophet, citing Isaiah, advised them to flee and hide. But who, the three asked, would then testify against the idols? Whereupon Ezechiel, consulting with God says: "Sovereign of the universe, Hananiah, Mishael, and Azariah seek to give their lives for the sanctification of Thy name. Wilt Thou stand by them or no?" God replied, "I will not stand by them, as it is written . . . 'As I live . . ., I will not be inquired of by you.' " (Ez. 20:3) Ezechiel broke into tears, for did not Scripture say that these three alone were left in Judah, and would not this small remnant now perish? Yet Hananiah, Mishael, and Azariah, informed of the divine reply, said: "Whether He stands by us or

> does not stand by us, we will sacrifice our lives for the sanctification of God's name."

Fackenheim comments on this harrowing account: "Who are the three pillars on which God has established the world? The Midrash ends with this question and replies that some say it is Abraham, Isaac, and Jacob; others, Hananiah, Mishael, and Azariah."[11]

This is more or less how Fackenheim ends his discussion on Abraham and modern philosophy, concluding with what he calls the "impossible question" (ibid.). Just as the midrash answers the question with another question, we can read Heine's story as an insistent reminder that the deep ethical predicament that the rabbi of Bacherach faces is not easily resolved. Rather, the situation renders any resolution impossible. But while the rabbi's fault might be his desire to escape the dilemma, Sarah nearly misses her cue to smile at the appearance of Isaac Abarbanel. Only upon the latter's insistence will they unite as friends at Schnapper-Elle's restaurant, reconstituting as it were a modern family relation that reimagines the biblical. Yet just like in the biblical account, this will only take place by way of the liberating power of laughter that, in this case, will reconstitute this family by imagining its relations anew. It is through laughter, and in Heine's story at the restaurant—the site of the openness of the life-sustaining force of tradition's creative power of internal difference—that Jewish tradition asserts its significance anew through "restoration." As the smile returns to Sarah and with it her ability to eventually laugh again, that is, to appreciate the openness of Jewish tradition, she and Abraham will find themselves able to conceive of Isaac and the future of the Jewish people as that internal other they welcome as their own, their lost son, as they open themselves to parenthood.

The role of Isaac assumes particular significance if Heine's employment of the Abarbanel family is given fuller attention. Born in Lisbon in 1437, Isaac Abarbanel was long the family's most prominent figure. A learned scholar of Jewish tradition, he not only authored a number of commentaries but also served as a high-ranking financial advisor at the courts of Portugal and Spain and later as advisor to the viceroy of Naples. It is however not him, but rather his oldest son, Yehuda Abarbanel, born in the 1460s, who would be the age-mate of the story's rabbi of Bacherach. Yehuda Abarbanel gained fame and recognition as a physician but became famous under the name Leone Ebreo as the author of one of the most widely read Renaissance texts, the *Dialoghi d'amore*. It is easy to see how Yehuda would capture Heine's imagination. An interlocutor of Pico della Mirandola, who likely inspired the composition of the *Dialoghi*'s reconciliatory approach to Aristotelian and Platonic philosophy as congenial rather than contradictory, Yehuda Abarbanel was one of the most prominent Jewish philosophers of the Renaissance. There was also a copy of the *Dialoghi d'amore* in the library of Spinoza, whose notion of *amor Dei* resonates with Leone Ebreo.[12] But why would Heine, whose notes on the Abarbanel family represent the largest excerpts he took while researching for the story in the 1820s, choose the name Isaac for a character that so strikingly resembles Leon Ebreo, Heine's alter ego in the *The Rabbi of Bacherach*?[13] The choice of the name of Isaac calls for attention. It is unclear whether or not Heine knew of Yehuda's son, who was named after his grandfather, Isaac. Born in 1491, the fate of this Isaac Abarbanel, grandson of the great scholar and courtier Isaac Abarbanel, was a particularly haunting one. In retaliation for his father's, Yehuda's, departure from Spain in 1492, King Ferdinand took the one-year-old son hostage and planned to subject him to forced baptism. Yehuda succeeded in having his son taken safely to Portugal. But the more liberal mood was soon to change in Portugal as well, and King João II took the five-year-old Isaac into custody, where he was subjected to forced baptism in 1497. This was to be his father Yehuda's most traumatic experience, dwarfing his many repeated experiences of escape and expropriation. It was, as Carl Gebhardt supposes, probably not until 1507 that Yehuda was reunited with his then sixteen-year-old son.[14] Whether or not Heine was aware of this remains an open question. But the story of Isaac, Leone Ebreo's son, gives Heine's reading of the Isaac story an unexpected historical dimension that sheds an illuminating light on Heine's reimagining of the story of the lost son who returns and is—despite his baptism—welcomed with open arms as the reanimating voice and force of Jewish tradition. Heine's story asks to be understood not as a narrative of (self-)justification but as an exploration of the deep and often profound ironies of history that all forms of teleological explanation must fail to comprehend.

If we have read Heine's *Rabbi of Bacherach* with Derrida, I would like to point out that we have read Derrida with Heine, as well: Derrida's other Abraham or other Abrahams. If Derrida gets succor from Kafka, Derrida is also to be seen in the context of modern renegotiations of Abraham. Kafka and Fackenheim are important voices in the chorus of that project. But so is, I argue, Heine. It is from the unique constellation of these interventions that a discourse on Abraham emerges that engages creatively with tradition as it reimagines it.

Reading Derrida with Heine gives us a richer context for tracing the Abrahamic traditions' multiplicity of origins as the liberating impulse that resides at the very heart of the biblical tradition of the figure of Abram/Abraham; the differance that informs the critical approach of thinking difference with and through Jewish thought. To say that Derrida resonates with a group of voices that engage creatively with Abraham is to highlight the fact that this shared concern is truly not external but critically intrinsic to a crucial strand that reflects the problem of in- and exclusion in Jewish tradition, and so addresses Jewish tradition as always already representing a multiplicity of origins. The one Abraham can thus represent the principle of emancipation and liberation because his monotheism is always already figured as a plurality of views that recognizes Sarah as a crucial part of the story. Equally, Isaac brings to their marriage the life, laughter, and the moment of recognition without which theirs would not be a family. With the story of Isaac as the lost son who returns, the story opens up not only the possibility of responding to the question of Christianity but also, albeit only implicitly as a possibility for a further midrashic intervention, the question of Hagar and Ishmael. Heine's reimagination of Abraham, Sarah, and Isaac as a modern day family presents an open rather than a closed notion of family as a dynamic, open-ended project rather than a fixed entity. If Hagar and Ishmael go unmentioned, Heine's story critically undoes the Christian opposition of Christ versus Abraham, Christian versus Jewish martyrdom, highlighting the profound symmetries between the two narratives Christian theology sought to mute.[15] But by exposing the hidden but profound affinity between the biblical narrative and the New Testament version, Heine's story opens up the narrative in principal terms, thus allowing, if not inviting, further renegotiations of the narrative of Abraham, Sarah, and Isaac.

But let us return to the story's ending, the gathering of the protagonists for dinner at Schnapper-Elle's kitchen. In Heine, food—and Jewish food in particular—plays a crucial role as catering not just to the body but also and in equal measure to the soul, or more precisely, the right food in the right society restores the individual's particularity as a human being. As the pleasures of Jewish cooking keep body and mind together, it becomes the restorative power that sustains Jewish tradition. Tradition lives on because the moment of transmission and reception goes through the kitchen. The pleasure of the shared meal, the communal interaction where difference and identity are negotiated, is thus the place where the division of mind and body is restored to the unity of the whole human being. An eminently social encounter, as Georg Simmel notes, the meal transforms the individual's need to eat and drink into a social affair that in the process is constitutive for the formation of sociability.[16] Or as Don Isaac puts it so cheekily:

> I like your cookery much better than your creed which wants the right sauce. (L 1, 235)
>
> Ich liebe Eur Küche weit mehr als Euren Glauben; es fehlt ihm die rechte Sauce. (B 1, 498)

After a few blasphemous comments, Isaac, who, after years apart, has just reunited with his friend rabbi Abraham who, with his wife, has just the night before escaped the pogrom in Bacherach, continues:

> My nose is not a renegade. When I once by chance came at dinner time into this street, and the well-known savoury odours of the Jewish kitchen rose to my nose, I was seized by the same yearning which our fathers felt for the fleshpots of Egypt—pleasant tasting memories of youth came unto

> me. I saw again in spirit the carp with brown raisin sauce which my aunt prepared so sustainingly for Friday eve—I saw once more the steamed mutton with garlic and horse-radish which might raise the dead, and the soup with dreamily swimming force-meat balls—the Klösschen—and my soul melted like the notes of an enamoured nightingale and since then I eat in the cookshop of my friend Donna Schnapper Elle. (L 1, 236f.)
>
> Meine Nase ist nicht abtrünnig geworden. Als mich einst Zufall um Mittagszeit in diese Straße führte, und aus den Küchen der Juden mir die wohlbekannten Düfte in die Nase stiegen: da erfaßte mich jene Sehnsucht, die unsere Väter empfanden, als sie zurückdachten an die Fleischtöpfe Ägyptens; wohlschmeckende Jugenderinnerungen stiegen in mir auf; ich sah wieder im Geiste die Karpfen mit brauner Rosinensauce, die meine Tante für den Freitagabend so erbaulich zu bereiten wußte; ich sah wieder das gedämpfte Hammelfleisch mit Knoblauch und Mairettig, womit man die Toten erwecken kann, und die Suppe mit schwärmerisch schwimmenden Klößchen . . . und meine Seele schmolz, wie die Töne einer verliebten Nachtigall, und seitdem esse ich in der Garküche meiner Freundin Donna Schnapper-Elle! (B1, 499)

Schnapper-Elle, the restaurateur, seems just as heretical as the perky Don Isaac. Bedecked with a silver necklace bearing all kinds of medallions, cameos, and other curiosities, a large picture of the city of Amsterdam commands attention where it rests, or rather seems to bob up and down, on Schnapper-Elle's heaving bosom (L 1, 224; B 1, 490). As Don Isaac seeks to ingratiate himself with her for a solid lunch (and possibly something more), his praise of her beauty and her bosom in particular concludes with the following panegyric:

> Oh, Senora, if the city of Amsterdam be as beautiful as you told me yesterday, and the day before, and every day, yet is the ground on which it rests far lovelier still. (L 1, 238)
>
> O Senora, ist auch die Stadt Amsterdam so schön, wie Ihr mir gestern und vorgestern und alle Tage erzählt habt, so ist doch der Boden, worauf sie ruht, noch tausendmal schöner. (B 1, 500)

While Amsterdam, the modern Jerusalem, beckons with a feast of the senses and Isaac's sweet talk seeks to seduce to the end of the enjoyment of Schnapper-Elle's culinary feats, the party approaches its destination, the restaurant, and is told that the soup has already been served. As everybody is waiting for the hostess, the story breaks off:

> That the soup was already served, and that the boarders were seated at table, but that the landlady was missing. (L 1, 240)

> daß schon längst die Suppe aufgetragen sei und die Gäste zu Tische säßen und die Wirtin fehle. – – – – – – (B 1, 501)

If the *Rabbi of Bacherach* highlights the necessity of rethinking Jewish tradition by considering its heretical impulses as its most liberating and empowering moments, the characters' expectant waiting for the hostess' arrival to have the supper begin restores the messianic impulse. Reclaiming Christianity's soteriological repurposing of Christ's last supper as the meal to come, the conclusion of the story gives the restorative function of the Passover meal new meaning as the reappropriation of the hope for the emancipation of all Jews and everybody else along with them—if only the hostess would finally arrive and let the celebration begin, that is, the "host nation" with all of its "guests." Difference, thanks to identity, or identity in difference, is the anticipated pleasure of enjoying the soup that is already served—if only we are ready to enter the kitchen where universal needs are satisfied by way of attention to the specificities of the preference of the particular. Schnapper-Elle's kitchen serves as the site of the continuing life of tradition, because it is a place where dissonant voices are welcomed as the life force of social existence, culture, and tradition. Not unlike Schnapper-Elle's kitchen—the site where the renewal of tradition takes place in a pleasurable exchange over a meal—the Frankfurt School's emancipatory vision grounds itself in the recognition of the sources of its weak messianic force, in the empowering pleasure of giving voice to critique as the enabling force of difference. While the soup is served and everybody is waiting to be seated, the purpose of Critical Theory lies not in its consummation—or consumption—but in the pleasure produced by the dissonance of the different voices that define the project of critique.

NOTES

Introduction: Heine's Jewish Difference and the Project of Critical Theory

1 For the critical significance of pleasure see for instance aphorism no. 37 in Theodor W. Adorno, *Minima Moralia*, trans. Edmund Jephcott (New York and London: Verso, 1974), 61: "He alone who could situate utopia in blind somatic pleasure, which, satisfying the ultimate intention, is intentionless, has a stable and valid idea of truth." ("Nur wer es vermöchte, in der blinden somatischen Lust, die keine Intention hat und die letzte stillt, die Utopie zu bestimmen, wäre einer Idee von Wahrheit fähig, die standhielte." Adorno, GS 4, 72).

2 MartinJay, *The Dialectical Imagination: A History of the Frankfurt School and the Institute of Social Research 1923–1950* (Boston and Toronto: Little, Brown, 1973), 33.

3 More recent studies include Steven E. Aschheim, *Beyond the Border: The German-Jewish Legacy Abroad* (Princeton and Oxford: Princeton University Press, 2007) and Jack Jacobs, *The Frankfurt School, Jewish Lives, and Antisemitism* (Cambridge: Cambridge University Press, 2014). See also for broader discussions of the context, Paul Mendes-Flohr, *Divide Passions: Jewish Intellectuals and the Experience of Modernity* (Detroit: Wayne State University Press, 1991) and Michael Löwy, *Redemption and Utopia. Libertarian Judaism in Central Europe: A Study in Elective Affinity*, trans. Hope Heany (Stanford: Stanford University Press, 1992).

4 See Michael Brenner, *The Renaissance of Jewish Culture in Weimar Germany* (New Haven and London: Yale University Press, 1996).

5 For Adorno's friendship with Scholem, see his correspondence and Asaf Angermann's illuminating account in Theodor W. Adorno and Gershom Scholem, *Briefwechsel: "Der liebe Gott wohnt im Detail" 1939–1969*, ed. Asaf Angermann (Frankfurt am Main: Suhrkamp, 2015).

6 For Heine as the first modern German intellectual, see Gerhard Höhn, "Heine und die Genealogie des modernen Intellektuellen," in *Heinrich Heine: Ästhetisch-politische Profile*, ed. Gerhard Höhn (Frankfurt am Main: Suhrkamp, 1991), 66–84 and Jürgen Habermas, "Heine and the Role of the Intellectual in Germany," in *The New Conservativism: Cultural Criticism and the Historian's Debate*, ed. Jürgen Habermas trans. Shierry Weber Nicholson (Cambridge, MA: MIT, 1989), 71–99.

7 Harvey Gross, "Adorno in Los Angeles: The Intellectual in Emigration," *Humanities in Society* 2, no. 4 (Fall 1979): 339–52, 349.

8 Martin Jay, "Adorno in America," in *Permanent Exiles: Essays on the Intellectual Migration from Germany to America*, ed. Martin Jay (New York: Columbia University Press, 1986), 120–37, 137.

9 For a recent affirmation, see Peter Stein's claim that "Heine the Wound" is the wound "that Heine has and *is*." (Emphasis by Stein.) Stein goes on to note that "Heine the wound" is also "Germany the wound," referring to the book-length essay by Walter Hinck *Die Wunde Deutschland: Heinrich Heines Dichtung im Widerstreit von Nationalidee, Judentum und Antisemitismus* (Frankfurt am Main: Insel, 1990). See Peter Stein, "Zu den Widersprüchen in der Rezeptionsgeschichte Heinrich Heines," in *"Die Emanzipation des Volkes war die große Aufgabe unseres Lebens": Beiträge zur Heinrich-Heine-Forschung anläßlich seines zweihunderststen Geburtstags 1997*, ed. Wolfgang Beutin, Thomas Bütow, Johann Dvorak, and Ludwig Fischer (Hamburg: von Bockel, 2000), 253–66, 253. However, this move shows a profound misreading, obscuring Adorno's critique of blaming the victim by supplanting it with the symptom's complex "Germany." For a symptomatic sideways move that Stein also cites on the same page, see Heiner Müller's claim that "Heine the wound is beginning to form a scar, though uneven; Woyzeck is the open wound." Heiner Müller, "Die Wunde Woyzeck," in *Büchner-Preis-Reden 1984–1994*, ed. Deutsche Akademie für Sprache und Dichtung (Stuttgart: Reclam, 1994), 42–4, 44. In exploring in his essay on Germany as Heine's wound, Hinck however is careful to distinguish Heine's "open wound" (*die nie geschlossene Wunde*, ibid., 9) from the German "discontent" (Unbehagen) that Adorno notes in his essay (ibid., 10).

10 Theodor W. Adorno, "Heine the Wound," in *Notes to Literature*, vol. 1, trans. Shierry Weber Nicholsen (New York: Columbia University Press, 1991), 80–5.

11 For Heine as the archetype of the modern exile, see Harry Slochower, "Attitudes towards Heine in German Literary Criticism" *Jewish Social Studies* 3 (1941): 355–74, 374: "The fate of the Jew as exile is determined by the same constellation of forces which renders all criticism and intellectual expression homeless."

12 Slochower, "Attitudes towards Heine," 370. Heinrich von Treitschke, who played a militant role in the 1880 Berlin anti-Semitism debate, turned Heine's phrase that Judaism is not a religion but a misfortune into the slogan "Die Juden sind unser Unglück!"—"*The Jews are our misfortune!*" For Treitschke and the ensuing controversy see *Der Berliner Antisemitismusstreit*, ed. Walter Boehlich (Frankfurt am Main: Insel 1965), for the quote: 11.

13 Theodor W. Adorno, *Aesthetic Theory*, trans. Robert Hullot-Kentor (Minneapolis: University of Minnesota Press, 1997), 110.

14 Heinrich Heine, *Shakespeares Mädchen und Frauen* in Heinrich Heine, *Sämtliche Schriften*, ed. Klaus Briegleb (Munich: Hanser, 2nd ed., 1975–85 and Munich: Deutscher Taschenbuch Verlag, 1997), vol. 4, 171–293. I will refer to this edition henceforth as B followed by volume and page number.

15 See also the comment in Robert C. Holub, "Heine and the Dialectic of Jewish Emancipation," in *"und die Welt ist so lieblich verworren": Heinrich Heines dialektisches Denken*, ed. Bernd Kortländer and Sikander Singh (Bielefeld: Aisthesis, 2004), 229–47, 244f: "Jewish emancipation is thus viewed as a cure for German maladies: the restrictions on Jews are portrayed humorously as the 'corns on the feet of the German state.' [. . .] Ultimately Heine recognizes that the dialectic of Jewish emancipation does not necessarily

lead to the dead end of apostasy or assimilation, but rather demands the overcoming of social and political barriers thwarting the emancipation of humanity as a whole." The "corns on the feet of the German state" is a quote from Heine's commemorative article "Ludwig Marcus Denkworte" (Heine, B 5, 175–91, 184).

16 See Miriam Leonard, *Tragic Modernities* (Cambridge MA: Harvard, 2015).

17 Ibid.

18 See Heine, *On the History of Religion and Philosophy in Germany*, trans. Pollack-Milgate, ed. Terry Pinkard (Cambridge: Cambridge University Press, 2007), 87 and Heine, B 3, 604. See also the above-mentioned, suggestive passage in Heine's *Travel Pictures*: "After the departure of the heroes, the clowns and graciosos enter with their baubles and lashes." L 2, 312 and Heine, B 2, 282.

19 Heine and Marx's appropriation of the motto is discussed at the opening of Chapter 5.

20 Walter Benjamin, *The Arcades Project*, trans. Howard Eiland and Kevin McLaughlin (Cambridge, MA: Harvard University Press, 2003), 486.

21 Walter Benjamin, *Das Passagen-Werk*, GS 5.1, 609.

22 For a discussion of Adorno, see Willi Goetschel, "Theory-Praxis: Spinoza, Hess, Marx, and Adorno," *Bamidbar: Journal for Jewish Thought and Philosophy*, 2 (2013): 16–28.

23 Paul Ricœur introduced the term "masters of suspicion" for Marx, Nietzsche, and Freud in his book *Freud and Philosophy: An Essay on Interpretation*, trans. Denis Savage (New Haven and London: Yale, 1970), 32f.

24 Theodor W. Adorno, *Negative Dialectics*, trans. E. B. Ashton (New York and London: Continuum, 2005), 3.

25 For a discussion of the Heine reception during this period, see Jeffrey Sammons, "Zur ausgeklammerten Heine-Rezeption: Beobachtungen zur ersten großen Zeit der Heine-Philologie," in *Heinrich Heine: Alternative Perspectives 1985–2005*, ed. Jeffrey L. Sammons (Würzburg: Königshausen & Neumann, 2006), 207–22 and George F. Peters, *The Poet as Provocateur: Heinrich Heine and His Critics* (Rochester: Camden, 2000).

26 For an early exception that stresses Heine's modernist aspects, see Barker Fairley, "Heine's Vaudeville," *University of Toronto Quarterly*, 3 (1934): 185–207.

27 Jean-Luc Nancy, *Hegel: The Restlessness of the Negative*, trans. Jason Smith and Steven Miller (Minneapolis and Londo: University of Minnesota Press, 2002).

28 See Heine's poem on the perils of Hegelian speculation, "Life and the World's too Fragmentary for Me!" D 99, "Zu fragmentarisch ist Welt und Leben!" B 1, 135.

29 For a discussion of the genealogical filiations of this view, see Willi Goetschel, "The Differential Character of Traditions," *Telos* no. 95 (2013): 161–70.

30 While modernity appears in English early on in the seventeenth century, the earliest references in German and French appear after the publication of Heine's text in 1827. For a reference of the word's first occurrence in German in this text by Heine, see *Digitales Wörterbuch der deutschen Sprache* at www.dwds.de under Deutsches Textarchiv https://www.dwds.de/r?corpus=dta;q=Modernit%C3%A4t, last accessed July 14, 2017. See also *Geschichtliche Grundbegriffe*, s.v. "Modern." By the time Baudelaire uses "modernité" in 1859, Heine's decisive

discussion was three decades old: "La modernité, c'est le transitoire, le fugitive, le contingent" (*Geschichtliche Grundbegriffe*, vol. 4, 110 n 66).

31 Heine, *Travel Pictures* in Heine, *Works*, vol. 2, 255. Reference to this edition is indicated by the letter L followed by the number of the volume and page number.

32 B 2, 235.

33 Heine's point gets lost in Leland's translation of *unerfreuliche Modernität* as "uncongenial modern fashion" (L 2, 257).

34 Reinhart Koselleck, "'Space of Experience' and 'Horizon of Expectation': Two Historical Categories," in *Past Futures: On the Semantics of Historical Time*, ed. Reinhart Koselleck, trans. Keith Tribe (New York: Columbia University Press, 2004), 255–75.

35 My translation. Leland translates "wide-spreading, uncongenial modern fashion," thereby passing over Heine's neologism "modernity"

36 Theodor W. Adorno, "Introduction to Benjamin's *Schriften*," in *Notes to Literature*, ed. Theodor W. Adorno, trans. Shierry Weber Nicholsen (New York: Columbia University, 1992), vol. 2, 227.

37 Adorno, "Einleitung in Benjamins 'Schriften,'" in Adorno, *Noten zur Literatur*, in GS 11, 575.

38 Benjamin, *Arcades Project*, 462.

39 Benjamin, *Passagen-Werk*, 576.

40 Benjamin, *Arcades Project*, 474; Benjamin, *Passagen-Werk*, 592f.

41 Benjamin, *Arcades Project*, 462.

42 Benjamin, *Passagen-Werk*, 577.

43 For a discussion of some of the striking affinities between Heine and Benjamin, see Albrecht Betz, "Marchandise et modernité: Notes sur Heine et Benjamin," in *Walter Benjamin et Paris*, ed. Heinz Wismann (Paris: Les Éditions du Cerf, 1986), 153–62. Betz notes the missed opportunity ("*acte manqué*," 153 and 162) or parapraxis (*Fehlleistung*, 19 and 30 in the German version cited below), respectively repression (*refoulement*, 162 or *Verdrängung*, 29) by Benjamin with regard to Heine as he concludes his article: "Tous deux partagent l'optique des déshérités et adoptent le point de vue des victimes d'histoire; en écrivant ils se souviennent de la souffrance, ils veulent tout à la fois démasquer l'imposture et libérer le désir. En outré, ils lient tous deux les motifs politiques aux motifs théologiques ; chez tous deux la pensée et l'imagination fonctionnent dans la tension des contradictions et des collisions, tous deux sont convaincus que la vérité ne s'exprime que dans la constellation" (162). For a German version of this essay, see Albrecht Betz, "Heine und Benjamin in Paris: Vom doppelten Exil zweier deutscher Intellektueller," in *Der Charme des Ruhestörers: Heine Studien. Ästhetik und Politik II*, ed. Albrecht Betz (Aachen: Rimbaud 1997), 19–30.

Chapter 1

1 Leon Trotsky, "Tolstoy, Poet and Rebel." Translated for the first time into English by John G. Wright. Published in *Fourth International* 12, no. 3, May–June 1951. https://www.marxists.org/archive/trotsky/1908/09/tolstoy.htm, accessed September 20, 2016.

2 For Metternich's admiration for Heine, see Karl August Varnhagen von Ense's letter from February 23, 1838, where he writes: "Have you already written to Prince Metternich? who estimates and considers your talent so extremely highly?" ("Haben Sie denn schon an den Fürsten von Metternich geschrieben? der Ihr Talent so äußerst hoch anschlägt und berücksichtigt!"), HSA 25, 166. See also Heine's draft of a letter in 1855 that mentions Metternich's appreciation of Heine's poetry, by which he was reportedly moved to tears. See HSA 23, letter no. 1655, 430.

3 Alfred Schumacher, "Heinrich Heine," *The Manchester Quarterly: A Journal of Literature and Art* 19 (1900): 272–97, 272.

4 See Frederic Ewen's substantial introduction "Heinrich Heine: Humanity's Soldier" in his edition *The Poetry and Prose of Heinrich Heine*, selected and edited with an introduction by Frederic Ewen (New York: Citadel Press [1948]), 3–50, 39.

5 Sol Liptzin, *The English Legend of Heinrich Heine* (New York: Bloch, 1954), 4f.

6 Randolph Bourne, "The Jew and Transnational America," *Menorah Journal* 2 (December 1916): 277–84. Bourne had earlier, in July 1916, published the essay "Trans-National America" in *The Atlantic Monthly* 118 (1916): 86–97. See Daniel Greene, *The Jewish Origins of Cultural Pluralism: The Menorah Association and American Diversity* (Bloomington and Indianapolis: Indiana University Press, 2011), 84.

7 Michael Löwy, *Redemption and Utopia: Jewish Libertarian Thought in Central Europe: A Study in Elective Affinity*, trans. H. Heaney (London: Athlone Press, 1992).

8 Gershom Scholem, *Tagebücher nebst Aufsätzen und Entwürfen bis 1923. 2. Halbband 1917–1923*, ed. Karlfried Gründer, Herbert Kopp-Oberstebrink and Friedrich Niewöhner with the assistance of Karl E. Grözinger (Frankfurt am Main: Jüdischer Verlag, 2000) vol. 2, 303; see Michael Löwy, "Le messianisme hétérodoxe dans l'œuvre de jeunesse de Gershom Scholem," in *Messianismes: Variations sur une figure juive*, ed. Jean-Christophe Attias, Pierre Gisel, and Lucie Kaennel (Genève: Labor et Fides, 2000), 131–45.

9 Scholem, *Tagebücher*, vol. 2, 359.

10 See the section on Heine in Löwenthal's series of articles "Judentum und deutscher Geist," in Leo Löwenthal, *Schriften 4: Judaica, Vorträge, Briefe*, ed. Helmut Dubiel (Frankfurt am Main: Suhrkamp, 1984), 20–9.

11 Leo Lowenthal "Heine's Religion: *The Messianic Ideals of the Poet*," *Commentary* 4, no. 2 (1947): 153–7, 157.

12 Martin Jay, "Leo Lowenthal and the Jewish Renaissance," in *Jews and the Ends of Theory*, ed. Shai Ginsburg, Martin Land, and Jonathan Boyarin (New York: Fordham University Press, 2018).

13 Thomas Wheatland, *The Frankfurt School in Exile* (Minneapolis: University of Minnesota Press, 2009), 157.

14 Ibid., 158.

15 See Enrique Krauze, "The Fury of Historical Redemptionism: An Interview with Joseph B. Maier, September 30, 1982," in *Surviving the Twentieth Century: Social Philosophy from the Frankfurt School to the Columbia Faculty Seminars*, ed. Judith T. Marcus (New Brunswick and London: Transaction Publishers, 1999), 37–48, 37–9. In his account, Maier refers to the unveiling

of the monument, but this might be an error. The monument had been in the Bronx for several decades though occasionally rededicated with the wreath-laying ceremonies presumably starting in 1934. *Aufbau*, the organ of the German-Jewish Club of New York reports in its first year of existence for February 17, 1935, the event as a "Kranz-Niederlegung," with Josef Maier as speaker. See also the front-page article of *Aufbau*, "Zur Feier am Heinedenkmal" in *Aufbau* February 1, 1935, pp. 1 and 7, which commemorates Heine as the first German Jewish literary exile. *Aufbau* also reports a wreath-laying ceremony for the following year. For the history of the monument, see Jeffrey L. Sammons: "The Restoration of the Heine Monument in the Bronx," *The Germanic Review* 74, no. 4 (1999): 337–9. For a biographical sketch of Maier, see Judith Marcus, "Joseph B. Maier's Life and Work: An Introduction," in *Surviving the Twentieth Century*, ed. Judith Marcus, 1–8, and Judith Marcus, "Remembering Joseph B. Maier: The Last Member of the Frankfurt School," *Logos: A Journal of Modern Society & Culture* 2, no. 1 (2003): 181–5.

16 Krauze, ibid., 38f.

17 See the short biographical sketches by Marcus.

18 If not otherwise referenced, all translations are mine.

19 For the history of the monument, see Paul Reitter, "Heine in the Bronx" and Jeffrey Sammons, "The Restoration of the Heine Monument in the Bronx" both in *The Germanic Review* 74 (1999): 327–36 and 337–9. For a social history of the Grand Course in the Bronx, where the park is located in which the monument was erected and still stands, and for the particular role of the area for burgeoning Jewish life in the Bronx in the 1930s, see Constance Rosenblum, *Boulevard of Dreams: Heady Times, Heartbreak, and Hope along the Grand Concourse in the Bronx* (New York and London: New York University Press, 2009). For a discussion of the monument and its history at that time, see Louis Untermeyer, *Heinrich Heine: Paradox and Poet* (New York: Harcourt, Brace, 1937), 366–8 including also two unusually sharp photographs of the monuments.

20 Erich de Jonge, "Des unheiligen Dritten Reiches jüdischer Prophet: Zur Heinefeier am 16. Februar 1936," *Aufbau* 2 no. 3 (February 1, 1936), 1–2.

21 Ludwig Vogelstein, "Heine in New York," *Aufbau* March 8, 1940, 3 responding to the article "Heine in the Bronx" in *Aufbau* February 9, 1940, 16.

22 The essay is discussed in Chapter 3.

23 For an exception, see Detlev Claussen, *Theodor W. Adorno: Ein letztes Genie* (Frankfurt am Main: Fischer, 2003), 38–42, who notes that the basic elements of Horkheimer and Adorno's magnum opus *Dialectic of Enlightenment* are already addressed in Heine's work and thematized in his ambivalent reception, which Adorno reads with different eyes in exile (40).

24 The proximity between the associates of the Institute for Social Research and the editors of *Commentary* had also a spatial component: they were all employed by the American Jewish Committee and housed in offices across the hall. See Wheatland, *The Frankfurt School in Exile*, 153–6.

25 For a discussion of family resemblances between Bloch and Heine, see *"Zuckererbsen für Jedermann": Literatur und Utopie. Heine und Bloch heute*,

ed. Norbert Otto Eke, Karin Füllner, and Francesca Vidal, Vormärz-Studien XXXV (Bielefeld: Aisthesis, 2014).

26 Gershom Scholem, "Ahnen und Verwandte Walter Benjamins," in *Walter Benjamin und sein Engel: Vierzehn Aufsätze*, ed. Gershom Scholem (Frankfurt am Main: Suhrkamp, 1983), 128–57, 133.

27 Howard Eiland and Michael W. Jennings, *Walter Benjamin: A Critical Life* (Cambridge, MA and London: Harvard University Press, 2014), 527. See also Gerhsom Scholem, *Walter Benjamin: The Story of a Friendship*, trans. Harry Zohn (New York: New York Review Books, 2003) 79, where Scholem notes Benjamin's sympathy for Platen, with whom Heine had a great fallout. Heine had responded to Platen's polemic insinuations about his Jewishness with the exposure of Platen's homosexuality. Scholem also notes a general disengagement of their generation with Heine at the time (ibid.).

28 See Gerhard R. Kaiser, "Baudelaire pro Heine contra Janin," *Heine-Jahrbuch* 22 (1983): 135–78.

29 Walter Benjamin, "Über einige Motive bei Baudelaire," in *Gesammelte Schriften* 1.2, ed. Walter Benjamin (Frankfurt am Main: Suhrkamp, 1980), 607–53, 607 and Walter Benjamin, "On Some Motifs in Baudelaire," in *Illuminations: Essays and Reflections*, ed. Walter Benjamin, trans. Harry Zohn, ed. Hannah Arendt (New York: Schocken, 1968), 155–200, 156. The English edition renders "Schwelle" erroneously with "watershed."

30 Heine also appears at the end of the essay's section 7, where Benjamin culls from an anthology of Heine's conversations, letters, and diaries that features Heine as a "student of the physiognomy of the big city" who, walking down one of the magnificent Paris boulevards, pointed out the "horror with which this center of the world was tinged," Benjamin, "On Some Motifs," 174, and Benjamin, "Über einige Motive," 629. The German edition provides as reference *Heinrich Heine, Gespräche, Briefe, Tagebücher, Berichte seiner Zeitgenossen*, ed. Hugo Bieber (Berlin: Welt-Verlag 1926), 163. In his collection "Zentralpark" associated with the Baudelaire project, Heine notes: "Die fleurs du mal sind das letzte Gedichtbuch von gesamteuropäischer Wirkung gewesen. Vor ihnen etwa: Ossian, das Buch der Lieder?" Cf. Benjamin, GS 1.2, 681.

31 Scholem, "Ahnen und Verwandte Walter Benjamins," 128: "In der Familie Benjamins war die Tradition lebendig, dass die väterliche Grossmutter mit Heine verwandt war, aber niemand wusste, wie der genaue Zusammenhang bestand."

32 For an early study of Heine's presence in America, see the dissertation by Baruch Sachs, *Heine in America* (Philadelphia: University of Pennsylvania Press, 1916).

33 Heine Heine's *Sämmtliche Werke* (Philadelphia: John Weik, 1856–67).

34 For a discussion of Leland, who started translating Heine in 1855 and whose revised last edition of Heine's works appeared in 1906, see Jeffrey Sammons, "Charles Godfrey Leland and the English-Language Heine Edition," in *Heinrich Heine: Alternative Perspectives 1985–2005*, ed. Jeffrey Sammons (Würzburg: Königshausen & Neumann, 2006), 163–87; for Emma Lazarus's translation, see *Poems and Ballads of Heinrich Heine*, trans. Emma Lazarus (New York: Hurst, 1881); for Louis Untermeyer's translation *Poems of Heinrich Heine* (New York: Harcourt, Brace, 1916; 2nd ed. 1923).

35 Sol Liptzin, "Heine and the Yiddish Poets," in *The Jewish Reception of Heinrich Heine*, ed. Mark Gelber (Tübingen: Max Niemeyer, 1992), 67–76. For a more recent discussion, see Julian Levinson, *Exiles on Main Street: Jewish American Writers and American Literary Culture* (Bloomington and Indiana: Indiana University Press, 2008), 125–30, see also 122f.

36 For a comprehensive discussion of the significance of the Menorah Society and its journal, see Greene, *The Jewish Origins of Cultural Pluralism*. For brief discussions of the role of the Menorah Society, its journal and contributors, see also Alan M. Wald, *The New York Intellectuals: The Rise and Decline of the Anti-Stalinist Left from the 1930s to the 1980s* (Chapel Hill and London: University of North Carolina Press, 1987), 27–33, and Nathan Abrams, *Commentary Magazine 1945–1959: "A Journal of Significant Thought and Opinion"* (London and Portland, OR: Vallentine Mitchell, 2007), 5–28.

37 S. Baruch, "One Hundred Years Ago: A 'Menorah' Anniversary," *Menorah* 6 (1920): 11–25.

38 Adolph S. Oko, *The Spinoza Bibliography* (Boston: G. K. Hall, 1964).

39 Oko's at some point closest friend, Waldo Frank, succinctly noted: "Oko's great literary loves were Spinoza, on whom he was an authority, and Heine." *Memoirs of Waldo Frank*, ed. Alan Trachtenberg (Amherst: University of Massachusetts Press, 1973), 176.

40 Ibid., 11, in the short summary of the article.

41 Baruch, "One Hundred Years Ago," 21.

42 Israel Abrahams, "Poetry and Religion: The Third Arthur Davis Memorial Lecture," 333.

43 Heinrich Heine, "Of Judaism and the Jews," *Contemporary Jewish Record* (October 1, 1943): 550–9, 550. A short sketch in the collection of the Adolph S. Oko Papers at the Jacob Rader Marcus Center of the American Jewish Archives at the Hebrew Union College in Cincinnati entitled "Heinrich Heine" that mirrors verbatim parts of the anonymous editorial introduction corroborates that Oko was the author. I would like to thank Elisa Ho of the American Jewish Archives for providing me with an electronic copy of Oko's sketch on Heine.

44 Abrams, *Commentary Magazine*, 32.

45 Hannah Arendt, "In Memoriam: Adolph S. Oko" in *Aufbau* (October 13, 1944). For the English translation, see Hannah Arendt, *Jewish Writings*, ed. Jerome Kohn and Ron H. Feldman (New York: Schocken, 2007), 229f., 229.

46 Hannah Arendt, "The Jew as Pariah: A Hidden Tradition," *Jewish Social Studies* (1944): 99–122, 106f.

47 For the background of the larger context of the politics in which Arendt's pointedly coded jab at Karl Kraus and his followers takes place and the enduring role of Kraus's conflicted essay "Heine and the Consequences," see Dietmar Goltschnigg, *Die Fackel ins wunde Herz: Kraus über Heine. Eine "Erledigung"? Texte, Analysen, Kommentar* (Vienna: Passagen, 2000) and Paul Peters's chapter "Karl Kraus und die Folgen" in his study *Die Wunde Heine* (Bodenheim: Philo, 1997), 119–53.

48 In contrast to Bourne who chose to privilege "the orthodox Jew" as a paradigmatic example for his multicultural model of American "transnationalism" (Bourne, "The Jew and Transnational America," 280), Arendt

pointedly embraced as her model the figure most vilified for his alleged assimilationist stance, Heine.

49 Heinz Politzer, "From Mendelssohn to Kafka: The Jewish Man of Letters in Germany" in *Commentary* 4 (1947): 344–51, 350.

50 In Palestine, Politzer had assisted Max Brod with the edition of Kafka. In 1947 he came to the United States to earn his PhD at Bryn Mawr College in 1950. In 1960 he became professor at Berkeley where he published *Franz Kafka: Parable and Paradox* in 1962, a study that would assume canonical importance. The biographical information accompanying this article in *Commentary* indicates that "he lives at present" in Palestine and suggests that it served Politzer as a calling card to announce his move to America. For biographical information, see http://texts.cdlib.org/view?docId=hb1j49n6pv&doc.view=frames&chunk.id=div00078&toc.depth=1&toc.id=, accessed December 12, 2016.

51 Elliott Cohen, "Jewish Culture in America: Some Speculations by an editor" in *Commentary* (May 1947): 412–20.

52 Abrams, *Commentary Magazine*, 32–5.

53 Elliot Cohen, "Jewish Culture in America," 417.

54 Ibid., 420.

55 Heinz Politzer, review, *Commentary* 6 (1948): 287f, 287.

56 David Suchoff, *Kafka's Jewish Languages: The Hidden Openness of Tradition* (Philadelphia: Pennsylvania University Press, 2012).

57 Martin Greenberg, "Heinrich Heine: Flight and Return. The Fallacy of Being Only a Human Being," *Commentary* 8 (1949): 225–31.

58 See Jacques Derrida, "Abraham, the Other," in *Judeities: Questions for Jacques Derrida*, ed. Bettina Bergo, Joseph Cohen, and Raphael Zagury-Orly, trans. Bettina Bergo and Michael B. Smith (New York: Fordham University Press, 2007), 1–35, for the critique of Sartre, see 21–30.

59 David Daiches. review of Israel Tabak, *Judaic Lore in Heine: The Heritage of a Poet* (Baltimore: Johns Hopkins University Press, 1948), *Commentary*, 405–7, 407.

60 Ibid., 207f. Continuing his discussion, Tabak poses the question he suggests to be a rhetorical one, but which has haunted and continues to haunt much of Heine reception: "Is it possible to draw a line of demarcation between these two cultural strains in Heine, and say, this is where the Jewish poet ends and the German poet begins? Is there necessarily a contradiction between these two elements when we regard them from a purely literary and artistic point of view?" (209).

61 Tabak, *Judaic Lore in Heine*, IX.

62 Greenberg, "Heinrich Heine: Flight and Return," 231.

Chapter 2

1 In provocative contrast to dominant views, Lucien Calvié, *Heine/Marx: Révolution, liberalism, démocratie et communisme* (Uzès: Inclinaison, 2013) argues that Heine's theoretical and political difference to Marx highlights a genuine blind spot in Marx rather than an insufficiency on Heine's part.

Putting Heine on an equal footing with Marx has not been a strong point of Marx and Heine scholarship. While itself occasionally bordering to the speculative, Calvié's study aptly identifies the problem that has long haunted the discussion of the relationship between Marx and Heine: an overwhelming awe of Marx's authority combined with a remarkable diffidence in Heine's philosophical and theoretical abilities that overshadow the views even of many of the most devoted Heine scholars. For the best studies on Heine and Marx, see Nigel Reeves, "Heine and the Young Marx," *Oxford German Studies* 7 (1972–3): 44–97 and Jean Pierre Lefebvre, "Marx und Heine," *Schriften aus dem Karl-Marx-Haus* 7 (Trier: Karl-Marx-Haus, 1972) and the slightly abridged version "Marx und Heine," in *Heinrich Heine: Streitbarer Humanist und volksverbundener Dichter*, ed. Karl Wolfgang Becker, Helmut Brandt, and Siegfried Scheibe (Weimar: Nationale Forschungs- und Gedenkstätte der klassischen deutschen Literatur, 1973), 41–61. See also Walther Victor, *Marx und Heine: Tatsache und Spekulation in der Darstellung ihrer Beziehungen* (Berlin: Henschel-Verlag, 1953); Johanna Rudolph, "Karl Marx ind Heinrich Heine," *Neues Deutschland*, February 17, 1953, 4; Joachim Müller, *Marx und Heine* (Berlin: Aufbau, 1953) published in the series *Vorträge zur Verbreitung wissenschaftlicher Kenntnisse*, a publication that stands out as the most sympathetic discussion of Heine's and Marx's "intellectual affinity" (*geistesverwandt*, 20), demonstrating that to toe the party line did not have to mean to subordinate Heine to Marx; the chapter "Heine und Marx," in Hans Kaufmann, *Politisches Gedicht und klassische Dichtung—Heinrich Heine: Deutschland. Ein Wintermärchen* (Berlin: Aufbau, 1959), 39–64; Ludwig Marcuse, "Heine and Marx: A History and a Legend," *The Germanic Review* 30 (1955): 110–24; Gerhard Schmitz, *Über die ökonomischen Anschauungen in Heines Werken* (Weimar: Arion, 1960); the chapter on Marx and Heine in Klaus Briegleb, *Opfer Heine? Versuche über Schriftzüge der Revolution* (Frankfurt am Main: Suhrkamp, 1986), 71–104; Michael Werner, "Heine und die französischen Frühsozialisten," *Internationales Archiv für Sozialgeschichte der deutschen Literatur* 7 (1982): 88–108; Renate Schlesier, "Homeric Laughter by the Rivers of Babylon: Heinrich Heine and Karl Marx," in *The Jewish Reception of Heinrich Heine*, ed. Mark H. Gelber (Tübingen: Niemeyer, 1992), 21–43; Anita Bunyan, "1843: Heinrich Heine and Karl Marx Meet for the First Time in Paris," in *Yale Companion to Jewish Writing and Thought in German Culture, 1096–1996*, ed. Sander L. Gilman and Jack Zipes (New Haven: Yale University Press, 1997), 171–7; Zvi Tauber, "Remarks on the Relationship Between Heine and Marx in 1844," *Tel Aviver Jahrbuch für deutsche Geschichte* 30 (2002): 402–13; Jost Hermand, "Das Gemeinsame im Trennenden: Heine und Marx," in *Heinrich Heine: Kritisch, Solidarisch, Umstritten*, ed. Jost Hermand (Cologne, Weimar, and Vienna: Böhlau, 2007), 85–103; Eleanor Courtemanche, "Marx, Heine, and German Cosmopolitanism: The 1844 Deutsch-Französische Jahrbücher," *Telos* 159 (2012 Summer): 49–63. For an example of the complicated forms that the negation of party line and philosophical conviction could assume when it came to an appreciation of the relationship between the two friends, see, for example, Wolfgang Harich's comments in the introduction to his edition of Heine's *Zur Geschichte der Religion und Philosophie in Deutschland* that first appeared in 1956 and that I quote according to the edition that appeared in Frankfurt am Main with Insel in 1965, 29–42.

2 Karl Marx, "Toward a Critique of Hegel's Philosophy of Right," in *Selected Writings*, 30.

3 For Marx using Heine's language, see Briegleb, *Opfer Heine?* 76.

4 HSA 23, 430. After Börne's death in 1837 and Heine's merciless settling of his scores, Heine had become the most prominent German voice of opposition in exile.

5 Karl Marx, "The German Ideology," in Marx, *Selected Writings*, 111.

6 Marx, *Economic and Philosophic Manuscripts* and *Capital*, in Marx, *Selected Writings*, 59 and 294.

7 For a review of a selection of passages dealing with money in Heine that suggestively resonate with Marx, see the chapter "Der gelbe Kuppler" in Schmitz, *Über die ökonomischen Anschauungen*, 25–33.

8 Französische Zustände, art. VIII, May 27, 1832, B 3, 192.

9 Georg Simmel will expand on the notion of the hydraulic nature of the laws of the flow of money in his *Philosophy of Money* (1900).

10 See Die Bäder von Lucca, B 2, 425 and Lutetia, article XXXII, March 31, 1841, B 5, 355.

11 Marx, *Selected Writings*, 161f.

12 Heine, *Ludwig Börne: A Memorial*, trans. Sammons, 19.

13 See also ChristianLiedtke, "'. . . die überwuchernde Macht des Kapitals.' Geld, Gold und Eisenbahnen im Spätwerk Heinrich Heines," in *". . . und die Welt ist so lieblich verworren": Heinrich Heines dialektisches Denken*, ed. Bernd Kortländer and Sikander Singh (Aisthesis: Bielefeld, 2004), 73–100.

14 See, for instance, Heine's letters to his mother and sister for fastest shipment of library books to Paris on July 25, 1850 (HSA 23: 47) and gifts from Paris to Hamburg on June 26, 1844 (HSA 23: 343), letters to his publisher Julius Campe for best shipments of proofs, copies of his publications, or reading material on October 18 and 24, 1844 (HSA 22: 138), October 21 and November 17, 1851, October 23, 1853, June 26 and October 3, 1854 (HSA 23: 139, 163, 300, 342, 372, 380) and to Michael Schloss, the owner of a lending library in Cologne on January 19, 1851 (HSA 23: 75).

15 Marx's letter to his father from November 10, 1837, MEW, Ergänzungsband, Schriften bis 1844, 9.

16 Paul Lafargue, *Reminiscences of Marx*, https://www.marxists.org/archive/lafargue/1890/xx/marx.htm, accessed December 19, 2016.

17 For a complete list of Marx's references in the 1840s lifted from volumes 5 and 6 of the MEW, see Reeves, "Heine and the Young Marx," 75 n.1.

18 Karl Marx, *Capital: A Critique of Political Economy*, vol. 1, trans. Samuel Moore and Edward Aveling, ed. Frederick Engels (1887), 432 n.50. https://www.marxists.org/archive/marx/works/download/pdf/Capital-Volume-I.pdf, accessed December 18, 2016.

19 Marx in a letter to Engels, January 17, 1855. See Briegleb, *Opfer Heine?* 76.

20 Briegleb, *Opfer Heine?* 71–104.

21 Briegleb, *Opfer Heine?* 82 and Briegleb's extensive notes to the editor's introductory note to a letter by Heine that the Neue Rheinische Zeitung published January 4, 1955. Marx was at that time the editor of the paper, B 5, 766.

22 Friedrich Nietzsche, *Ecce Homo* in Nietzsche, *The Complete Works*, vol. 17, trans. Anthony M. Ludovici (New York: Macmillan, 1911), 39f.

23 *Ecce homo* (um 1888), section *Warum ich so klug bin*, 4. Abschnitt, KSA 6, 286. In the preceding section, "Warum ich so weise bin," Nietzsche describes himself provocatively as a Polish aristocrat without a drop of bad blood: "Ich bin ein polnischer Edelmann pur sang, dem auch nicht ein Tropfen schlechtes Blut beigemischt ist, am wenigsten deutsches." Ibid., 268.

24 For Adorno's own admiration of, and indebtedness to Nietzsche, see his comment in the lectures in Theodor W. Adorno, *Probleme der Moralphilosophie* (Frankfurt am Main: Suhrkamp, 1996), 255: "[Nietzsche] dem ich, wenn ich aufrichtig sein soll, am meisten von allen sogenannten großen Philosophen verdanke—in Wahrheit vielleicht noch mehr als Hegel."

25 See the opening sentence in Georg Lange, "Heine und Nietzsche," *Österreichische Rundschau* 64 (1920): 190–202.

26 J. P. Stern observed in 1964 that Nietzsche's debt to Heine has never been explored. See J. P. Stern, *Re-interpretations: Seven Studies in Nineteenth-Century German Literature* (London: Thames and Hudson, 1964), 217. This has since changed if only in parts. For a discussion of the significance of Heine for Nietzsche, see also Arno Carl Coutinho, "Nietzsche, Heine, und das 19. Jahrhundert," *PMLA* 53, no. 4 (December 1938): 1126–45; Sander Gilman, "Nietzsche and Heine," in *Nietzschean Parody: An Introduction to Reading Nietzsche*, ed. Sander Gilman (Aurora, CO: Davies, 2nd ed. 2001), 65–86; Hanna Spencer, "Heine und Nietzsche?," in *Dichter, Denker, Journalist: Studien zum Werk Heinrich Heines*, ed. Hanna Spencer (Bern: Peter Lang, 1977), 65–100; Reinhold Grimm, "Antiquity as Echo and Disguise: Nietzsche's 'Lied eines theokritischen Ziegenhirten,' Heinrich Heine, and the Crucified Dionysus," *Nietzsche Studien* 14 (1985): 201–48 and the shorter version, Reinhold Grimm, "Heine und Nietzsche: Bemerkungen zu einem lyrischen Pastiche," in *Heinrich Heine und das neunzehnte Jahrhundert: Signaturen*, ed. Rolf Hosfeld (Berlin: Argument, 1986) 98–107; Herwig Friedl, "Heinrich Heine und Friedrich Nietzsche," in *Heinrich Heine im Spannungsfeld von Literatur und Wissenschaft*, ed. Wilhelm Gössmann and Manfred Windfuhr (Essen: Hobbing, 1990), 195–214; Linda Duncan, "Heine and Nietzsche. Das Dionysische: Cultural Directive and Aesthetic Principle," *Nietzsche-Studien* 19 (1990): 336–45; Adrian Del Caro, Adrian, "Heine's 'Deutschland. Ein Wintermärchen' reflected in Nietzsche," *Heine-Jahrbuch* 33 (1994): 194–201; Gerhard Höhn, "'Farceur' und 'Fanatiker des Ausdrucks': Nietzsche, Heineaner *malgré lui*?," in *Heinrich Heine: Neue Wege der Forschung*, ed. Christian Liedtke (Darmstadt: Wissenschaftliche Buchgesellschaft, 2000), 198–215; and the short but pointed entry by Gerhard Höhn, "Heine und Nietzsche, Kritiker des Christentums," in *Ich Narr des Glücks*, ed. Joesph A. Kruse (Stuttgart: Metzler1997), 357–60; Welisar Iliev, "Nietzsche und Heine: Chronik einer (lebenslänglichen?) Beziehung," *Germanica: Jahrbuch für deutschlandkundliche Studien* 4 (1997): 247–66; Walter Gebhard, "Heine und Nietzsche: historische und literarische Formen der Aufklärungsarbeit," in *Heine gehört auch uns*, ed. Zhang Yushu (Beijing: Peking University Press, 1998) 268–304; Stefanie Winkelnkemper, "Der Hass des 'Nazareners': Heinrich Heine antizipiert die

Psychologie des Ressentiments," *Nietzscheforschung* 13 (2006), 211–18; David Midgley, "Heine bei Nietzsche," in *Harry . . . Heinrich . . . Henri . . . Heine: Deutscher, Jude, Europäer*, ed. Dietmar Goltschnigg, Charlotte Grollegg-Edler, and Peter Reeves (Berlin: Erich Schmidt, 2008), 301–6; Ronald James Floyd, "Heine and Nietzsche: Parallel Studies in Paradox and Irony," a 1969 University of Washington dissertation, touches with its title a central aspect of the connection between Heine and Nietzsche. The dissertation is, however, disappointing and often unreliable. Nicolas S. Humphrey's 1986 Johns Hopkins dissertation "Heinrich Heine and Friedrich Nietzsche: Dance as Metaphor and Theoretical Imagery" presents a suggestive approach to address a central point of connection between Heine and Nietzsche. For a comprehensive exploration of the significance of the relationship between Nietzsche and Heine, see the dissertation by Alexander Soros, "Jewish Dionysus: Heine, Nietzsche, and the Politics of Literature" (Berkeley: University of California Press, 2018).

27 In a letter to Sophie Ritschl, the wife of his mentor Friedrich Ritschl and the woman who enabled the later encounter with Wagner, Nietzsche writes on July 2, 1868: "But I have unfortunately a preference for the Paris feuilleton, for Heine's Travel Pictures etc." ("Aber ich habe leider die Neigung für das pariser Feuilleton, für Heines Reisebilder usw."). See KSB 2, 299. For Sophie Ritschl, see Julian Young, *Friedrich Nietzsche: A Philosophical Biography* (Cambridge: Cambridge University Press, 2010), 66. Sophie was Jewish and an early love interest of Nietzsche who certainly knew to appreciate the twinkle in Nietzsche's eye when he addressed this line to her.

28 Friedrich Nietzsche, *Human, All Too Human: A Book for Free Spirits*, trans. R. J. Hollimgdale (Cambridge: Cambridge University Press, 1986), 120. The translation has three words of the sentence in italics. The German has no such emphases and the italics seem only confusing.

29 Cf. also Nietzsche's comment about Heine's significance for French poetry, KSA 11, 600f.

30 KSB 8, 359f. Nietzsche was so upset that he wrote the same day to his close friend Overbeck about the cancellation of his subscription to the *Kunstwart*, a journal that had hoped to count Nietzsche among its contributors. Cf. Nietzsche, *Briefe*, vol. 8, 362. For a full commentary on the letter, see Friedrich Nietzsche, *Briefwechsel, Kritische Gesamtausgabe*, section III, vol. 7.3, ed. Norbert Miller, Renate Müller-Buck, and Annemarie Pieper (Berlin and New York: de Gruyter, 2004), 348.

31 The editors Colli and Montinari fix the date for the last addendum, the passage on Heine, for December 29, 1888. Cf. KSA 14, 475.

32 KSB 8, 534: "Ich rechne die Heiterkeit zu den *Beweisen* meiner Philosophie . . . Vielleicht beweise ich diesen Satz durch die zwei Bücher, die ich Ihnen hiermit vorlege." The quote is from a draft. The original letter has been lost. For Bourdeau's reply to this letter, see his response from December 27, 1888, in Friedrich Nietzsche, *Kritische Ausgabe, Briefe* (Berlin: de Gruyter, 1984), vol. 3: 6, 403.

33 For this change that does not take shape until the 1870s, see Harro Müller, "Taubenfüße und Adlerkrallen: Friedrich Nietzsche's Sprach- und Stilkonzeption," in *Taubenfüße und Adlerkrallen: Essays zu Nietzsche,*

Adorno, Kluge, Büchner und Grabbe, ed. Harro Müller (Bielefeld: Aisthesis, 2016), 13–34, 27f.

34 For an incisive discussion of Nietzsche's text with regard to his language philosophy and style, see Müller, "Taubenfüße und Adlerkrallen: Friedrich Nietzsche's Sprach- und Stilkonzeption," 13–34.

35 For Nietzsche's "Über Wahrheit und Lüge im aussermoralischen Sinne," see KSA 1, 873–90, and "On Truth and Lying in a Non-Moral Sense," in *The Birth of Tragedy and Other Writings*, ed. Friedrich Nietzsche, trans. Ronald Spiers, ed. Raymond Geuss and Ronald Spiers (Cambridge: Cambridge University Press, 1999), 139–53.

36 Thomas Mann, "Notiz über Heine," in Mann, *Reden und Aufsätze*, vol. 2 (Frankfurt am Main: Fischer, 1965), 680.

37 Nietzsche, KSA 7, 138; Heine, S 36; Heine, B 4, 45.

38 Heine B 4, 399–423; L 6, 293–375.

39 Heine, "An meinen Bruder Max," DHA, Bd. 3.1, 404.

40 Renate Stauf mentions in passing the two poems as linked through the theme of falling into disrepute and exile: "Götter, und mit ihnen die Kunst, verlieren ihr Ansehen und gehen ins Exil." Renate Stauf, *Heinrich Heine: Gedichte und Prosa* (Berlin: Erich Schmidt, 2010), 49. And indeed, the resonance of the two is suggestive. If we read these two literally "extravagant" poems together, following the cue of the relation between center and periphery, they interestingly resonate with each other. Whether Apollo/Faibisch/Dionysus indeed departs for exile is unclear, as the directions of movement in the poem are contrary: the nun elopes to libertine Holland while the boat with Apollo and the debauched entourage goes river up (recently having been spotted in Amsterdam, he is now floating on the Rhine).

41 For a discussion of "Der Apollogott" that addresses its dissonant character, see especially Siegbert S. Prawer, *Heine, The Tragic Satirist: A Study of the Later Poetry 1827–56* (Cambridge: Cambridge University Press, 1961), 158–67, and Siegbert S. Prawer, *Heine's Jewish Comedy: A Study of his Portraits of Jews and Judaism* (Oxford: Clarendon Press, 1983), 531–51.

42 I owe the suggestion of the allusion to the tableau-like quality of the staging of this scene to Catriona MacLeod.

43 Nietzsche, *The Birth of Tragedy and Other Writings*, 104.

44 Nietzsche, Die Geburt der Tragödie, in Nietzsche, KSA 1, 140.

45 Nietzsche, *The Birth of Tragedy*, 113f.

46 In a letter to his friend Moses Moser, Heine writes about his urge "den großen Judenschmerz (wie ihn Börne nennt) auszusprechen." HSA 20, 97.

47 Walter Kaufmann, *Nietzsche: Philosopher, Psychologist, Antichrist* (New York: Vintage, 3rd ed., 1968), 377. See also Dolf Sternberger, *Heinrich Heine und die Abschaffung der Sünde* (Hamburg and Düsseldorf, 1972), 156–60.

48 Mann, "Notiz über Heine," 382.

49 For Heine's critical engagement of the distinction, see the chapter "Hellenes, Nazarenes, and Other Jews: Heine the Fool," in Willi Goetschel *The Discipline of Philosophy and the Invention of Modern Jewish Thought* (New York: Fordham, 2013), 21–38 and Willi Goetschel, "Tangled Genealogies: Hellenism, Hebraism, and the Discourse of Modernity," *Arion* 21 no. 3 (2014): 181–94. For Matthew Arnold, see Ilse-Maria Tesdorpf, *Die*

Auseinandersetzung Matthew Arnolds mit Henrich Heine, des Kritikers mit dem Kritiker: Ein besonderer Fall von konstruktivem Missverstehen und eigenwilliger Entlehnung (Frankfurt am Main: Athenäum, 1971).

50 Friedrich Nietzsche, *On the Genealogy of Morality*, trans. Carol Diethe, ed. Keith Ansell-Pearson (Cambridge: Cambridge University Press, 1994), first essay, §10, 21.

51 The primary references that come to mind in Heine are his obituary to a dying God in "On the History of Religion and Philosophy" and the witty aside in *Journey from Munich to Genoa* that, given the comfortable coolness in Italian churches, Catholicism is a convenient summer religion.

52 For one of the first discussions of Freud's relationship to Heine, see Hermann Levin, "Heine und Freud" (1956) now in Goldschmidt, *"Der Rest bleibt": Aufsätze zum Judentum*, ed. Willi Goetschel (Vienna: Passagen, 1997), 197–209. For crucial insights, see also Norbert Altenhofer, *Die verlorene Augensprache: über Heinrich Heine* (Frankfurt am Main: Insel, 1993). See also Michael Levine, "Heine and the Dream Naval: Reframing the Question of Censorship," in *Writing through Repression: Literature, Censorship, Psychoanalysis*, ed. Michael Levine (Baltimore: Johns Hopkins University Press, 1994), 43–70; Sander Gilman, "The Jewish Reader: Freud Reads Heine Reads Freud," in *The Jew's Body*, ed. Sander Gilman (New York: Routledge 1991), Jay Geller, "'Of Snips . . . and Puppy Dog Tails': Freud's Sublimation of Judentum," *American Imago* 66, no. 2 (2009): 169–84; Jocelyn Kolb, "Heine as Freud's Double in 'Der Witz und seine Beziehung zum Unbewußten,'" *Heine-Jahrbuch* 31 (1992), 137–62; Willi Goetschel, "Heine und der Traum," in *Palimpseste*. Zur Erinnerung an Norbert Altenhofer, ed. Pascal Nicklas and Joachim Jacob (Heidelberg: Carl Winter, 2004), 41–61.

53 Freud, *The Interpretation of Dreams*, in SE 5, 434.

54 Freud, *Traumdeutung*, SA 1, 420.

55 Freud, *Traumdeutung*, 471.

56 Heine's poem is number LVIII in the section "Heimkehr" ("Homecoming") of *Buch der Lieder* (*Book of Songs*) and starts with the line "Zu fragmentarisch ist Welt und Leben!" (B 1, 135), for an English translation, see Draper's rendering D 99.

57 Stéphane Mosès, "'Selten habt Ihr mich verstanden,' Zur Funktion eine Heine-Zitats in Freud, *Traumdeutung*," in *Heine und Freud: Die Enden der Literatur und die Anfänge der Kulturwissenschaft*, ed. Sigrid Weigel (Berlin: Kadmos, 2010), 91–8.

58 The poem is in the cycle "Die Heimkehr," number LXXVIII.

59 Gerhard Höhn, *Heine-Handbuch: Zeit, Person, Werk* (Stuttgart: Metzler, 3rd ed., 2004), 477.

60 Sander Gilman, *The Jew's Body* (New York: Routledge 1991), chapter 6: "The Jewish Reader: Freud Reads Heine Reads Freud," 168.

61 Freud, *Der Witz und seine Beziehung zum Unbewussten*, SA 4, 219; Freud, *Jokes and their Relation to the Unconscious* in SE 8, 235.

62 Louis Untermeyer, *Heinrich Heine: Paradox and Poet* (New York: Harcourt, Brace, 1937), 303. For Heine's importance for Freud's discussion of jokes, see also Yael Kupferberg, *Dimensionen des Witzes um Heinrich Heine: Zur*

Säkularisation der poetischen Sprache (Würzburg: Königshausen & Neumann, 2011).

63 Freud, SA 4. 125: "Der Witz ist nun als ein psychischer Machtfaktor erkannt [. . .]." Freud SE 8, 132: "A joke is now seen to be a psychical factor possessed of power."

64 Translation modified. Strachey's version "any more affable" suggests the opposite of Freud's German that exempts his aunt from the family's negative attitude.

65 Freud, SE 8, 140.

66 Freud, *The Future of an Illusion* in SE 21, 1–56, 49.

67 The Standard Edition provides its own translation from the German. Draper's is "The heavens we can safely leave/To the angels and the sparrows" (D 484).

68 Freud, SA 9, 183, end of section 11.

69 See 199f. For the reference, see Freud, *Der Witz und seine Beziehung zum Unbewussten*, SA 4, 75 and Freud, *Jokes and Their Relation to the Unconscious*, SE 8, 76.

70 Freud, *Civilization and its Discontents* in *SE* 21, 57–146.

71 Freud, *Das Unbehagen in der Kultur*, in SA 11, 239.

72 Responding to an inquiry by a journal, Freud lists Heine's "Lazarus," a cycle of poems at the end of "Lamentations," part 2 of *Romanzero*, as one of his two favorite books, the other being Milton's *Paradise Lost*. See Freud's letter to Hugo Heller from November 1, 1906, in Sigmund Freud, *Briefe 1873–1939*, ed. Ernst and Lucie Freud (Frankfurt am Main: Fischer, 1980), 267.

73 Freud, "The Acquisition and Control of Fire," in SE. 22, 183–94, 191; Freud, "Zur Gewinnung des Feuers," in SA 9, 454; B 6.1, 301–4, 304: verse 117f.

Chapter 3

1 See especially the three essays by Gerhard Höhn, "Kontrastästhetik: Heines Programm einer neuen Schreibart," in *Heinrich Heine: ein Wegbereiter der Moderne*, ed. Paolo Chiarini and Walter Hinderer (Würzburg: Königshausen and Neumann, 2009), 43–66, "'Sauerkraut mit Ambrosia': Heines Kontrastästhetik," *Heine Jahrbuch* 48 (2009): 1–27, and "Paris, ein Fest fürs Leben und Wende des Schreibens: Heines Kontrastästhetik," in *"Was die Zeit fühlt und denkt und bedarf": die Welt des 19. Jahrhunderts im Werk Heinrich Heines*, ed. Bernd Kortländer (Bielefeld: Aisthesis, 2014), 115–36.

2 Ernst Simon, "Heine und die Romantik," in *Essays Presented to Leo Baeck on the Occasion of His Eightieth Birthday* (London: East and West Library, 1954), 127–57, 156. The passage from the young Heine's early play *Almansor* (B 1, 318) is worth citing for the particular effect of dissonance it produces. For a further discussion of this passage, see the end of this section.

3 Heinrich Heine, *Poems of Heinrich Heine*, trans. Louis Untermeyer (New York: Harcourt, Brace 1916), 219. See also, for a more contemporary version D 334. I prefer the Untermeyer version for diction and flow.

4 Written in 1832, this poem is # 10 from the cycle "Seraphine" in the part titled "Verschiedene" of *Neue Gedichte*, B 4, 327.

5 Heine, *Deutschland. Ein Wintermärchen*, B 4, 578; D 484.

6 Untermeyer's translation in *Poems of Heinrich Heine*, 87f. See also D 76f.
7 Willi Goetschel, *German Studies in a Post-National Age*. The 2009 Craig Lecture, Rutgers German Studies Occasional Papers 9 (New Brunswick: Rutgers University, 2010), 12–17.
8 Theodor W. Adorno, *Ästhetische Theorie*, in Adorno, *Gesammelte Schriften*, ed. Rolf Tiedemann (Frankfurt am Main: Suhrkamp, 1997), vol. 7, 168. Henceforth I refer to this edition as GS followed by volume number and page number. For the English translation, see Theodor W. Adorno, *Aesthetic Theory*, trans. Robert Hullot-Kentor (New York and London: Continuum, 2002), 110.
9 Ibid.
10 For the significance of Kafka and Beckett for Adorno, see David Suchoff, "Dissonant Lineages: Adorno, Beckett, Blanchot, Kafka, Rosenzweig," *The Germanic Review* 90 (2015): 335–57. The Beckett scholar Marx Nixon, for instance, notes the decisive importance of Heine for Beckett: "Einer der bedeutendsten Schriftsteller dieses neuen Zeitalters war Heinrich Heine, der nach 1945 auf Beckett eine starke Wirkung ausübte." Mark Nixon, "Beckett liest die deutsche Literatur: Eine Übersicht," in *Samuel Beckett und die deutsche Literatur*, ed. Jan Wilm and Mark Nixon (Bielefeld: transcript Verlag, 2013), 23. I owe this reference as well as the insight into the critical role Heine plays in Kafka and Beckett to David Suchoff. For a reading of Kafka that illustrates this point, see also David Suchoff, *Kafka's Jewish Languages: The Hidden Openness of Tradition* (Philadelphia: University of Pennsylvania Press, 2012).
11 Adorno, *Ästhetische Theorie*, GS 7, 113; Adorno, *Aesthetic Theory*, 72.
12 Adorno, *Dissonanzen: Musik in der verwalteten Welt*, GS 14, 18.
13 Theodor W. Adorno, "On the Fetish-Character in Music and the Regression in Listening" in Adorno, *Essays on Music*, ed. Richard Leppert, trans. Susan H. Gillespie (Berkeley and Los Angeles: University of California Press, 2002), 288–317, 291.
14 On this, Heine and Adorno resonate with Freud and Spinoza who both stress the dynamic role the affects play in defining what constitutes happiness. See especially Sigmund Freud, *Civilization and Its Discontents* (SE 21, 57–146) and Spinoza's definitions of joy and sadness as functions of transitions from lesser to greater and greater to lesser perfection, respectively. See Spinoza's definitions 2 and 3 at the end of part 3 of his *Ethics*, in *The Collected Works of Spinoza*, vol. 1, ed. and trans. Edwin Curley (Princeton: Princeton University Press, 1985), 531.
15 Adorno, *Negative Dialektik*, GS, vol. 6, 207.
16 Adorno, *Negative Dialectics*, trans. Ashton 207. Notice that the verb quench has an annihilating quality, meaning to put out or extinguish a fire or light, while the decisively more peaceful "stillen" has a nursing quality. In other words, the English translation has the physical urge (*leibhafter Drang*) neutralized and extinguished while Adorno's German would have the bodily need nursed, satisfied, gratified, pacified, and assuaged: "gestillt." In German, the spirit is not "reconciled"—by whom? Rather, the German has the spirit reconcile itself with the bodily urge. However, in the English rendering, Adorno's use of the reflexive verb, a hallmark of Adorno's style, is elided and the active verb "to reconcile itself" replaced by a passive construction that shifts the agency from *Geist* or spirit to

an unknown, unnamed agent that assumes authority over brokering the spirit's reconciling with the bodily needs. And finally, while the English translation has the "spell of material conditions" refuse to "let" *Geist* satisfy material needs, the German verb *verweigern* indicates that this denial is an intentional refusal on the part of *Geist* that denies the physical needs what is rightfully theirs.

17 Theodor W. Adorno, *Philosophy of New Music*, trans. Robert Hullot-Kentor (Minneapolis and London: University of Minnesota Press, 2006), 11.

18 Adorno, *Philosophie der neuen Musik*, GS 12, 18.

19 Adorno, "Toward a Reappraisal of Heine," in GS, 20.2, 441–52, 441. For the excited report about the success of this talk, see the comments by Gretel and Theodor Adorno in their letter to Adorno's parents on December 2, 1948, in Theodor A. Adorno, *Briefe an die Eltern*, ed. Christoph Gödde and Henri Lonitz (Frankfurt: Suhrkamp, 2003), 482f. In this letter, Adorno notes that a recording was made. Unfortunately, it has been impossible to locate the recording.

20 Adorno, *Philosophy of New Music*, 158.

21 Adorno, *Philosophie der neuen Musik*, GS 12, 196.

22 Adorno, *Minima Moralia*, GS 4, 245; Adorno, *Minima Moralia*, trans. Jephcott 215.

23 For Marx's famous line, see his *Communist Manifesto* in Marx, *Selected Writings*, 161f.

24 Karl Kraus, "Heine und die Folgen," in *Die Fackel* 1910, rpt. in Karl Kraus, *Ausgewählte Werke*, ed. Dietrich Simon (Munich: Langen Müller, 1977), vol. 1, 290–312; for an English translation, see the bilingual edition by Jonathan Franzen, *The Kraus Project: Essays by Karl Kraus*, trans. Jonathan Franzen with assistance and additional notes from Paul Reitter and Daniel Kehlmann (New York: Farrar, Straus and Giroux, 2013), 6–133.

25 For the classic locus, see Max Horkheimer, *Die Juden und Europa* in Horkheimer, *Gesammelte Werke*, vol. 4 (Frankfurt am Main: Fischer, 1988), 308f.

26 On Louis Untermeyer, see Jeffrey Sammons's fine essay "Retroactive Dissimilation: Louis Untermeyer, the 'American Heine,'" in Sammons, *Heinrich Heine: Alternative Perspectives 1985–2005* (Würzburg: Königshausen & Neumann, 2006), 223–42.

27 Heine, *Poems*, trans. Untermeyer, 36. Cf. also Draper's translation D 31.

28 Jacob and Wilhelm Grimm, *Deutsches Wörterbuch*, vol 30, col. 1773, the line is from Heine's "Die Grenadiere," B 1, 47.

29 Gerhard Höhn, "Adorno face à Heine ou le couteau dans la plaie," in *Revue d'Esthétique* 8 (1985): 137–44, 144.

30 Theodor W. Adorno, "Die Wunde Heine," in *Noten zur Literatur* in GS 11, 100; Theodor W. Adorno, "Heine the Wound," in *Notes to Literature*, vol. 1, trans. Shierry Weber Nicholsen (New York: Columbia University Press, 1991), 80–5, 85.

31 See especially Adorno's essay "Was bedeutet: Aufarbeitung der Vergangenheit," Adorno, GS, 10.2, 555–72, 557; "The Meaning of Working Through the Past," in *Critical Models: Interventions and Catchwords*, ed. Theodor W. Adorno, trans. Henry Pickford (New York: Columbia, 1998), 89–103, 91. On Adorno's strategic word choice of *Wunde* rather than trauma in "Heine the Wound,"

see Katya Garloff, "Essay, Exile, Efficacy: Adorno's Literary Criticism," *Monatshefte* 94, no. 1 (Spring 2002): 80–95, 87f.

32 Max Horkheimer and Theodor W. Adorno, *Dialectic of Enlightenment: Philosophical Fragments*, trans. Edmund Jephcott (Stanford: Stanford University Press, 2002), 213–14.

33 Max Horkheimer and Theodor W. Adorno, *Dialektik der Aufklärung: Philosophische Fragmente* (Frankfurt am Main: Fischer, 1988), 274.

34 Horkheimer and Adorno, *Dialectic of Enlightenment*, 214.

35 Ibid., 275.

36 Katya Garloff's essay brilliantly engages in a critique of Peter Uwe Hohendahl's discussion of Adorno's essay. Ulrich Plass, who follows both Hohendahl and Garloff, repeats, however, some of the claims that Garloff demonstrates as displaying a problematic reading on the part of Hohendahl. While I agree with many of Garloff's tenets, I part company when it comes to a collapsing of the positions evidenced in the *Dialectic of Enlightenment* and Adorno's later, more differentiated approach. See Garloff, "Essay, Exile, Efficacy"; Peter Uwe Hohendahl, *Prismatic Thought: Theodor W. Adorno* (Lincoln: University of Nebraska Press, 1995), 105–17; and Ulrich Plass, *Language and History in Theodor W. Adorno's Notes to Literature* (New York and London: Routledge, 2007), 115–52. For Hohendahl's claim that Adorno criticized Heine for his writing's inauthenticity, see also the more recent Peter Uwe Hohendahl, *Fleeting Promise of Art: Adorno's Aesthetic Theory Revisited* (Ithaca, NY: Cornell University Press, 2013), 155: "When Adorno turns his attention to Heinrich Heine, the reader has to keep in mind the resistance of German literary criticism of the 1950s to Heine because of his Jewish background. On the other hand, there is also the issue of Adorno's own doubts about Heine's poetry because of its supposed inauthenticity, an evaluation that Adorno took over from the famous Austrian critic Karl Kraus."

Uwe Peter Hohendahl, *Heinrich Heine: Europäischer Schriftsteller und Intellektueller* (Berlin: Erich Schmidt, 2008) presents a similar view. Just as in his other publications, the chapter "Adorno als Leser Heines" ignores Adorno's Los Angeles talk on Heine from 1948/9. In a selective reading of "Heine the Wound," Hohendahl curiously identifies Adorno with the very position he seeks to critically expose. The chapter is a translation of "Adorno as a Reader of Heine," which appeared earlier in *Reason and its Other: Rationality in Modern German Philosophy and Culture*, ed. Dieter Freundlieb and Wayne Hudson (Providence and Oxford: Berg and New York: St. Martin's Press, 1993), 229–40.

37 Adorno's earlier essay on Heine "Towards a Reappraisal" appeared in 1985 in GS 20.2.

38 Gerhard Höhn, "Adorno face à Heine ou le couteau dans la plaie," *Revue d'esthétique* 8 (1985): 137–44, 138.

39 Adorno, "Die Wunde Heine," GS 11, 97; Adorno, "Heine the Wound," 82.

40 Adorno, "Heine the Wound," 82.

41 Adorno, "Die Wunde Heine," GS 11, 97f.; Adorno, "Heine the Wound," 82.

42 Adorno, "Heine the Wound," 82.f.

43 See, especially, Adorno, "Wörter aus der Fremde," in *Noten zur Literatur*, GS 11, 219, broadcast a year after the print version of "Heine die Wunde": "Keine Sprache, auch die alte Volkssprache nicht, ist wozu restaurative Lehren sie machen möchten, ein Organisches, Naturhaftes" (ibid.) and "Über den

Gebrauch von Fremdwörtern" (Adorno, *Noten zur Literatur* in GS 11, 644). Adorno's indictment that there is no such thing as a "Sprachontologie," the underlying tenor of *Jargon der Eigentlichkeit* and *Negative Dialectics*, as well as his *Aesthetic Theory* resonates profoundly with the ideas he articulates in "Die Wunde Heine." I thank David Suchoff for alerting me to Adorno's critical position in this essay with regard to the question of language. See also David Suchoff, "Dissonant Lineages."

44 Adorno, "Heine the Wound," 83.

45 Ibid., 83.

46 Ibid..

47 Adorno, "Die Wunde Heine," 98f; Adorno, "Heine the Wound," 83.

48 Ibid.

49 Theodor W. Adorno, *Minima Moralia: Reflections on a Damaged Life*, trans. Edmund Jephcott (New York and London: Verso, 1974), 110.

50 Theodor W. Adorno, *Minima Moralia: Reflexionen aus dem beschädigten Leben*, GS 4, 125.

51 Theodor W. Adorno, "Words from Abroad," in *Notes to Literature*, vol. 1, 185–99, 189.

52 For a discussion of "Der Apollogott" see Chapter 2, **(page numbers) – **.

53 The centerpiece is the middle piece of the three parts of the poetic insert: L 2, 111–13; B 2, 132–4.

Chapter 4

1 Untermeyer, *Poems of Heinrich Heine*, trans. Louis Untermeyer (New York: Harcourt, Brace, 1916; 2nd ed. 1923), 49.

2 The entry dates from 1882. Bd. 12, Sp. 1819–22. http://woerterbuchnetz.de/DWB/?sigle=DWB&mode=Vernetzung&hitlist=&patternlist=&lemid=GM02662#XGM02662 (accessed June 3, 2016).

3 David Suchoff, *Kafka's Jewish Languages: The Hidden Openness of Tradition* (Philadelphia: University of Pennsylvania Press, 2012), 51f.

4 I follow the translation by Suchoff, ibid., 51. For a slightly different translation, see S 15f.

5 Suchoff, ibid., 51f.

6 Paul Mendes-Flohr, "Hermann Levin Goldschmidt and the Legacy of German-Jewish Humanism," Hermann Levin Goldschmidt Memorial Lecture 2011. This comment was given in the oral presentation but not included in the published version. www.dialogik.org/memorial-lectures.

7 For Goethe's critical attitude with regard to self-entitled claims of inheritance, see Faust's comment that inheritance will have to be earned in order to be owned. Goethe, *Faust I*, in *Sämtliche Werke*, vol. 5, 164, verses 682–3.

8 Goethe, "Deutsche Sprache," in *Sämtliche Werke*, vol. 14, 267.

9 "Von der Ausbildung der Teutschen Sprache, in Beziehung auf neue, dafür angestellte Bemühungen," which drew Goethe's attention to its author, was published with Heinrich Meyer's mediation in *Nemesis, Zeitschrift für Politik und Geschichte*, ed. Heinrich Luden, 8, no. 3 (1816): 337–86. See Daniel Jacoby, "Ruckstuhl, Karl," in *Allgemeine Deutsche Biographie* 53 (1907), 576–80. http://www.deutsche-biographie.de/sfz77204.html (accessed June 6,

2016). Ruckstuhl had been a student and then a teacher at Johann Heinrich Pestalozzi's in Yverdon.

10 See also Goethe's comments on translation in the section "Übersetzungen" of the appendix to *West-östlicher Divan*, vol. 3, 554–7.

11 Friedrich Nietzsche, "Über Wahrheit und Lüge im aussermoralischen Sinne," see KSA 1, 873–90 and "On Truth and Lying in a Non-Moral Sense," in Friedrich Nietzsche, *The Birth of Tragedy and Other Writings*, trans. Ronald Spiers, ed. Raymond Geuss and Ronald Spiers (Cambridge: Cambridge University Press, 1999), 139–53. See also Chapter 2 for a discussion of Heine's significance for Nietzsche with regard to language.

12 An earlier version of this section appeared in my article "Nightingales Instead of Owls: Heine's Joyous Philosophy," in *A Companion to the Works of Heinrich Heine*, ed. Roger F. Cook (Rochester, NY: Camden House, 2002), 139–68, 142–6.

13 Norbert Altenhofer, "Chiffre, Hieroglyphe, Palimpsest: Vorformen tiefenhermeneutischer und intertextueller Intepretation im Werk Heines," in Altenhofer, *Die verlorene Augensprache: Über Heinrich Heine* (Frankfurt am Main: Insel, 1993), 104–53. For a discussion of the romantic discourse on hieropglyphs, see Gideon Stiening, "Die Metaphysik des Hieroglyphischen," *Jahrbuch des Freien Deutschen Hochstifts* (1999): 121–62.

14 Altenhofer, *Die verlorene Augensprache*, 150.

15 Ibid., 151.

16 The term is borrowed from Barbara Johnson's translation of Jacques Derrida, *Plato's Pharmacy*, in Derrida, *Dissemination*, trans. Barbara Johnson (Chicago: University of Chicago Press, 1981), 63.

17 Walter Benjamin, *The Origin of German Tragic Drama*, trans. John Osborne (London and New York: Verso, 1998),162.

18 Walter Benjamin, *Ursprung des deutschen Trauerspiels* in Benjamin, *Gesammelte Schriften*, ed. Rolf Tiedemann (Frankfurt am Main: Suhrkamp, 1978), 1, 339.

19 Benjamin, *Origin of German Tragic Drama*. 167.

20 Benjamin, *Trauerspiel*, 344

21 Benjamin, *Origin of German Tragic Drama*, 176.

22 Karl Marx, *The German Ideology*, in Marx, *Selected Writings*, 117.

23 Marx and Engels, "Deutsche Ideologie," in MEW, vol. 3, 30.

24 The Briegleb has "Papagoi" while the DHA has "Papagoy."

25 On Heine's particular spelling, see the commentary in DHA 5, 808: "[Papagois] Heine gebraucht meist diese Form, z. B. in der Stadt Lukka (DHA VII, 164; vgl. auch 92) und im Schnabelewopski außerdem noch 181,38 und 182,4. Grimms Deutsches Wörterbuch (VII, 1433) bezeichnet sie als niederdeutsch. In Belegen des 16.–18. Jahrhunderts begegnet sie aber auch außerhalb dieses Bereichs."

26 Heine's affinities are clearly with the nightingales and also at one point with the finch (*Gimpel*), with which he identifies as well. For the finch, see *Buch der Lieder*, "Lyrisches Intermezzo," poem LIII (B 1, 97).

27 Turtle dove is used in German to refer to a lovebird, an "almanac nightingale," suggests an author of "applied" poetry such as might be found in an almanac; a gander might be the male equivalent of a silly goose; and a "house rooster" invokes someone with the personality of a cock.

28 Arendt, "The Jew as Pariah: A Hidden Tradition" in *Jewish Social Studies* 6, no. 2 (April 1944): 99–122.

29 For a discussion of the character and its background, see Prawer, *Heine's Jewish Comedy*, 133–42; for identification of Heine and his character, resp. Hirsch-Hyazinth as self-parody, see also Freud, *Jokes and their Relation to the Unconscious* in SE 8, 140; Freud, *Der Witz und seine Beziehung zum Unbewussten*, in SA 4, 133.
30 For an illuminating reading of the passage to which this reading of the *Florentine Nights* owes many suggestions, see Birgit R. Erdle, *Literarische Epistemologie der Zeit: Lektüren zu Kant, Kleist, Heine und Kafka* (Munich: Fink, 2015), 105–33.
31 This and the next paragraph are based on the introduction coauthored with David Suchoff to the special theme issue *Displaced Philology* published in *The Germanic Review* 93, no.1 (2018): 1–6, here 3–4.
32 Translation modified.
33 Jacques Derrida, *Specters of Marx*, trans. Peggy Kamuf (New York and London: Routledge, 1994), 10.
34 Theodor W. Adorno, "Words from Abroad," in *Notes on Literature*, ed. Theodor W. Adorno, trans. Shierry Weber Nicholsen (New York: Columbia University Press, 1991), 188.
35 The name Le Grand appears as another challenge for translation: what is "grand" about the drum major is precisely his down-to-earth attitude, devoid of any pretense of grandeur.
36 See above pp. 133–6.
37 I tacitly restored Heine's way of listing the sections. Leland's rendering makes the list nonsensical, but at the expense of obfuscating the parodistic thrust of Heine's imitation of Hegel's formal organization of his texts.
38 In Spinoza, ideas can only exist as ideas of a particular body and an idea of an idea has reality only insofar as it is tied to an idea of a body. Ideas in other words do not exist in and of themselves. For Spinoza's discussion of the nature and function of ideas and the idea of an idea, see his *Ethics* and the *Treatise on the Emendation of the Intellect* in *The Collected Works of Spinoza*, ed. and trans. Edwin Curley (Princeton: Princeton University Press, 1985).
39 G. F. W. Hegel, *Outlines of the Philosophy of Right*, trans. T. M. Knox and ed. Stephen Houlgate (Oxford: Oxford University Press, rev. ed., 2008), 14.
40 See, for instance, Theodor W. Adorno, *Negative Dialectics*, 11–12, 153–5.
41 For a discussion of this aspect of Heine's text, see Willi Goetschel, *The Discipline of Philosophy and the Invention of Modern Jewish Thought* (New York: Fordham, 2013), 27–33.

Chapter 5

1 Karl Marx, *The Eighteenth Brumaire of Louis Bonaparte*, in Marx, *Selected Writings*, 187–208, 188.
2 Marx, *Der achtzehnte Brumaire des Louis Bonaparte*, MEW, vol. 8, 115.
3 Marx, *Selected Writings*, 188f.
4 Marx, MEW 8, 115.
5 Marx, "Toward a Critique of Hegel's Philosophy of Right" in Marx, *Selected Writings*, 27–39, 31.

6 Marx, MEW, vol. 1, 382.

7 See Lefebvre's comment that "Heine's influence is not limited to quotations: it can be detected everywhere in Marx's language. His extraordinary polemical vivacity, the joy in metaphorical invention—one think only of *The Eighteenth Brumaire*—immediately recall Heine's style." Lefebvre, "Marx und Heine," 60. Cf. also Reeves, "Heine and the Young Marx," 76–8.

8 Marx, *Selected Writings*, 196; MEW 8, 123.

9 For the significance of this passage for Marx, see also Paul-Laurent Assoun's entry on historical repetition in *Dictionnaire critique du marxisme*, ed. Georges Labicia and Gérard Bensussan (Paris: Presse universitaires de France, 2nd ed., 1982), 993–5, 994.

10 For a discussion on Marx's view on the tragic, see Miriam Leonard, *Tragic Modernities* (Cambridge, MA: Harvard University Press 2015), 27–34.

11 Benjamin, *Arcades Project*, section "N."

12 Ernst Bloch, *Erbschaft dieser Zeit* in Bloch, *Gesamtausgabe* (Frankfurt am Main: Suhrkamp, 1977), 104–26. For a discussion of Heine and Bloch, see Mathias Richter, "Hermeneutik der Emanzipation: Heine und Bloch als Gesellschaftsanalytiker," in "Zuckererbsen für Jedermann": *Literatur und Utopie. Heine und Bloch heute*, ed. Norbert Otto Eke, Karin Füllner, and Francesca Vidal (Bielefeld: Aistehis, 2014), 135–53.

13 For Freud, see the discussion that follows in this chapter; for Simmel, see Georg Simmel, "The Problem of Historical Time," in *Essays on Interpretation in Social Science*, trans. Guy Oakes (Manchester: Manchester University Press, 1980), 127–44 where *Nachträglichkeit* however is translated as "retrospective syntheses" (139). See Georg Simmel, "Das Problem der historischen Zeit" in *Simmel, Brücke und Tür: Essays*, ed. Michael Landmann together with Margarete Susman (Stuttgart: Köhler, 1957), 43–58, 53; for Derrida, see Jacques Derrida, *Specters of Marx*, trans. Peggy Kamuf (New York and London: Routledge, 1994).

14 Hayden White, *Metahistory: The Historical Imagination in Nineteenth-Century Europe* (Baltimore: Johns Hopkins University Press, 1973), 139.

15 Walter Benjamin, "Eduard Fuchs, Collector and Historian," in *Selected Writings, vol. 3: 1935–1938*, ed. Walter Benjamin, trans. Edmund Jephcott, Howard Eiland, et al., ed. Howard Eiland and Michael W. Jennings (Cambridge, MA: Harvard University Press, 2008), 260–302; Benjamin, "Eduard Fuchs, der Sammler und der Historiker" in GS 2, 465–505.

16 See Benjamin, "Eduard Fuchs," 287 note 6; Benjamin, GS, 467 note 3.

17 See, for instance, Howard Caygill, "Walter Benjamin's Concept of Cultural History," in *The Cambridge Companion to Walter Benjamin*, ed. David S. Ferris (Cambridge: Cambridge University Press, 2006), 73–96, esp. 89–94.

18 Marx, *A Contribution to the Critique of Political Economy* in Marx, *Selected Writings*, 209. As Benjamin rightly observes, Marx had developed many of the ideas that inform the preface in the section on Feuerbach in *The German Ideology*. See MEW 3, 26f.; Marx, *Selected Writings*, esp. 111f.

19 For Engels's review of Marx, see MEW 13, 470.

20 Engels to Conrad Schmidt, August 5, 1890. https://www.marxists.org/archive/marx/works/1890/letters/90_08_05.htm (accessed April 10, 2018).

21 Engels in a letter to Conrad Schmidt, August 5, 1890, MEW 37, 436. See also Hermann Braun, s.v. "Materialismus" in *Geschichtliche Grundbegriffe*, ed.

Otto Brunner, Werner Conze, and Reinhart Koselleck (Stuttgart: Klett-Cotta, 2004), vol. 3, 1005f.

22 MEW 22, 287–311; for "historischer Materialismus," see 292, for Baco and Hobbes esp. 292–4, for England's repression of its own materialist tradition and its current return, see 295–311. Initially written as the introduction for his English edition of *Socialism: Utopian and Scientific* (London: Swan Sonnenschein and New York: Scribner, 1892), Engels translated the introduction into German and published the text the same year in *Die Neue Zeit* under the title "Über historischen Materialismus" (cf. MEW 22, 608).

23 MEW 21, 259–307, for Marx's theses on Feuerbach, see MEW 3, 533–5.

24 Frederick Engels, *Ludwig Feuerbach and the End of Classical German Philosophy*. https://www.marxists.org/archive/marx/works/1886/ludwig-feuerbach/index.htm (accessed June 28, 2018). Müller, *Marx und Heine*, 16, calls this a "downright monumentally sounding sentence."

25 Braun, "Materialism," 1006 and Müller, *Marx und Heine*, 33, who notes that in Heine we can find "essential propositions of dialectical and historical materialism, especially that of the mutual relation [*Wechselwirkung*] between theory and praxis." Plekhanov in his Russian translation of this text calls Heine's *On the History of Religion and Philosophy in Germany* a "splendid work," thus suggesting the long-term impact Heine had beyond Marx and Engels for later Marxist discussions. See Plekhanov's first note to his Russian edition of Engels's *Ludwig Feuerbach and the End of Classical German Philosophy*. https://www.marxists.org/archive/plekhanov/1892/engels/notes1.html (accessed April 10, 2018).

26 Marx, *Selected Writings*, 210f.

27 See Heine's comment that intentions are indeterminable in history: B 3, 536 and OH 28.

28 For an insightful discussion of the life of ideas in Spinoza see Hasana Sharp, *Spinoza and the Politics of Renaturalization* (Chicago and London: Chicago University Press, 2011), 62f.

29 Translation modified. Leland curiously renders the German *Gestirne* with "starry intellects," suggesting that Heine had thought here of the constellation of minds. However, Leland's version seems to confuse rather than clarify.

30 See also Benjamin's comment that a philosophy is of no worth unless it includes the possibility of soothsaying from coffee grounds: "A philosophy that does not include the possibility of soothsaying from coffee *grounds* and cannot explicate it cannot be a true philosophy." Gershom Scholem, *Walter Benjamin: The Story of a Friendship*, trans. Harry Zohn (New York: New York Review Book, 2003), 73.

31 For an illuminating discussion of this text and Heine's reflections on history more generally, see Kristina Mendicino, "Newswriting, Historiography, and the Controversion of the Present (after Heine)," *diacritics* 44, no.3 (2016): 80–112.

32 Heine eventually published a part of the draft of the introduction in his *Shakespeares Frauen und Mädchen*, B 4, 214–17.

33 For a study of Heine's "French Painters," see Irmgard Zepf, *Denkbilder: Heinrich Heines Gemäldebericht* (Munich: Fink, 1980). See also András Sándor, "The Oak Tree and the Ax: Delaroche's Painting and

Heine's Montage," in *Paintings on the Move*, ed. Susanne Zantop (Lincoln and London: University of Nebraska Press, 1989), 51–74. For a discussion of Heine addressing absence in the exhibit's paintings, see Renate Stauf, "Imaginäre Galerien: Heines Gemäldekommentare zum Salon von 1831," in *Poetische Zeitgenossenschaft: Heine-Studien*, ed. Cord-Friedrich Berghahn (Heidelberg: Winter, 2015), 161–81.

34 The art work represents the issue of terror rather than horror because the revenge acts of the Greek Gods are not merely random acts, but function according to a repressive regime of despotic rulers that control any form of expressed dissent rather than any kind of unaccountable force. The story of Laocoon's death is the story of exactly this type of explanation that serves as an example, itself a crucial function of terror.

35 G. W. F. Hegel, *Phenomenology of Spirit*, trans. A. V. Miller (Oxford: Oxford University Press, 1977), 360.

36 For a succinct discussion of the situation of terror in postrevolutionary Europe, see Rebecca Comay, *Mourning Sickness: Hegel and the French Revolution* (Stanford: Stanford University Press, 2011).

37 Heinrich Heine, "French Painters," in *Paintings on the Move*, trans. David Ward, 121–72, 143f

38 For a brief discussion of Heine's presentation of the paintings, see the section "Geschichtsbilder" (history paintings) in Zepf, *Denkbilder*, 111–17.

39 Cf. Jeffrey Sammons's note on the passage: "No such rabbi has been identified, nor does Heine seem to have gone to Cracow during his visit to Poland. The scene is probably fictional." S 103, note 179.

40 For a discussion of the passage on the Messiah in Heine, see also Tamara Eisenberg, "Neither Christ nor Barbarossa: Heinrich Heine's Messiah in Golden Chains," in *Benjamin—Agamben: Politics, Messianism, Kabbalah*, ed. Vittoria Borsò, Claas Morgenroth, Karl Solibakke, and Bernd Witte (Würzburg: Königshausen & Neumann, 2010), 219–27.

41 The apparatus of the Heine Düsseldorf edition lists the medieval mystical "Midrash Konen" dating from around 1000 as reference and gives as reference for the relevant passage the collection *Bet ha-Midrash*, ed. Adolph Jellinek, Jerusalem 1938, part I, no. 2, 29, that Ernst Simon provided and translated for the edition in DHA 11, 610. Ernst Simon, a close friend of Martin Buber and Gershom Scholem, was not only the author of numerous studies on Jewish tradition but has also published a fine essay on Heine and romanticism in the festschrift collection of *Essays Presented to Leo Baeck on the Occasion of His Eightieth Birthday* (London: East and West Library, 1954), 127–57.

42 For a lively description of the Sabbatian tradition, see Gershom Scholem's magnum opus *Sabbatai Sevi: The Mystical Messiah*, trans. R. J. Zwi Werbloswky (Princeton: Princeton University Press, 1973), esp. 490 and 585.

43 Hermann Levin Goldschmidt, "Mitzeitgenosse Turel," in *Werke*, ed. Hermann Levin Goldschmidt, vol. 8 (Vienna: Passagen, 1995), 227–46, 230. For the source, see Adrien Turel, *Generalangriff auf die Persönlichkeit und dessen Abwehr* (Zurich: Adrien Turel, 1955). Turel uses the question as the title of part 2 of the book.

44 This sentence is left out in Leland's translation.

45 I have modified Leland's translation to reflect Heine's point.

46 Leland renders the passage simply as reflections "which now go sweeping about" (L 3, 107) omitting the haunting image of abandoned stray dogs.
47 The dash is missing in the English translation.
48 Translation modified. Leland has "world's history."
49 The motif recurs in in B 2, 344, 346, 356, 366, 388, 617. For a discussion of the role of the motif of the dead Maria in Heine, see Michel Espagne, "Die tote Maria: ein Gespenst in Heines Handschriften," *Deutsche Vierteljahrsschrift für Literaturwissenschaft und Geistesgeschichte* 57 (1983): 298–320.
50 Sigmund Freud, *Moses and Monotheism*, in SE 23 (1937–9): 1–138, 29.
51 Freud, SA 9, 480; for Heine see B, 4, 420f., 420: Heine has the second line in the nominative, Freud sets it in the accusative. For an English translation, see D 399: "The plague they carried from the grim Nile valley, / The old Egyptian faith so long unhealthful."
52 Heine composed the poem "The New Israelite Hospital in Hamburg," from which Freud quotes, to celebrate the generous donation by his uncle Salomon Heine who had the hospital built.
53 Freud, *Moses and Monotheism*, 6; Freud, *Der Mann Moses*, 459.
54 Heinrich Heine, "Confessions," in *Heine's Prose Writings*, intro. Havelock Ellis (London: Walter Scott, 1887), 307; Heine, *Geständnisse*, B 6.1, 481.
55 Heine, "Confessions," 307. Ellis omits the sentence put in brackets. The translation of this sentence is mine.
56 Heine calls himself "ich armer Exgott" (B 6.1, 476) in this revocation of any divine claims.
57 Miriam Leonard, *Socrates and the Jews: Hellenism and Hebraism from Moses Mendelssohn to Sigmund Freud* (Chicago: University of Chicago Press, 2012). See also my review essay "Tangled Genealogies: Hellenism, Hebraism, and Discourse of Modernity." Review essay of Miriam Leonard, Socrates and the Jews: Hellenism and Hebraism from Moses Mendelssohn to Sigmund Freud, *Arion* 21, no.3 (2014): 111–24.
58 For a discussion of Heine's approach to the issue, see the chapter "Hellenes, Nazarenes, and Other Jews: Heine the Fool," in *The Discipline of Philosophy and the Invention of Modern Jewish Thought*, ed. Willi Goetschel (New York: Fordham, 2013), 39–57.
59 Heine, "Confessions," 308.
60 Freud, *Der Mann Moses*, 537; Freud, *Moses and Monotheism*, 89.
61 See Harold Bloom, *The Anxiety of Influence: A Theory of Poetry* (New York: Oxford University Press, 1997).
62 Heine, *The City of Lucca*, L 3, 305; B 2, 513.
63 Johann Wolfgang Goethe, *West-östlicher Divan* in Goethe, *Sämtliche Werke*, ed. Ernst Beutler (Zurich: Artemis, 1948 and 1977), vol. 3, 514.
64 Benjamin, *Arcades Project*, N, 19, 1486; Benjamin, *Passagen Werk*, GS 5, 609.
65 The following discussion of "Hebrew Melodies" is based on my discussion in Willi Goetschel, "Nightingales Instead of Owls: Heine's Joyous Philosophy," in *A Companion to the Works of Heinrich Heine*, ed. Roger F. Cook (Rochester, NY: Camden House, 2002), 156ff.
66 For a detailed discussion of the poem, see the chapter "Tradition as Innovation in Heine's 'Jehuda ben Halevy': Counterhistory in a Spinozist Key." in Willi

Goetschel, *Spinoza's Modernity: Mendelssohn, Lessing, and Heine*, 266–76 (Madison: University of Wisconsin Press, 2004).

67 Benjamin, *Arcades Project*, N, and Adorno, *Minima Moralia*, trans. E. F. N. Jephcott (London and New York: Verso, 2005), concluding paragraph, 247.

68 Marx, *Selected Writings*, 161f.

Chapter 6

1 For an illuminating study of Heine's relationship to the Saint-Simonists, see Nina Bodenheimer, *Heinrich Heine und der Saint-Simonismus (1830–1835)* (Stuttgart: Metzler, 2014).

2 For a detailed study of the critical role of sensualism in Heine, see Olaf Hildebrand, *Emanzipation und Versöhnung: Aspekte des Sensualismus im Werk Heinrich Heines unter besonderer Berücksichtigung der "Reisebilder"* (Tübingen: Niemeyer, 2001). For a succinct discussion of Heine research on sensualism, see esp. 4–6. While Hildebrand correctly highlights Spinoza's critical importance for Heine's conception of sensualism, he reduces it to a foundational role limited to aspects of philosophy of religion in the 1830s and early 1840s (246f.). However, Heine connects with Spinoza on a range of shared concerns that Heine's sensualist attitudes articulate.

3 Maximilian Heine, *Erinnerungen an Heinrich Heine und seine Familie* (Berlin: Dümmler, 1868), 32.

4 Ibid., 32.

5 See, for instance, Willi Goetschel, "Heine's Spinoza," *Idealistic Studies* 33, no.2–3 (2003): 207–21 and the two concluding chapters in Willi Goetschel, *Spinoza's Modernity: Mendelssohn, Lessing, and Heine* (Madison: University of Wisconsin Press, 2004).

6 For the Spinoza reception of Lessing and Mendelssohn as the project of their ongoing dialogue see Goetschel, *Spinoza's Modernity*.

7 Ehrenfried Walther von Tschirnhaus, *Medicina mentis* (Amsterdam, 1687).

8 Immanuel Wolf, "Über den Begriff einer Wissenschaft des Judenthums," *Zeitschrift für die Wissenschaft des Judenthums* 1 (1823): 1–24, 14.

9 See Willi Goetschel, *The Discipline of Philosophy and the Invention of Modern Jewish Thought* (New York: Fordham, 2013), 41.

10 L 3, 249; DHA 6, 736. Briegleb's edition does not provide this passage, which Heine had inserted in the first edition of 1827 but deleted in later editions. For a later reference by Freud to Heine's coinage—this time as referring to Heine, not Spinoza—see p. 85.

11 The passage is in Spinoza's *Political Treatise*, chapter 2, § 8. Baruch de Spinoza, *The Collected Works*, trans. Edwin Curley (Princeton and Oxford: Princeton University Press, 2016), vol. 2, 511. See the discussion that follows later.

12 This point is repeated in the *Theological-Political Treatise* and the later *Political Treatise*. For a recent in-depth discussion of this point, see Martin Saar, *Die Immanenz der Macht: Politische Theorie nach Spinoza* (Frankfurt am Main: Suhrkamp, 2013).

13 Spinoza, *The Collected Works*, vol. 2, 507.

14 Baruch de Spinoza, *Politischer Traktat: Tractatus Politicus*, trans. and ed. Wolfgang Bartuschat (Hamburg: Meiner, 1994), chapter 2, §3, 14. Cf. also ibid., part chapter, §8 and *Theological Political Treatise*, chapter 16, §2. For a discussion of the passage, see Goetschel, *Spinoza's Modernity*, 69f.

15 For discussion of Spinoza's critical notion of power, see Goetschel, *Discipline of Philosophy and the Invention of Modern Jewish Thought*, 166–70. See also Warren Montag, *Bodies, Masses, Power: Spinoza and his Contemporaries* (London and New York: Verso, 1999) and Saar, *Die Immanenz der Macht*.

16 See Jacobi's 1781 polemics against Wieland, "Über Recht und Gewalt, oder philosophische Erwägung eines Aufsatzes von dem Herrn Hofrath Wieland, über das göttliche Recht der Obrigkeit," in *Kleinere Schriften*, ed. Friedrich Heinrich Jacobi, vol. 1 (1771–83), ed. Mark Georg Dehrmann, Catia Goretzki, and Walter in Jacobi, *Werke, Gesamtausgabe*, vol. 4.1, ed. Klaus Hammacher and Walter Jeschke vol. 4.1 (Hamburg: Meiner, and Bad Cannstatt, Stuttgart: Frommann-Holzboog, 2006), 259–87, esp. 271–6.

17 For Heine's incisive critique of Jacobi's role in the Pantheism Dispute, see his caustic comments in OH 59; B 3, 571f.

18 See discussion of the passage below.

19 DHA 8.1, 296.

20 It is worth noting that Kafka's short text "The Truth about Sancho Panza" casts Sancho Panza not as a subaltern character but turns the tables around, presenting Don Quixote as a figment of Panza's imagination. But Kafka's ultimate point is, like Heine's, the deep codependence of the two, and might well be a variation on Heine. Cf. Franz Kafka, *The Complete Stories*, ed. Nahum Glatzer (New York: Schocken, 1971), 430.

21 My translation. The rest of the quotes follow the identical wording Heine lifted from the pages of the *Travel Pictures' The City of Lucca* and are taken from the English translation there.

22 While in the *Travel Pictures* the sentence is linked to the preceding quote by a semicolon after which the narrative continues with an "and," the introduction to Cervantes separates the two parts of the quotation with a period.

23 In a letter, Heine's publisher Julius Campe ironically called himself "your Sancho Panza." HSA 24, letter 192, from July 23, 1834, 268.

24 Adorno, *Negative Dialektik*, in GS 6, 29.

25 Max Horkheimer and Theodor W. Adorno, *Dialectic of Enlightenment: Philosophical Fragments*, trans. Edmund Jephcott (Stanford: Stanford University Press, 2002), 193.

26 Max Horkheimer and Theodor W. Adorno, *Dialektik der Aufklärung: Philosophische Fragmente* (Frankfurt am Main: Fischer, 1988), 246.

27 For a brief discussion of Adorno's affinity to Spinoza, see Willi Goetschel, "Theory-Praxis: Spinoza, Hess, Marx, and Adorno," *Bamidbar: Journal for Jewish Thought and Philosophy* 2 (2013): 16–28.

Chapter 7

1 L 6, 60; B 3, 479. The discussion of Goethe follows my discussion in "Secularization Theories and Their Discontents," the introduction to a special

theme issue of *The Germanic Review* 95 (2015): 2–5, 2f. on secularization theories, coedited with Nils Roemer.

2 Hans Blumenberg, *The Legitimacy of the Modern Age*, trans. Robert M. Wallace (Cambridge, MA: MIT, 1985), 139. See Tracie Matysik, "Hans Blumenberg's Multiple Modernities: A Spinozist Supplement to *Legitimacy of the Modern Age*," *The Germanic Review* 90, no. 1 (2015): 21–41.

3 Franz Overbeck, *Über die Christlichkeit unserer heutigen Theologie. Streit- und Friedenschrift* (Leipzig: Fritzsch, 1873), 10; quoted in Blumenberg, *The Legitimacy of the Modern Age*, 119. For Nietzsche's collaboration, see Andreas Urs Sommer, *Der Geist der Historie und das Ende des Christentums. Zur "Waffengenossenschaft" von Friedrich Nietzsche und Franz Overbeck* (Berlin: Akademie Verlag 1997).

4 See Siegbert Prawer, *Heine's Jewish Comedy: A Study of his Portratits of Jews and Judaism* (Oxford: Clarendon Press, 1983).

5 Karl Marx, "Toward a Critique of Hegel's Philosophy of Right" in *Selected Writings*, 27–39, 30.

6 Leland's translation omits Heine's irreverent misattribution to the *Vulgata*.

7 See Heine's letter to his friend Moses Moser from October 14, 1826 (HSA 20, 265), where he writes "der nie abzuwaschende Jude" ("the Jew never to be washed off"). In an earlier letter to Moser, Heine pointed out the strange fact that ever since his baptism he had been decried as a Jew: "Isn't it crazy, as soon as I am baptized I am decried as a Jew." ("Ist es nicht närrisch, kaum bin ich getauft so werde ich als Jude verschrieen.") Letter from January 9, 1826 (HAS 20, 235). See also Willi Goetschel, "Kommentar zu Heinrich Heine" (Heinrich Heines Theorie des Judenhasses), in *Theorien über Judenhass—eine Denkgeschichte: Kommentierte Quellenedition (1781–1931)*, ed. Birgit Erdle and Werner Konitzer, Wissenschaftliche Reihe des Fritz Bauer Instituts (Frankfurt am Main and New York: Campus, 2015), 140–50.

8 Heine continues "What is an idea?"—A question he pursued in the *Travel Pictures*' "Ideas. The Book Le Grand" discussed at the end of Chapter 4.

9 Heine's approach resonates with Spinoza's insight concerning the dynamics of the life of ideas. For a good discussion of Spinoza's view, see the chapter "Renaturalizing Ideology: Spinoza's Ecosystem of Ideas," in *Spinoza and the Politics of Renaturalization*, ed. Hasana Sharp (Chicago: University of Chicago Press, 2011), 55–84.

Chapter 8

1 This chapter is written with Derrida's discussion in his "Abraham, the Other" in mind as an illuminating intervention in the discussion on Abraham in which Kierkegaard, Kafka, and Fackenheim among others represent important interlocutors. Cf. Jacques Derrida, "Abraham, the Other," in *Judeities: Questions for Jacques Derrida*, ed. Bettina Bergo, Joseph Cohen, and Raphael Zagury-Orly, trans. Bettina Bergo and Michael B. Smith, 1–35 (New York: Fordham University Press, 2007). For Kierkegaard, see Soren Kierkegaard, *Fear and Trembling: Dialectical Lyric by Johannes de silentio*, trans. Alastair Hannay (London: Penguin, 1985). For Derrida's preceding

discussion of Kierkegaard, see also Jacques Derrida, *The Gift of Death*, trans. David Wills (Chicago and London: Chicago University Press, 2nd ed., 2007).

2 B 1, 463.

3 Whereas some critics assert the possibility that the two strangers are renegades willing to betray their people, the wording of the passage suggests otherwise. In addition to using the Christian terms of membership in a community of faith that accentuates faith as the defining feature of their belonging—rather than the Jewish sense of historical belonging—the revealing clue is that they declare themselves in the first place rather than simply asking permission to join. Their Freudian slip, as it were, is to declare a Jewish identity precisely to claim a false identity. While the confessional nature of Christian discourse requires an unequivocal declaration of oneself as Christian, the Jewish minority position leads to the very opposite: the silent implication that anyone who seeks admission to a Jewish community is, other evidence notwithstanding, Jewish. For who else would want to join? Of course, the ultimate reason why Jews would not need to declare themselves as Jews is simply the rigorously implemented dress code for Jews that in the 15th century makes them easily and obviously recognizable.

4 For a discussion of the role of Father Rhine and the changing of meaning by repetition, cf. Aamir Mufti, *Enlightenment in the Colony: The Jewish Question and the Crisis of Postcolonial Culture* (Princeton: Princeton University Press, 2007), 85–7 and 87f.

5 I owe this point to Ben Cruchley and John Koster who kindly relayed it to me. The afikomen is that part of a half-broken matzah that the rabbi would hide for children to find later on.

6 See Heine's discussion on the dynamic fluidity of changing perspectives in history in *Travel Pictures* (*Die Nordsee III*), L 2, 231; B 2, 221. This passage is discussed in Chapter 5.

7 For a discussion of Heine's poem "Jehuda ben-Halevy," see Willi Goetschel, *Spinoza's Modernity: Mendelssohn, Lessing, and Heine* (Madison: University of Wisconsin Press, 2004), 266–76. For a discussion of "Disputation" and Queen Blanche's sniffish comment, see Willi Goetschel, "Nightingales Instead of Owls: Heine's Joyous Philosophy," in *A Companion to the Works of Heinrich Heine*, ed. Roger F. Cook (Rochester, NY: Camden House, 2002), 139–68, 162.

8 Cf. Derrida's critique of Kierkegaard's radical but problematically reductive and abstract concretism in his *Gift of Death*. In his discussion of the philosophical challenge of rethinking Abraham in *Encounters between Judaism and Modern Philosophy*, Emil Fackenheim poses a similar paradox in the face of the Holocaust: What is more important, saving Judaism or saving the life of Jews and how could the two possibly be distinguished?

9 Emil Fackenheim, *Encounters between Judaism and Modern Philosophy* (New York: Basic Books, 1973).

10 For an illuminating reading of Kafka that has helped me in my reading of Heine's recognition of the openness of Jewish tradition, see David Suchoff, *Kafka's Jewish Languages: The Hidden Openness of Tradition* (Philadelphia: University of Pennsylvania Press, 2012).

11 Emil Fackenheim, *Encounters between Judaism and Modern Philosophy* (New York: Basic Books, 1973), 76. For the source, see *Midrash Rabbah: Song*

of Songs, trans. Maurice Simon, ed. Harry Freedman and Maurice Simon (London: Soncino, 1939), 293–5.

12 All information concerning the Abarbanel family is taken from Carl Gebhardt's classic introduction to his edition of Leone Ebreo, *Dialoghi d'Amore* (Heidelberg: Carl Winter, 1929), 1–110.

13 For the excerpts, see the critical apparatus and commentary in DHA, 5, 762–8.

14 I would like to thank Moshe Idel for reminding me of this haunting episode and for pointing out its significance for the understanding of Heine's story.

15 Cf. Yvonne Sherwood, "Spectres of Abraham," in *Judaism in Contemporary Thought: Traces and Influence*, ed. Agata Bielik-Robson and Adam Lipszyc (New York and London: Routledge, 2014), 26–38.

16 Georg Simmel, "The Sociology of the Meal," in *Simmel on Culture*, ed. David Frisby and Mike Featherstone (London, Thousand Oaks, CA, and Delhi: Sage, 1997), 130–5.

BIBLIOGRAPHY

Heine, Heinrich. "Confessions." In *The Prose Writings of Heinrich Heine*, ed. Havelock Ellis, 290–327. London: Walter Scott, 1887.
Heine, Heinrich. "French Painters." In *Paintings on the Move: Heinrich Heine and the Visual Arts*, ed. Suzanne Zantop, 121–72. Lincoln: University of Nebraska Press, 1989.
Heine, Heinrich. "Of Judaism and the Jews." *Contemporary Jewish Record* (October 1943): 550–9.
Heine, Heinrich. *Poems and Ballads of Heinrich Heine*. Trans. Emma Lazarus. New York: Hurst, 1881.
Heine, Heinrich. *Poems of Heinrich Heine*. Trans. Louis Untermeyer. New York: Harcourt, Brace, 1916; 2nd ed. 1923.
Heine, Heinrich. *The Poetry and Prose of Heinrich Heine*. Ed. Frederic Ewen. New York: Citadel Press, 1948.
Heine, Heinrich. *Zur Geschichte der Religion und Philosophie in Deutschland*. Ed. Wolfgang Harich. Frankfurt am Main: Insel, 1965.

Anonymous. "Zur Feier am Heinedenkmal." *Aufbau* (February 1, 1935).
Abrahams, Israel. "Poetry and Religion: The Third Arthur Davis Memorial Lecture." *Menorah Journal* 6, no. 6 (December 1920): 322–36.
Abrams, Nathan. *Commentary Magazine 1945–1959: "A Journal of Significant Thought and Opinion."* London and Portland, OR: Vallentine Mitchell, 2007.
Adorno, Theodor W. *Aesthetic Theory*. Trans. Robert Hullot-Kentor. Minneapolis: University of Minnesota Press, 1997.
Adorno, Theodor W. *Briefe an die Eltern*, ed. Christoph Gödde and Henri Lonitz. Frankfurt: Suhrkamp, 2003.
Adorno, Theodor W. "Heine the Wound." In *Notes to Literature*, vol. 1, trans. Shierry Weber Nicholsen, 80–5. New York: Columbia University Press, 1991.
Adorno, Theodor W. "Introduction to Benjamin's *Schriften*." In *Notes to Literature*, vol. 2, trans. Shierry Weber Nicholsen, 220-32. New York: Columbia University, 1992.
Adorno, Theodor W. *Minima Moralia: Reflections on a Damaged Life*. Trans. Edmund Jephcott. New York and London: Verso, 1974.
Adorno, Theodor W. *Negative Dialectics*. Trans. E. B. Ashton. New York and London: Continuum, 2005.
Adorno, Theodor W. "On the Fetish-Character in Music and the Regression in Listening." In *Essays on Music*, ed. Richard Leppert, trans. Susan H. Gillespie, 288–317. Berkeley and Los Angeles: University of California Press, 2002.
Adorno, Theodor W. *Philosophy of New Music*. Trans. Robert Hullot-Kentor. Minneapolis and London: University of Minnesota Press, 2006.

Adorno, Theodor W. *Probleme der Moralphilosophie*. Frankfurt am Main: Suhrkamp, 1996.

Adorno, Theodor W. "The Meaning of Working through the Past." In *Critical Models: Interventions and Catchwords*, trans. Henry Pickford, 89–103. New York: Columbia, 1998.

Adorno, Theodor W. "Words from Abroad." In *Notes on Literature*, vol. 1, trans. Shierry Weber Nicholsen, 185–99. New York: Columbia University Press, 1991.

Adorno, Theodor W., and Gershom Scholem. *Briefwechsel: "Der liebe Gott wohnt im Detail" 1939–1969*. Ed. Asaf Angermann. Frankfurt am Main: Suhrkamp, 2015.

Altenhofer, Norbert. *Die verlorene Augensprache: über Heinrich Heine*. Frankfurt am Main: Insel, 1993.

Arendt, Hannah. "The Jew as Pariah: A Hidden Tradition." *Jewish Social Studies* 6, no. 2 (April 1944): 99–122.

Arendt, Hannah. *Jewish Writings*, ed. Jerome Kohn and Ron H. Feldman. New York: Schocken, 2007.

Aschheim, Steven E. *Beyond the Border: The German-Jewish Legacy Abroad*. Princeton and Oxford: Princeton University Press, 2007.

Benjamin, Walter. "Eduard Fuchs, Collector and Historian." In *Selected Writings, vol. 3: 1935–1938*, trans. Edmund Jephcott, Howard Eiland, et al., ed. Howard Eiland and Michael W. Jennings, 260–302. Cambridge, MA: Harvard University Press, 2008.

Benjamin, Walter. "On Some Motifs in Baudelaire." In *Illuminations: Essays and Reflections*, trans. Harry Zohn, ed. Hannah Arendt, 155–200. New York: Schocken, 1968.

Benjamin, Walter. *The Arcades Project*. Trans. Howard Eiland and Kevin McLaughlin. Cambridge, MA: Harvard University Press, 2003.

Benjamin, Walter. *The Origin of German Tragic Drama*. Trans. John Osborne. London and New York: Verso, 1998.

Jellinek, Adolph, ed. *Bet ha-Midrash*. Jerusalem: Bamberger & Wahrmann, 1938.

Betz, Albrecht. *Der Charme des Ruhestörers: Heine Studien. Ästhetik und Politik II*, 19–30. Aachen: Rimbaud 1997.

Betz, Albrecht. "Marchandise et modernité: Notes sur Heine et Benjamin." In *Walter Benjamin et Paris*, ed. Heinz Wismann, 153–62. Paris: Les Éditions du Cerf, 1986.

Bieber, Hugo, ed. *Heinrich Heine, Gespräche, Briefe, Tagebücher, Berichte seiner Zeitgenossen*. Berlin: Welt-Verlag, 1926.

Bloch, Ernst. *Erbschaft dieser Zeit*. Vol. 4, *Gesamtausgabe*. Frankfurt am Main: Suhrkamp, 1977.

Bloom, Harold. *The Anxiety of Influence: A Theory of Poetry*. New York: Oxford University Press, 1997.

Blumenberg, Hans. *The Legitimacy of the Modern Age*. Trans. Robert M. Wallace. Cambridge, Mass: MIT, 1985.

Bodenheimer, Nina. *Heinrich Heine und der Saint-Simonismus (1830–1835)*. Stuttgart: Metzler, 2014.

Boehlich, Walter, ed. *Der Berliner Antisemitismusstreit*. Frankfurt am Main: Insel 1965.

Bourne, Randolph. "The Jew and Transnational America," *Menorah Journal* 2, no. 5 (December 1916): 277–84.

Bourne, Randolph. "Trans-National America." *Atlantic Monthly* 118 (1916): 86–97.

Brenner, Michael. *The Renaissance of Jewish Culture in Weimar Germany*. New Haven and London: Yale University Press, 1996.

Briegleb, Klaus. *Opfer Heine? Versuche über Schriftzüge der Revolution*. Frankfurt am Main: Suhrkamp, 1986.

Bunyan, Anita. "1843: Heinrich Heine and Karl Marx Meet for the First Time in Paris." In *Yale Companion to Jewish Writing and Thought in German Culture, 1096–1996*, ed. Sander L. Gilman and Jack Zipes,171–7. New Haven: Yale University Press, 1997.

Calvié, Lucien. *Heine/Marx: Révolution, liberalisme, démocratie et communisme*. Uzès: Inclinaison, 2013.

Caygill, Howard. "Walter Benjamin's Concept of Cultural History." *The Cambridge Companion to Walter Benjamin*, ed. David S. Ferris, 73–96. Cambridge: Cambridge University Press, 2006.

Claussen, Detlev. *Theodor W. Adorno: Ein letztes Genie*. Frankfurt am Main: Fischer, 2003.

Cohen, Elliot. "Jewish Culture in America: Some Speculations by an Editor." *Commentary* (May 1947): 412–20.

Comay, Rebecca. *Mourning Sickness: Hegel and the French Revolution*. Stanford: Stanford University Press, 2011.

Courtemanche, Eleanor. "Marx, Heine, and German Cosmopolitanism: The 1844 Deutsch-Französische Jahrbücher." *Telos* 159 (Summer 2012): 49–63.

Coutinho, Arno Carl. "Nietzsche, Heine, und das 19. Jahrhundert." *PMLA* 53, no. 4 (December 1938): 1126–45.

Daiches, David. Review of *Judaic Lore in Heine: The Heritage of a Poet*, by Israel Tabak. *Commentary* (October 1949): 405–7.

de Jonge, Erich. "Des unheiligen Dritten Reiches jüdischer Prophet: Zur Heinefeier am 16. Februar 1936." *Aufbau* (February 1, 1936).

Del Caro, Adrian. "Heine's 'Deutschland. Ein Wintermärchen' Reflected in Nietzsche." *Heine-Jahrbuch* 33 (1994): 194–201.

Derrida, Jacques. "Abraham, the Other." In *Judeities: Questions for Jacques Derrida*, ed. Bettina Bergo, Joseph Cohen, and Raphael Zagury-Orly, trans. Bettina Bergo and Michael B. Smith, 1–35. New York: Fordham University Press, 2007.

Derrida, Jacques. *The Gift of Death*. Trans. David Wills. Chicago and London: Chicago University Press, 2nd ed. 2007.

Derrida, Jacques. *Plato's Pharmacy*. In *Dissemination*, trans. Barbara Johnson, 61–172. Chicago: University of Chicago Press, 1981.

Derrida, Jacques. *Specters of Marx*. Trans. Peggy Kamuf. New York and London: Routledge, 1994.

Dictionnaire critique du marxisme, ed. Georges Labicia and Gérard Bensussan. Paris: Presse universitaires de France, 2nd ed., 1982.

Duncan, Linda. "Heine and Nietzsche. Das Dionysische: Cultural Directive and Aesthetic Principle." *Nietzsche-Studien* 19 (1990): 336–45.

Ebreo, Leone. *Dialoghi d'Amore*. Heidelberg: Carl Winter, 1929.

Eiland, Howard, and Michael W. Jennings. *Walter Benjamin: A Critical Life*. Cambridge, MA and London: Harvard University Press, 2014.

Eisenberg, Tamara. "Neither Christ nor Barbarossa: Heinrich Heine's Messiah in Golden Chains." In *Benjamin—Agamben: Politics, Messianism, Kabbalah*, ed. Vittoria Borsò, Claas Morgenroth, Karl Solibakke, and Bernd Witte, 219–27. Würzburg: Königshausen & Neumann, 2010.

Eke, Norbert Otto, Karin Füllner, and Francesca Vidal, eds. "*Zuckererbsen für Jedermann*": *Literatur und Utopie. Heine und Bloch heute*, Vormärz-Studien XXXV. Bielefeld: Aisthesis, 2014.

Engels, Frederick. Frederick Engels to Conrad Schmidt, August 5, 1890. marxists.org. Accessed April 10, 2018. https://www.marxists.org/archive/marx/works/1890/letters/90_08_05.htm,

Engels, Frederick. *Ludwig Feuerbach and the End of Classical German Philosophy*. marxists.org. Accessed June 28, 2018. https://www.marxists.org/archive/marx/works/1886/ludwig-feuerbach/index.htm

Engels, Frederick. *Socialism: Utopian and Scientific*. Trans. Edward Aveling. London: Swan Sonnenschein and New York: Scribner, 1892.

Erdle, Birgit R. *Literarische Epistemologie der Zeit: Lektüren zu Kant, Kleist, Heine und Kafka*. Munich: Fink, 2015.

Espagne, Michel. "Die tote Maria: ein Gespenst in Heines Handschriften." *Deutsche Vierteljahrsschrift für Literaturwissenschaft und Geistesgeschichte* 57 (1983): 298–320.

Fackenheim, Emil. *Encounters between Judaism and Modern Philosophy*. New York: Basic Books, 1973.

Fairley, Barker. "Heine's Vaudeville." *University of Toronto Quarterly* 3 (1934): 185–207.

Floyd, Ronald James. "Heine and Nietzsche: Parallel Studies in Paradox and Irony." PhD diss., University of Washington, 1977.

Frank, Waldo. *Memoirs of Waldo Frank*. Ed. Alan Trachtenberg. Amherst: University of Massachusetts Press, 1973.

Franzen, Jonathan. *The Kraus Project: Essays by Karl Kraus*, trans. Jonathan Franzen with assistance and additional notes from Paul Reitter and Daniel Kehlmann. New York: Farrar, Straus and Giroux, 2013.

Freud, Sigmund. *Briefe 1873–1939*. Ed. Ernst and Lucie Freud. Frankfurt am Main: Fischer, 1980.

Friedl, Herwig. "Heinrich Heine und Friedrich Nietzsche." In *Heinrich Heine im Spannungsfeld von Literatur und Wissenschaft*, ed. Wilhelm Gössmann and Manfred Windfuhr, 195–214. Essen: Hobbing, 1990.

Garloff, Katya. "Essay, Exile, Efficacy: Adorno's Literary Criticism." *Monatshefte* 94, no. 1 (Spring 2002): 80–95.

Gebhard, Walter. "Heine und Nietzsche: historische und literarische Formen der Aufklärungsarbeit." In *Heine gehört auch uns*, ed. Zhang Yushu, 268–304. Beijing: Peking University Press, 1998.

Geller, Jay. "'Of Snips . . . and Puppy Dog Tails': Freud's Sublimation of Judentum." *American Imago* 66, no. 2 (2009): 169–84.

Geschichtliche Grundbegriffe, ed. Otto Brunner, Werner Conze, and Reinhart Koselleck. Stuttgart: Klett-Cotta, 2004.

Gilman, Sander. *The Jew's Body*. New York: Routledge 1991.

Gilman, Sander. "Nietzsche and Heine." In *Nietzschean Parody: An Introduction to Reading Nietzsche*, 65–86. Aurora, CO: Davies, 2nd ed., 2001.

Goethe, Johann Wolfgang von. *Sämtliche Werke*. Ed. Ernst Beutler. Zurich: Artemis, 1948 and Munich: Deutscher Taschenbuch Verlag, 1977.

Goetschel, Willi. "The Differential Character of Traditions." *Telos* no. 95 (1993): 161–70.

Goetschel, Willi. *The Discipline of Philosophy and the Invention of Modern Jewish Thought*. New York: Fordham, 2013.

Goetschel, Willi. "German Studies in a Post-National Age." The 2009 Craig Lecture, Rutgers German Studies Occasional Papers 9. New Brunswick: Rutgers University, 2010.

Goetschel, Willi. "Heine und der Traum." In *Palimpseste. Zur Erinnerung an Norbert Altenhofer*, ed. Pascal Nicklas and Joachim Jacob, 41–61. Heidelberg: Carl Winter, 2004.

Goetschel, Willi. "Heine's Spinoza." *Idealistic Studies* 33, no. 2/3 (2003): 207–21.

Goetschel, Willi. "Kommentar zu Heinrich Heine" (Heinrich Heines Theorie des Judenhasses.). In *Theorien über Judenhass—eine Denkgeschichte: Kommentierte Quellenedition (1781–1931)*, ed. Birgit Erdle and Werner Konitzer. Wissenschaftliche Reihe des Fritz Bauer Instituts, vol. 26. Frankfurt am Main and New York: Campus, 2015, 140–50.

Goetschel, Willi. "Nightingales Instead of Owls: Heine's Joyous Philosophy." *A Companion to the Works of Heinrich Heine*, ed. Roger F. Cook, 139–68. Rochester, NY: Camden House, 2002.

Goetschel, Willi. "Secularization Theories and Their Discontents." *The Germanic Review* 95 (2015): 2–5.

Goetschel, Willi. *Spinoza's Modernity: Mendelssohn, Lessing, and Heine*. Madison: University of Wisconsin Press, 2004.

Goetschel, Willi. "Tangled Genealogies: Hellenism, Hebraism, and Discourse of Modernity." Review of *Socrates and the Jews: Hellenism and Hebraism from Moses Mendelssohn to Sigmund Freud*, by Miriam Leonard. *Arion* 21, no. 3 (2014): 111–24.

Goetschel, Willi. "Theory-Praxis: Spinoza, Hess, Marx, and Adorno." *Bamidbar: Journal for Jewish Thought and Philosophy* 2 (2013): 16–28.

Goetschel, Willi and David Suchoff. "Displaced Philologies." *The Germanic Review* 93, no. 1 (2018): 1–6.

Goldschmidt, Hermann Levin. *Werke*, ed. Willi Goetschel. Vienna: Passagen, 1992–2014.

Goltschnigg, Dietmar. *Die Fackel ins wunde Herz: Kraus über Heine. Eine "Erledigung"? Texte, Analysen, Kommentar*. Vienna: Passagen, 2000.

Greenberg, Martin. "Heinrich Heine: Flight and Return. The Fallacy of Being Only a Human Being." *Commentary* (March 1949): 225–31.

Greene, Daniel. *The Jewish Origins of Cultural Pluralism: The Menorah Association and American Diversity*. Bloomington and Indianapolis: Indiana University Press, 2011.

Grimm, Jacob and Wilhelm Grimm. *Deutsches Wörterbuch*. 16 Bde. in 32 Teilbänden. Leipzig: Hirzel, 1854–1961.

Grimm, Reinhold. "Antiquity as Echo and Disguise: Nietzsche's 'Lied eines theokritischen Ziegenhirten,' Heinrich Heine, and the Crucified Dionysus." *Nietzsche Studien* 14 (1985): 201–48.

Grimm, Reinhold. "Heine und Nietzsche: Bemerkungen zu einem lyrischen Pastiche." In *Heinrich Heine und das neunzehnte Jahrhundert: Signaturen*, ed. Rolf Hosfeld, 98–107. Berlin: Argument, 1986.

Gross, Harvey. "Adorno in Los Angeles: The Intellectual in Emigration." *Humanities in Society* 2, no. 4 (Fall 1979): 339–51.

Habermas, Jürgen. "Heine and the Role of the Intellectual in Germany." In *The New Conservativism: Cultural Criticism and the Historian's Debate*, trans. and ed. Shierry Weber Nicholson, 71–99. Cambridge, MA: MIT, 1989.

Hegel, G. W. F. *Outlines of the Philosophy of Right*. Trans. T. M. Knox, ed. Stephen Houlgate. Oxford: Oxford University Press, rev. ed. 2008.

Hegel, G. W. F. *Phenomenology of Spirit*. Trans. A. V. Miller. Oxford: Oxford University Press, 1977.

Heine, Maximilian. *Erinnerungen an Heinrich Heine und seine Familie*. Berlin: Dümmler, 1868.

Hermand, Jost. *Heinrich Heine: Kritisch, Solidarisch, Umstritten*, 85–103. Cologne, Weimar, and Vienna: Böhlau, 2007.

Hildebrand, Olaf. *Emanzipation und Versöhnung: Aspekte des Sensualismus im Werk Heinrich Heines unter besonderer Berücksichtigung der "Reisebilder."* Tübingen: Niemeyer, 2001.

Hinck, Walter. *Die Wunde Deutschland: Heinrich Heines Dichtung im Widerstreit von Nationalidee, Judentum und Antisemitismus*. Frankfurt am Main: Insel, 1990.

Hohendahl, Peter Uwe. "Adorno as a Reader of Heine." In *Reason and Its Other: Rationality in Modern German Philosophy and Culture*, ed. Dieter Freundlieb and Wayne Hudson, 229–40. Providence: Berg, 1993.

Hohendahl, Peter Uwe. *Fleeting Promise of Art: Adorno's Aesthetic Theory Revisited*. Ithaca, NY: Cornell University Press, 2013.

Hohendahl, Peter Uwe. *Heinrich Heine: Europäischer Schriftsteller und Intellektueller*. Berlin: Erich Schmidt, 2008.

Hohendahl, Peter Uwe. *Prismatic Thought: Theodor W. Adorno*. Lincoln: University of Nebraska Press, 1995.

Höhn, Gerhard. "Adorno face à Heine ou le couteau dans la plaie." *Revue d'esthétique* 8 (1985): 137–44.

Höhn, Gerhard. "'Farceur' und 'Fanatiker des Ausdrucks: Nietzsche, Heineaner *malgré lui*?" In *Heinrich Heine: Neue Wege der Forschung*, ed. Christian Liedtke, 198–215. Darmstadt: Wissenschaftliche Buchgesellschaft, 2000.

Höhn, Gerhard. *Heine-Handbuch: Zeit, Person, Werk*. Stuttgart: Metzler, 3rd ed. 2004.

Höhn, Gerhard. "Heine und die Genealogie des modernen Intellektuellen." In *Heinrich Heine: Ästhetisch-politische Profile*, ed. Gerhard Höhn, 66–84. Frankfurt am Main: Suhrkamp, 1991.

Höhn, Gerhard. "Heine und Nietzsche, Kritiker des Christentums." In *Ich Narr des Glücks*, ed. Joseph A. Kruse, 357–60. Stuttgart: Metzler 1997.

Höhn, Gerhard. "Kontrastästhetik: Heines Programm einer neuen Schreibart." In *Heinrich Heine: ein Wegbereiter der Moderne*, ed. Paolo Chiarini and Walter Hinderer, 43–66. Würzburg: Königshausen and Neumann, 2009.

Höhn, Gerhard. "Paris, ein Fest fürs Leben und Wende des Schreibens: Heines Kontrastästhetik." In "*Was die Zeit fühlt und denkt und bedarf*": *die Welt des 19. Jahrhunderts im Werk Heinrich Heines*, ed. Bernd Kortländer, 115–36. Bielefeld: Aisthesis, 2014.

Höhn, Gerhard. "'Sauerkraut mit Ambrosia': Heines Kontrastästhetik." *Heine Jahrbuch* 48 (2009): 1–27.

Holub, Robert C. "Heine and the Dialectic of Jewish Emancipation." In "*und die Welt ist so lieblich verworren*": *Heinrich Heines dialektisches Denken*, ed. Bernd Kortländer and Sikander Singh, 229–47. Bielefeld: Aisthesis, 2004.

Horkheimer, Max. *Gesammelte Werke*, vol. 4. Frankfurt am Main: Fischer, 1988.

Horkheimer, Max, and Theodor W. Adorno, *Dialectic of Enlightenment: Philosophical Fragments*, trans. Edmund Jephcott. Stanford: Stanford University Press, 2002.

Horkheimer, Max, and Theodor W. Adorno, *Dialektik der Aufklärung: Philosophische Fragmente*. Frankfurt am Main: Fischer, 1988.

Humphrey, Nicolas S. "Heinrich Heine and Friedrich Nietzsche: Dance as Metaphor and Theoretical Imagery." PhD diss., Johns Hopkins, 1986.

Iliev, Welisar. "Nietzsche und Heine: Chronik einer (lebenslänglichen?) Beziehung." *Germanica: Jahrbuch für deutschlandkundliche Studien* 4 (1997): 247–66.

Jacobi, Friedrich Heinrich. "Über Recht und Gewalt, oder philosophische Erwägung eines Aufsatzes von dem Herrn Hofrath Wieland, über das göttliche Recht der Obrigkeit." In *Kleinere Schriften*, vol. 1 (1771–83), ed. Mark Georg Dehrmann, Catia Goretzki, and Walter, vol. 4.1, *Werke, Gesamtausgabe*, ed. Klaus Hammacher and Walter Jeschke, 259–87. Hamburg: Meiner and Stuttgart-Bad Cannstatt: Fromman-Holzboog, 2006.

Jacobs, Jack. *The Frankfurt School, Jewish Lives, and Antisemitism*. Cambridge: Cambridge University Press, 2014.

Jay, Martin. *Permanent Exiles: Essays on the Intellectual Migration from Germany to America*, 120–37. New York: Columbia University Press, 1986.

Jay, Martin. *The Dialectical Imagination: A History of the Frankfurt School and the Institute of Social Research 1923–1950*. Boston and Toronto: Little, Brown, 1973.

Jay, Martin. "Leo Lowenthal and the Jewish Renaissance." In *Jews and the Ends of Theory*, ed. Shai Ginsburg, Martin Land, and Jonathan Boyarin. New York: Fordham University Press, 2018.

Kafka, Franz. *The Complete Stories*, ed. Nahum Glatzer. New York: Schocken, 1971.

Kaiser, Gerhard R. "Baudelaire pro Heine contra Janin." *Heine-Jahrbuch* 22 (1983): 135–78.

Kaufmann, Hans. *Politisches Gedicht und klassische Dichtung—Heinrich Heine: Deutschland. Ein Wintermärchen*, Berlin: Aufbau, 1959.

Kaufmann, Walter. *Nietzsche: Philosopher, Psychologist, Antichrist*. New York: Vintage, 3rd ed. 1968.

Kierkegaard, Soren. *Fear and Trembling: Dialectical Lyric by Johannes de silentio*, trans. Alastair Hannay. London: Penguin, 1985.

Kolb, Jocelyn. "Heine as Freud's Double in 'Der Witz und seine Beziehung zum Unbewußten.'" *Heine-Jahrbuch* 31 (1992), 137–62.

Koselleck, Reinhart. *Past Futures: On the Semantics of Historical Time*, trans. Keith Tribe. New York: Columbia University Press, 2004.

Kraus, Karl. "Heine und die Folgen." In *Ausgewählte Werke*, vol. 1, ed. Dietrich Simon, 290–312. Munich: Langen Müller, 1977.

Krauze, Enrique. "The Fury of Historical Redemptionism: An Interview with Joseph B. Maier, September 30, 1982." In *Surviving the Twentieth Century: Social Philosophy from the Frankfurt School to the Columbia Faculty Seminars*, ed. Judith T. Marcus, 37–48. New Brunswick and London: Transaction Publishers, 1999.

Kupferberg, Yael. *Dimensionen des Witzes um Heinrich Heine: Zur Säkularisation der poetischen Sprache*. Würzburg: Königshausen & Neumann, 2011.

Lafargue, Paul. *Reminiscences of Marx*. marxists.org. Accessed December 19, 2016. https://www.marxists.org/archive/lafargue/1890/xx/marx.htm

Lange, Georg. "Heine und Nietzsche." *Österreichische Rundschau* 64 (1920): 190–202.

Lefebvre, Jean Pierre. "Marx und Heine." In *Heinrich Heine: Streitbarer Humanist und volksverbundener Dichter*, ed. Karl Wolfgang Becker, Helmut Brandt, and Siegfried Scheibe, 41–61. Weimar: Nationale Forschungs- und Gedenkstätte der klassischen deutschen Literatur, 1973.

Lefebvre, Jean Pierre. *Marx und Heine*. Schriften aus dem Karl-Marx-Haus 7. Trier: Karl-Marx-Haus, 1972.

Leonard, Miriam. *Socrates and the Jews: Hellenism and Hebraism from Moses Mendelssohn to Sigmund Freud*. Chicago: University of Chicago Press, 2012.

Leonard, Miriam. *Tragic Modernities*. Cambridge, MA: Harvard 2015.

Levine, Michael. *Writing through Repression: Literature, Censorship, Psychoanalysis*. Baltimore: Johns Hopkins University Press, 1994.

Levinson, Julian. *Exiles on Main Street: Jewish American Writers and American Literary Culture*. Bloomington and Indiana: Indiana University Press, 2008.

Liedtke, Christian. "'. . . die überwuchernde Macht des Kapitals'. Geld, Gold und Eisenbahnen im Spätwerk Heinrich Heines." In *". . .und die Welt ist so lieblich verworren": Heinrich Heines dialektisches Denken*, ed. Bernd Kortländer and Sikander Singh, 73–100. Aisthesis: Bielefeld, 2004.

Liptzin, Sol. *The English Legend of Heinrich Heine*. New York: Bloch, 1954.

Liptzin, Sol. "Heine and the Yiddish Poets." In *The Jewish Reception of Heinrich Heine*, ed. Mark Gelber, 67–76. Tübingen: Max Niemeyer, 1992.

Lowenthal, Leo. "Heine's Religion: *The Messianic Ideals of the Poet*." *Commentary* 4, no. 2 (1947): 153–7.

Löwenthal, Leo. "Judentum und deutscher Geist." In *Schriften 4: Judaica, Vorträge, Briefe*, ed. Helmut Dubiel, 20–9. Frankfurt am Main: Suhrkamp, 1984.

Löwy, Michael. "Le messianisme hétérodoxe dans l'œuvre de jeunesse de Gershom Scholem" In *Messianismes. Variations sur une figure juive*, ed. Jean-Christophe Attias, Pierre Gisel, and Lucie Kaennel, 131–45. Genève: Labor et Fides, 2000.

Löwy, Michael. *Redemption and Utopia. Libertarian Judaism in Central Europe: A Study in Elective Affinity*. Trans. Hope Heany. Stanford: Stanford University Press, 1992.

Lukács, Georg. *Deutsche Realisten des 19. Jahrhunderts*. Berlin: Aufbau, 1951.

Mann, Thomas. "Notiz über Heine." In Thomas Mann, *Reden und Aufsätze*, vol. 2. Frankfurt am Main: Fischer, 1965.

Marcus, Judith. "Joseph B. Maier's Life and Work: An Introduction." In *Surviving the Twentieth Century: Social Philosophy from the Frankfurt School to the Columbia Faculty Seminars*, ed. Judith T. Marcus. New Brunswick and London: Transaction Publishers, 1999, 37–48.

Marcus, Judith. "Remembering Joseph B. Maier: The Last Member of the Frankfurt School." *Logos: A Journal of Modern Society & Culture* 2, no. 1 (2003): 181–5.

Marcuse, Ludwig. "Heine and Marx: A History and a Legend." *The Germanic Review* 30 (1955): 110–24.

Marx, Karl. *Capital: A Critique of Political Economy*, vol. 1. Trans. Samuel Moore and Edward Aveling, ed. Frederick Engels. marxists.org. Accessed December 18, 2016. https://www.marxists.org/archive/marx/works/download/pdf/Capital-Volume-I.pdf

Matysik, Tracie. "Hans Blumenberg's Multiple Modernities: A Spinozist Supplement to *Legitimacy of the Modern Age*." *The Germanic Review* 90, no. 1 (2015): 21–41.

Mendes-Flohr, Paul. *Divided Passions: Jewish Intellectuals and the Experience of Modernity*. Detroit: Wayne State University Press, 1991.

Mendes-Flohr, Paul. "Hermann Levin Goldschmidt and the Legacy of German-Jewish Humanism," Hermann Levin Goldschmidt Memorial Lecture 2011. www.dialogik.org/memorial-lectures.

Mendicino, Kristina. "Newswriting, Historiography, and the Controversion of the Present (after Heine)." *diacritics* 44, no. 3 (2016): 80–112.

Midgley, David. "Heine bei Nietzsche." In *Harry . . . Heinrich . . . Henri . . . Heine: Deutscher, Jude, Europäer*, ed. Dietmar Goltschnigg, Charlotte Grollegg-Edler, and Peter Reeves, 301–6. Berlin: Erich Schmidt, 2008.

Midrash Rabbah: Song of Songs. Trans. Maurice Simon, ed. Harry Freedman and Maurice Simon. London: Soncino, 1939.

Montag, Warren, *Bodies, Masses, Power: Spinoza and his Contemporaries*. London and New York: Verso, 1999.

Mosès, Stéphane. "'Selten habt Ihr mich verstanden'. Zur Funktion eine Heine-Zitats in Freuds *Traumdeutung*." In *Heine und Freud: Die Enden der Literatur und die Anfänge der Kulturwissenschaft*, ed. Sigrid Weigel, 91–8. Berlin: Kadmos, 2010.

Mufti, Aamir. *Enlightenment in the Colony: The Jewish Question and the Crisis of Postcolonial Culture*. Princeton: Princeton University Press, 2007.

Müller, Harro. *Taubenfüße und Adlerkrallen: Essays zu Nietzsche, Adorno, Kluge, Büchner und Grabbe*. Bielefeld: Aisthesis, 2016.

Müller, Heiner. "Die Wunde Woyzeck." In *Büchner-Preis-Reden 1984–1994*, ed. Deutsche Akademie für Sprache und Dichtung, 42–4. Stuttgart: Reclam, 1994.

Müller, Joachim. *Marx und Heine*. Berlin: Aufbau, 1953.

Nancy, Jean-Luc. *Hegel: The Restlessness of the Negative*. Trans. Jason Smith and Steven Miller. Minneapolis and London: University of Minnesota Press, 2002.

Nietzsche, Friedrich. *Briefwechsel, Kritische Gesamtausgabe*, ed. Giorgio Colli, Mazzino Montinari continued by Norbert Miller, Annemarie Pieper (Berlin and New York, 1974–2004).

Nietzsche, Friedrich. *Ecce Homo*. In *The Complete Works*, vol. 17, trans. Anthony M. Ludovici, New York: Macmillan, 1911.

Nietzsche, Friedrich. *Human, All Too Human: A Book for Free Spirits*, trans. R. J. Hollimgdale Cambridge: Cambridge University Press, 1986.

Nietzsche, Friedrich. *On the Genealogy of Morality*, trans. Carol Diethe, ed. Keith Ansell-Pearson Cambridge: Cambridge University Press, 1994.

Nietzsche, Friedrich. "On Truth and Lying in a Non-Moral Sense." In *The Birth of Tragedy and Other Writings*, trans. Ronald Spiers, ed. Raymond Geuss and Ronald Spiers, 139–53. Cambridge: Cambridge University Press, 1999.

Nixon, Mark. "Beckett liest die deutsche Literatur: Eine Übersicht." In *Samuel Beckett und die deutsche Literatur*, ed. Jan Wilm and Mark Nixon, 19–32. Bielefeld: transcript Verlag, 2013.

Oko, Adolph S. [Baruch, S.] "One Hundred Years Ago: A 'Menorah' Anniversary." *Menorah Journal* 6, no. 1 (1920): 11–25.

Oko, Adolph S. [Anonymous] Introduction to Heinrich Heine, "Of Judaism and the Jews." *Contemporary Jewish Record*, October 1 (1943): 550–9.

Oko, Adolph S. *The Spinoza Bibliography*. Boston: G. K. Hall, 1964.

Overbeck, Franz. *Über die Christlichkeit unserer heutigen Theologie. Streit- und Friedenschrift*. Leipzig: Fritzsch, 1873.

Peters, George F. *The Poet as Provocateur: Heinrich Heine and His Critics*. Rochester: Camden, 2000.

Peters, Paul. *Die Wunde Heine*, Bodenheim: Philo, 1997.

Plass, Ulrich. *Language and History in Theodor W. Adorno's Notes to Literature*. New York and London: Routledge, 2007.

Plekhanov, Georgi. "Notes to Engels' Book Ludwig Feuerbach." marxists.org. Accessed April 10, 2018. https://www.marxists.org/archive/plekhanov/1892/engels/notes1.html

Politzer, Heinz. *Frank Kafka, Parable and Paradox*. Ithaca, NY: Cornell University Press, 1962.

Politzer, Heinz. "From Mendelssohn to Kafka: The Jewish Man of Letters in Germany." *Commentary* (April 1947): 344–51.

Politzer, Heinz. "The Threshold of Emancipation." Review of *An Autobiography*, by Salomon Maimon; and *The Rabbi of Bacherach: A Fragment*, by Heinrich Heine. *Commentary* (March 1948): 286–8.

Prawer, Siegbert S. *Heine, the Tragic Satirist: A Study of the Later Poetry 1827–56*. Cambridge: Cambridge University Press, 1961.

Prawer, Siegbert S. *Heine's Jewish Comedy: A Study of his Portraits of Jews and Judaism*. Oxford: Clarendon Press, 1983.

Reeves, Nigel. "Heine and the Young Marx." *Oxford German Studies* 7 (1972–3): 44–97.

Reitter, Paul. "Heine in the Bronx." *The Germanic Review* 74, no. 4 (1999): 327–36.

Richter, Mathias. "Hermeneutik der Emanzipation: Heine und Bloch als Gesellschaftsanalytiker." In *"Zuckererbsen für Jedermann": Literatur und Utopie. Heine und Bloch heute*, ed. Norbert Otto Eke, Karin Füllner, and Francesca Vidal, 135–53. Bielefeld: Aisthesis, 2014.

Ricœur, Paul. *Freud and Philosophy: An Essay on Interpretation*, New Haven: Yale University Press, 1970.

Rosenblum, Constance. *Boulevard of Dreams: Heady Times, Heartbreak, and Hope along the Grand Concourse in the Bronx*. New York and London: New York University Press, 2009.

Ruckstuhl, Karl. "Von der Ausbildung der Teutschen Sprache, in Beziehung auf neue, dafür angestellte Bemühungen." *Nemesis, Zeitschrift für Politik und Geschichte* 7, no. 3 (1816), 337–86.

Rudolph, Johanna. "Karl Marx und Heinrich Heine." *Neues Deutschland*, February 17, 1953.

Saar, Martin. *Die Immanenz der Macht: Politische Theorie nach Spinoza*. Frankfurt am Main: Suhrkamp, 2013.

Sachs, Henry Baruch. *Heine in America*. Philadelphia: University of Pennsylvania Press, 1916.

Sammons, Jeffrey L. *Heinrich Heine: Alternative Perspectives 1985–2005*. Würzburg: Königshausen & Neumann, 2006.

Sammons, Jeffrey L. "The Restoration of the Heine Monument in the Bronx." *Germanic Review* 74, no. 4 (1999): 337–9.

Sándor, András. "The Oak Tree and the Ax: Delaroche's Painting and Heine's Montage." In *Paintings on the Move*, ed. Susanne Zantop, 51–74. Lincoln and London: University of Nebraska Press, 1989.

Schlesier, Renate. "Homeric Laughter by the Rivers of Babylon: Heinrich Heine and Karl Marx." In *The Jewish Reception of Heinrich Heine*, ed. Mark H. Gelber, 21–43. Tübingen: Niemeyer, 1992.

Schmitz, Gerhard. *Über die ökonomischen Anschauungen in Heines Werken.* Weimar: Arion, 1960.

Scholem, Gershom. *Walter Benjamin und sein Engel: Vierzehn Aufsätze.* Frankfurt am Main: Suhrkamp, 1983.

Scholem, Gershom. *Sabbatai Sevi: The Mystical Messiah.* Trans. R. J. Zwi Werbloswky. Princeton: Princeton University Press, 1973.

Scholem, Gershom. *Tagebücher nebst Aufsätzen und Entwürfen bis 1923. 2. Halbband 1917–1923.* Ed. Karlfried Gründer, Herbert Kopp-Oberstebrink, and Friedrich Niewöhner with the assistance of Karl E. Grözinger. Frankfurt am Main: Jüdischer Verlag, 2000.

Scholem, Gershom. *Walter Benjamin: The Story of a Friendship.* Trans. Harry Zohn. New York: New York Review Book, 2003.

Schumacher, Alfred. "Heinrich Heine." *Manchester Quarterly: A Journal of Literature and Art* 19 (1900): 272–97.

Sharp, Hasana. *Spinoza and the Politics of Renaturalization.* Chicago and London: Chicago University Press, 2011.

Sherwood, Yvonne. "Spectres of Abraham." In *Judaism in Contemporary Thought: Traces and Influence*, ed. Agata Bielik-Robson and Adam Lipszyc, 26–38. New York and London: Routledge, 2014.

Simmel, Georg. *Brücke und Tür: Essays*, ed. Michael Landmann together with Margarete Susman (Stuttgart: Köhler, 1957).

Simmel, Georg. *The Philosophy of Money*. Ed. David Frisby and trans. Tom Bottomore and David Frisby from a first draft by Kaethe Mengelberg. London and New York: Routledge, 3rd ed., 2004.

Simmel, Georg. "The Problem of Historical Time." In *Essays on Interpretation in Social Science*, trans. Guy Oakes, 127–44. Manchester: Manchester University Press, 1980.

Simmel, Georg. "The Sociology of the Meal." In *Simmel on Culture*, ed. David Frisby and Mike Featherstone, 130–5. London, Thousand Oaks, CA, and Delhi: Sage, 1997.

Simon, Ernst. "Heine und die Romantik." In *Essays Presented to Leo Baeck on the Occasion of His Eightieth Birthday*, 127–57. London: East and West Library, 1954.

Slochower, Harry. "Attitudes towards Heine in German Literary Criticism." *Jewish Social Studies* 3 (1941): 355–74.

Sommer, Andreas Urs. *Der Geist der Historie und das Ende des Christentums. Zur "Waffengenossenschaft" von Friedrich Nietzsche und Franz Overbeck.* Berlin: Akademie Verlag, 1997.

Soros, Alexander. "Jewish Dionysus: Heine, Nietzsche, and the Politics of Literature." PhD diss. University of California, Berkeley, 2018.

Spencer, Hanna. *Dichter, Denker, Journalist: Studien zum Werk Heinrich Heines.* Bern: Peter Lang, 1977.

Spinoza, Baruch de. *The Collected Works of Spinoza*. Ed. and trans. Edwin Curley. Princeton: Princeton University Press, 1985.

Spinoza, Baruch de. *Politischer Traktat: Tractatus Politicus*. Trans. and ed. Wolfgang Bartuschat, Hamburg: Meiner, 1994.

Stauf, Renate. *Heinrich Heine: Gedichte und Prosa*. Berlin: Erich Schmidt, 2010.

Stauf, Renate. *Poetische Zeitgenossenschaft: Heine-Studien*, ed. Cord-Friedrich Berghahn. Heidelberg: Winter, 2015.

Stein, Peter. "Zu den Widersprüchen in der Rezeptionsgeschichte Heinrich Heines." In *"Die Emanzipation des Volkes war die große Aufgabe unseres Lebens": Beiträge zur Heinrich-Heine-Forschung anläßlich seines zweihundertsten Geburtstags 1997*, ed. Wolfgang Beutin, Thomas Bütow, Johann Dvorak, and Ludwig Fischer, 253–66. Hamburg: von Bockel, 2000.

Stern, J. P. *Re-interpretations: Seven Studies in Nineteenth-Century German Literature*. London: Thames and Hudson, 1964.

Sternberger, Dolf. *Heinrich Heine und die Abschaffung der Sünde*. Hamburg: Claassen Verlag 1972.

Stiening, Gideon. "Die Metaphysik des Hieroglyphischen." *Jahrbuch des Freien Deutschen Hochstifts* (1999): 121–62.

Suchoff, David. "Dissonant Lineages: Adorno, Beckett, Blanchot, Kafka, Rosenzweig." *The Germanic Review* 90 (2015): 335–57.

Suchoff, David. *Kafka's Jewish Languages: The Hidden Openness of Tradition*. Philadelphia: University of Pennsylvania Press, 2012.

Tabak, Israel. *Judaic Lore in Heine: The Heritage of a Poet*. Baltimore: Johns Hopkins University Press, 1948.

Tauber, Zvi. "Remarks on the Relationship between Heine and Marx in 1844." *Tel Aviver Jahrbuch für deutsche Geschichte* 30 (2002): 402–13.

Tesdorpf, Ilse-Maria. *Die Auseinandersetzung Matthew Arnolds mit Henrich Heine, des Kritikers mit dem Kritiker: Ein besonderer Fall von konstruktivem Missverstehen und eigenwilliger Entlehnung*. Frankfurt am Main: Athenäum, 1971.

Trotsky, Leon. "Tolstoy, Poet and Rebel." Trans. John G. Wright. marxists.org. Accessed September 20, 2016. https://www.marxists.org/archive/trotsky/1908/09/tolstoy.htm.

Tschirnhaus, Ehrenfried Walther von. *Medicina mentis*. Amsterdam: Magnum and Rieuwerts Jr., 1687.

Turel, Adrien. *Generalangriff auf die Persönlichkeit und dessen Abwehr*. Zurich: Adrien Turel, 1955.

Untermeyer, Louis. *Heinrich Heine: Paradox and Poet*. New York: Harcourt, Brace, 1937.

Victor, Walther. *Marx und Heine: Tatsache und Spekulation in der Darstellung ihrer Beziehungen*. Berlin: Henschel-Verlag, 1953.

Vogelstein, Ludwig. "Heine in New York." *Aufbau* (March 8, 1940).

Wald, Alan M. *The New York Intellectuals: The Rise and Decline of the Anti-Stalinist Left from the 1930s to the 1980s*. Chapel Hill and London: University of North Carolina Press, 1987.

Weiller, Hermann E. "Heine in the Bronx." *Aufbau* (February 9, 1940).

Werner, Michael. "Heine und die französischen Frühsozialisten." *Internationales Archiv für Sozialgeschichte der deutschen Literatur* 7 (1982): 88–108.

Wheatland, Thomas. *The Frankfurt School in Exile*. Minneapolis: University of Minnesota Press, 2009.
White, Hayden. *Metahistory: The Historical Imagination in Nineteenth-Century Europe*. Baltimore: Johns Hopkins University Press, 1973.
Winkelnkemper, Stefanie. "Der Hass des 'Nazareners': Heinrich Heine antizipiert die Psychologie des Ressentiments." *Nietzscheforschung* 13 (2006): 211–18.
Wolf, Immanuel. "Über den Begriff einer Wissenschaft des Judenthums." *Zeitschrift für die Wissenschaft des Judenthums* 1 (1823): 1–24.
Young, Julian. *Friedrich Nietzsche: A Philosophical Biography*. Cambridge: Cambridge University Press, 2010.
Zepf, Irmgard. *Denkbilder: Heinrich Heines Gemäldebericht*. Munich: Fink, 1980.

INDEX